Jonson and Elizabethan Comedy

L. A. Beaurline

Jonson and Elizabethan Comedy

ESSAYS IN DRAMATIC RHETORIC

THE HUNTINGTON LIBRARY
SAN MARINO
1978

COPYRIGHT © 1978
HENRY E. HUNTINGTON LIBRARY AND ART GALLERY
LIBRARY OF CONGRESS CATALOG CARD NUMBER L.C.77-75148
ISBN 0-87328-071-7
PRINTED IN THE UNITED STATES OF AMERICA
BY PUBLISHERS PRESS
DESIGNED BY WARD RITCHIE

Contents

v

Illustrations

Preface

The subject of this book is the rhetoric of Ben Jonson's comedies, approached from various directions to show the diversity of some of his accomplishments within an Elizabethan and early seventeenth-century setting. The great problem is understanding Jonson's development as he tried new ways of instructing and moving the public without completely abandoning what was useful about the old ways. Our difficulties are compounded by his attempts to give the impression that he followed a consistent program in his "studies" from start to finish. Since his work, seen with a discerning eye, is not as homogeneous as literary historians lead us to think, we do little justice to the special pleasures of his comedies if we iron out the differences between them, being content to describe them as just satiric, learned, neoclassical, or sternly didactic comedies. He wrote for audiences and actors as well as for his "understanding readers," making it necessary for him to adapt to contemporary taste and not to isolate himself in an impregnable poetic creed. He apparently accepted the challenge to be successful as well as right in a number of ways, sometimes accommodating his art to the baser elements of his audience and sometimes reaching for heights of thought or mirth that appealed to none or few. In his comedies he never failed to mix his appeals (although it is hard to be sure whether consciously or unconsciously), but he always seems to have been asking for more than the obvious meaning, some unforeseen or latent effect. There is evidence to suggest that as Jonson matured he became more tentative about his judgments of life and more accommodating in his plays; he was an entertainer, yet he wanted to be understood differently by the better part of his public.

Most of the essays here are comparative, placing the comedies in some kind of historical context, where their conventional and original techniques can be understood only by comparison with the art of Shakespeare and other Elizabethan comic dramatists. Jonson may not have been the soul of his age, but in many ways he was a child of it, even when he deliberately turned against it. The tone and texture of that complex reaction interest me, and I am often delighted by the way his sense of fun becomes part of the strategy that mediates between him and his contemporaries without ever making peace.

I have not tried to cover all the comedies, because I did not have something to say about every one, nor have I given a systematic account of all aspects of his art in the plays that are discussed. Jonas Barish has done so well in *Ben Jonson and the Language of Prose Comedy* with style and characterization, and Edward B. Partridge has done so well in *The Broken Compass* with themes and images, that I have more or less avoided those topics. Instead, my main concerns have been with Jonson's attempts to speak to, to fool, or to enlighten his audiences. The first essay examines his attitudes toward the theater and contrasts them with Shakespeare's. The following studies look at the ways these attitudes were realized or expressed in his comedies, so to that extent there is adumbrated here a rhetoric of his comedies, his techniques of communicating with spectators and readers. Three chapters describe the critical and dramatic evidence for a special kind of Elizabethan comedy and Jonson's adaptation of it in the so-called comical satires, mixing caustic laughter with admiration. His striving for these effects culminated in the best of his early plays, *Poetaster* (excepting the revised *Every Man in His Humor* because its final form belongs to his middle years). The next chapter investigates the force of dramatic speech, illustrated from *Volpone*, showing his mature ability to write superbly evocative language. The design of Jonson's plots reveals more about his changing dramatic methods at mid-career in *The Alchemist* and *Epicoene* as he aims to please a mixed audience. The essay on *Bartholomew Fair* analyzes his most volatile mixture, a brilliant combination of materials calculated to appeal to radically different sensibilities, as the comedy succeeds most when it borders on travesty. Jonson's later plays, such as *The Staple of News, The New Inn, Tale of a Tub,* and the unfinished *Sad Shepherd,* worked out distinct aspects of what he had achieved in *Bartholomew Fair,* when he had settled into a moderated contempt and wise playfulness in his dealings with the theater and with life. He really meant it when he said that the stage was loathsome, but since he continued to write for the theater, and sometimes very well, it must have been important to him and more than just a living. A certain spirit of mirth, provoking wise laughter, sometimes shines through at surprising moments in those last attempts to accommodate his art to a new audience.

My debts to Madeleine Doran's *Endeavors of Art* and Muriel Bradbrook's *The Growth and Structure of Elizabethan Comedy* are more general than notes can record. Portions of chapters 5 and 6 appeared in *Studies in the Literary Imagination,* 6, no. 1 (1973), and in *PMLA,* 84, no. 1 (1969), and I am grateful to the publishers for allowing me to reprint the essays, considerably revised. Parts of other chapters were presented in lecture form to groups at the Huntington Library, the Southern California Renaissance Society, the University of California at Davis, and the University of California at Riverside. My friend Arthur Kirsch read several chapters and made many useful suggestions, and Robert Sanoff and Harold Weber were particularly helpful in correcting details. A grant from the Cooperative Program in the Humanities at the University of North Carolina-Duke, in 1968-69, enabled me to begin these studies, and a grant from the Huntington Library, 1973-74, helped me to finish. Although Chapel Hill and San Marino are very different places, they both have a protective and stimulating atmosphere that fosters a love of learning and beauty. I thank James Thorpe and O. B. Hardison for their support and encouragement, and I rejoice in the resources of the Folger and Huntington Libraries.

Charlottesville, Virginia
September, 1975

Jonson and Elizabethan Comedy

1.

Jonson, Shakespeare, and the Divided Audience

Drama of the Elizabethan and Jacobean age is distinguished for many things — it has immense human vitality, its dialogue, even if we exclude Shakespeare's, contains some of the best dramatic poetry in the language, and its social and moral themes continue to engage the sympathies of people far removed in time and place. It is also distinguished because it is eminently playable. Since the dramas were written for actors, the lines have power to come across to spectators, as many recent commentators have noticed. Actors probably always knew it. These plays were for stages that encouraged an intimate contact with their audience, not very different from conditions at popular or courtly festivals. Coming before doctrines of verisimilitude had gripped the theater, before actors had to contend with constricting rules about truth of representation, not to mention the proscenium arch, elaborate scenery, and the recessed stage (rather than the apron stage jutting into the auditorium) that tended to separate the actors from the spectators, the theaters of Renaissance England gave playwrights an opportunity to exploit artifice as well as life.[1] There prevailed a greater technical liberty, and there must have been a quicker interaction between the stage and the galleries that modern drama has only lately rediscovered. I do not mean to imply that the conventions of performance were uniform, rude, and simple, for indeed they were in many ways various, complex, and sophisticated.

I

Jonson and Elizabethan Comedy

Although Shakespeare and Jonson wrote for a pre-illusionist theater, they did not find its forms to be just a continuation of medieval conventions. The conditions of playing had recently been legitimized for professional troupes of actors in established theaters, and more skillful acting had to blend with old traditions of sport or "game." Under royal and artistocratic patronage, the companies flourished in public theaters and gamehouses, in private theaters and great halls. Presenting a play at court before important people was a troupe's reason for existing and for its protection from Puritan attack. Therefore the display of skill in entertainment probably increased even as the style of acting became more natural. From the audience's point of view, playing may very well have seemed formal to some and natural to others, depending on their experience with the theater. By 1600, anyway, the old style in Cambyses' vein struck some fine sensibilities as crude mouthing, and Tamburlaine's vociferous vaunts had gone out of favor, in preference for dialogue that seemed more natural, closer to common language. But the best of Burbage was still probably rather formal by comparison with natural acting of the twentieth century.

At any rate the new professional standards amidst surviving liberties of drama as a game created a lively self-awareness. Special effects of art might be perceived in a play as deliberate reassertion of slightly archaic devices set off from more sophisticated techniques, or new methods might cut a figure against a background of convention. As appropriate to the context, actors delivered either natural or highly mannered speeches, some in plain style and some consciously artificial; yet they used their art to evoke something like real feelings, as is suggested by much contemporary testimony. The face of Desdemona, as she lay dying on her bed, implored the pity of Jacobean audiences, and they were moved to tears. They were expected to respond with sorrow, guilt, admiration, and delight, as they enjoyed themselves, and perhaps some also might have found a "cure" for their faults or diseased minds, partly because auditors were encouraged to see reflections of real experience as well as of ideas of virtue and images of vice. Nowhere were these conditions of performance more clearly shown than in the comedies of the time.

The signs of an especially self-aware theater survived in comedies because there were so many more occasions to sport with the pit or with gallants on the stage. Ample evidence exists that the Admiral's Men, the Chamberlain's Men, and later the King's Men, as well as children's companies, provided lively entertainment. Music was heard during pauses in the performances at private theaters; and at public theaters perhaps there was a jig afterwards,[2] these activities doing what opening and closing the curtain did for performances later in the seventeenth century. On off days some stages, the "gamehouses," were used for fencing demonstrations, vaulting, acrobatic shows, cockfights, or bearbaiting; consequently it was natural that a definitely local sport at the Globe would have been seen in *Twelfth Night* in the mock duel between Sir Andrew Aguecheek and Viola, or it was a clever touch in *Epicoene,* at Whitefriars, that the vexations of Morose should have a tinge of bearbaiting,[3] an instance of a sport excluded from private theaters but allowed as entertainment in the comedies presented there.

Therefore, it seems likely that a playwright who, like Jonson, wanted control over the production of his work would capitalize on stage conventions. He had other opportunities in addition to the common use of male/female disguises and its conventional sport with boys in women's parts. Rather than let Tarleton or Kempe improvise, the comic dramatist might write episodes into the script to control what would otherwise have been inane fooling around. For instance, the Christopher Sly induction to *Taming of the Shrew* is a kind of jig, essentially a practical joke with a theatrical point, since it effectively spoofs at remarks from the audience (" 'Tis a very excellent piece of work, madam lady. Would 'twere done") and at the same time demonstrates how spectators are induced to accept the reality of a fictional world. For similar reasons Jonson and his contemporaries repeatedly use preliminary maneuvers with surrogate audiences in "unplanned" conversation with the stage keeper or with the prologue. This kind of induction is the dramatic equivalent of the mock "accident" at the beginning of courtly festivities. When Queen Elizabeth approached the gates of Kenilworth Castle starting Leicester's famous entertainment in 1575, a huge porter blocked the way, pretending that he did not know the queen and her entourage. He roared in a rough speech, full of passions, but "in meter aptly made to the purpose." He burst out "in a great pang of impatience to see such uncouth trudging to and fro, such riding in and out with such din and noise of talk." But when he laid eyes on the monarch, he was transfixed; this must be a goddess; and he fell on his knees, giving her the key and asking her forgiveness.[4]

I suspect that the concluding theatrical sports of the Nine Worthies in *Love's Labor's Lost* and the playlet of Pyramus and Thisbe in *A Midsummer Night's Dream* were absurd counterparts of the conventional jigs,[5] and perhaps the masque near the end of *The Tempest* and the palinode closing *Cynthia's Revels* were more serious counterparts. After the first trial scene in *Volpone* when the comedy seems to be finished, Volpone proposes one more trick "to vex 'em all," and Jonson calls attention to this as if it were an afterpiece, by the question, "Shall we have a jig now?" (V.ii.59). Moreover, the puppet shows in *Tale of a Tub* and *Bartholomew Fair* seem to be spoofs at fifth-act shows within the dramas.

There must have been some formal or ceremonial pressure felt by theater people when they wanted a festive close for the afternoon. This form of closure also gave the author a chance to comment on his play and to emphasize the game the actors were playing, raising a laugh and encouraging applause — for which actors and writers have always had an unlimited appetite. It gave the audience an extra moment of detachment to look back at the drama from an oblique perspective and to reflect upon it, if they were so inclined.

Those playful moments at the start and finish of a drama seem to be most theatrical when actors and audience are moving in and out of the fictional world together and when actors have more chance to talk about what they are doing.[6] During the play itself, extradramatic moments (as they are misnamed) were used as early as the medieval cycles, and they continued to be common enough through the first half of the seventeenth century. Highly mannered speeches, soliloquies, asides, and various kinds of *coups de théâtre* were an important part of the pre-illusionist theater. I do not mean to suggest that the drama encouraged no illusion, but rather that there was a free play of fact and fiction. The inductions, the formal close, prologues, and epilogues show actors commenting on these things and show them getting into the intimate mood; these conventions suggest the partial survival of a medieval conception of drama as playing a game — actors as gamesters.[7] As I understand the game of drama, there was less difference between Jacobean and Elizabethan stages than we have been led to think, less distinction between children's companies and the adult ones (which still used children, after all). The theatricality of Marston and Jonson's dramaturgy may not have been as original as we suppose, because there never was a realistic or strictly illusionist theater that preceded them. They were not breaking an illusion or surprising audiences with their daring so much as they were exploiting time-honored devices of artificial stage-playing at a time that called for a more professional style of acting. Jonson and Marston did not invent these self-referring devices, but they mocked and dissimulated with them in an original way.[8] From Jonson's practice I see many shifts of tone and strategy as he moves back and forth between public and private theaters, but his theatricality remains fairly constant. And in the early seventeenth century the premier company of London actors easily served both kinds of stages with apparently the same repertory.

The point is not so much who actually saw the plays in what theaters, although much information has accumulated about the price of admission, the classes of people who went to the private or public theaters, where they sat, and the like. Granted there has been useful speculation about their different tastes, based mostly on our knowledge of the repertories of various companies.[9] And certainly subject matter, allusions, and degree of sophistication would often vary between plays for public or private performance, but what governed the construction and the art of plays was not so much how they liked it but how the dramatist thought they would like it. In other words, we come closer to a playwright's art if, as we keep in mind the actual conditions of presentation, we try to discover the power of the script. Is it a medium for actors, and what might be its potential effect on an audience? And how is it governed by the special perceptions of a given dramatist? Eventually the problem returns to the playwright's conception of his task, his ethos, and his public. Every playwright understood certain postulates, even if he never formulated them explicitly, that helped him function in a complex social and theatrical milieu. These postulates are open to investigation, and they can be useful for interpretation if we do not think of them as all-purpose solutions or skeleton keys to the plays, but merely as interesting hypotheses, ideas to be tested on the pulses of dramatic experience. For the plays themselves were often larger than critical categories.

I. LOVING AND UNDERSTANDING

A familiar assumption about drama that everyone shared complemented rather than opposed the custom of playing as a game. There was widespread agreement in ancient and medieval theory, surviving in the Renaissance alongside newer ideas of comedy, that drama was a neighbor of oratory and that comedy was its nearest neighbor, since it dealt as a lawyer did with the common conditions of men.[10] Like an orator, the comic poet had to play his game in a sort of courtroom trial to appeal to two kinds of auditors, the better and the worse. Quintilian, the standard source of sixteenth- and seventeenth-century rhetorics, had acknowledged the degrees of difference in almost any public gathering when he remarked that if all juries were made of wise men, orators need not appeal to emotion nor try to charm, soothe, nor exhort. They might use only bare argument. ''Since however our judges are the people or drawn from the people, and since those who are appointed to give sentence are frequently ill-educated and sometimes mere rustics, it becomes necessary to employ every method that we think likely to assist our case,'' and these artifices must be shown in writing as well as in speech (*Inst.* 12.10.52-53). That distinction influences oratorical style too, because some listeners are moved by bombast and licentious diction, others by finer eloquence. Quintilian avoids an absolute division of audiences, nevertheless, saying that even the rough sort of listeners can be stirred by better eloquence, for "every effort of the voice inspires a natural pleasure in the soul of man." Although discriminating listeners reject false brilliance and although the multitude approves things that are in poor taste, no one is unmoved by good speaking (12.10.73-76).

Elizabethan prologues and epilogues reveal the common attitude that such a theory might generate in a culture that was nursed on a rhetorical education, and they show what would occur to a playwright trying to address a mixed crowd. Conventionally the audiences were "judging spectators" — combined judges and juries — and the legal metaphors easily followed in both comedy and tragedy. The audience must "kindly judge our play," not "condemn," "tax," or "censure." Accord with the assembly was achieved by means of "bonds," "indentures," and "covenants," the most elaborate being the mock-legal articles of agreement between the author and the audience in the induction to *Bartholomew Fair*. The "decision" at the end of a play was almost invariably "judgment" or "doom" that would "save," "free," "release," "acquit," or "pardon" the play.[11] It was probably not accidental that the comedies themselves often led to a climactic trial scene, as in *The Merchant of Venice, Poetaster,* and *Volpone, Volpone* outdoing the others by giving us two bizarre trials. Many comedies at least ended with some definitely legal disposition of the drama, as in *Comedy of Errors, Measure for Measure,* Middleton's *Michaelmas Term,* and Jonson's *Every Man in His Humor*,[12] Legal difficulties often were a part of the *donné* of a comic plot, as well. Northrop Frye points out that there was often an irrational law explained at the start of a play, out of which the argument of the comedy proceeds: the rule that women may not enter the academy of Navarre and that the men must take an oath of celibacy for three years, the law that any citizen of Syracuse must pay with his life if he is found in Ephesus, the law that all lechery is punishable by death, and the law of obligatory marriage in *A Midsummer Night's Dream*. Compacts like the venture tripartite in *The Alchemist* between Dol Common, Face, and Subtle — their common cause and the little game to see who will cozen the best in one day — this

7

and the statute against sorcery generate much of the action in that play. The legal metaphor, thus, often becomes a literal fact in the world of the play.

Hamlet best expressed the usual educated opinion that in the audience there were two kinds of people, the unskillful and the judicious. He advised the players not to use base rhetoric fit for the groundling's wit, overdone style that may make the "unskillful laugh cannot but make the judicious grieve, the censure of the which one must in your allowance o'erweigh a whole theater of the others." For Hamlet the censure of one discriminating person means more than the approval of the common multitude (III.ii.28-32).[13] He preferred a play that was never acted "or if it was not above once," something like Marlowe's *Dido Queen of Carthage*. It never pleased the million, only him and a few others with better judgments who thought it modest, cunning, and unaffected; no sallets in the lines to make the matter savory to the general multitude — or to people like Polonius who wants a jig or a tale of bawdry, else he sleeps (II.ii. 440-71, 503-05). Hamlet sounds like a literary critic strayed into the playhouse, a critic with views that Jonson would approve of.

But Shakespeare went beyond Hamlet's elitist separation between levels of taste, and in the process he departed from common theories, turning Quintilian's idea of an address to the natural pleasure of everyone's soul into a completely different relationship. Shakespeare's most frequent appeals came from a self-deprecating actor, aware of his imperfections, who modestly pointed out defects in his art and who asked for charity. In this way the dramatist, identifying with the actors, used a finer rhetoric than Quintilian knew. His usual method was to welcome a loving auditory who had a capacity to forgive and an imagination to mend the actor's faults. He closed his plays in the same way. For instance, in the epilogue to *The Tempest* Prospero pleads for "good hands" and "gentle breath" from the spectators to send him back to Milan, now that he has renounced his quasi-dramatic magic:

> Now I want
> Spirits to enforce, art to enchant;

> And my ending is despair
> Unless I be relieved by prayer,
> Which pierces so that it assaults
> Mercy itself and frees all faults.
> As you from crimes would pardoned be,
> Let your indulgence set me free.

Ceremonial applause sets the actor free from both his fictional role and his faults. Furthermore the choruses to *Henry V* ask for an active, generous imagination that can transform the inadequate facilities of the stage and the small band of actors into a heroic English army. "Piece out our imperfections with your thoughts," "your thoughts that now must deck our kings." For a comic application of this idea of a gracious imagination, Theseus in *A Midsummer Night's Dream* remarks on the crudities of performance in Pyramus and Thisbe: "The best in this kind are but shadows: and the worst are no worse if imagination amend them." When Hippolyta objects that it is his imagination not the actors', his reply gets to the heart of Shakespeare's gentle view and appeals to the audience's better feelings: "If we imagine no worse of them than they of themselves they may pass for excellent men. Here come two noble beasts in, a man and a lion" (V.i.214-71).

That attitude suggests a creative kindness that a monarch might display when great scholars came with premeditated welcome to meet him at his approach to a city. Although they shivered and looked pale, made periods in the middle of sentences, misplaced accents, and finally broke off in silence, Duke Theseus responded with generous condescension.

> Trust me, sweet,
> Out of this silence yet I picked a welcome . . .
> Love, therefore, and tongue-tied simplicity
> In least speak most, to my capacity.

(V.i.99-105)

In short, noble respect for the intent of the actor makes a good listener. Hamlet himself advises this noble respect toward players when he tells Polonius to treat the players not according to their merits, but "after your own honor and dignity — the less they

9

deserve the more merit is in your bounty." "Use every man after his desert, and who shall scape whipping?" (II.ii.533-59). Such a theory still allowed Shakespeare to contrast the gracious with the ungracious audiences, no doubt, and he illustrated the distinction in the ill-behaved gentlemen of Navarre in *Love's Labor's Lost*. The princess reproves them for unkind treatment of the fools in the fifth act pageant, asking the gentlemen to remember that true mirth lies where "zeal strives to content, and the contents/ Dies in the zeal of that which it presents." So the distinction is there even though we do not hear much about it, because after all Shakespeare identifies with the actor who must strive to content; therefore his main emphasis when he speaks of performances is one of love, not critical judgment. Sonnet 23 nicely combines the feeling of a lover and the theatrical metaphor close to Shakespeare's heart:

> As an unperfect actor on the stage,
> Who with his fear is put besides his part,
> Or some fierce thing replete with too much rage,
> Whose strength's abundance weakens his own heart;
> So I, for fear of trust, forget to say
> The perfect ceremony of love's rite,
> And in mine own love's strength seem to decay,
> O'er charged with burden of mine own love's might.
> O, let my looks be then the eloquence
> And dumb presagers of my speaking breast,
> Who plead for love, and look for recompence,
> More than that tongue that hath more expressed.
>> O, learn to read what silent love hath writ:
>> To hear with eyes belongs to love's fine wit.

If Shakespeare sought a loving audience among his judges, Jonson sought an understanding one. Shakespeare conceived of a harmony of poet, actors, and audience, in a bond of hearts that ties with more than words. Jonson felt a threatening tension between himself, the stage, and his audience, with the consequent need to control them, to subordinate them, in the service of his art. Awareness of this tension is fundamental for an appreciation of Jonson, and it has valuable implications that I want to explore in the following essays. Ultimately, however, there is not an absolute

contrast between Shakespeare and Jonson, because Jonson was by
no means simple nor single-minded. He was writing plays, not
moral or intellectual treatises, writing comedies, not just satires, and
he was a man in the theater, if not of the theater, who knew the
demands he had to satisfy.[14] (For that matter neither was Shakespeare completely averse to satiric judgment, in a character like
Malvolio or Thersites.)[15]

An extreme instance of Jonson's awareness of the audience,
and of his theatrical game playing, occurs in the induction to
Cynthia's Revels (1600). (It was his first production for a private
theater, but he used the induction much as he had in his previous
play for the Chamberlain's Men, *Every Man out of His Humor.*)
After the second sounding of trumpets, three of the children walk on
stage quarreling about who should deliver the prologue. To the
audience this appears to be an unplanned foul-up among inexperi-
enced young actors. One Boy has the official prologue's cloak, but
2. Boy claims he has memorized the piece better, and 3. Boy insists
that the author wants him to speak it. One Boy confidently calls for a
vote of the assembly, but the boys decide in all fairness to draw lots
instead, leaving it to fortune. One Boy proves his right to be wearing
the cloak, for he wins the draw; however he hints at an unseen guiding hand behind it all: "Fortune was not altogether blind in this."
Recognizing the trick that the author has played on him, 3.Boy feels
trapped in the script of what the audience had at first thought was an
unrehearsed, earnest quarrel. Thus Jonson emphasizes right off the
distinction between game and earnest: 1. and 2.Boys are presumably playing the game, 3.Boy seems earnest. Three Boy is determined to break out somehow and to get his revenge on the poet:
"I'll go tell all the argument of his play aforehand, and so stale [pun
on "urinate"] his invention to the auditory before it come forth."
The other two boys try to interrupt his nonstop recitation of the plot
because it is a spoil-sport kind of thing; it spoils the feast, giving the
audience an inventory of the cates aforehand, as if they dined in a
tavern. That is hardly a fitting routine for this select gathering.

So far Jonson accomplishes a number of things by such fooling
around. He flatters the high-class audience, who presumably do not

11

eat in taverns and who need no bill-of-fare. Under the guise of not doing the proper thing, he does it, while summarizing the argument of a rather complicated play. And if anyone accuses him of being pedantic, he can claim a special decorum, because a rebellious actor said the offending things, he did not. Finally, and most important, he creates an atmosphere of improvisation and unpredictability. As actors and audience move out of the world of fact and exactly when they discover that this silly business of boys quarreling really may be part of the play, 3.Boy becomes earnest, spoiling the fiction. Nevertheless his plot summary is obviously the author's work too and is properly within the conventions of a preliminary skit. Human perversity of actors threatens to take charge of the stage, but the author's game is big enough to contain it. So unpredictability is really controlled chance. By means of an apparent dramatic license the poet has shown how much he really is following certain conventional laws. These interplays between game and earnest, laws and license, author and actors increase our sense that we must be on guard. This is not going to be an ordinary comedy, and it will take an extraordinary act of attention.

The rest of the induction reinforces that impression, as Jonson toys with various attitudes of the spectators while he jabs at their understanding. At first it was a struggle between actors and author; now it changes to a struggle between the author and actors on one hand and the audience on the other. Out of this second struggle Jonson clarifies his conception of the divided audience. After he has summarized the argument of the play, 3.Boy next borrows the cloak and pretends he is an ignorant gentleman-critic, sitting on the stage, railing at actors — "rascally tits," they are, who act like "so many wrens or pismires." Between puffs on his tobacco pipe, he complains of the abominable music and their lamentable songs, "like the pitiful fellows that make them — poets." The smell of the actors' bodies would be intolerable if he had not tobacco to mask it. He'd as soon visit fifteen jails or a dozen hospitals as come near them. So much for the ignorant rebellious critic. Next 3. Boy changes his role to that of a "more sober or better-gathered gallant" who is a friend or well-wisher of the house. He offers to speak for the "more judicious part" of the assembly who advocate a reform of stage wit in unmistakably urbane terms. As points for negotiation with the author, he advocates that they banish immodest and obscene writing, stale apothegms, and other men's jests, that they abstain from "penuriously" taking wit from every laundress or hackney man, or wit derived from servile imitation of the "common stages" and from observation of the people who frequent them.

These hieratic opinions are likely to be Jonson's own, transposed but slightly, for they seem to ask for his characteristically fresh invention, above the common sort. At any rate the division is made between the uninformed railer and patrons of new wit; old wit presumably goes with ignorance, since Jonson always prided himself on his well-informed originality. Two Boy, who stands as "attorney" for the poet, affirms that this play is untouched by any breath of servile or common writing, but he will not be dictated to by any spectators, and everyone better watch out, because he can see through the pretentions of most of the gallants. Finding "tokens" of the auditory right there in the hall, 2.Boy rips through a series of five caricatures of gallant playgoers, scoring each for his defective wit. One judges by authority of his fine clothes — a smelling civet wit. Another swears that old Hieronimo (as it was first acted with all its bombast, that is before Jonson's equally bombastic additions to the script) was the only best and judiciously penned play in Europe. Another favors the French taste of twenty years ago when the Duke of Alençon visited. A fourth miscalls everything "fustian" that his grounded capacity cannot aspire to. "A fifth, only shakes his bottle head, and out of his corky brain squeezeth out a pitiful-learned face, and is silent" (215-17). The conclusion is left to the understanders: as we reject old wit in the play, so should we scorn it in the audience.

This demonstration puts down 3.Boy, and in tribute to the poet he renounces the cloak, giving it to 1.Boy — a symbolic gesture sealing the bond between actors, poet, and the judicious part of the audience. Three Boy even regrets his misbehavior and gives his blessing of sorts: "Here, take your cloak and promise some satisfaction in your prologue, or (I'll be sworn) we have marred all." Two

Boy replies in equally genial terms, "Tut, fear not, Sal" (that is, Salomon Pavy, Jonson's favorite, who must have played 3.Boy), "fear not Sal, this will never distaste a true sense" (219-23). In other words, the true understanders will know that the quarrel was mock and that the poet was up to something else.[16]

Now that rebellious actors and a rebellious audience have been put in their places, the prologue can go on in due form, and there is no question but that the poet is in command. He asks for gracious silence, sweet attention, quick sight, and "quicker apprehension." The author hopes the spectators have all these qualities, and if they do, he opens himself to them. To weaker minds he closes his labors, lest he prostitute their virgin offspring to "every vulgar and adulterate brain." His muse aims for originality that only "learned" ears can perceive, and she avoids popular applause or "foamy praise that drops from common jaws." The true function of the auditory's quick apprehension is to admire, to wonder, to weave not bays but a garland of light that should crown his poesy, and the garland is made only by those who can censure, understand, and define. The poet knows, equally well, that their understanding will be complete only if his poesy gives precedence to "Words above action, matter above words." In other terms, dialogue before spectacle, ideas before dialogue: for an audience must see with its ears and hear with its mind. This is Jonson's creed, that seems to bind him with his audience, fit though few. It is essentially a manifesto, setting forth his hierarchy of dramatic values, and even when Jonson speaks in a coterie theater, where he might expect a more educated audience, he feels the need to distinguish between the worse and the better understanders of these values. Yet is it not significant that he needs to go through that playful ritual before he comes to this conclusion? Might there be some analogy between his art and Bottom's dream?

II. FROM REFORMATION TO ACCOMMODATION

Jonson never abandoned his critical spirit, though he condescended to entertain the Jacobean and Caroline ages in more than thirty years of dramatic writing. Lorenzo Junior's defense of poesy in the early version of *Every Man in His Humor* (acted 1598) set the tone of Jonson's career, when he contrasted the idea of poetry in its blessed, eternal, and true state with poesy as she appeared in many poor, lame, and patched remnants and old, worn rags. Invention those days was half-starved, but if we could conceive of poetry as a majestic spirit we would know that she is fit only for grave and consecrated eyes, nor can she be blemished by lean, ignorant and blasted wits, brainless gulls, and the fat judgments of the multitude (V.v.312-43). Ever after, Jonson somehow managed to suggest that his work was above cheapness and worn-out conventions — "fools and devils and those antique relics of barbarism" (dedication to *Volpone,* 1606), even when he put fools and devils on the stage. Good judging spectators give "justice" because they do not depend on "fortune that favors fools" (prologue to *The Alchemist,* 1610). The dramatist would "have you wise,/ Much rather by your ears than by yours eyes" (prologue to *Staple of News,* 1625). "He will not woo the gentle ignorance so much. But careless of all vulgar censure, as not depending on common approbation, he is confident it shall super-please judicious spectators" (induction to *Magnetic Lady,* 1632).[17]

The strongest assertions came in his early satiric comedies, when he was more on the defensive, as he thundered at errors of the stage and cast bolts at envious slanderers. *Poetaster* (1601) begins both the quarto and folio texts with Envy in a grotesque, snakey costume, impersonating hostile members of the audience who might blast our pleasures and destroy our sports with "wrestings, comments, applications,/ Spy-like suggestions, privy whisperings/ And thousand such promoting slights" (24-26). Poet-apes or players come to spy, pervert, and poison — in short, they use envy's snakes to arm themselves with triple malice. Envy goads on these people in the auditorium, "Here take my snakes among you, come and eat,/ And while the squeezed juice flows in your black jaws,/ Help me to damn the author. Spit it forth/ Upon his lines" (44-47). Since no one comes forward to take the snakes, Envy prepares to leave the stage, but the Prologue appears — representing the author's "well-erected confidence." And although open malice and illiterate detraction have been, in effect, charmed out of the theater, the play itself, he says, will step on envy's head, fright its pride, and laugh its folly away.

As with the three boys in *Cynthia's Revels,* the overtones and complications of Envy's speeches seem nearly as interesting as the doctrine. Although words are still above action, stage action has not been slighted, and although matter remains above words, the words are powerfully dramatic and inflammatory. It is hard to miss the zest, the aggressive intimidation, and the caricature of the audience when, with a certain relish, Envy asks them to choose the longest vipers "to stick down/ In your deep throats, and let the heads come forth/ At your rank mouths" (49-51). The mood turns to self-congratulation when the loftier and free-spirited author agrees to entertain his friends while he complacently pities his enemies. In effect, the induction and prologue of *Poetaster* ritually silence the opposition and clear the air — for now, presumably, only friends are present. The opening ceremonies have seized their minds, anesthetized objections, poisoned the wells of debate, and forced opponents into ignominious roles. At its worst the poet's address might be called bluster, but in Jonson's terms it was the erected confidence — that same mental equanimity that Horace displays in the drama that follows. But confidence comes forth only after some vigorous and grotesque conjuring of evil spirits. Indeed, I wonder if these theatrical maneuvers do more than preach sermons about reform. Although Jonson is a protestant of the theater, as Aldous Huxley called him,[18] he seems to reach out by these devices to more catholic responses that modify the reforming dogma. If so, we are in danger of distorting his artistic power when we take Jonson at his word, depending only upon his much advertised literary theories. He was a praiser of "master spirits," who wanted to be a master spirit himself, to steer the minds of the people. "I shall raise the despis'd head of poetry again, and [like Luther] stripping her out of those rotten and base rags, wherewith the times have adulterated her form, restore her to her primitive habit, feature, and majesty, and render her worthy to be embraced, and kissed, of all the great and master spirits of our world" (dedication to *Volpone,* 129-34). But his manner of doing those things was so explosive and so provocative that it was not easy to control. License or "allowed" fooling and various softening appeals, therefore, became indispensable to Jonson.

An appeal to the spectators' charity is one of the ways he softened the thunderbolts. In *Poetaster,* for instance, the prologue implores that we should not think the poet is arrogant when he says his play is good; he hopes that free souls will allow him the liberty to follow his own strength. In *Every Man in His Humor* (prologue to the folio text), he deplores conventions and errors of the stage, but he hopes that the audience can learn from a just image of the times expressed in language such as men do use. If poets do not pander to "ill customs of the stage" and do not make the audience love their "popular errors" (as a flatterer would), the spectators can learn to laugh at such faults:

> Which when you heartily do, there's hope left, then,
> You, that have so graced monsters, may like men.

(29-30)

Apparently there is a saving remnant in people at large, but in Jonson's opinion, although we may naturally love good drama, we have become corrupted by bad habit. The need is to develop a capacity to laugh at the truly ugly in order to come again to love the natural. Asper lacks nearly every touch of graciousness when he welcomes spectators to *Every Man out of His Humor* and describes his program. He invites them to be critical, but

> Yet here, mistake me not, judicious friends,
> I do not this to beg your patience,
> Or servilely to fawn on your applause,
> Like some dry brain despairing in his merit:
> Let me be censured, by th' austerest brow,
> Where I want art, or judgment, tax me freely.

(56-61)

Mild Cordatus, however, in the same induction, plays the gracious role, asking the audience not to misjudge the dramatist's intention.

> Kind gentlemen, we hope your patience

17

Jonson and Elizabethan Comedy

Will yet conceive the best, or entertain
The supposition that a madman speaks.

(148-50)

He gives us a way of saving face and of saving the poet from being responsible for Asper's sharp attacks. The players' endeavors should be how to please, Cordatus insists, and Asper agrees, but to please whom? The better auditors, of course.

In prologues and inductions Jonson continues to hector the audience of play after play. He quarrels with their love of tired old devices and "monsters" that Shakespeare, among others, gave them, and he reproves the ingorance and bad taste of his readers to the end of his career. Yet the tolerance that was needed to support zestful good fun became more and more important in his relationship with the theater.

An open appeal to tolerance, at least from the better kind of critics, appears later in a number of forms, especially with regard to violations of comic law: though the catastrophe of *Volpone* may, "in the strict rigor of comic law, meet with censure, as turning back to my promise, I desire the learned, and charitable critic to have so much faith in me, to think it was done of industry" (Dedication, 109-12). *The Alchemist* ends on a similar note, when Face steps forward to confess that his part fell a little in the last scene:

> Yet 'twas decorum. And though I am clean
> Got off, from Subtle, Surley, Mammon, Dol,
> Hot Ananias, Dapper, Drugger, all
> With whom I traded; yet I put my self
> On you, that are my country: and this pelf,
> Which I have got, if you do quit me, rests
> To feast you often, and invite new guests.

(V.v.159-65)

Since England is the best place for mirth, Face is willing to be judged by a jury of his countrymen, and the riches of cozening he has accumulated — his pelf — will continue to feast the comic audience.[19] There is an important shift here from stern judging to indulgent, though proper, mirth.

Lovewit, who lives up to his name, has the same inclinations that are expected from the audience. He helps the events to imitate justice with regard to some of the rogues and fools when he mulcts bawds and rivals to Face's game, but to the master brain of the whole fantastic scheme Lovewit feels forgiveness and indulgence. Face is an "allowed" jester. The benefits of mirth and wit outweigh the offenses for, he says,

> That master
> That had receiv'd such happiness by a servant
> In such a widow, and with so much wealth,
> Were very ungrateful, if he would not be
> A little indulgent to that servant's wit,
> And help his fortune, though with some small strain
> Of his own candor.
>
> (V.v.146-52)

Lovewit seems to apologize for his liberality, suggesting that it is within the bounds of propriety, as he explains in the rest of the same speech:

> Therefore, gentlemen,
> And kind spectators, if I have out-stripped
> An old man's gravity, or strict canon, think
> What a young wife, and good brain may do:
> Stretch age's truth sometimes, and crack it too.
>
> (152-56)

The poet's brain is also allowed that liberty, to stretch art's truth and crack it too. In a variation on Lovewit's liberality, the actor playing Volpone steps forward at the end of his play and asks the audience to take a different view of justice from that in the drama:

> The seasoning of a play is the applause.
> Now, though the Fox be punished by the laws,
> He, yet, doth hope there is no suff'ring due,
> For any fact, which he hath done 'gainst you;
> If there be, censure him: here he doubtful stands,
> If not, fare jovially, and clap your hands.
>
> (V.xii.152-56)

In other words, Volpone was punished in the play, but if the actor has done no personal harm to anyone in the auditorium, he ought to

be rewarded or set free with jovial applause.[20]   The prologue to
The Alchemist turns this point into an explicit distinction, wishing
nothing be left to chance: justice for the author but grace to the
players.

The clearest evidence of Jonson's greater emphasis on pleasure
and liberty comes from the prologue to *Epicoene* (1609), where he
asks for less and gives more to the spectators than the carefully
hedged joviality of Volpone or the justice and mirth of Lovewit. He
presents *Epicoene* explicitly as a public feast for the pleasure of a
mixed audience. The rhetorical maneuvers to silence and belittle
spectators give way to the old art of making plays to content the
people. Some writers care only for "particular likings" and will not
taste anything popular, but our play is to please not the cook but the
guests. Nevertheless, Jonson is less than ingenuous, for he assures
"cunning" palates that they can come to his feast and still get a
place and good treatment. Furthermore, when some of these with
cunning palates leave their seats, they will have found things in the
play that will make them admit: "Who wrote that piece, could so
have wrote a play:/ But that he knew this was the better way"
(14-15). Again, we have the suggestion that Jonson consciously
deviates from certain laws of comedy, and he expects better people
to understand that some decorum may be invoked to justify it. It
would not have been fine cookery otherwise.

> For to present all custard, or all tart,
> And have no other meats, to bear a part,
> Or to want bread, and salt, were but coarse art.
>
> (16-18)

And the prologue concludes with a promise that the whole feast will
have things

> fit for ladies: some for lords, knights, squires,
> Some for your waiting wench, and city wires,
> Some for your men, and daughters of Whitefriars.
>
> (22-24)

That amounts to the full range of society from ladies and lords down
to prostitutes. The suggestion is strong here of a principle of artistic

accommodation — how a writer can keep his integrity and yet satisfy different expectations of his public.

This softened attitude of accommodation to the pleasures of a mixed audience changed Jonson's rhetorical strategies gradually. Although the attitude was latent in his early comedies, I think he learned by experience how important it was to be ingratiating and to evoke delight for all who came to his plays. His efforts to write masques for court that began in 1605, the heady success of *Volpone* (1606), which won the approbation of learned spectators at Oxford and Cambridge as well as spectators of the public stage at the Globe, and the failure of his uncompromising *Sejanus* (1603) must have left an impression. He began revising *Every Man in His Humor*, probably in 1605,[21] to adapt it to English mirth, and in the same year he collaborated with Marston and Chapman on a jolly London comedy, *Eastward Ho!*

Jonson also could have found theoretical justification for his new pliability in Horace's *Ars Poetica*. He announced in the address to the readers of *Sejanus* that he was preparing a translation and commentary to Horace's epistle, and he repeated the promise to publish it soon, in the dedication to *Volpone* (1607). By 1619, when he read the commentary to Drummond, it included a dialogue, with John Donne cast in the role of Criticus, but instead of being an apology for poetry, it was an apology for *Bartholomew Fair*. And we should remember that this play is the most accommodating of all Jonson's comedies, written at the height of his powers, acted at the Hope in 1614, and published with a dedication to the memory of King James. Written to the meridian of the lowest and dirtiest stage in London, *Bartholomew Fair* celebrates and ridicules grossness and bad taste such as no other comedy has ever done. It reaches out to the coarsest kind of pleasure in the auditors, and yet through masterful sleight-of-hand, parody, and spoof it has the power to delight the most judicious critics.

Unfortunately the commentary and dialogue on Horace was burned in the fire of Jonson's library, but from his translation of the text (literal and wooden as it is), we can be fairly certain what was relevant. Jonson surely accepted Horace's central premise about audience response, and he repeated it more than half a dozen times in his writings:

> Poets would either profit, or delight,
> Or mixing sweet, and fit, teach life the right.
>
> $(477\text{-}78)^{22}$

Like Jonson, Horace concerned himself with diversity of response.

> The poems void of profit, our grave men
> Cast out by voices; want they pleasure, then
> Our gallants give them none but pass them by;
> But he hath every suffrage, can apply
> Sweet mixed with sower, to his reader, so
> As doctrine and delight together go.
>
> (511-16)

The point of observation will influence a viewer's response, and that is the meaning of Horace's much misunderstood analogy of poetry and painting:

> As painting, so is poesie, some man's hand
> Will take you more, the nearer that you stand:
> As some the farther off: this loves the dark;
> This fearing not the subtlest judge's mark,
> Will in the light be viewed: this, once, the sight
> Doth please: this, ten times over, will delight.
>
> (539-44)

The rest of Horace's epistle is sometimes baffling and contradictory; sometimes Jonson misread it, but its consistent preoccupations are obviously with problems of audience — fitting the drama to the language of the times, the audience's social interests, and the conventions that prevailed — all the while the poet aiming at solid judgment, being new, but not too new, traditional but not reactionary.

I presume that Jonson interpreted Horace's remarks on accommodation in the light of that protean concept of decorum that prevailed in much sixteenth-century criticism, since the idea of decorum came mainly from Horace in the first place. As Puttenham and Sidney took decorum, so did Jonson, understanding it as both artistic and social justification for certain levels of diction, tone, and

22

ideas, adapted to specific characters, readers, and occasions. The clearest examples may be seen in his epigrams and songs, where decorum appears to be the equivalent of "tact."[23] With regard to drama, his most common synonyms were "propriety" and "fitness" of character, scene, and style. The decorum of speech is proper when it is consistent with a person's character, but decorum may also be determined by the general tenor of a scene or by the place where a play is performed.[24] This unsystematic application of decorum is not far from Horace's shifting justifications for spectators' preferences, for custom, and for certain liberties in language and character. A dramatist must give due consideration to the custom of each person's age and nature in his audience (215-25); Horace recommends dissimulation if it is necessary, for a poet should hide his faults and should mix truth with falsehood to conceal what he despairs of handling (213-18, 285-86). If you want to avoid severe criticism, treat novel subjects rather than common ones (183-94); it is proper for rude satyrs to break jests if they are introduced at the right time and when the spectators are in the right mood (320-27), but if you appeal too overtly to the "nutcrackers" in the audience, you may displease the gentry (355-64). In some circumstances a right "humoured" poem with no grace may delight more than a graceful but empty composition (453-60).

In the same way, Jonson insisted that dramatists always had liberty to adapt ancient forms "according to the elegancy and disposition of those times wherein they wrote" (*EMOH*, Induction, 265). The classical chorus was not needed nor hardly possible on the modern stage, as "the old state and splendor of dramatic poems" interfered with "popular delight" (*Sejanus*, To the Readers). Jonson said he would explain this concession to popular delight more in his observations on Horace's *Art of Poetry*. But in one respect Jonson differed with Horace, who had objected to Plautus' scurrile wit and irregular verse, whereas many critics thought Plautus was the parent of all conceit and sharpness.[25] Jonson had something at stake in any apology for Plautus, since he had for over two decades imitated Plautus more than any other ancient writer. He had a close affinity with the Latin master of farce, who could appeal to

23

bondmen as well as to gentle Romans. The case for Plautus, as Heinsius made it, and Jonson copied it into his *Discoveries,* was largely a social and moral one. Aristophanes, according to Heinsius, was much more personally abusive than Plautus, appealing to baser passions and more diseased minds, as when he attacked Socrates. Plautus presumably had more of the better kind of jests — the true and natural ones that scarce raise a laugh with the beastly multitude. We can see here the pull toward "sharpness" and "conceit" that Terence does not have and the revulsion from what too much sharpness leads to — obscene and sinister rhetoric that Aristophanes practices. Plautus represents the rational mean between the bland deficiency of Terence and the vicious excess of wit in Aristophanes. Proper wit, thus, seems to be a kind of urbanity — that savors of equity, truth, perspicuity, and candor. It is suited to learned palates or wise tastes, and although it may have a touch of bitterness, it provokes only a smile as it instructs and informs us. Plautus, no doubt, made his compromises with the stage, but he avoided the worst scurrility.

III. DISSUMULATION AND SYMBIOSIS

Accommodation may be necessary, but woe unto the poet who panders to genuinely evil practices of the contemporary stage or feeds the base appetite of a diseased audience (*EMIH,* Prologue, 1-6). Jonson was acutely conscious of the danger in accommodation, for he did not want to be a hypocrite, like modern journalists who titillate readers while reprehending nudity. John Marston, in *The Metamorphosis of Pigmalion's Image* (1598) or in his two Antonio plays, seems to have gone over the line between adaptation to contemporary taste and artistic hypocrisy because he could not control his desire to revel in the very things he claimed to attack. In practice Jonson did not always succeed in staying on the honest side of the line between accommodation and pandering, but in his pronouncements we can see that he tried to maintain the ideal standard. Thus his comical satires purported to attack generic evils while leaving it to the audience to apply the scourge to themselves, if they so deserved. In that way he claimed to be innocent of vicious libel. There is little doubt, however, that he sometimes caricatured "low" people like Captain Hanum in Tucca, Marston and Dekker in Crispinus and Demetrius, and a number of other specific targets in the plays (and some more distinguished people like Lord Mayor Hayes in Adam Overdo). And in 1607 he admitted that his work had "sharpness," but he disassociated himself from playwrights who attack "public persons," the general order, or the state, those who "make themselves a name with the multitude, or (to draw their rude and beastly claps) care not whose living faces they entrench, with their petulant styles; may they do without a rival for me" (dedication to *Volpone*, 70-77). A bad dramatist will cozen an unsuspecting or naive person by "concupiscence of dances and antics" that "so raineth as to run away from nature and be afraid of her." That kind of art tickles the spectators, through their vice of judgment, because after all, the multitude favors common errors. Sordid, vile, and copious writing is equally dangerous, but the right-minded poet is not so unrestrained, because he uses "election and a mean" to achieve "composed" art (*Alchemist*, To the Reader). Thus style seems to have great importance, since it can redeem potentially vile subjects. I think Jonson referred to this role of style when he urged that literal truth in comedies is not to be aimed at, but things like truth, well feigned (*Epicoene*, Prologue). He imitates natural follies, "but so shown/ As even the doers may see and yet not own" (*Alchemist*, Prologue). By implication, the audience is better pleased by this dissembling manner than by a literal presentation of fact. Jonson even recommends that the guilty spectator dissemble his disease, if he can, to gain at least a public respect — presumably putting himself on the road to health (dedication to *Volpone*, 57-60).

As a last resort, an accommodating dramatist could assure the world that although he wrote for the theater, he kept himself haughtily remote in his composed spirit, his erected confidence, like Crites, the inventor of a court masque in *Cynthia's Revels*. And Jonson unashamedly displayed his proper pride before theater audiences and to readers of his poetry — for example in his two odes to himself, one of them appended to *The New Inn*. Once a man achieves such a lofty self-conception, he has at hand many devices for dealing with lesser creatures. Erasmus dissimulated with mock praise, Sir Thomas More with elusive irony, but Jonson's method was less exquisitely poised, more blunt and more suited to a dramatist; he simply shifted the blame to the other fellow. His strategy appears to have been motivated by his real fear of hypocrisy or flattery. His witty epigram "To my Muse" (lxv) describes his dismay when he finds that his muse has betrayed him into praising a noble lord who did not deserve the honor. This false vision caused him to commit fierce idolatry; he would rather live in poverty and manliness than let his art smell of the parasite. At first he renounces his muse, telling her to leave him, but at the last moment he repents: "Stay. Whoe'er is raised,/ For worth he has not, he is taxed not praised" (15-16). What was written as praise turns into satire if the subject is unworthy. He justified his extravagant praise of the court in *Cynthia's Revels* by another shift; he meant to adumbrate the ideal of what a court should be and how it should propagate virtue. In his masques, too, he set a high standard for courtiers to live by, for he was not praising persons but their states or offices, not their clothes but their forms of virtue.[26] Although he admitted that he had sometimes praised men too much, it was "with purpose to have made them such" ("Epistle to Selden," *Underwood*, no. 14, l.22).

We can interpret his dissimulation unfavorably as a device to exculpate the poet from responsibility for his words, but such harsh judgment overlooks the art and grace and thought that are involved in the execution of a comedy or an epigram. In other words, there are intrinsic and perhaps mixed, even contradictory, values in art if it is strongly related to a social occasion. Patrons, actors, and audiences impose special requirements that must be grappled with and worked upon, and once an artist begins accommodating, there are consequences in the work that must be allowed to develop even if they are exorcized later. As in the art of teaching, the dramatist has to meet his public at their level, in some way, before he can lift them to a higher level. For this reason, there cannot be much pure poetry or unalloyed high seriousness in a practical art like the drama. Some playwrights, like Thomas Dekker or Tennessee Williams, holding a low opinion of their public, settle for a strong popular appeal and little else. Others, like Shakespeare or Chekhov, try to remove the differences between high and low by an appeal to sympathy and imagination. Others, like Jonson and Bernard Shaw, are unusually aware of the need to be both high and low, and they make their work into a kind of serious spoof.[27] They turn themselves into outrageous figures, at one moment clowning, at the next dead serious. Their art seems to be a blend of dissimulation, tact, shock, jest, and earnest — all in a wonderful flow of words, so that the spectators never know exactly where they stand. Surface impressions are untrustworthy, so the judicious observer must exert an extraordinary power of mind. Oddly, these playwrights seem to need popularity even as they disdain it. They thrive on opposition and ignorant critics so much that I wonder if they do not have a symbiotic relationship with their worst audiences. What would Shaw have done without middle-class morality rampant in the theater, or what would Jonson have done without people who like puppet shows, hobby horses, gingerbread, ballads, quaking custards affrighted by fierce teeth, scenical strutting, and some moldy tale like *Pericles*? It is natural that the poet who came up from a common bricklayer should need to distinguish himself from the vulgar multitude, even as he entertained them.

There are scattered signs of this complex attitude toward low entertainers in Jonson's later career. In *The New Inn,* for instance, Mine Host welcomes high-born patrons and laughs at low fellows (as he nurtures them) in his theaterlike haven, and he encourages the playlike antics of the zany Tipto or the crude Mr. and Mrs. Stuff and the stableman as much as he delights in the courtly games of Prue and Lady Franpul. The life of a gypsy seems to have fascinated Jonson in the 1620s, inducing him to put a gypsy into the role of presentor in his most popular masque, apparently another version of the puppeteer from *Bartholomew Fair*.[28] Jonson himself took a walking tour to Scotland and back in 1619, where he consorted with the great and small, sang for his supper like a comic parasite, as he sponged on the hospitality of his admirers, teasing and cajoling simple and grand folks. The canting vagabond, a disguise of

27

Penniboy Senior, delivers his son from evil habits in *The Staple of News,* just as Mine Host (a former vagabond living with gypsies, and a father with a guilty conscience) liberates his daughter from her affectations. The suggestion emerges from these examples that the comic poet-gypsy-father lowers himself in disguise to charm and to elevate his "children" or audience. In psychological terms, joking itself could relieve enough of the father's anger or disapprobation to permit the free flow of indulgence and forgiveness.

One last example of Jonson's later attitude toward his public demonstrates how mellow he became and how his comic strategies had permeated his rhetoric, so much so as to suggest a symbiotic relationship. In the induction to *The Staple of News* (acted at Blackfriars, 1626) he seems aware that he still had to contend with a divided audience, part judicious and part foolish. And he had good reason to be annoyed by the public, more reason to despair at the continued corruption of opinion, in spite of his years of instruction. But since he was now more content to tease than to hector, his results were much funnier and more elusive than in *Cynthia's Revels.* Overtly he still ridiculed people for low taste in order to silence them, and covertly he still wooed them, but his playfulness had become so large a part of the scene that the emphasis had essentially shifted. He subtly mediated his hostility by a curious self-mockery, so that in the upshot he merely chided the actors and the greater part of the audience. A genial air pervaded the formal welcome while, nonetheless, a sly, tickling pleasure was given to the judicious. The whole induction deserves a careful look to see Jonson's efforts to achieve an essentially Lucianic air of improvisation.

Like an antimasque, the induction interrupts and hence impedes the start of the play. The duly authorized Prologue enters and begins his conventional appeal to an attentive audience: "For your own sake and not ours — " It is a familiar dissimulation, saying, in effect, "We aren't acting this play for our benefit, so if you will just listen, you'll see it's worth a lot for you." But the Prologue is cut off in mid-sentence by four garrulous females, the embodied spirits of Mirth, Tattle, Expectation, and Censure.

The Divided Audience

> *Mirth.* Come Gossip, be not ashamed. The play is *The Staple of News,*
> and you are the mistress and Lady of Tattle, let's ha' your opinion
> of it: Do you hear Gentleman? What are you? Gentleman-usher to
> the play? Pray you help us to some stools here.
> *Prologue.* Where? O' the stage, ladies?
> *Mirth.* Yes, o' the stage; we are persons of quality, I assure you, and
> women of fashion; and come to see, and to be seen. My Gossip
> Tattle here, and Gossip Expectation, and my Gossip Censure, and
> I am Mirth, the daughter of Christmas, and spirit of Shrovetide.
> They say, "It's merry when Gossips meet," I hope your play will
> be a merry one! (2-13)

Again we have the surrogate spectators, only this time they are
actors imitating ladies who are imitating gallant gentlemen. Like the
gallants, they come to see and to be seen, not to listen. I suppose the
regular audience recognized the vaudeville trick — the "plants"
among the spectators—but the gimmick probably was not so transparent then as in modern illusionist theater, where a break in the
presentation is always carefully planned (except in the most recent
improvised performances). And there was at least one outrageous
afternoon at the Fortune Theater when the notorious Marion Firth
"in man's apparel and in her boots and with a sword at her side" sat
on the stage, played her lute, and sang. She told the company there
present that many thought she was a man; but if they came to her
chamber they would soon find she was a woman.[29] Unlike Moll
Firth, Jonson's Tattle, Expectation, Censure, and Mirth exploit their
allegorical attributes right from the start, even as they talk in the
idiom of city gossips. The mingled effect is like that in Jonson's
masque, "Love Restored," where the god of money and Robin
Goodfellow intrude on the opening speeches. There, too, worlds of
game and fact confuse a mock apology to the audience, and they
throw us off our bearings.

In *The Staple of News* the action of the next sixty lines is a
struggle for physical possession of the stage and for the authority to
"arraign" plays and their poets that goes along with it. Mirth
imperiously asks for stools; and her wondering if the Prologue is
gentleman-usher to the play suggests her kind of false perception,
implying that the Prologue should serve her needs. The ensuing

dialogue alternates between the ladies' utter banalities and the Prologue's unobtrusive replies, which seem genial and inoffensive unless you are listening very carefully. Mirth wants the play to be merry but she better watch out, for the merry part may be Mirth herself. The gossips want to arraign plays as the noblemen and grave wits do, and the Prologue says go ahead and "enjoy your delight freely," but they should not expect more than they can understand. The Prologue quietly explodes their asinine logic, and he leads Curiosity, Lady Censure, to caricature herself — for she judges plays entirely by the cut of the costumes.

Now the Prologue almost has control of the situation, although he conceded part of the fictive space on stage to the ladies, and he wants to continue with his part of the play. As the tiremen prepare the lights, he hopes to give light to the business. In a confidential way he lets them peep behind the stage.

> The truth is, there are a set of gamesters within in travail of a thing called a play and would fain be delivered of it, and they have entreated me to be their man-midwife, the Prologue, for they are like to have a hard labor on't. (54-57)

His use of the generic term "gamesters" for players may be another concession to the ladies' outmoded view of drama, just as it refers to Volpone's private entertainers when Nano says "Now room for fresh gamesters" (I.ii.1). But the ladies will not be patronized, and Tattle interrupts again, objecting that the poet has abused himself; any mother would know it, if he thinks this man-midwife will help the actors through a hard labor. Furthermore Mirth, daughter of Christmas fun and spirit of Shrovetide, has already been backstage, so she turns the comment on its head in the most remarkable speech of the induction. Now defending the poet against the actors, she implies that the actors will abuse the poet enough, and he need not do it to himself. In another shift, she proceeds to describe (and to abuse) the agitated poet she has just seen in the dressing room. There follows a mocking caricature of the fat old dramatist, such as no one but Jonson could pen, and no one but Jonson would put it in the mouth of so unreliable a commentator:

Yonder he is within (I was i' the tiring-house a while to see the actors dressed) rolling himself up and down like a tun, i'the midst of 'em, and spurges, never did vessel of wort or wine work so! His sweating put me in mind of a good shroving dish (and I believe would be taken up for a service of state somewhere, an't were known) a stewed poet! He doth sit like an unbraced drum with one of his heads beaten out: for, that you must note, a poet hath two heads, as a drum has, one for making, the other repeating, and his repeating head is all to pieces: they may gather it up i' the tiring house: for he hath torn the book in a poetical fury and put himself to silence in dead sack, which, were there no other vexation, were sufficient to make him the most miserable emblem of patience. (61-74)

The speech is a charming piece of comic dissimulation, with Mirth as Jonson's stalking horse, from behind which he shoots at the players, at authors who take the stage too seriously, and at the public image of himself. It is all in the language of a voluble lady — a sappy Ursula, with a sharp tongue and a capacity for delightful insinuations. The whole piece is calculated to raise the level of mirth indeed, because there is something in it to tickle everyone. The poet's self-caricature is funniest because it capitalizes on well-known Jonsonian traits. Jonson had often advertised his mountain belly and his rocky face, and had pointed out how "the whole lump [was] grown round, deform'd" and drooping, although a woman still might embrace it — for even the great Heidelberg Tun had hoops. Jonson was known for his passion for wine, especially for Canary sack, and for his love of reciting verses.[30] Surely some people knew of his unusual concern for quality acting and of his hovering about the playhouse to censure the players lest they mouth his speeches. One epilogue had special fun with this over-anxiousness:

> The author (jealous how your sense doth take
> His travails) hath enjoined me to make
> Some short and ceremonious epilogue;
> But if I yet know what, I am a rogue:
> He ties me to such laws as quite distract
> My thoughts; and would a year of time exact.
> I neither must be faint, remiss, nor sorry,

31

Sour, serious, confident, nor peremptory,
But betwixt these.

(Epilogue to *Cynthia's Revels,* 3-11)

The old stage keeper in *Bartholomew Fair* confides to the spectators: "I am looking, lest the poet hear me, or his man Master Brome, behind the arras . . . . He has kicked me three or four times about the tiring house . . . for offering to put in with my own experience" (Induction, 7-8, 28-30). But above all, Jonson had advertised his pride and his violent feelings, carefully masked under the guise of Horace's long-suffering patience.

The miserable emblem of patience is the figure that finishes the portrait, not without a sad note, capping it like a prose epigram. (And it has an incidental dramatic function, since the ladies need to be taught patience before the Prologue can go on.) But the most ludicrous touches are at the beginning: Jonson's rolling himself up and down like a tun, and the playful pun on "sweating" — which reminds Mirth of a sweating or loaded dish of food at a Shrovetide feast. She may also connote the sweating cure for venereal disease, because her appellation — a stewed poet — has similar hints. However, the plain sense of "stewed" — bathed in perspiration — is enough to depict the poet's fear and frustration, especially after he had indeed for a good many years been "taken up for a service of state" (that is, writing masques, but now out of favor). *The Staple of News* was his first stage play in ten years, and he was, in his proud way, trying to make a comeback.

At last the Prologue can pick up where he began, but in the first line the point of view has changed:

For your own sakes, not his, he bad me say . . .

Since the conditions have changed, the original defense of actors — "For your own sake, not ours" — is changed into the author's personal message to the audience.[31] Jonson's shift of perspective in the induction has put everyone in his place, emphasizing that actors, too, belong a few steps below the poets, and below them belong the town ladies. Now, with little dissimulation, he can use actors for his appeal over their heads. All is presumably honest and straightforward. In other words, the induction amounted to a genial contest, ending with a bargain between players and potentially hostile or foolish members of the popular audience. Now the Prologue speaks for the serious poet, trying to raise judgment a little higher. Having passed through a facetious ordeal, his formal address has earned his superior attitude and his disdain for mere spectacle. The reverse of Shakespeare in Sonnet 23, he calls for attentive ears, not eyes, to discern the poet's true meaning.

> Would you were come to hear, not see a play.
> Though we his actors must provide for those,
> Who are our guests, here, in the way of shows,
> The maker hath not so; he'ld have you wise
> Much rather by your ears than by your eyes. . . .

The maker, too, asks for attention, but he expects something better, discrimination:

> Great noble wits, be good unto your selves
> And make a difference 'twixt poetic elves
> And poets: All that dabble in the ink
> And defile quills are not those few can think,
> Conceive, express, and steer the souls of men
> As with a rudder, round thus with their pen.

(19-24)

The poet itches to have control over men's minds. He yearns for the power of a great orator who can play on the most significant thoughts and feelings of his listeners, who can think of his matter, conceive the design, express it in words, and steer the souls of men as with a rudder. Yet he cannot define this power without thinking of all those miserable poetic elves, too. He has steered our souls through seas of banality and folly before we have landed on the blessed isles of noble wit.

The ideal poet must instruct the young and maintain mature men at their full perception of truth; he must ''enterprise this work'' — which I take to mean he must undertake or venture his artistic commitment in this endeavor. On the other hand, the ideal auditors should be both active and passive to mark the poet's ways —

33

Jonson and Elizabethan Comedy

What flight he makes, how new; and then he says
If that not like you, that he sends to night
'Tis you have left to judge, not he to write.

(28-30)

The bold claim, following an impressive demonstration of Jonson's comic writing, probably deserves our indulgence. In the poet's eyes it is proper pride, and after all, we have already been treated with his more than proper humility. In the induction he lowered himself to raise mirth, and at the end of the prologue he elevates himself to raise the audience as well.

The gap between Jonson the buffoon and Jonson the noble wit seems as wide as he conceived the division to be in his audience, but there are hints of certain ceremonial lifelines between them. He needed both kinds of people to fill a theater, and given his commitment, he needed both purposes for his art to operate successfully. Dissimulation and jesting were inevitable. As Shaw remarked, "Vulgarity is a necessary part of a complete author's equipment; and the clown is sometimes the best part of the circus." And as Shaw also said, "When a thing is funny, search it for a hidden truth."[32] Ultimately for Jonson, the vulgar stage was loathed, but pragmatically, in order to survive in that world, he came to see the need to accommodate his work to the "meridian" of his audience,[33] hoping that the plays would produce delight and sport, all the while being somehow "honest." We can imagine how difficult this dramatic program must have been for Jonson, and it is little wonder that his results did not always please. Fortunately for him, he always had a way of making the poet come off best. When the plays were good, they were very very good, and when they were bad — that was the fault of the crowd. He made that particular boast so often that it must have been intended as a joke or a jest in earnest. But in performance how can we separate the entertainer from the poet when, at the end of a play about pride, he explodes with "By God, 'tis good, and if you like it you may"?[34]

34

2.

Comedy of Admiration

Since drama is above all an art of provoking responses — no response, no drama — and since comedy above all teases an audience, pricks it, and convulses it with laughter, we would then expect a first-rate comedian like Jonson to frame his plays for that purpose. His peers, Aristophanes and Molière, usually built their plays around some huge joke, and although Jonson came to master that art too in his mature work, he began more cautiously. In his apprenticeship he was apparently content to follow the traditional theory of new comedy descending from Donatus' commentary on Terence, elaborated in school texts and imitated in popular examples like *The Comedy of Errors*, George Chapman's comedies, and Henry Porter's *Two Angry Women of Abington*. Jonson's earliest surviving plays, *The Case is Altered* (ca. 1598) and *Every Man in His Humor* (1598), clearly belong to that academic tradition. The Donatine theory conceived of comedy as a ridiculous imitation of the common errors of life, involving men of lower birth (not kings or nobles) in order to make audiences laugh at their follies and vanities. The commentators repeated the definition attributed to Cicero, that comedy is "the imitation of life, the mirror of custom, and the image of truth." Comedy's action begins in trouble and ends in happiness. As the definition never represented Latin comedy adequately, so it did not exactly fit the Elizabethan imitations, and many variations developed.

35

Jonson and Elizabethan Comedy

One alternative kind of comedy emerged in the later sixteenth century, what may be called comedy of admiration. It had partial support from critical theory of the time, and it flourished on the stage. There is evidence of an interest in comedies that violated the Donatine formula, plays that deliberately combined "mirth" and "care," low comedy and serious matter, like Richard Edwards' *Damon and Pythias* (1564-65) and George Whetstone's *Promos and Cassandra* (1578). In his dedication Whetstone identified these elements as characteristic of English comedy with its "devils from hell," "gods from heaven," conquerors, rustics, children, strumpets. The intermingled actions were such that the grave could instruct and the pleasant could delight. Other playwrights may have disseminated the form, but from surviving texts it appears that John Lyly polished this sort of comedy by adding elegant dialogue in *Campaspe,* and he gave it a definite courtly quality in *Sapho and Phao. Endymion* and the rest of his comedies, aside from *Mother Bombie,* repeated and varied the pattern that made Lyly the most influential comic dramatist of the age. It was essential to Lyly's comedy of admiration that it include courtly compliment, great heroes like Alexander or princesses like Sapho thrust in among common folk; and it might also include more or less spectacle with its deities, spirits, dreams, magic, music, dance, and maskings. Most important, it had to provoke a delicate laughter amidst elevated feelings and thought. After Lyly, Shakespeare exploited comic admiration in his early plays, particularly in *A Midsummer Night's Dream,* and there are some features of it (minus the deities) in some of his other comedies up through *Twelfth Night.*

I am persuaded that three of Jonson's early comedies belong to this alternative tradition and that although they are called comical satires on their title pages, the satiric elements are not nearly so interesting nor provocative as the elements of comic wonder. As was noted in the previous chapter, the split between Jonson the entertainer and Jonson the noble wit appeared early in his career, and after a few years of pleasing the multitude at the Theater, Curtain, and the Rose, he suspected that maybe laughter alone had not enough dignity about it; it was not always the effect of good comedy.To the noble mind, laughter might even be a fault, as he copied into his notes years later, "a kind of turpitude that depraves some part of a man's nature without a disease," and to seem ridiculous is a part of dishonesty and foolishness. True wit, which is natural and perspicuous, seldom raises a laugh from the common folk in the audience (*Discoveries,* VIII, 2631-59). The earliest hint of this attitude comes at the end of *Every Man in His Humor,* where he seems to cast about for additional effects — something that would raise his art to a distinction that poetry deserves. His next three plays, written in as many years, abandoned new comedy entirely and explored the possibilities of a better sort of play, adapting the more elegant successes of Lyly and Shakespeare to his own purposes. He became very good at evoking wonder and made it an important purpose of *Every Man out of His Humor, Cynthia's Revels,* and *Poetaster.*

This chapter sketches the critical background of comic admiration, and the next chapter suggests some of its uses in Elizabethan comedy before Jonson. I do not try to be exhaustive but only to call attention to the rich variety of thoughts about this mode that were available to a writer in 1599. Aside from the general growing interest in comic admiration, I think Sir Philip Sidney formulated theories that were especially important to explain the best kind of English comedy; his theories were distinct from and much broader than the conventional ideas of ridiculous comedy, based on Donatus. The rhetorical and religious traditions behind Sidney are valuable for the way they bring out certain nuances of feeling that cling to the language of praise in drama as well as in poetry. Modern readers are likely to miss the point if they assume too quickly that the familiar phrases in Elizabethan sonnets, for instance, are simply "Petrarchian conventions" or clichés, but if we have reason to believe that otherwise sincere and thoughtful writers could have meant what they said, and if we can see that there were articulate ideas behind their words, rooted in the cultural past and present, the literature takes on a new life for us. In this respect, I agree with C.S. Lewis that the vitality of Elizabethan literature may have been caused by a new feeling for magic, a "higher magic" that came in with humanism and Neoplatonic theology.[1] Certain words like "clear spirit," "idea," "the mirror of the soul," "the charmed soul," and the "magic of her voice" denoted actual powers from an invisible world that could be apprehended by the elevated mind, and they denoted undercurrents of feeling that writers were trying to describe. Comedy of admiration not only described those feelings and ideas, but it was calculated to evoke them.

I. THE RELIGIOUS AND HUMANIST TRADITIONS

Educated Elizabethans believed in the power of oratory and, like many good speakers, they hoped their words would affect listeners, especially the perceptive and thoughtful people who could imagine things beyond common experience. John Rainolds, reader of Greek at Merton College, Oxford, delivered an important *Oratio in Laudem Artis Poeticae* about 1572, emphasizing this very point. Since Rainolds is known to have been tutor of Stephen Gosson and the main influence upon Lyly in his formation of the Euphuistic style, we should listen to him. He is trying to describe wonder:

> One thing I especially ask: that you be like those who when they take up Plato's works, which could not be written in greater detail, nevertheless surmise something still nobler concerning Socrates than is shadowed in those copious writings; so I beg that when you listen to my praises of poetry, even though they are so spoken that my limitations keep me from noble expression, you nevertheless think more highly of it than my few poor words will urge you. For I come to the task of telling its praises, not as one who is most able, but as one who is most willing; not as one who most eloquently, but as one who most earnestly, desires to render its adornments as ornate as possible. . . . . But if, because of the barren dryness of my wit, I cannot do justice to the greatness of the work I have undertaken, . . . I trust you will praise my good intentions.[2]

Here are the hallmarks of wonder that we shall see again and again in both theory and practice: the greatness of the subject, the inability of the speaker to do justice to it, although he sincerely wants to be equal to the task, and the audience's responsibility to fill in the gaps with their surmises. The shadows of an idea can be cast on the ground, but the observer must deduce imaginatively what is the real thing. In this way of thinking, Socrates, the hero of ancient philosophy, must have been greater than Plato could have told us, and Plato was the most eloquent philosopher of them all. The technique is elaborately hyperbolical, resting upon a *ne plus ultra* which the mind must overreach.

The response is not unfamiliar to modern audiences either, for our pleasure in science fiction depends upon similar effects, and it presupposes our considerable faith in the unseen powers commanded by a Captain Kirk and Mr. Spock. Scholars and art historians go through a process of reconstruction that is a function of their wonder when, for instance, they try to imagine an original, lost Greek statue that stands behind a Roman copy. Because they assume that the original by Scopas was far better than the copy, they search for hints of the original inspiration.

In the theater it is a matter of transference of feeling from the breast of the actor to the audience, even though their understanding be imperfect. Thomas Dekker explains the process in the prologue to *If This Be Not a Good Play, the Devil is in It* (1612). He praises the true sons of poetry "whose quick clear eyes can view poesy's pure essence," that essence so magnificent that it is like the sun or lightning, and as impossible to approach, weigh, touch, or comprehend. An actor speaking the prologue calls for a playright who can capture some of poetry's powers, lure the audience into the theater, and "tie his ear with golden chains to his melody"; and can force the audience to reach up

> And (from rare silence) clap their brawny hands,
> T'applaud what their charmed soul scarce understands.
> That man give me, whose breast fill'd by the muses
> With raptures, into a second, them infuses:
> Can give an actor, sorrow, rage, joy, passion,
> Whilst he again (by self-same agitation)
> > Commands the hearers, sometimes drawing out tears,
> > Then smiles, and fills them both with hopes and fears.[3]

Shakespeare made his characteristic point, closer to Rainolds, that the medium of communication itself may be imperfect, requiring that the audience fill in the gaps by reference to the higher or truer subject. The magnificent prologue to *Henry V* (1599) asks for a muse of fire (like Dekker's sun or lightning) worthy to present so "great an object" as warlike Harry or so great an event as the battle of Agincourt. Nothing short of real kings and a real battlefield could do it, but he begs the audience to allow the actors, mere "ciphers to this great account," to work on their "imaginary forces."

> Suppose within the girdle of these walls
> Are now confined two mighty monarchies,
> Whose high upreared and abutting fronts
> The perilous narrow ocean parts asunder.
> Piece out our imperfections with your thoughts:
> Into a thousand parts divide one man,
> And make imaginary puissance.

And in a later chorus he asks us to "Still be kind/ And eke out our performance with your mind." This attitude, which has already been noted in *A Midsummer Night's Dream,* throws part of the artistic responsibility upon the audience, and their active response is greatest when they feel wonder toward grand things. The wonder, in turn, intensifies other emotions and ideas by raising "spirits" in the blood. Of course the actors must do their part too, and if they do it well, they can enchant the spectators, as Thomas Heywood explains: "as if the personator were the man personated, so bewitching a thing is lively and well-spirited action, that it hath power to new mold the hearts of the spectators and fashion them to the shape of any noble and notable attempt."[4]

The roots of this dramatic rhetoric are in ancient thought and literary theory, the trunk and branches in Renaissance culture, and much of the story has been told of its transmission to the artists and poets of the High Renaissance. Erwin Panofsky traced the philosophical tradition, in his *Idea: A Concept in Art Theory,* through Plato, Artistotle, Cicero, and Plotinus, and he illustrated the application of the Idea in fifteenth- and sixteenth-century theories of painting.[5] Raphael, Lomazzo, Zuccaro (whom Sidney must have met on the painter's visit to England), and Vasari absorbed the Idea differently into their theories, but in general they suggested that inner thoughts can be depicted on canvas and that the artist must know the subject under appearances. He must have a prior conception or Idea of his composition, a kind of ground or platform which he rests on or imitates. As Alberti said, a finished painting should depict a "movement of the soul" of each man painted (like Sidney's *energia*), so that the beholder's soul can be equally moved. The observer, therefore, seeks to respond to more than the sensuous impressions of a painting, to recover the original Idea, a conception better than nature, more perfect than any single living woman, more heroic than any natural man. J.V. Cunningham examined the genealogy of wonder in the theory of tragedy, and he illustrated it in *Hamlet* and other Shakespearean plays, showing that pity and fear were displaced as the ultimate tragic effects by emotions of woe and wonder, more congenial to the Renaissance.[6] But the role of wonder in the Neoplatonic revival has more importance for poetry and drama than Cunningham and Panofsky suggest.

The place of wonder in the history of rhetoric can be described as a series of changes in the relationship between love and the art of speaking. In the *Phaedrus* Plato subordinated the usual concerns of rhetoric — style, organization, and knowledge of the subject — to the love of the soul; and love of the soul naturally led a thinking person to the love of truth itself. So good speaking was finally indistinguishable from good dialectic and the quest for the highest good. Wonder was the expression of the mind's growing spiritual awareness. Cicero learned Platonic rhetoric of wonder from the Greek originals, which he adapted to civic oratory and stoic philosophy. True wonder was for him the contemplation of a supremely good man like Socrates. St. Augustine, who knew Plontinus, not Plato, and gathered his rhetoric from Cicero, adapted it to Christian charity and the love of God. Man's wonder, according to Augustine, is best expressed by silence in the presence of divine wisdom. Among medieval writers, Petrarch was the staunchest advocate of Ciceronean eloquence, but he owed as much to St. Augustine as to Cicero himself. Although noble eloquence appropriate to public honor could enhance one's fame and support the state, private feelings in the depths of understanding and love, like his love for Laura, required another kind of eloquence — the rhetoric of understatement or even silence appropriate to a vision. Ficino in turn blended the doctrines of Petrarch, Plotinus, and Augustine into a new synthesis of art and love, closer to magic or spiritualism. Love is a metaphysical power that art imitates in language, sound, and sight, even smell; wonder is an effect of God's drawing the world to Himself, as we wish to draw closer to God.

It is not possible in a few pages to explain the complexities of these ideas as they touched sixteenth-century English culture at almost every level, but we can imagine some of the implications of wonder in two of its important manifestations. One was the emotional force that came with religious devotion, especially in the Reformation. The other was the respectable "higher magic" that attended humanist philosophy. The two were seldom distinct, although they can be recognized in various writers with differing emphases. For convenience, I will call one Augustinian piety and the other Neoplatonic philosophy, and since both had something to do with dramatic theory and practice, I ask the reader's indulgence for a few pages as I sketch the backgrounds of the two.

The religious connotations of wonder arise from the example of the Psalms, from a few passages in Isaiah, and from the interpretations of St. Paul. Isaiah is the most haunting and eloquent when he talks of the "wondrous work of God" and of man's inadequacies (according to the gloss in the Geneva version). God's communication with man begins with the warning that He will humble us, besiege us as in circle, fight against us as on a mount, and will cast up ramparts against us. We shall be made to feel so miserable and so small that our voices shall be "as out of the dust . . . like him that hath a spirit of divination," and our talking "shall whisper out of the dust." When the full force of the spirit comes into the flesh, it will be an apocalyptic experience: "Thou shalt be visited of the Lord of Hosts with thunder and shaking, and a great noise, a whirlwind, and a tempest, and a flame of a devouring fire." But men will not understand, for it will seem to them as an illusion. The fool in the eyes of this world may overturn the wise and the prudent when the vision is vouchsafed him. The low, the humble, and the stupid will know a deeper truth than blind wise men, and revelation may lie in a sealed book, to be known only by those with sincere faith (29:4-14, Geneva version). To receive this revelation we must have a prepared heart, waiting for a message; for "since the beginning of the world they have not heard, nor understand with the ear, nor hath the eye seen another God beside thee which doth so to him that waiteth for him" (64:4).

For sixteenth-century readers, these passages were cross referenced to St. Paul's similar promise in 1 Cor. 2:9 with the "same kindle of admiration . . . marvelling at God's great benefit shewed to his church by the preaching of the Gospel." Paul describes the evidence of a promise to man in the incarnation, the secret wisdom, virtue, and grace which Christ imparted to us by living on earth. The fulfillment of the promise will come to us later: "The things which eye hath not seen, neither ear hath heard, neither came into man's heart are which God hath prepared for them that love him." Commentators went further to grander interpretations as they found it agreeable to the context to say that Isaiah seems to "fly away in admiration from the incarnation and manhood of Christ to the celestial glory, which is the fruit and end of the incarnation."[7] In support of this extension, it was common to cite St. Bernard's fourth sermon on the Vigil of the Nativity where Bernard meditates; "Eye hath not seen that unapproachable light, ear hath not heard that incomprehensible peace . . . And why is it that it has not ascended into the heart of man? Surely because it is a spring and cannot ascend. For we know that the nature of springs is to seek the rivers in the valleys and to shun the tops of the mountains; for God resisteth the proud, but giveth grace to the humble."[8]

The problem for the true humble believer is one of inward feeling that can be articulated only by words that rely upon outward images. If expression fails in the presence of the incomprehensible, perhaps plain words will do; so St. Paul explained to his followers that he spoke in humbleness, fear, and trembling. He did not use the enticing speech of wise men but the "plain evidence of the spirit and of power." Paul did not speak the wisdom of the princes or of riches, "which come to nought." He rather spoke the wisdom of God, "even the hid wisdom, which God has determined before the world, unto our glory" (1 Cor. 2:4-7). Paul rejected mere rhetoric because it got in the way of his message of salvation, for on the day of deliverance "Where is the wise? Where is the scribe? Where is the disputer of this world? Hath not God made the wisdom of this world foolishness?" (1 Cor. 1:20). "If any man among you seem to be wise in this world, let him be a fool that he may be wise" (1 Cor. 3:18). This and similar passages in the Bible inaugurated the tradition in comic literature of the wise fool; like St. Paul, true believers are fools for Christ's sake.

St. Augustine saw the fascinating paradoxes of Paul's homiletics of the "plain truth" and the "hidden wisdom," in which he saw a special eloquence. He learned from St. Ambrose the central principle of religious discourse — that "the letter killeth but the spirit giveth life" (2 Cor. 3:6), and as Scaliger believed after him, Augustine put a higher value on matter (*res*) than on words (*verba*). Consequently he could penetrate the mystery of passages in scripture which, taken according to the letter, seemed to teach foolish or perverse doctrine *(Confessions* 6.4). He could look past "unskillful speech" in scripture toward the heart of the message (*Christian Instruction,* 4.10).[9] From Ambrose he also learned silent admiration as he read scripture, his eye traveling across the page, his heart seeking into the sense.[10]

In keeping with Augustine's emphasis on meaning rather than words, interpretation of the Bible required that the Law of Love be followed. By the Law of Love, he began with the assumption that those truths in scripture which are necessary for salvation must eventually be clear; the Holy Spirit would not have allowed it to be otherwise. And if men cannot understand the letter, they must follow the spirit. Since a basic sympathy with the intended meaning exists in his mind from the start, when Augustine came to a passage that seemed obscure, he said "This seems contradictory" or "How can this be?" and his reply was "Something lies hidden."

The Law of Love applies to other writing and preaching too, whenever one feels admiration for the object of praise (and here

Augustine is consistent with Shakespeare's interest in a loving relationship between actor and audience). Like a good teacher in any age, a speaker loves his auditors; nothing wearies him; going over the same material can be a delightful experience because he finds enjoyment enriched by the students' reactions, and old things become new for him. By the same principle an auditor should love a speaker, should forgive grammatical errors, mispronunciations, or confused pauses. Although such errors should be corrected, they should also be taken in the spirit of tolerance and piously borne by those who have come to know the difference between the Forum and the Church (*On Catechizing,* 11.17, 9.13). Respect for the profound message and for the speaker's good intentions enables the listener to rise above foolish words.

The Law of Love is most important and most difficult to follow in the praise of God. When we admire God's creation we are so acutely aware of the deficiencies of our language, the great disparity between our speech and our thought, that it makes us unwilling to speak and we naturally fall silent. Yet we are enjoined to give thanks to God and to express our delight. But "we cannot express our feeling; let us shout for joy. God is good. What sort of good, who can say? Lo, we cannot say, and we are not allowed to be silent . . . let us neither speak nor be silent . . . Let us shout for joy" (*Exposition of the Psalms,* 5.45, on Psalm 103).Using the high style when praising God's glory calls for the greatest effort, although the result may be imperfect. No one praises glory fittingly, but no one fails to praise it one way or another (*Christian Instruction,* 4.38).

The mirror metaphor also plays an important role in Augustine's poetics of praise (as it did in many medieval and renaissance writers) because of its use by St. Paul to suggest divine revelation. The Platonic image of the mirror or divining glass (*speculum*) was identified with the magic glass in 1 Cor. 13:12: We now see through a glass darkly, but in paradise we will look on God face to face. We will see the glorious countenance of God (2 Cor. 3:7-8), as promised by the beauty of the Word that gives us the perfect Law of Liberty (James 1:23-25).

The mirror of custom was frequently quoted as part of the

Ciceronean definition of comedy, and it was frequently interpreted as an ambiguous mirror, since it shows evil customs as they are and it awakens us to knowledge of good behavior. It corrects manners and reflects manners. The same ambiguity resides in St. Paul's mirror: it reflects things as they are but it is also a prophetic glass through which we can divine better things. By representing our outward appearance it suggests some inward truths, darkly hinting at an image of things as they should or will be.[11] Even vain and false things (that are interesting to comic dramatists, of course) can be mirrors if they are adapted to the understanding of God, where we see them as enigmas that we must labor to see right.[12] Hugh of St. Victor, for instance, explains the metaphor in moral terms. We should read the book of *The Rule of St. Augustine* until we know it by heart, and it is right to call it a mirror, for we can see in it as in a mirror what state we are in, whether beautiful or deformed, just or unjust.[13]

Many English writers saw that a mirror was also in the mind itself, reflecting the "clear spirit" that was identified with a noble mind, and it became a favorite topic of literary praise. The mirror and the clear spirit were not exclusively religious metaphors, for they are found in secular uses up and down the humanist tradition and sometimes with mixed religious and secular meanings. Petrarch in particular elevated the rhetoric of praise for semidivine beauty that evoked a clear spirit, and it is hard to say exactly where Laura stops and a religious ideal begins.[14] In later humanism, the clear spirit owes something to Neoplatonic philosophy and to Ficino especially, to whom we must now turn. The road through Neo-platonic thought eventually takes us to critical theory in the sixteenth century.

A fresh interest in the relations of art and love and knowledge came with Marsilio Ficino. Ficino was the central figure of the Platonic Renaissance because, under the patronage of the Medici, he translated all of Plato's dialogues into Latin, wrote commentaries (mainly within the Plotinian world view), and appeared to have reconciled Plato with Christianity. Moreover Ficino influenced a large number of writers and artists, including Ben Jonson.[15] What

Jowett's translation is to us Ficino's was to sixteenth-century Europe. Roughly speaking, by equating God with the Idea of the Good and by appropriating terms from the Bible and from Augustinian Christianity, he, in effect, cleansed pagan idealism, making it safe for Medici plutocracy and humanist poetics. Ficino was a syncretist by method, and, although he incorporated ideas from Cicero, Aristotle, Hermetic philosophy, and Stoicism, the most abstract or Neoplatonic ideas tended to rise to the surface. He was fascinated with spiritual magic and astrology, and he apparently believed that aerial spirits could be communicated with. Between men and God, he said, the air is peopled with good daemons, our protectors and governors of the lower world, ministers of God we might call them. The daemons emanating from the world soul distribute divine gifts into men's souls, and moreover, some wise men like Socrates are special friends of daemons, to whom they speak. On the intellectual level, there is a spirit of God in all men that enables them to aspire toward perfection, if they will, toward pure being, to something more than human, even to the godhead. This is possible because the soul is a mirror in which the divine image can be seen; self-knowledge by a clear spirit is, therefore, a means to achieve knowledge of God (see the Proemium to his *Platonic Theology*).[16] Man's aspiring spirit as a function of self-knowledge is felt as a species of awe or wonder, and these assumptions govern Ficino's related conceptions of love, poetry, and music.

According to Ficino, all art is a reflection of metaphysical ideas that rest in the world's soul. Divine beauty creates love in everything, that is, desire for its ideal self; so as God draws the world to himself, the world is attracted to Him. Every earthly thing is alive and beautiful as it gives evidence of its identity with the spirit of beauty and with its own Idea. On the sensual level, we can smell the aroma of God in our beloved, we yearn for the indistinguishable flavor of deity in her. Lovers lament because they are losing, destroying, and ruining themselves; they rejoice because they transform themselves into something better (*Commentary on Symposium*, p. 141). Sensual love itself is a magician with power to

47

enchant (with the help of daemons), because love holds the world together, and the daemons understand the relationships of natural things (pp. 199-200). The eye is the highest of the senses by which men behold beauty, and all beautiful creatures have a bewitching power, sharing their loved ones "with the powers of rhetoric and the meters of poetry, as though with some incantation; moreover they overcome and take possession of them with worship and rewards exactly as though with magic potions" (p. 200).

Ficino's theory of music and song was also suggestive because he thought sound had a powerful effect on the spirits, too. A musical tone by a movement of air moves the body; "by purified air it excites the aerial spirit which is the bond of body and soul, by emotion it affects the sense." Without words the spirit can go no higher, but with words set to music it touches the soul. "By meaning it works on the mind: finally, by the very movement of the subtle air it penetrates strongly: by its contemperation it flows smoothly: by the conformity of its quality it floods us with a wonderful pleasure: by its nature, both spiritual and material, it at once seizes and claims as its own man in his entirety." Ficino's contribution to music theory is important because he was seriously interested in effects, practical effects, as illustrated by his composition and performance of astrological music. He wrote odes to the sun and various planets, and he probably sang them in religious rites, by which means he expected to be cured of harmful humors, perturbations of the spirit (a tempting analogy with Jonson's cure of humors). Furthermore, Ficino gave high importance to the words of songs; the tones alone in music are sensual; the tone together with poetic verses contains the real spiritual force, an attractive theory for poets who write songs for plays and masques with musical accompaniment.[17]

It is possible to think of Ficino, Pico, Castiglione, Leone Ebreo, and their followers as extreme Neoplatonists, even monists, but there were many ways that Ficino, like his disciples, tried to accommodate his theories to a practical world; for instance, he recognized two Venuses and two faces of the soul, like Plato's two horses pulling the chariot of the soul. The soul is another Janus "with a face of gold turned toward eternity and a face of silver turned toward temporal things — one, Saturnine, the other Jovial" (*Op. Omnia,* I.657.2, cited by Marcel, p. 653), and the silver face recognizes forms in the world, too. At any rate, in practical treatises on the sister arts of poetry and painting in the sixteenth century, the concern was less with transcendant ideas and more with the conception in a workman's mind. A poet could conceive either of these worlds, framing a model by nature's pattern, or he could improve on nature and appeal to a pattern of ideas closer to the mind of God. The two orders are not always kept clearly distinct, and sometimes both seem to be signified, making it difficult for us to say exactly where a distinction has been made.

Sixteenth-century literary theorists only gradually came to appreciate, as did writers on painting, the power of admiration for a Platonic idea. But at base many critics accepted the humanist doctrine of a preexisting model in the mind of the poet or orator, and their interpretations ranged over a wide territory. Giordano Bruno, in his *De gli eroici* (1585), dedicated to Sidney, was an extreme Platonist in such matters, and he insisted that the idea was a literal *furor poeticus.*[18] At the beginning of the century, Giovanni Pontano presented a typical rhetorical view: the aim of poetry is simply to move and carry away the listener and reader, to impress admiration on his soul.[19] A representative opinion from the middle of the century comes from J. C. Scaliger's *Poetics* (1561), a work worth attention because it is known to have influenced Sidney and Jonson in many matters.[20] Scaliger made *Idea* the central concept of his *Poetics,* and in typical Renaissance fashion *Idea* is a composite of all knowledge, expecially knowledge of nature; it is the matter, the *res* of art, more important than the *verba.* Reality is the *res* of poetry, the literal truth of things, and as we discover in science what man is, so in poems we see what man should be. Communication of the *Idea* to readers and spectators, therefore, is the end of poetry. "These things, which are thus constituted by nature, must be discovered in the bosom of nature, and plucked out therefrom, must be exposed beneath the eyes of men." However, he adds this important qualification: "If we would do this as perfectly as possible, we must ask

49

examples from him who alone is worthy of the name of Poet . . .
Virgil, from whose divine poem we shall establish the various kinds
of persons."[21] Godlike Virgil has made a world more perfect than
Nature, although he has taken the elements from Nature herself.

Since nature alone is not sufficient for the poet, he must be like
the painter — try to discover the universal patterns in nature, and
occasionally even try to "give laws" to nature. Therefore, Virgil's
example is necessary to the poet.

> So far we have shown by the use of Virgilian examples how the forms
> [*ideae*] of things may be drawn from nature itself. For I think that in
> his poetry the same thing has come about as in paintings. Now
> sculptors and those who use color take their ideas from things
> themselves, of which they imitate the lines, light, shade, and relief.
> Whatever they find of most excellent in everything they carry over
> from many things into one of their works; thus they seem not to have
> learned from nature, but to have vied with her, or rather to have been
> able to give laws to her. Who indeed believes that there was ever any
> woman, any such beauty that it did not leave something to be desired
> by an expert judge? For even though there is a universal perfection in
> the very patterns and dimension of nature, to them many blemishes are
> brought by the mixture of either parent, by time, by weather, by place.
> Thus we could not take from any one work of nature herself the
> examples which we have borrowed from one work of Virgil.[22]

It is that something-to-be-desired addition, like Phideas' idea of
perfect beauty and Cicero's idea of a better Socrates, that raises
Virgil's work to distinction.

When Scaliger talks of the general effects of poetry, he says
that it teaches by means of pleasure, and pleasure is a disposition of
the soul in a sound body. By the instrument of poetry the soul is
reflected in itself, and it brings forth from its "celestial store
whatever there is within it of divinity."[23] Pleasure is part of our
admiration for the mind of the poet, and it is aroused by rhythm and
harmony, by "relief" (song, mime, and parody), by suspense, and
by poetry's relation to truth. It is clear that the last point, poetry's
adherence to universal truth, occupies the major position in
Scaliger's theory, so it is not surprising that he finds comedy less
important than serious poetry. "We are pleased either by subjects

for mirth, as in the case of comedy, or by serious subjects if they are more like truth; for the greater part of men hate falsehood'' (III.xcvi, p. 144; Padelford, p. 60). Since Scaliger's theory of verisimilitude rests on this assumption, he insists that ''The subject matters themselves are to be composed and ordered in such a way that they approach the truth as closely as possible.'' But again it is a carefully arranged truth distilled into poetry to fit the needs of an admiring audience.

When he gets down to details concerning comedy and tragedy, Scaliger is less interesting, more conventional, and far removed from his general theory of poetry. Comedy, like tragedy, is fashioned on examples of human life, and it differs from tragedy in the status of characters, the quality of circumstances, and the ending. In comedy the old men, the slaves, and the women are of humble station and are brought in from the country. The beginnings are somewhat troubled and the endings happy. The language is that of the common people. All is familiar, from the Donatine tradition of commentaries on Terence, and we see it repeated again and again in English treatises (the most notable being Heywood's *Apology for Actors,* 1612). About the only departures from convention in Scaliger's remarks on comedy are his greater respect for Aristophanes and his slight revision in the analysis of comic plots. Donatus had said that Terence's plots were divided into protasis, epitasis, and catastrophe; Scaliger said they should be in four units — protasis, epitasis, catastasis, and catastrophe.[24] But we must turn to other Italian critics for specific conceptions of comedy that improve on or reinterpret the Donatine commentaries. What we find is an emerging recognition of an alternative kind of comedy, more concerned with wonder and relatively different from the traditional imitation of common conditions of men and ridicule of their follies.

As sixteenth-century criticism was periodically overlaid with Aristotelian, Horatian, and Platonic theories, various complementary accounts of the specific genres and the ends of poetry appeared, and eventually, in more consistent writers, the concerns in one part of a theory began to influence other parts. The movement of *admiratio* from the general theory of all poetry into tragic theory, and eventually into comedy, occurred over a number of years. It first established itself in epic and tragic forms so that, by the mid-sixteenth century, there was little dispute about the effects of tragedy on this score: instead of pity and fear, the usual effects were deemed to be sorrow and admiration.[25] The broad eclecticism of most of the critics made almost any theory unstable as ideas passed from one part of a treatise to another. Discrimination was not nearly so highly valued as the synthesis of past ideas. Consequently almost any striking thing said by an ancient was likely to find a place in later theory. In the more systematic thinkers, as we observed with Ficino, the most general ideas usually prevailed, and these were usually Platonic. And according to Weinberg it was the Platonic thought that more or less triumphed by the end of the sixteenth century. It may be that the inclination to see epic and tragedy as a species of epideictic rhetoric accelerated some of these changes because if poetry must either praise or blame, it is easy to assign praise to those forms that represent persons of high social station and doers of heroic deeds. From Aristotle's time, admiration had always been the effect of marvels and wonderful events, and the *Aeneid* supplied notable examples of bravura passages for the admiration of the reader, like the description of the serpent coming out of the sea to strangle Laocoon or the description of Rumor recited in Jonson's *Poetaster*. Therefore, when sixteenth-century writers praised the better kinds of poetry, they thought of them in terms of admiration.

In the last half of the century many things about poetry were wonderful. For instance Diason Denores (1553) found that metaphor produces admiration because we derive knowledge from the resemblance, and this evokes admiration. In a later treatise (1586), Denores says that each device used in a poem must be capable of causing wonder and admiration in the audience. "Therefore every poem is founded on the marvelous. For if this were not so, it would not engender in our minds that pleasure which the audience desires" (Weinberg, pp. 427, 622). Francisco Patrizi (1586) went even farther, insisting that admiration was the only quality common to all poetry; it originated in the divine furor of a poet's soul, and in the poem it was manifested by the improbable and marvelous: "All poetry must have as its object the incredible." Its effect on the audience was, as we might have suspected by now, admiration — a kind of contemplation of ideas (Weinberg, pp. 772-75, 785). Patrizi's consistency extends to comedy as well, for he says that a comic poem entirely incredible would be just ridiculous and laughable; therefore, poets should mix the credible and incredible (Weinberg, p. 774).

It is clear that these critics, particularly those with more than a slight Platonic bias, were using the term admiration in the expanded sense, to signify not just a reaction to supernatural marvels, but to suggest a high regard for an author's talents, a good opinion of the characters, and a reverence for abstract ideas behind or in nature, perhaps leading to a contemplation of the highest things. The admiration of tragicomedy that touched the sensibilities of half of Europe, therefore, must inevitably wash over comedy, too.

Robortello, Vincenzo Maggi, and Giovanni Pigna specifically associated *admiratio* with comic effects. Robortello was cautious and hedging in the matter but forthright enough to illustrate a tendency. Since the great end of all poetry, said Robortello (1548), was pleasure through imitation which excites virtue, the pleasures from various forms cannot be totally different from each other. The audience is "refined" by experiencing such pleasures, and comedy should be no exception. The pleasure from comedy is not unlike that from tragedy — both arouse admiration, but tragedy is superior because it requires greater effort to express. Therefore we regard it with greater admiration. And since the marvelous is less credible, it must be mingled with the trivial or common in forms such as comedy where verisimilitude is essential.[26] The assumption is that a playwright would do well to mix his comedy with other forms involving the marvelous, if he is to provoke grief, joy, or hope.

Maggi thought the end of poetry is achieved by "imitating human actions in delightful discourse, to render the soul refined," like Robortello, to embellish the soul with the best moral dispositions. In his treatise *De ridiculis* (1550), he extracts passages from Cicero, Quintilian, and Pontano, to suggest that comedy produces the same kind of admiration that is required of tragedy and epic, and it is accomplished by use of variety and novelty. New circumstances produce laughter and admiration, because potential knowledge is always involved (Weinberg, pp. 412-17). Maggi cited Plato's *Theatetus* to explain this moving power of wonder: "Men are moved to the study of wisdom by wonder." Apparently the sudden perception of new ideas heightens the spirits of the audience, even though the comic figures or events be *"turpitudine."* [27]

Giovanni Pigna, in a treatise on romance (1554), made a similar association between newness and comic admiration. Comparing Ariosto's *Cassaria* to the *Suppositi*, he consistently preferred the *Cassaria*. Among other reasons, he said its devices were newer, more original inventions, causing increased admiration and greater pleasure. But in general Pigna still retained the basic medieval distinctions between the decorum of tragedy and comedy. Tragedy represents royal life, in long discourses, showing the consequences of fortune, and its end is grave teaching and majestic sorrow. Comedy presents the life of the people in short repartees, by means of cunning, to produce delight, joy, and playfulness, and to give many warnings about private life (Weinberg, pp. 451-52). At any rate, Pigna acknowledges, like the others, that the delight of comedy involves that degree of admiration proper to the form. I cite the views of Robortello, Maggi, and Pigna not as useful comic theory nor as any known sources of Elizabethan thought on the subject but as illustrations of the status that *admiratio* had attained by the middle of the century. Each of the critics felt a need to make a place for some sort of admiration in his account of comedy, a sign of the temper of critical thought.

The human and divine uses of wonder in Renaissance thought that we have looked at so far are stated neatly by the English essayist Owen Feltham (1628). Like many of his predecessors, Feltham brings together the religious and the Neoplatonic implications when he meditates on God's works and man's art — the "soul's perspective glass" (and typical of the age, the mirror now becomes a telescope) by which we see God as if He were nearer at hand. "All endeavors aspire to eminency; all eminencies do beget admiration."

Therefore, he feels that the worship of God is a kind of admiration, a sublime bowing of the soul to the godhead. This inclination spreads to all serious contemplation — of masques, of feminine beauty, song, epic poetry, and essay.

> Whatsoever is rare and passionate carries the soul to the thought of eternity. And, by contemplation, gives it some glimpses of more absolute perfection than here 'tis capable of. When I see the royalty of a state show, at some unwonted solemnity, my thoughts present me something, more royal than this. When I see the most enchanting beauties, that earth can show me; I yet think, there is something far more glorious; methinks I see a kind of higher perfection, peeping through the frailty of a face. When I hear the ravishing strains of a sweet-tuned voice, married to the warbles of the artful instrument; I apprehend by this a higher diapason; and do almost believe, I hear a little Deity whispering, through the pory substance of the tongue. But this I can but grope after. I can neither find, nor say what it is. When I read a rarely sententious man, I admire him to my own impatiency. I cannot read some parts of Seneca above two leaves together. He raises my soul to a contemplation, which sets me a-thinking on more than I can imagine. So I am forced to cast him by, and subside to an admiration. Such effects works poetry, when it looks to towering virtues. It gives up a man to raptures, and irradiates the soul with such high apprehensions that all the glories which this world hath hereby appear contemptible.[28]

So Feltham reacted to serious and grave works, but, also like many of his contemporaries, he saw no place for admiration simply in "light airs" that turn us into "spriteful actions" and breathe away quickly in "loose laughter," leaving behind not half the impression that serious works do. This attitude created a difficulty for comic writers who wished to entertain and to praise seriously. Sir Philip Sidney was aware of the difficulty and tried to solve it as well as anyone in the age did.

II. SIDNEY'S APOLOGY FOR RIGHT COMEDY

Sir Philip Sidney was in the tradition of English humanists like John Colet, Sir Thomas Elyot, Roger Ascham, and Thomas Wilson, who mixed their enthusiasm for good writing with veneration for

55

Christian morals and patriotism, but his outlook was European. His *Apology for Poetry* (ca. 1580-83) is a treatise in praise of poetry — what it can be in the great world — and it is a practical analysis of the deficiencies of English achievements. It begins with expansive generalizations describing the ideal of good poetry, which Sidney conceives in Neoplatonic terms; later the treatise points out departures from the "right use" of the art.[29] Sidney's general theory of poetry disposed him toward both the humanist and religious sides of *admiratio,* and it led him to a particular analysis of comedy for which something very close to admiration was necessary.

From the humanists he accepted the notion of the poet as maker, whose mind reflects not only the created world but, like the *speculum vivens,* manufactures its own intellectual species, creating images of another nature, in the same way that God created things.[30] Although the famous passage in the *Apology* that sets forth the concept of "another nature" is an elaboration of a statement in Scaliger (*Poetics,* I.i.5-6), Sidney's exalted tone changes it greatly. The poet, Sidney says, does not merely look to nature but to an ideal in his own mind: "in making things either better than Nature bringeth forth, or, quite anew, [he invents] forms such as never were in Nature, as the heros, demigods, cyclops, chimeras, furies, and such like; so as he goeth hand in hand with Nature, not enclosed within the narrow warrant of her gifts but freely ranging only within the zodiac of his own wit" (p. 100). Sidney related the mental operation of the poet to a distinctly Platonic theory of knowledge whereby, knowing himself, the poet knows the world and Ideas of a more perfect world, for Nature's world is an inferior, brazen copy; the poet's world is golden. Each artificer's skill stands most of all in "that *Idea* or fore-conceit of the work, and not in the work itself" (p. 101). The poet manifests his fore-conceit in order to represent accurately what is in his mind, but most of all he tries to create a provocative instrument, a model for men to imitate in their lives. Like Scaliger the emphasis, therefore, is upon subject matter rather than upon words because Sidney was bound to show the ethical effects of poetry upon its audience.

The poet represents a "right prince" in Cyrus, a constant

friend in Pylades, a true lover in Theagenes, so as to bestow upon readers and listeners the power to reconstruct and admire the ideal. He aims "to bestow a Cyrus upon the world to make many Cyruses, if [men] will learn aright why and how the maker made him"(p. 101). In this sense a poem is truly a "speaking picture" because it speaks to the mind's eye of readers.[31] The religious side of Sidney's theory emerges at this point. Since the fall of Adam the world has been corrupted, but our "erected wit" is assisted by God to conceive anew the perfect world, a perfect world beyond nature. For that reason poets should bring forth things surpassing nature's doing, even though our "infected will" prevents us from ever reaching perfection. The speaking picture of poetry can at least teach us how to strive. The best and original poets were prophets who spoke above human understanding and who sang hymns in praise of God; and in worldly affairs poets function as educators, master wits who teach and delight by imitation of the Idea, so as to cure our moral defects and lead us to good action.

Unlike the philosopher, who speaks in crabbed or misty generalities, or the historian, who writes of particular and contradictory events, the poet uses delightful, concrete images to draw men's minds toward more perfect ideas. All learning leads and draws us "to as high a perfection as our degenerate souls, made worse by their clayey lodgings, can be capable of . . . to lift up the mind from the dungeon of the body to the enjoying his own divine essence" (p. 104). The best effect of teaching, as Ficino and other humanists said, is virtuous action and knowledge of one's self, and poetry's delightful teaching best brings us to this end. The use of concrete images awakens the "powers of the mind" better than a description or a philosopher's definition, and poetry moves men to use what they know or it makes them desire to know; it entices the mind by delight, more effectively than any other art (p. 107).

Sidney, therefore, uses many of the coins of Renaissance theory, and his debts appear to be heavy to Neoplatonic humanism, although specific borrowings are hard to identify. He surely read Plato and Scaliger; some close parallels have been found with Fracastoro's *Naugerius,* and a striking similarity in describing the artist's Idea has been noticed with Zuccaro's mannerist treatise on painting. His conception of "fore-conceit," which Jonson was to make so much of, was widely understood in sixteenth-century theory to be the artists' "platform," plan, or design, and his respect for the creative activity of the mind to make images of things beyond the observed facts of experience suggests the mind as *speculum*.

When he comes to admiration, Sidney also seems contemporary: for instance in his peroration, where he catalogs the stupendous benefits from poetry claimed by various authorities, he "conjures" us

> to believe with Aristotle that [the poets] were the ancient treasurers of the Grecians' divinity; to believe with Bembus [i.e. Cardinal Bembo] that they were the first bringers-in of all civility; to believe with Scaliger that no philosopher's precepts can sooner make you an honest man than the reading of Virgil; to believe with Clauserus, the translator of Cornutus, that it pleased the heavenly Deity, by Hesiod and Homer, under the veil of fables, to give us all knowledge, Logic, Rhetoric, Philosophy natural and moral, and *quid non?;* to believe with me that there are many mysteries contained in Poetry, which of purpose were written darkly, lest by profane wits it should be abused; to believe with Landino, that they are so beloved of the gods that whatsoever they write proceeds of a divine fury; lastly to believe themselves when they tell you they will make you immortal by their verse. (pp. 141-42)

Sidney's aim here is to dazzle us into an admiration, to demonstrate his conviction that poetry is ever praiseworthy and full of virtue-breeding delight.

Divine poetry, such as the Psalms, is vatic, and Sidney describes his own profound admiration for the ability of holy David making us, as it were, "see God coming in His majesty, his telling of the beasts' joyfullness, and hills leaping." David almost "showeth himself a passionate lover of that unspeakable and everlasting beauty to be seen by the eyes of the mind, only cleared by faith" (p. 99), a description worthy of Augustine's exposition of the Psalms. It is especially suited to religious admiration that the eyes of the mind have been cleared by faith, the belief that qualifies one for the vision of inconceivable excellence of God. Secular poetry, according to Sidney, is limited to human skill, the best a human can accomplish without divine inspiration; yet "right poets" must try to bridge the gap between ideal and actual worlds if poetry is to make men good; it should "take naughtiness away and plant goodness even in the secretest cabinet of our souls" — presumably our consciences (p. 106). Thus secular poetry also has an elevating power. It works positively and negatively by creating notable images of virtues and vices in which we see our own filthiness and achieve proper reconciliation with honor and truth (pp. 103, 115). The heroes of epics not only teach and move us to truth, but a lofty image of such worthies will inflame our desire to make magnanimity shine throughout all misty fearfulness. We are "wonderfully ravished" by the love for virtue which the epic poet sets forth in all her beauty "to the eye of any that will deign not to disdain until they understand" (p. 119). Let Aeneas be kept in the tablet of your memory and he will be more fruitful in your actions than all the moral philosophers. Thus the Idea is something we must live by. Tragedy, too, evokes wonder as we witness the rise and fall of tyrants "that with stirring the affects [emotions] of admiration and commiseration, teacheth the uncertainty of this world and upon how weak foundations gilden roofs are builded" (p. 118).

Sidney's appreciation of ballads is often quoted: "I never heard the old song of Percy and Douglas that I found not my heart moved more than with a trumpet" — but the full context shows that he is demonstrating for us the effects of wonder, comparable to Duke Theseus' generous reaction to the acting of Pyramus and Thisbe. What amazes Sidney is not only the valor of the old heroes but the fact that the song is performed "by some blind crowder with no rougher voice than rude style," and Sidney characterizes the crude language as like "the dust and cobwebs of that uncivil age," all the while he muses upon what an effect the song might have if it were trimmed in the "gorgeous eloquence of Pindar" (p. 118). He conceives not only an image of a dead hero who has more power than a live trumpet, but his improving imagination leaps to the better poem it might be. Pindar after all was the poet most fit to awaken thoughts from the sleep of idleness to the embrace of honorable enterprises; so again the Idea is turned to practical action through the operation of our admiring souls.

So much for Sidney's general theory of poetry. His extensive remarks on comedy reveal two fairly distinct theories. At first, while defending poetry's moral usefulness, he emphasizes comedy's extreme ridiculousness, defining it in the fashion of the Donatine tradition: "comedy is an imitation of the common errors of our life, which [the poet] representeth in the most ridiculous and scornful sort that may be, so that it is impossible that any beholder can be content to be such a one. Now as in geometry the oblique must be known as well as the right, and in arithmetic the odd as well as the even, so in the actions of our life who seeth not the filthiness of evil wanteth a great foil to perceive the beauty of virtue" (p. 117). We no sooner see evil men represented, but by a reflex we look at the inward idea of beauty and virtue, and we wish the evil punished. Like Donatus, Sidney says that comedy handles private and domestic matters, although he explains the purpose of such a representation as both mental and moral teaching. A picture of evil generates useful concepts to help us perceive base actions correctly. Our eyes are opened when we see evil "contemptibly set forth." Thus far his emphasis is on comedy as instructive ridicule.

Later in the *Apology* where he examines the state of English poetry, Sidney redefines comedy, in a shift from a single effect theory to one of double or ambiguous effects that arise from "right comedy." No longer dwelling on the single operation of ridicule, he distinguishes between a better and a worse sort of comedy. He probably thought that the worse was an abuse of the better (as he implies in other parts of the *Apology*), but his analysis isolates different ways of provoking an audience by means of different comic motives. The explanation has confused some readers, I think, because they have taken his remarks out of context, regardless of the trend of the main argument. Sidney seems to be trying to do two things at once, here: to maintain the hegemony of his general theory of the great ends of poetry and to separate the various genres enough so that "mungrel tragicomedy" does not prevail over pure-bred tragedy and comedy. In the face of his general theory, punitive tragedy (opening "great wounds") and scornful comedy ("the filthiness of evil") cannot prevail; otherwise the elevating effects will never emerge from the dramas. "Admiration and comiseration" and "right sportfulness," therefore, replace the old punitive concerns, and a certain amount of controlled indecorum or mixture is allowed without losing the purity of old forms.

So, Sidney says of comedy that the worse sort depends entirely upon ridicule as it causes just "loud laughter." The better sort depends upon some joyful events which produce delight, and they may be mixed with the ridiculous. He seeks by means of this better sort to raise the effects of delightful comedy to a level at least analogous to the admiration we feel for tragedy. The "whole tract of a comedy should be full of delight, as tragedy should be still maintained in a well-raised admiration."[32] And Sidney's remarks on comic delight suggest that, as an ethical Platonist, he is trying to bring comedy under the more acceptable influence of poetry's general purpose. He begins by objecting to loud laughter and ends with a conception of mixed comic effects.

> Our comedians think there is no delight without laughter; which is very wrong, for though laughter may come with delight, yet cometh it not of delight, as though delight should be the cause of laughter; but well may one thing breed both together. Nay, rather in themselves they have, as it were, a kind of contrariety: for delight we scarcely do but in things that have a conveniency [i.e. fitness, agreement, accordance] to ourselves or to the general nature; laughter almost ever cometh of things most disproportioned to ourselves and nature. Delight hath a joy in it, either permanent or present. Laughter hath only a scornful tickling. For example, we are ravished with delight to see a fair woman, and yet are far from being moved to laughter. We laugh at deformed creatures, wherein certainly we cannot delight. We delight in good chances, we laugh at mischances; we delight to hear the happiness of our friends and country, at which he were worthy to be laughed at that would laugh. (p. 136)

Delightful comedy, therefore, has sportfulness or joy as its end in a reflection of ourselves and nature; its subject might be the appropriate representation of fair women, good fortune, and happiness for

61

those things dear to our hearts, things we approve of. From this kind of experience Sidney thought there was something good to learn: citing Aristotle (as Jonson does later) on the great fault of laughter, he says, "I speak to this purpose, that all the end of the comical part be not upon such scornful matters as stir laughter only, but mix it with delightful teaching which is the end of poesy" (pp. 136-37).

His explanation of the mixture of delight and ridicule suggests that we should not confuse his theory with the modern distinction in Shakespeare criticism between laughing *at* (Dogberry, Armado, the Falstaff of *Merry Wives*) and laughing *with* (Berowne, Rosalind, and the Falstaff of *Henry IV*), which amounts to two kinds of ridicule — one directed at the comic figure, the other directed by the jester toward himself and other objects. Sidney distinguishes ridicule from another quite different comic effect where laughter is inappropriate. He does not deny that laughter and delight sometimes go together, although they are separate, almost contrary, things. "For as in Alexander's picture well set out we delight without laughter, and in twenty mad antics we laugh without delight, so in Hercules, painted with his great beard and furious countenance, in woman's attire, spinning at Omphale's commandment, it breedeth both delight and laughter" (p. 136). In this example, Hercules in the painting (Figure 1) is not mocking himself, parodying, nor teasing like Rosalind or Berowne; nor does it seem that we are invited to laugh with him; and although Sidney may have understood that audiences sympathize with the person ridiculed, he did not make that point. Rather he emphasized the idea of the speaking picture: Hercules' great beard and his furious countenance imply his "strange power," and that such a powerful demigod should be in love is amazing, hence it "procureth delight." We see that great energy can be under the commandment of love, and at the same time we laugh at the ignominious sight of Hercules in women's clothes wielding a distaff instead of a club.

The choice of Alexander and Hercules as objects of delight in comedy is especially significant because they were traditionally the types of ancient wisdom, valor, and justice — in the group of heroes who most readily aroused admiration. Wonder had kept the heroic

Fig. 1. *Hercules and Omphale,* by Lucas Cranach, 1537, Hercules in women's clothing

ideal alive in the minds of men, as Hercules wondered at his father Jupiter, Theseus admired Hercules, Achilles admired Theseus, and Alexander, viewing a dramatic representation of the destruction of Troy, was inspired to shape his action ''after that pattern'' (Heywood, *Apology,* sig. B3). According to Sidney, Alexander read Homer's account of Achilles and found ''more bravery of mind by the pattern of Achilles than by hearing the definition of fortitude'' (p. 127). In the same way Caesar was moved by the images of Alexander in the Temple of Hercules, and he was ''never in any peace of thoughts till by his memorable exploits he had purchased to himself the name of Alexander: as Alexander till he thought himself of desert to be called Achilles: Achilles Theseus, Theseus till he had sufficiently imitated the acts of Hercules, and Hercules till he held himself worthy to be called the son of Jupiter'' (Heywood, sig. B3v). This apostolic succession in the images of heroes affects our minds too, inflaming them with desire and informing us with counsel how to be worthy (Sidney, p. 119). It is apparent, therefore, that the picture of fierce Hercules spinning in women's clothes signifies the archetypal hero in a ridiculous situation, and it was delightful not because Hercules was a sympathetic person, but because he was an image of great moral force, for the moment out of his character, masculine power under feminine government — a speaking picture indeed for Elizabethans.[33] Although his potential inner nature is appropriately suggested, the outer garments and his situation make us laugh. These are two distinct yet simultaneous responses, the effects of jest and earnest.

In this light, Sidney's other examples of comic characters make sense: "a busy loving courtier, a heartless threatening Thraso, a self-wise-seeming schoolmaster, a wry transformed traveller — these if we saw [them] walk in stage names, which we play naturally; therein were delightful laughter, and teaching delightfulness; as in the other, the tragedies of Buchanan do justly bring forth divine admiration" (p. 137). Sidney does not insist that "heartless threatening Thraso" be sympathetic, but that he should be naturally acted, "lively and well spirited," and yet be a type of human nature, of "general nature," even when he falls into ridiculous situations. The vigorous language and dramatic force of character should be made in such a way that the actor can affect his teaching delightfulness by some movement of the soul, as Alberti would have said. Sidney, therefore, conceives of a comedy that will have the *energia* of forcibleness of expression that carries conviction, making us feel men's strong passions. The sweet, charming force of poesie lies in this *energia,* which strikes and pierces the soul or possesses the sight more than philosophy ever can.[34] Delightful comedy will therefore flourish as it evokes a "true lively knowledge" or "heart ravishing knowledge" in dramatic action.

In this sketch of various meanings of admiration in Renaissance culture, I have suggested that the two traditions are different but related. However differing in emphasis and purpose, both make admiration an essential part of the rhetoric of praise, and both strive to express thoughts above our understanding. The religious tradition has more to do with emotions. It begins with the feeling of inadequacy, silence, and the small voice out of the dust. It proceeds to a delight in the rich beauty of God's gifts, along with the sense of mystery of the hidden truth — salvation — known only to the pure in heart and seen only in a glass darkly. The law of love is the imperative: that we should interpret scripture and treat others with deep understanding of the spirit, although in the eyes of the world we seem fools. The philosophic and rhetorical tradition has to do with emotions, too, but emotions and reason directed toward the will and its ethical or civic consequences. Our response is a lifting of the intellect above common, sensual things, an operation of the rational soul, thus a kind of self-criticism. We may see a reflection of the idea in actual things, and we may invent things beyond nature. Our enchantment comes from an awareness of a greater power — perhaps a higher magic — by which, according to some humanists, man is stimulated to make himself into another kind of being. Although love is involved, its pleasure culminates in know- ledge which is the equivalent of virtue. Selected elements of both of these tendencies of thought can be found in Sidney's *Apology,* and like some other sixteenth-century theorists Sidney attempted to bring a delight, like admiration, into a conception of right comedy. After the building of James Burbage's Theater (1576) and the association of John Lyly with a children's company at Blackfriars (1582) and the writing of Sidney's *Apology* (ca. 1580-82), the stage was set in more ways than one for a series of delightful comedies.

3.

Lyly and Shakespeare

In the two or three decades before Lyly was active, school comedies based on Terence and Plautus and imitations of Italian comedies offered a distinct kind of entertainment. Coming out of Westminster School and St. Paul's, as well as from groups of choir boys, they had frequent exposure at court, as the Revels accounts suggest. Probably typical were plays like *Roister Doister* (before 1552), and *The Bugbears* (ca. 1563-65); but jolly farce and Italianate comedy had to vie with an obvious preference for mythological tales and moralities, if titles of lost plays mean anything: *Cupid, Venus, and Mars* (1553); *Cloridon and Radiamanta* (1572); *Narcissus* (1572); *Paris and Vienne* (1572); *Perseus and Andromeda* (1574); *Truth, Faithfulness, and Mercy* (1574); and *The Marriage of Mind and Measure* (1579). Interest in more exalted persons and in love and marriage, always latent in Latin comedy, may have been greatly enlarged in this romance material. The stories could now focus on the first encounter of heroic lovers, their difficulties telling of their feelings, the barriers between them, their separation; but the final reunion may frequently have been denied them, for Queen Elizabeth did not approve of her courtiers' marrying. Certainly the titles *Narcissus, Perseus and Andromeda,* and *Dido* do not suggest happy endings of conventional comedy, but, of course, some could have been tragedies. The new emphasis appears to have spread to the popular stage as well, for Leicester's Men acted *Mamillia* and

66

Preddor and Lucia in 1573 and Sussex's Men did *The Rape of the Second Helen* in 1579. In any case, we know that by the mid-1580s plays representing heroic persons from classical legend or romance thrived in boys' companies, and on the public stage a few years later. The comedies may not have corresponded exactly to Sidney's right comedy, but the bare titles indicate a possible trend in that direction before *The Apology* was written.

Among the surviving comedies before Lyly there are examples to support the impression that the English tended toward mixed forms. Perhaps Sidney had something like Edwards' *Damon and Pythias* (ca. 1564-65) in mind when he objected to "mungrel tragi-comedy," and the dedication to Whetstone's *Promos and Cassandra* (1578) openly defended comedy that mixed vice and virtue to produce scorn and delight, although the author distinguished it from the worst abuses of English plays. Like Sidney, he wanted to keep decorum of character better than others had, and for decorum's sake he separated the comical discourses into two plays: the first showed "the insufferable abuse of a lewd magistrate, the virtuous behaviors of a chaste lady, the uncontrolled lewdness of a favored courtesan, and the undeserved estimation of a pernicious parasite." The second showed "the magnanimity of a noble king in checking vice and favoring virtue . . . the ruin and overthrow of dishonest practices, with the advancement of upright dealing."[1] Like Sidney he seems to have felt a tension between a more serious purpose of comedy and its need to please; consequently he wished to avoid a vain and indiscreet mixture of "impossibilities" and gross indecorum, to keep his comedies true to the proper social types or kinds of men, but he still wanted to keep people's attention and to please them by intermingling the grave with the delightful. Unfortunately Whetstone's crude plays fell miserably short of his intent; nevertheless their wretched dialogue and undeveloped scenes gave Shakespeare a lot of room for redesigning the story in *Measure for Measure,* for a theater more receptive to radical mixtures.

In the 1580s Lyly succeeded where others had failed to reconcile the conflicting needs of right comedy. After experimenting with *Alexander and Campaspe,* he achieved a delicate equilibrium in *Sapho and Phao* of learned, satiric, and sophisticated material, and he did it mainly with dialogue in carefully constructed scenes, built around ambiguous situations. Especially as they show the indignity or embarrassment of some figure of great power under the sway of irresistible love — a conquering emperor subjugated to the beauty of his prisoner, a princess in love with a boatman — these seem calculated to evoke a quiet smile and delight. The other party to the love affair was also touched and possibly ennobled by the experience even as he was threatened. Although the situations resemble the examples that Sidney gave of mixed comedy, Alexander and Hercules in love, Lyly included other elements that enhanced the plays' courtly entertainment and their wonder, for behind the noble and common folk were spirits and deities, set forth with music and spectacle that created an air of magic, dreams, and playful but dangerous masquerade. The plays turn on themselves to comment on the spectacle or to direct our attention to a point without ever saying exactly what is meant.

Shakespeare testifies to his interest in Lyly's kind of comedy in *A Midsummer Night's Dream,* where Lyly's inner and outer transformations reappear most wonderfully adapted to the richer possibilities of experience. The folly of human love and the strange effects of the Queen of the Fairies' love for Bottom lift that play to a special distinction, and the whole creates a mood that pervades some of Shakespeare's other early comedies. In this chapter I will comment on the two plays by Lyly and on *A Midsummer Night's Dream* as definitive examples of comedy of admiration. Though something could be said about similar plays like *Endymion, The Arraignment of Paris, Friar Bacon and Friar Bungay, The Cobbler's Prophecy, Summer's Last Will and Testament,* and perhaps *As You Like It* and *Love's Labor's Lost,* I will not, because the purpose of this essay is just to suggest the possibilities of the form clearly enough before we go on to Jonson's peculiar use of it.

1. *Sapho and Phao*

In Lyly's *Sapho and Phao,* the scholar, Pandion, has come

from the university in Athens to live in the court of Syracusa, and it is clear from his debate with Trachinus that this was a move from a life of contemplation to a life of action, from a study of times past and a prophecy of future times to action in time present, "in perfection, not by devise as fables but in execution as truths."[2] Apparently his new position has altered him in some unspeakable way and he feels shame. He expresses his melancholy feelings indirectly, through cryptic sayings and witticisms, often enough to suggest the cause: he sees the contradiction between the ideal from which he came and the actual in which he is embroiled. He agrees that Princess Sapho is a virtuous woman without compare, but the society about her is inhabited by dangerous dissemblers. Threatened by the iniquity of flatterers, a courtier must continually dissemble. Since "it is harder to shape a life to dissemble, than to go forward with the liberty of truth," he is discontented (I.ii.32-35); nevertheless he still feels drawn to the court, and as he departs, Tachnis, the cynical courtier, explains Pandion's divided feelings — the aphorism that caps the scene: "you flatter that which you seem to mislike and seek to disgrace that which you most wonder at" (I.ii.67-69). After spending some time at court, Pandion has learned his lesson well, for when asked if he thinks that the virgin princess's mysterious illness is caused by love, he equivocates: "Of men we learn to speak, of gods to hold our peace. Silence shall digest what folly hath swallowed, and wisdom wean what fancy hath nursed" (III.i.27-29).

If this situation were not presented in the usual brilliant banter of Lyly's plays, we might expect to find Pandion in a tragedy, muttering "Something is rotten in Sicily." But Lyly has clothed his potentially serious situation in such bright fancies that we are kept at a suitable distance, neither so emotionally disturbed nor so intellectually awakened to remove the spirit of mirth. The bright and elaborate pattern of talk, laid over actions and characters, attains a fine self-sufficiency. Although we may feel that within or beneath the charming texture of his work there is some stronger emotion and probably some significant references to the court of Queen Elizabeth, we are merely teased by such hints. Unlike Sidney, Lyly obviously puts words before matter, but there is always the suggestion of some important matters indeed, just beyond our reach. We may feel that wisdom must try to wean what fancy hath nourished, and in our silence we should try to digest what folly has given us to swallow, but Lyly does not allow us much time to reflect, for every episode is quickly carried forward to an equally playful and dazzling scene. The mind, like the ear, is never at rest, for it must be continually alert for the sharp little antithesis or a suddenly suggestive analogy that has been woven like a thin silver thread through the fabric of the dialogue.

It is easy to deplore the excesses of modern scholars' interpretations that find Queen Elizabeth and her ever-impending marriage to someone — the earl of Leicester, the earl of Oxford, duc d'Alençon, or Philip II of Spain — hidden behind various characters. But it is hard to deny that Lyly has given many opportunities for conjecture. There are simply too many loose ends, such as the dreams of Endymion and Sapho (which I will comment upon below), or suggestive details, such as Midas' desire to conquer the island of Lesbos. We are positively encouraged by this art to toy with local meanings, especially flattering to the queen, and in this respect Lyly is a practitioner (but not the originator) of what Jonson, Marston, and Chapman later exploited.[3] The very restraint Lyly exercises in handling delicate subjects encourages us to fill in the silences, for he chooses most often to present an image of a court, sometimes with a virgin queen at its head, like Sapho, and often with certain unspoken or dangerous sentiments on the tips of everyone's tongues. This method — and it is a method of allusion, not allegory — works, I think, in the same way that pastoral poetry, under the guise of wolves and sheep and the pretty talk of country affairs, seems to glance at the larger urbane world. So it is almost inevitable that court entertainment of this kind should arouse speculation about allusions to real social and political issues at court. Because of the explosiveness of the subject, Lyly keeps most of his thoughts secure in a vague or remote place, like Jonson's Gargaphie or Shakespeare's Bohemia. Since *Endymion* is "a tale of the Man in the Moon," says Lyly, do not apply it to our times. Just as the method is not allegorical, it is not simply archetypal or mythic either,[4] because the actual presence of the monarch at the play needs always to be kept in mind, as she was probably in the minds of the audience. She is a dangerous and yet magnetic person with real power; hence the desires to advance and retreat are strong, and the playwright has an obligation to say something true and yet to say something pleasing, to give the play important ideas but also to pay a compliment.

We should not make a mere political paradigm of each of Lyly's plays, for they are after all charming comedies, and as G. K. Hunter has shown, the very conditions of performance prevented Lyly from making extensive and systematic comments on politics (pp. 92, 97). Elizabeth did not like personal reference, and presumptuous courtiers were disciplined severely, although her vanity and coyness may sometimes have seemed to provoke advances beyond decorum. An entertainer was in a difficult position. He had to imply just enough of general importance in his spectacle but not specific enough to bring offense. He had to keep a nice balance, which itself lent just that necessary amount of tension to bring Lyly's plays to their comic achievement. The result was a brilliant surface appeal, to dazzle, to amuse with soft smiles, to elevate the mind with half-formed thought, and perhaps to insinuate a little, but finally to charm it all away. This is Lyly's kind of comedy, and I think it was understood to be a kind of comedy that approached the very ideal of poetry, to teach delightfully, yes, but to delight with a tinge of comic wonder, in the face of the inexplicable and powerful. Basically, I assume that certain passages in each play were calculated to excite special, now-forgotten, associations, but that these passages were sparsely scattered, more like a few grains of pepper in a salad. They give the plays zest, and they are there to enhance the taste of the rest of the composition. The way Lyly manages his plays in order to raise this delightful response is the concern of the following remarks.

Part of the delight involved lifting the minds of an audience to an idea, such as the idea of a monarch. In fact, as we have seen in the sixteenth-century critics, the powerful operation of wonder was to go beyond the local and physical impression, toward some grander thought and feeling. So that even if the queen herself is part of the subject of the plays, Lyly is leading us to thoughts about the Idea of a queen, rather than about her person.[5] Lyly is interested in what it means to *be* a monarch, *vis à vis* what it means to be a philosopher, an artist, a soldier, a virtuous virgin, or a woman. Once we know what each kind of person is, we are to be amused in our contemplation of the inner harmony of their minds temporarily disturbed by false desire.

Campaspe (ca. 1580-84), probably Lyly's first play, has some of the elements of his later comedies, but in execution it barely moves away from the conventions of academic debate, and it does not quite achieve the artfulness of his mature plays. One other play, *Mother Bombie,* adapts the conventions of Latin farce and only incidentally uses the means to provoke admiration. The rest of his plays bear enough family resemblances to suggest that the author worked within a definite form. In so far as they present general ideas, these plays seem to crack a smile and to stir thought about the contingencies of human existence and the way a good man meets them. Our inward delight comes from our understanding what it means to be human and how the forces of nature, destiny, the gods impinge upon us. The conduct of Lyly's typical comedy leads its heroes through a series of defining experiences, toward a final discovery of their true selves, their true minds. The questions most frequently asked are those of the humanist orator: What sort of behavior is "becoming" and what is "not becoming" in a soldier, virgin, monarch, and so forth. To this degree, I might be describing the design of *Campaspe* as well as later plays, for Alexander must learn what is becoming of a heroic conquerer. He has to see that there is a distinct difference between his role and that of a philosopher like Diogenes or that of a painter like Apelles. The little episode where Alexander tries to draw a picture in Apelles' studio is a good example of Lyly's tricks of dialogue that make the idea clear. At first Alexander is headstrong and opinionated (as Caesar sometimes was to be in Jonson's *Poetaster),* about how he should do it; he would begin by painting the eyes; Apelles says he must begin with the outline of the face. "If you will paint as you are a king, your majesty may begin where you please, but as you would be a painter you must begin with the face" (III.iv.73-75). Aided by Apelles' gentle wit, Alexander gradually sees the foolishness of trying to be an artist:

> *Alexander.* Lend me thy pencil Apelles, I will paint, and thou shalt judge.
> *Apelles.* Here.
> *Alexander.* The coal breaks.
> *Apelles.* You lean too hard.
> *Alexander.* Now it blacks not.
> *Apelles.* You lean too soft.
> *Alexander.* This is awry.
> *Apelles.* Your eye goeth not with your hand.
> *Alexander.* Now it is worse.
> *Apelles.* Your hand goeth not with your mind.
> *Alexander.* Nay, if all be too hard or soft, so many rules and regards, that one's hand, one's eye, one's mind must all draw together, I had rather be setting of a battle, than blotting of a board. But how have I done here?
> *Apelles.* Like a king.
> *Alexander.* I think so: but nothing more unlike a painter.
>
> (III.iv.97-113)

It could not be more explicit, a lesson in being yourself in a social context. The final lesson of Alexander involves the highest virtues of a monarch, magnanimity. He must see that it is beneath a king to love a common woman and be rival to a painter for her affections. He must grandly renounce his claim to Campaspe, remove all dissembling, subdue his affections, and give his blessing to Apelles and Campaspe — the "two loving worms." "Go Apelles," he says, "take with you your Campaspe, Alexander is cloyed with looking on that which thou wond'rest at." The magnificent thing is that Alexander can resist love, like a monarch, "as he list." Hephestion stands back in proper admiration: "The conquering of Thebes was not so honorable as the subduing of these thoughts." And Alexander concludes with a solemn declaration of his understanding.

It were a shame Alexander should desire to command the world, if he could not command himself. But come, let us go, I will try whether I can better bear my hand with my heart, than I could with mine eye. And good Hephestion, when all the world is won, and every country is thine and mine, either find me out another to subdue, or on my word I will fall in love. (V.iv.150-55)

The ending of the play is gracefully carried off, pulling important threads together and pointing out the magnificent generosity of Alexander. It demonstrates that Lyly has an interest in grand effects even in his earliest work. Nevertheless the play lacks something we find in his later comedies. Although the hero is set forth for our admiration, the execution of the play suggests a humanist's dialogue or a simple exemplum, whereas the later comedies seem more independent of a mere lesson when they act out an irreducible and somewhat inexplicable human predicament. Lyly's special way of making them delightful comes from the plays' mysteries. We sense the mystery, a teasing charm of action, and that leads us on strangely. It probably arises from our awareness of a fundamental discontinuity and ultimate irrationality. In *Alexander and Campaspe* when the hero comes to his final discovery and resolve, he finds his right role easy and satisfying. The tinge of regret and humor implied by "find me out another to subdue, or on my word I will fall in love," does not encourage much speculation because everything else is tidy and decorous. In later comedies this sense of tidiness is still present, in the sentence structure for instance, but it is often disturbed in the action, and in the development of many scenes the issues seem more momentous. The whole atmosphere is touched with a sense of power. This new ingredient seems to make Lyly's mature comedies more typically delightful and wonderful. *Sapho and Phao,* written about the same time that Sidney composed his *Apology for Poetry,* will serve as an illustration of the dramatic method that was, with variations, to be the case in *Endymion, Midas, Love's Metamorphosis, The Woman in the Moon,* and *Gallathea.*

The subject of *Sapho and Phao* concerns the minds and the fortunes of the title characters, a great princess and a boatman. Their happiness is destroyed by Venus' arbitrary intervention in human affairs. Venus acts merely because she wants to prove her power over humans. "Sapho shall know, be she never so fair, that there is a Venus, which can conquer, were she never so fortunate." Cupid warns that this will be hard, for they say that Sapho "hath her thoughts in a string, that she conquers affections and sendeth love up and down upon errands; I am afraid she will yerk me, if I hit her" (I.i.39-41). Not easily discouraged, Venus makes Phao astonishingly beautiful and Cupid shoots arrows at Sapho. Although Sapho and Phao fall in love, their station in life is so impossibly different that neither feels willing to make a simple declaration of passion. Each resists the irresistible desire; Sapho from shame, Phao from fear. At the crisis, they approach the disastrous truth, but they do not quite compromise themselves. The disaster is averted unwittingly by Venus herself, as she, too, begins to lust after the beautiful Phao. New arrows are made for Cupid, and she instructs him to shoot an arrow of disdain into the heart of Sapho but an arrow of love for Venus into Phao's heart. After Cupid shoots disdain into Sapho's heart, Cupid is overcome by her kindness; he confesses all, and he agrees to give her control over his arrows. Thus she again has power to send love up and down upon errands, and her first order sends him to shoot an arrow of disdain for Venus into the heart of Phao. The play ends with Phao's declaration that he will leave Syracuse, reject Venus, and continue to worship Sapho in his mind, as his lust is transformed into contemplation of virtue.

The action is presented in three more or less static situations: before, during, and after; or in terms of the three emotional states: content, passionate anxiety, and stoic resolution. Phao stands in front of the audience more than Sapho, for she figures importantly only in the middle scenes and is given only the briefest moments on stage near the beginning and end. But she is in the thoughts and on the tongues of everyone almost constantly. Phao's long soliloquies and his consultations with the soothsayer occupy the main events of Acts I-II. In Act III the crisis involves the fuller depiction of Sapho's warring feelings, with her ladies-in-waiting standing by, with her alone, and with Phao at her bedside. Venus' intrigue is represented in Act IV and the surprising victory of Sapho in Act V, concluded by her "courteous" forgiveness of Phao. The play ends with Phao's noble resolution, as he leaves to pick up his oars:

> Oh Sapho! thou hast Cupid in thine arms, I in my heart; thou kissest him for sport; I must curse him for spite yet will I not curse him, Sapho, whom thou kissest. This shall be my resolution, wherever I wander to be as I were ever kneeling before Sapho; my loyalty unspotted, though unrewarded. With as little malice will I go to my grave, as I did lie withal in my cradle. My life shall be spent in sighing and wishing, the one for my bad fortune, the other for Sapho's good. (V.iii.14-22)

Although the main action is clear, the play as a whole leaves us with uncertainties. The plot turns in a circle, as Lyly admits in his epilogue, and that makes some "giddiness." It is as if we have trod a maze and "at the last come out where [we] entered in." He fears that he has led us all this while "in a labyrinth of conceits"; he has repeated one "device" diverse times, and brought us to the end where we first began. It is like a dance of fairies in a circle, and Lyly seems to apologize for its simplicity, promising hereafter to try his hand at "all forms." (I am not sure what *all forms* means: perhaps he means other forms besides the circle, or forms aside from the one device he mentions above. I doubt if he means devices of style, for he excuses himself on account of the "necessity of the history." The plainest sense may be "all forms of human entanglement, not just one pattern of love and disdain.") Simple as it seems, he wishes everyone in his audience a thread of understanding, to lead them out of "the doubts" wherewith they are entangled, "that nothing be mistaken by [his] rash oversights or misconstrued by [their] deep insights." It reminds me of Jonson's solicitude for the same understanding: "A good play is like a skein of silk, which, if you take the right end, you may wind off at pleasure on the bottom or card of your discourse, in a tale or so; how you will; but if you light on the wrong end, you will pull all into a knot or elf-lock, which nothing but the shears or a candle will undo or separate" (*Magnetic Lady,* Induction, 136-41).

The image of the thread that will lead us out of confusion is the same as Sybilla's description of her counsel to Phao: "a straight thread to lead you out of those crooked conceits" (II.i.38). From the play itself we get the beginning of ideas about what the counsel must be, but the whole is remarkably glossy and slick, resisting an interpretation. Lyly presents the actions to us to make what we can of them, and they have about them a suggestiveness that tickles thought. A good many doubts cluster around the meaning of destiny, Phao's destiny, and the responsibility of the gods. Things do occur to Phao by chance, and Lyly is at pains to show Phao's complete innocence at the beginning of the play. Phao is perfectly satisfied with his humble life, which is as distinct from court life as Pandion's university is, for his thoughts are no higher than his fortune, nor are his desires greater than his calling. Like a shepherd in Arcadia he praises an obscure life. "As much doth it delight thee to rule thine oar in a calm stream, as it doth Sapho to sway the scepter in her brave court," he says to himself. "Thou farest delicately, if thou have a fare to buy anything. Thine angle is ready, when thine oar is idle, and as sweet is the fish which thou gettest in the river, as the fowl which other buy in the market. Thou needest not fear poison in thy glass, nor treason in thy guard" (I.i.6-14). Wind and rough weather are his only enemies, and to find shelter for himself his only policy. In a thatched cottage he relishes his "sweet life," seldom found under a "golden covert." Apparently Phao is an entirely accidental instrument of Venus' willful demonstration of power. On the other hand we are at times led to think of Venus as an abstraction or metaphor of lovers' desires. Venus says nobody can resist love; "can mortal creatures resist that which the immortal gods cannot redress?" But Cupid balances her argument with the objection that Sapho controls her affections, whereas the gods are amorous and "therefore willing to be pierced" (I.i.44-45). In other words, if Sapho and Phao are amorous they will be shot with love; the act only confirms an inclination.

Lyly does not allow the audience to make up their minds between the "necessitarian" view suggested by events and the inclination view held by Cupid. The uncertainty may arise from the Renaissance use of classical deities in the first place, for unless the play tells us, we are never certain whether they are a Christian God's instruments or metaphors for psychological states in the characters. A similar instability and uncertainty comes to mind after reading the *Mirror for Magistrates*. Popular astrology of the time did not hold a single point of view, either: some astrologers said that the stars did not compel men, but only inclined; others believed that a stricter force of destiny was necessary and complete.[6] Neither does contemporary theology give a definite answer to the question, although most protestant theologians held that in matters of salvation predestination was a part of the ''secret wisdom'' of God, but in matters of practical moral choice no overriding necessity obtains. A man in his day-to-day life had to make moral decisions, and he was obliged to act, not to withdraw. In Lyly's plays, the religious concern for salvation does not arise, for the moral world he creates is a narrow humanist's world, with choices between wisdom and folly, virtue and vice, not sin and salvation. But when Lyly injects supernatural agents who disturb the natural course of men's lives, the humanist equilibrium becomes unstable. When the oracles talk darkly about destiny and when the gods roam the landscape, the moral freedom of dramatic characters begins to erode.

Later scenes do not remove our uncertainty. On the one hand Venus' transformation of Phao threatens to corrupt his will; on the other hand his reaction to Sybilla's advice shows a certain stubborn independence. His weakened resistance is emphasized in the first soliloquy of Act II. His new beauty, he complains, is not becoming for it has given him a proud heart and a disdaining mind. Even before he has seen the beauteous Sapho, he recognizes the inappropriateness of his position. ''Phao thy mean fortune causeth thee to use an oar, and thy sudden beauty a glass,'' causing a clash between his need in his natural estate and his pride for his beauty imposed from above. Therefore he consults a soothsayer, in her cave, lest he be benighted on his journey of life. The ''straight thread'' of Sybilla's counsel fails to lead him out of his crooked conceits, for all she can tell him is that he must not be coy, should not think too much of his beauty, and should yield to love. She admits that her advice will not remove the dangerous effects of what has happened, that she cannot interfere with history, but she can at least show the causes. A personal dignity in Phao or some foreboding suggests that he should not yield to love. "I am driven by your counsel into diverse conceits, neither knowing how to stand or where to fall: but to yield to love is the only thing I hate." Sybilla commits him to fortune, adding some light and dark prophecies about the "effects."

> Thou shalt get friendship by dissembling, love by hatred; unless thou perish, thou shalt perish: in digging for a stone, thou shalt reach a star; thou shalt be hated most, because thou art loved most. Thy death shall be feared and wished: so much for prophesy, which nothing can prevent. (II.i.124-28)

As for counsel, her last advice is to keep no company with deceitful courtiers, be careful of treachery and guarded in speech. "If any talk of the eclipse of the sun, say thou never sawest it." Phao properly objects, "Alas! madam, your prophecy threateneth miseries, and your counsel warneth impossibilities," meaning, I suppose, that he sees a miserable or perhaps a glorious, impossible end for himself, even though he has no intention of becoming entangled in court intrigue. Like Pandion, he wants to keep his mind clear, his virtue unspotted, but he fears that the instability of circumstances and passion may destroy him. His self-knowledge and self-restraint go together, but they are not enough.

So far, neither he nor the audience has seen Sapho, and the first encounter is handled in a cool way, without the attendance of Cupid. We do not see when the arrow of love strikes them, whether they are inclined or forced by external influence. Perhaps they were ready for love, like the sonneteer who loves an idea of his mistress before he sees her. Certainly the idea of temptation by love has already been present to Phao's mind.

> *Phao.* Unhappy Phao! — But soft, what gallant troup is this? What gentlewoman is this?
> *Cryticus.* Sapho, a lady here in Sicily.
> *Sapho.* What fair boy is that?
> *Trachinus.* Phao, the ferryman of Syracusa.
> *Phao.* I never saw one more brave: be all ladies of such majesty?
> *Cryticus.* No, this is she that all wonder at and worship.

79

Sapho. I have seldom seen a sweeter face; be all ferrymen of that fairness?

Trachinus. No, madam, this is he that Venus determined among men to make the fairest.

Sapho. Seeing I am only come forth to take the air, I will cross the ferry, and so the fields, then going in through the park, I think the walk will be pleasant.

Trachinus. You will much delight in the flattering green which now beginneth to be in his glory.

Sapho. Sir boy, will ye undertake to carry us over the water? Are you dumb, can you not speak?

(II.ii.1-19)

Phao, struck by wonder, stands in silence. When he finds his tongue, he tells her he is purblind and wishes he had never been given eyes at all. After reaffirming his content with a lowly life, he nevertheless immediately agrees to forsake his ferry and enter the court as a page. We know that choice is significant, but its meaning is never stated. The scene has symmetry and a formal simplicity that neither confirms nor denies conflicting implications.

The rest of the play proceeds in the same way, with alternating stretches of monologue and dialogue; the monologues stir thought and the actions follow their more or less destined path. The effect is analogous to that found in Marlowe's tragedies, where actions flowing from character and situation seem equivocal, and no single moral can be extracted. The long speeches are disjunct from the action because they are almost orations, all that might be said on the occasion. The disjunction, for instance in *Faustus,* becomes a critical problem; in Lyly it enhances the sense of wonder, without breaking the plays apart, for Lyly's smooth and serene tone is efficient enough on the surface to make ideas seem to belong to the action.

For the history of drama, this practice of Marlowe and Lyly represents a coming of age, the appearance of mimetic drama freed from the tyranny of a single programmatic concern because now actions begin to exist in their own right, not merely to illustrate ideas. So we get a new sense of people doing and suffering things in their capacity as men. We admire them as people as well as exemplars. The particular kind of comedy that results is Lyly's accomplishment, a comedy that breeds puzzlement and wonder mixed with a gentle irony, combining entertainment with thought. In the prologue to *Sapho and Phao,* he announces, "Our intent was at this time to move inward delight, not outward lightness; and to breed (if it might be) soft smiling not loud laughing: knowing it to the wise to be as great pleasure to hear counsel mixed with wit, as to the foolish to have sport mingled with rudeness." Moving inward delight to please the wise is echoed in the prologue to *Campaspe,* less pointedly: "We have mixed mirth with counsel and discipline with delight." It suggests a delightful teaching that Sidney and Maggi found proper to comedy. Because Lyly, like Sidney, distrusts "loud laughing," he seeks to arouse "soft smiling" and inward joy.

His use of fancies and dreams also seems to contribute to the elegant wonder of his plays. In his usual self-deprecating way, he tells the audience that the drama is a mere toy, a trivial pastime, a dream, and since these are creations of fancy, the audience should not take the events as real. "Whatsoever we present, whether it be tedious (which we fear) or toyish (which we doubt), sweet or sour, absolute or imperfect, or whatsoever, in all humbleness we all, and I on knee for all, entreat, that your Highness imagine yourself to be in a deep dream, that staying the conclusion, in your rising your Majesty vouchsafe but to say, *and so you awaked." The Woman in the Moon* (ca. 1590) is "our author's dream" for "Our poet slumbering in the Muses' laps,/ Hath seen a woman seated in the moon, . . . and as it was so he presents his dream." He assures us that *Endymion* (ca.1588) is incredible, a fiction, mere fancies. Perhaps this is another manifestation of his *sprezzatura,* but I incline to take his dreams a little more seriously, just as laughter can have its inward meaning. Dreams may be a form of prophecy of events in this world, or they could help us imagine an alternative world, a distinct order of things in the imaginative life of gods and fairies. This literary convention was encouraged by both Christian and pagan traditions of gods using dreams to communicate with men. The sensitive or overwrought mind sees images in his nightly visions which have a power over the waking imagination. Some writers held that they represented unconscious desire,[7] and there can be no question but that the dreams in *Endymion* and *Sapho and Phao* have serious import. In one way or another they reveal superior truths, to privileged characters in the plays. Again, I focus upon one example in *Sapho and Phao*.

Until the end of Act III Sapho has managed to conceal her unbecoming love for the boatman by retiring to her bed, feigning sickness. But her true, conflicting feelings come out in her dream. A stock dove tried to build a nest in a cedar tree, but he kept losing his feathers the more he worked; striving to get into the nest, he fell from the tree. As the bird looked up into the tree, he spoke in terms that might either "condemn the nature of such a tree or the daring of such a mind." Meanwhile the ants and caterpillars eating on the tree caused more leaves to fall than feathers from the bird. In her dream Sapho pitied both the fortune of the bird and the misfortune of the tree, but by this time the quills began to bud again on the bird, which made him look as though he would fly up. "And then wished I that the body of the tree would bow, that he might but creep up the tree; then, and so — Hey ho!" "And so what?" asks one of her ladies. "Nothing, Mileta: but and so I waked" (IV.iii.18-22). With that Sapho changes the subject. The hint of something unspeakable in her dream is enough to set the imagination to work.

Nothing ever comes of Sapho's dream, and no one interprets it; it is simply given for what we can make of it. We must not assume that this method was merely a happy chance, since Endymion's dream is recounted in the same way, its "strangeness" offering a "delight" to the listeners on stage (V.i.79,138). Like Sapho, we question "What dreams are these, Mileta? And can there be no truth in dreams?" (IV.iii.1-2). Ismene and Mileta give a partial answer, obliquely, when they interpret the other ladies' dreams as if they were prophecies. In disagreement, another lady, Eugenia, says that dreams are "mere dotings," just memories of the day or effects of food, which are presented to the imagination through the agency of "common sense" (IV.iii.46). The interpretations that follow con-tain a mixture of advice, warning, and psychological insight, but the net effect is to leave possibilities open for the audience. At any rate they show the different powers and conditions of love. The "loving humor" is a flame, only partly quenched by "counsel," and it will lead to death (Mileta's dream). Love brings gold into one's lap, but the gold turns to shameful dust (Canope's dream). It is the sting of a tarantula that will be cured by marriage, like the sympathetic vibrations of two lutes (Lamia's dream). In a woman's hard heart, once the heat of love penetrates, love will never cool; "women are scorched sometimes with men's eyes, though they had rather consume than confess" (Favilla's dream). All these thoughts might be applied to Sapho's predicament, but instead of enlightening us, she cuts the discussion short: "Cease your talking; for I would fain sleep, to see if I can dream whether the bird hath feathers, or the ant wings. Draw the curtain" (III.iii.93-95). Only one thing is certain. Sapho feels profound passions, and at the moment she can gratify her desires only in dreams.

The scenes that build to this muted climax show the same interest in dangers, uncertainties, and natural barriers suggested in Sapho's dream. Our first major impression of Sapho comes from her long soliloquy, while alone in her boudoir. She complains bitterly of her "extremities," depicting an irreconcilable clash within her mind, between love and pride. Reason tries to act as an agent of her self-respect, urging her to resist love now, before it is too late. Soon her soul will be corrupted by desire: "Strains are caught as well by stooping too low, as reaching too high . . . eyes are bleared as soon with vapors that come from the earth, as with beams that proceed from the sun." Possibly it is already too late, because "glutting" herself on Phao's face has made her desire more desperate. "There is an herb (not unlike unto my love) which the farther it groweth from the sea, the saltier it is; and my desires the more they swerve from reason, the more seem they reasonable. When Phao cometh, what then? wilt thou open thy love? Yes. No! Sapho: but staring in his face till thine eyes dazzle, and thy spirits faint, die before his face; then this shall be written on thy tomb, that though thy love were greater than wisdom could endure, yet thine honor was such as love could not violate" (III.iii.105-13).

Like the inevitable antithesis of the sentences, the princess' feelings are perfectly at odds. The heart may rage, reason may be corrupted, but her soul will keep the idea of honor inviolate. Death is the only end she foresees, tearing apart body and soul. As if she cannot control her actions, Sapho proceeds to glut herself on Phao's face, to seek "remedies" that he can bring to her bed. She will live and die by love. "Let him not come at all: yes, let him come: no, it is no matter: yet will I try, let him come" (III.iii.127-28). The war in her mind is like the one between prudence and jealousy in Master Kitely's, in *Every Man in His Humor,* except that here a great princess is talking.

The lovers confront each other in a guarded yet self-revealing dialogue, one of the liveliest exchanges in the play, calculated to raise soft smiles. Neither wants to dissimulate; yet both want to avoid an open declaration. As the need to tell begins to overwhelm them, the necessity to dissimulate becomes stronger. Decorum and danger, shame and desire thrust them into equivocating language. The love is a "disease," gratification a "medicine"; Jason and Medea their classical analogue. They cannot keep apart no matter how circumspect they seem. Phao brings "simples" to cure Sapho, but assures her that no herb will make lovers sleep but "heart's ease":

Sapho. But why do you sigh so, Phao?

Phao. It is my use, madam.

Sapho. It will do you harm, and me too: for I never hear one sigh, but I must sigh also.

Phao. It were best then that your ladyship give me leave to be gone: for I can but sigh.

Sapho. Nay stay, for now I begin to sigh, I shall not leave though you be gone. But what do you think best for your sighing to take it away?

Phao. Yew, madam.

Sapho. Me?

Phao. No, Madam, yew of the tree.

Sapho. Then will I love yew the better. And indeed I think it would make me sleep too, therefore all other simples set aside, I will simply use only yew.

Phao. Do madam, for I think nothing in the world so good as yew.
(III.iv.68-84)

Phao had said in jest that "there is nothing at the bottom of a woman's heart, that cometh not to her tongue's end," and he sees in the evil of dissembling another female habit he may be drawn into, a "painted truth" that is more appropriate to Venus than to himself. In spite of this knowledge and of Sapho's protestations of honor, truth and an unspotted mind, the agitated scene shows that they are drawn into a vortex of destructive passion. No human agency can save them, and the wonderful comic trick that delivers them is very strange, indeed, for Venus too falls in love — although she is old and "the crow's foot is on her eyes, and the black ox hath trod her foot" (one of the most delightful lines in Lyly). She gives Cupid new arrows to make Phao love her and hate Sapho.

But Cupid betrays his mother, and by the two arrows Sapho is made to disdain Phao and Phao to disdain Venus. Most wonderful of all, Cupid becomes the "son" of Sapho, so that henceforth she can be a better queen of love than Venus. She will direct Cupid's arrows better, "rule the fancies of men and lead Venus in chains like a Captive" (V.ii.66). As a consequence "Every rude ass shall not say he is in love. It is a toy for ladies" which she will reserve for them only. There will be sport left in the world, no doubt, but the important thing seems to be the way that humans respond to these happenings. If they can know themselves and maintain a kind of mental allegiance to that idea, they will have done their best. So, although at the end they do not enjoy the happy fortunes of comic heroes, Sapho extends her understanding to Phao with great dignity; Phao renounces his ambitious hopes and at the same time wishes for Sapho's good — he continues to blazon her virtues. Like Endymion he keeps his own unspotted loyalty, but destiny calls him away from Syracusa. Sybilla warns him as he leaves, "Other things hang over thy head, which I must neither tell nor thou inquire." Again we are left with something unspoken, and we can only smile and wonder at its meaning. Fortune, like love, is a smoke which vanishes in the seeing and yet hurts whilst it is seen.

II. *A Midsummer Night's Dream*

Shakespeare reified the comedy that Lyly fashioned, lending it greater dignity and power, for Shakespeare dared to present a more robust experience than Lyly's delicate playthings could suggest. Lyly carefully poised his mixed comedies between wise counsel and delight, keeping the audience at a discreet distance from his material, as he quietly insinuated the sense of inward pleasure, decorously teasing us with thought and soft smiles. In a play such as *A Midsummer Night's Dream* Shakespeare boldly seized Lyly's comic situations — a conquering monarch subdued by love (*Campaspe*), the intervention of rival gods in human affairs (*Love's Metamorphosis* and *Gallathea*), sudden transformations (*Gallathea* and *The Woman in the Moon*), and crossed lovers tyrannized by unpredictable passion (*Sapho and Phao*). Into the fabric of these he wove his coarser characters of Athenian artisans. If, as is usually assumed, Shakespeare wrote *A Midsummer Night's Dream* for an aristocratic wedding, he paid the bride, groom, and guests a compliment that only a master playwright could tender, for the drama demands as much from the actors as it gives to the spectators.[8] He increased the audience's sense of wonder because he was willing to call upon his dramatic resources to realize more fully men's feelings in the very action of the play. Whereas Lyly kept the mystery of passion partly hidden from us, Shakespeare gave only the spectators the understanding of things not revealed to any of the human participants on stage. His language is more expressive, invented episodes more ingenious, the folly lower and yet more luminous, and the spectacle variously lighted with wonder and loud laughter. Shakespeare's achievement, using drama to express the inexpressible, is managed in several different ways: in the first few acts our wonder is engendered by the fairies and our laughter by the inadequacies of the people. Later, the wonder and laughter come together in the most affecting and perplexing fun.

Above all, Shakespeare's fairies breathe a magic lacking in Lyly's pale, humanized gods. They are distinctly aerial spirits — invisible, or visible, tinier than an acorn cup, swifter than the wandering moon, girdling the earth in minutes — those intermediate spirits between heaven and earth so important to common folk and magicians.[9] They are intimately connected with the stars, planets, and other heavenly influences, hence they affect the weather and the seasons. They meet in moonlight, dance to the whistling wind by the blanched margent of the sea, and trace through the wild forests. Like Ficino's good daemons, they guard certain select persons, as Titania watches over Theseus and Oberon maintains "high credit" for Hippolyta, so they have come to the environs of Athens to bless that marriage and give joy and prosperity to the heroic bed (II.i.73). Although her name may suggest the moon, Titania is a more fruitful, even wanton, generative spirit, whose votaress gave birth to the lovely boy whom she dotes on and crowns with flowers "and makes all her joy" (27). She tells Bottom that she is "a spirit of no common rate:/ The summer still doth tend upon [her] state" (III.i.151-52) — that is, she maintains the burgeoning green life of the landscape, her servant. Both the king and queen are the "parents and original" of natural processes on earth; thus when they quarrel and when their sports are disturbed the winds become unhappy, sucking up fog, the moon weeps, the land is flooded, and the world suffers a distemperature or ill-humor. The green corn rots in the fields, the cattle are sick, and frosts put their hoary caps on the crimson rose. The seasons mock due decorum, changing their liveries so that the amazed world does not know which is which. A greater "progeny of evils" comes from this, opposite the good progeny that comes from their love (II.i.87-115). When the fairies return to harmony, giving up their debate and dissension, they shake hands, and they rock the ground beneath the sleeping lovers (IV.i.84-85), signifying their power over human concord.

As intermediate spirits, the fairy monarchs mirror both human and divine attributes, liberally mixed. They use a magic beyond ordinary men but like the whimsies of human love, and it is quite innocent magic, invisible power to create illusions that latch on the eyes of mortals (and other spirits, too), that affect their imaginations as well as passions. At least Puck is not infallible; Titania claims that she can purge Bottom of his mortal grossness by her love, so

87

that he too can be "an airy spirit." Both monarchs keep a court, no doubt a model for human rulers; thus Oberon has knights in his train and a court jester, Puck; Titania has a battery of maids in waiting and attendant spirits, some who go in advance like royal forerunners to deck the cowslips, her "pensioners," wearing her livery of gold coats and ruby freckles. Her servants fetch jewels from the deep and sing magical charms to caress and protect their queen from newts, hedgehogs, spiders, and spotted snakes. Oberon's philandering with amorous females and buskined mistresses suggests not only mortal kings but also Zeus, as Titania's jealousy suggests Hera, and both dote on a lovely boy, as the Greek gods were wont to do. By these signs the audience, in contemplation of the spirits, is encouraged to glance from heaven to earth and earth to heaven, observing them in moonlit darkness, as they aid the forces of light as best they can.

Act I of the comedy presents foolish discord in the distressed lovers, Hermia's heavy father, and a slightly insensitive Duke Theseus, who will arbitrarily enforce a cruel choice upon Hermia: either she marries as her father wishes or she dies or enters a nunnery, to spend her life chanting faint hymns to the cold, fruitless moon. Apparently Hermia and Lysander love each other truly, and Demetrius' affection is a selfish dotage, as the audience can judge by the lovers' speeches and attitudes during the next three acts, for the true lovers have mutual affection, and they swear earnest oaths. Lysander is considerate, gentle, and courteous enough to sleep a few feet away from Hermia. Theirs is a virtuous love that unites two hearts, and they expect theirs to be a constant love (always the synonym for true love in Shakespeare), until Puck makes his dreadful mistake. Demetrius, this spotted and inconstant man, has already wooed Helena, who dotes on him; now since he has Hermia's father's love — a more useful possession — he has shifted his attentions to the other girl. Hermia's father cannot see Lysander through his daughter's eyes, and since he prefers Demetrius, he simply assumes that Lysander has bewitched his daughter by moonlight, poetry, and love tokens. Moreover, Theseus seems unable to imagine any point of view but the sovereignty of a father, even though he is about to marry his own chosen love. If that is not enough discord, Helena, feeling slighted by Demetrius and jealous of Hermia, turns her desires into absurd self-flagellation; to be in sight of her beloved Demetrius for a few painful hours, she will betray her former friend's plan of escape. The audience, therefore, sees the ridiculous mismatches, the evil effects of discord and love, before they see the deeper spiritual causes that are revealed in Act II but never shown to the lovers.

Throughout the forest scenes we are lifted to a superior level of awareness, at moments even superior to the daemons. A good production of the play, like the film done with the Royal Shakespeare Company, under the direction of Peter Hall (1968), should make the magical air of the fairies clearly contrast with the faulty earthbound sight of the lovers. This was done in the film by some good acting on the part of Demetrius and Lysander, showing in their faces alternate perplexity and stubborn resolution. Lysander's sensitivity and his pock-marked face distinguish him from Demetrius' hard, almost brutal, way of talking and his even features. Hermia's smooth, in contrast to Helena's knitted, brow helps to keep their feelings distinct, too. An especially vivid device of the film that seems an appropriate extension of the text was that the lovers fall again and again into creeks and mud holes, gradually streaking their faces with filth as much as their clothes. Yet they go on relentlessly praising their mistaken beloved of the moment, as "transparent Helena" or a Hermia who looks as "bright, as clear, as yonder Venus in her glimmering sphere." Consequently, their delusions become extremely funny, and what pains them in their compulsive earnestness raises laughter in an audience that knows how little danger they are in. All the while disembodied spirits rush through the woods unmarked by cuts, bruises, or mud; they shine in eerie colors and glisten with droplets of water in the dim light. Oberon wants to right the wrongs that he sees between the lovers, and he sends Puck on those errands. Puck's contact with the humans occurs while they sleep, so presumably he works through visions in their dreams, the juice of love-in-idleness putting images in their minds' eyes — conceits of their beloved — that they act upon when they wake and project upon the first visible humans.

89

Jonson and Elizabethan Comedy

Without the strange adventures of Bottom and Titania, however, *A Midsummer Night's Dream* might have come down to us as mostly another variation on *The Comedy of Errors,* or the mistakes of the night. Even *The Comedy of Errors* had referred to the mysteries of perception and identity, as well as some supposed magic spells, so the difference between it and this play might have seemed small. But with Bottom and his friends we are given the brilliant fifth act with all its opportunities for deep laughter in reflection upon the right relations between lovers, poets, actors, and audience. And in the forest scenes we are given the curious earthbound fantasy of the encounter between the crudest man and the queen of the fairies. Without Bottom and Titania the play would be alternatively astonishing and amusing, but with them the wonder and laughter come together. As we noticed with the lovers, the audience sees the natural perspective of human foolishness first and gets the wonderful supernatural insight later, but for analysis, I will reverse that order.

When Bottom rejoins his friends, they are immediately plunged into preparations for their play. The practical problems of costume naturally occupy his talk, and like children putting on a little show, their make-believe quickens in the outward symbols.

> Get your apparel together, good strings to your beards, new ribbons to your pumps. . . . In any case, let Thisby have clean linen; and let not him that plays the lion pare his nails, for they shall hang out for the lion's claws. And most dear actors, eat no onions nor garlic, for we are to utter sweet breath; and I do not doubt but to hear them say, it is a sweet comedy. (IV.ii.31-40)

Bottom, who is usually talkative, says little about his recent transformation, although he could "discourse wonders." He is dying to tell, but somehow he cannot.[10] In the scene before, just as he awakes, he is a little more expressive. He awakens as if still in the midst of his rehearsal of "Pyramus and Thisby," waiting for his cue to enter. The description he gives of his "most rare vision" identifies it as something high, mysterious, somehow religious, but ineffable. "I have had a dream, past the wit of man to say what dream it was. Man is but an ass, if he go about to expound this dream. . . . Methought I was — and methought I had — but man is but a patched fool if he will offer to say what methought I had'' (IV.i.204-11). We in the audience should not be fooled out of expounding at least part of his dream, for we have seen that in theatrical life; it was a real experience and not exactly a dream. The greatest fool of them all was vouchsafed a communion with a great spirit. The queen of the fairies and all her servants loved him and ministered unto his every whim. No other person was given that privilege. The experience was a palpable demonstration, eminently sensuous and ridiculous.

The quasi-religious importance of his encounter seems to strike even Bottom; he tries to recall a wonderful passage from scripture, but, as in all else, he botches it marvelously. It comes from Paul's First Epistle to the Corinthians, 2:9-10 — the same text that Augustine, Bernard, Bonaventure, and other Christian visionaries went to for the deepest mysteries of God's grace. Paul has been telling of the need for concord among Christians at Corinth: all should be enriched by the knowledge of Christ and await his coming. Paul asks that they all preach the same thing and that there be no divisions among them, that they be perfectly joined in mind and in the judgment. Unlike other eloquent preachers, he does not give them the wisdom of words but of salvation; he goes on to contrast the two sorts of auditors for his preaching, compatible to the two kinds of awareness we have noticed in *Midsummer Night's Dream* — the knowing and the unknowing.

> For Christ sent me not to baptize, but to preach the Gospel, not with wisdom of words, lest the cross of Christ should be made of none effect. For the preaching of the cross is to them that perish, foolishness: but unto us, which are saved, it is the power of God. For it is written, I will destroy the wisdom of the wise, and will cast away the understanding of the prudent. Where is the wise? where is the scribe? where is the disputer of this world? Hath not God made the wisdom of this world foolishness? For seeing the world by wisdom knew not God in the wisdom of God, it pleased God by the foolishness of preaching to save them that believe. . . . For the foolishness of God is wiser than men, and the weakness of God is stronger than men. (Geneva version)

This is Paul's attack on the affected eloquence of false apostles in

Corinth (according to the gloss). In his defense of his simple preaching of the gospel, he appeals to experience of the "plain evidence of the Spirit and power" illuminated by faith which the world "calleth folly" (says the gloss). "But we speak the wisdom of God in a mystery, even the hid wisdom, which God had determined before the world, unto our glory" (2:7). For him his preaching is a combination, therefore, of plainness, folly, and mystery, depending upon the point of view.

None of the princes of this world knows the hidden mystery, says Paul, only the foolish lovers of God receive his promise of paradise in the right spirit.

> But we preach as it is written, things which eye hath not seen and ear hath not heard, neither have entered into man's mind, which things God hath prepared for them that love Him. But God hath opened them unto us by his Spirit, for the Spirit searcheth all things, yea, the *bottom* of God's secrets. (2:9-10)[11]

Bottom describes his rare vision that cannot be expounded "because it hath no bottom," in unmistakably similar yet delightfully garbled terms;

> The eye of man hath not heard, the ear of man hath not seen, man's hand is not able to taste, his tongue to conceive, nor his heart to report, what my dream was. (IV.i.211-13)

Both St. Paul and Bottom are trying to express something wonderful. Paul tries to suggest the beauty of paradise and eternal love, and all the accompanying associations were expounded in the *Book of Homilies,* in accord with the Augustinian tradition. But it would be a gross error to infer from these parallels that Bottom has had a true vision of paradise and that he has undergone religious "initiation" comparable to a mystical experience.[12] First of all, the fairies are not completely divine; they are aerial spirits, not celestial gods. Although religious writers had taken the *Golden Ass* of Apuleius seriously, and Augustine for one alluded to it as a record of a genuine religious experience, Shakespeare does not present Bottom's experience in exactly the same light.

Abundant evidence suggests that we should see it to be *like* a vision of paradise, but that Bottom does not *have* such an experience in the fullest sense, because he does not understand it. In the words of scripture, he sees but he cannot perceive. Consequently our response should be a mixture of wonder and laughter, witnessing a conjunction of great power and superb ignorance. Titania in love with Bottom is like Hercules in women's clothes under the amorous control of Omphale. Shakespeare makes the most of the contradictions, and the luminous folly of these scenes is one of his most impressive achievements. If it were a real religious experience, the mists of error and delight would blow away in a moment, brief as the lightning in the collied night, and Shakespeare would have violated the mood of the forest scenes irreparably.

For instance, Bottom does not know he has an ass's head on his shoulders (in more ways than one) as he comes out of the thicket, and he yells at the terrified Snout, "What do you see? You see an ass head of your own, do you?" (III.i.116-17). Here, of course, is the beginning of the differences from Lucius' experience in *The Golden Ass*. Shakespeare may very well have read W. Adlington's translation published in 1566 and frequently reprinted, but if he did, he found reason to change the impact of the tale. Lucius knows he has been changed into an ass, suffers shame and ignominy when he is seduced by the beautiful, rich woman; he flees from feminine embraces, sees the goddess in a dream, repents his sensuous appetites, and prays for deliverance. The queen of the gods, Isis, who is described in all the terms of admiration, accepts his repentance and allows him to turn back into a man (by eating roses); thenceforth he is a new man, worthy to be initiated into the secrets of worship of Isis and Osiris. But Shakespeare depicts Bottom's experience differently; for example, his next remark is typically transparent as he tries to conceal his fears from himself. "I see their knavery. This is to make an ass of me, do what they can. I will walk up and down here, and will sing, that they shall hear I am not afraid." In his song about the woosel cock so black of hue, Titania hears the voice of an angel. For the rest of the scene, each detail emphasizes the four-cornered contradiction between fact and imagination: the earthy reality against Titania's absurd illusion, the

93

beauty and delicacy of the fairies against Bottom's unperceptive responses. He is wooed by the queen of the fairies (whereas Lucius had been feasted and seduced by lecherous, fleshly women), and Bottom treats it matter-of-factly, more interested in food and drink and in scratching where he itches.

Titania's eye is enthralled by his shape, as her ear is enamored by his music, and his "fair virtue's force" moves her to declare that she loves him. Bottom replies fatuously — and under the fatuousness we see truer meanings:

> Methinks, mistress, you should have little reason for that. And yet, to say truth, reason and love keep little company together nowadays; the more the pity, that some honest neighbors will not make them friends. Nay I can gleek upon occasion. (III.i.143-48)

Out of the mouth of a babe comes a fitting comment on the loves we have seen. Oberon and Puck may hide their marvels from the wise and prudent and reveal them to a fool; they have, in the words of Paul, "chosen the weak things of the world to confound the mighty things." But he who sees does not perceive, although Titania's confounded reply makes the point more explicit: "Thou art as wise as thou art beautiful." She gives Bottom the complete service of her fairies, and she will try the impossible, to purge his mortal grossness into spirit, but neither her ministrations nor Moth's, Mustardseed's, nor Peasblossom's do anything of the kind (again, unlike Isis). Bottom responds to them with innocent, gabbling formality, as if he were introduced to an alderman or a rich tradesman: "I cry your worship's mercy, heartily." "I pray you commend me to Mistress Squash, your mother, and to Master Peascod, your father." He is, indeed, the shallowest thickskin of the barren sort of people. Titania must have them tie up his tongue in order to bring him silently to her bower. So, he may still be a wise fool in God's eyes.

When we next see Titania and Bottom, she would kiss his fair, large ears, and she invites him to sit by her (IV.i.1 ff). Nevertheless, he keeps his character through it all — apparently no inner transformation. If he sees God, he sees her in terms of his reduced experience. As usual, he likes giving orders: he will have his head scratched by Peasblossom, Cobweb should bring some honey. The point of his essential limitations is made again when he says "I must to the barber's monsieur, for methinks I am marvelous hairy about my face, and I am such a tender ass, if my hair do but tickle me, I must scratch." For music he still prefers his familiar "tong and bones" when he might have the music of the ministering spirits or all the unheard tunes of the magic wood. Like King Midas, Bottom proves that he deserves ass's ears, choosing the harsh pipe of Pan over the lyre of Apollo. For food he will have a bottle of hay and some dried peas, when he could have fairy-delivered apricots, blackberries, purple grapes, and green figs. Instead of love he feels an exposition of sleep come upon him, and as Titania wraps her beautiful white arms about his rough body, she again emphasizes her dotage, making a heaven of her hell:

> So doth the woodbine the sweet honeysuckle
> Gently entwist: the female ivy so
> Enrings the barky fingers of the elm.
> O, how I love thee! How I dote on thee!

Oberon's attitude toward Bottom and Titania is equally clear. He cast her into this spell where by tormenting her she would give up the changeling boy. He hopes she will pursue "some beast: lion, bear, wolf, or bull; meddling monkey or busy ape — with the soul of love." Oberon takes the love juice from Puck, wraps himself in a snake skin and hurries off to her bower. Like Eve's bower, it is

> a bank where the wild thyme blows,
> Where oxlips and nodding violet grows,
> Quite over-canopied with luscious woodbine,
> With sweet musk-roses, and with eglantine:
> There sleeps Titania sometime of the night,
> Lulled in these flowers with dances and delight;
> And there the snake throws her enameled skin,
> Weed wide enough to wrap a fairy in.
> And with the juice of this I'll streak her eyes,
> And make her full of hateful fantasies.

(II.i.249-58)

He plans, therefore, to play a devilish role, bringing ugly dreams like an incubus come in the night.[13] Although he is like a devil in this prank, we should not jump to the conclusion that he is the Devil. We have seen that all evidence from the play suggests that both Oberon and Titania are natural spirits of the air, whereas evil spirits inhabited the earth. I grant that some references to serpents in the play are more than natural, especially in the charm to sing Titania asleep which includes a prohibition against "spotted snakes with double tongue" (II.ii.9), that is, deceiving powers. A hundred lines later Hermia awakes from a dream crying to Lysander to "pluck this crawling serpent from my breast," apparently a forecast of her jealousy of Helena. Two scenes later, Hermia thinks she has found a serpent, Demetrius, and she accuses him of being the adder with a double tongue who killed Lysander sleeping. And Lysander, later in the same scene, applies the image to Hermia, when he wishes to shake her from him "like a serpent" (III.ii.261). Finally, the image is transformed into a joke by Puck in his epilogue — "to scape the serpent's tongue"; lest the audience should hiss at this dream, he promises to mend the players' imperfect acting, if the audience pardons their faults. In these images, we have the associations of acting, dreams, imagination, and whimsical love, but the Christian connotations are vague, and the serpent, if not innocent, is only a disturbing illusion.

In any case, Bottom is the "vile thing" that Titania dotes upon, and she seems sufficiently aware of her pain to cause her to comply with Oberon's request.[14] She returns the changeling to be released from her eye's "monster's view," the "hateful fool," who disgraces the very flowers she puts on his head. Having possession of the boy, Oberon intends to undo this "hateful imperfection of her eyes" and to remove the ass's head:

> That he, awakening when the other do,
> May all to Athens back again repair,
> And think no more of this night's accidents
> But as the fierce vexation of a dream.

(IV.i.65-68)

After Oberton puts the juice of Dian's bud on Titania, she loathes the visage of Bottom, and as Puck takes off the ass's head, he leaves no doubt of his attitude: "Now, when thou wak'st, with thine own fool's eyes peep." The fairy king and queen symbolize their renewed concord by dancing round the sleeping figures, blessing pairs of the "faithful lovers" to be wedded with Theseus and Hippolyta "all in jollity."

The fairies have used Bottom as their instrument to bring concord to their lives as well as harmony to the world. The scene in Titania's bower should be a foretaste of paradise for a Christian Bottom, but it exists, if at all, only as a potential that the audience might recognize. Now the main idea is harmony, like the harmony in musical confusion of Theseus' baying hounds that immediately follows the dance of the fairies, bringing us back to daylight. The dogs' musical discord of tuned voices, hunting beasts whose voices are subhuman, still manage to "echo in conjunction." It represents most of the qualities of comic wonder that the play contains — how creatures following their natural desires can, with the help of a special point of view, body forth something of an ideal form. But it is an *unplatonic* ideal, in our amused admiration, and since it remains singularly earthbound, indwelling and invisible, our hearts go out to Bottom as he strains to express the mighty dream he has had, beyond the comprehension of man.

The wedding festivities in the court of Theseus repeat and enrich the admirable, unplatonic art of the forest scenes, and the play of "Pyramus and Thisby" can make us weep tears of joy if it is well acted. In itself the tedious brief scene would not appear to fulfill Theseus' needs for his revels. At least his Master of the Revels thinks not. Theseus had asked him to stir the Athenian youths to merriments and to the "pert and nimble spirit of mirth." Since the little play is hardly pert or nimble, its mirth must lie elsewhere. Several critics have been quick to see that the little play burlesques the romantic love of the main action in the first four acts, and it is apparent that the workingmen's absurd amateurism traves-ties the effort of the professional Lord Chamberlain's Men to entertain at a noble court wedding. (But inversely it can imply a flattering contrast with their skill.) In this way the play comments upon itself, a common device in self-conscious drama, rediscovered

97

and now tiresomely overdeveloped in our time.[15] Also it is fair, but not very profound, to say that "Pyramus and Thisby" is to the court of Theseus as *A Midsummer Night's Dream* is to its audience. But I think that the whole of *A Midsummer Night's Dream* suggests a great deal more than these interpretations offer. The theatricalism here leads to something more important than the idea of a play, and it works with an art more skillful and feelings more powerful than mere self-reference.

The reactions of the stage audience show that one function of the little play is to define and to toy with various responses. Lysander and Demetrius use the play as an occasion for their wit. "One lion may [speak], when many asses do," says Demetrius. Hippolyta thinks the play is "the silliest stuff that I ever heard." But Theseus instructs us all in the graceful, generous reaction: "the best of this kind [of plays or players] are but shadows; and the worse are no worse, if imagination amend them." Hippolyta makes the sensible objection, "It must be your imagination then, and not theirs." Theseus partly agrees with her — it is partly his imagination — but he does not assume that the players have no imagination themselves. A charitable imagination is necessary to enter their thoughts. "If we imagine no worse of them than they of themselves they may pass for excellent men." He is conscious that the lion is the "very goose of discretion" in warning the ladies that he is not a real lion; on the other hand, Theseus can delight in the great errors "It appears by [moonlight's] small light of discretion, that he is on the wane," says Theseus, "but yet in courtesy, in all reason, we must stay the time." So he obviously feels a tension between laughter and courtesy. And this is the sort of situation that is most likely to bring tears while we laugh, for we feel some obligation to hold back what we cannot, like not stifling laughter when someone really may have hurt himself in a ridiculous pratfall or trying to keep a straight face in church at some silly mishap.

A further clue lies in Theseus' remarks just before the rude mechanicals enter. Perhaps Theseus was attracted to the title of the Revels' list, because it promised to be "brief" although tedious. "That is hot ice and wondrous flaming snow. How shall we find the concord of this discord?''[16] — a problem for the audience of the whole play, mingled as it is with lovers, spirits, monarchs, and clowns "thrust head and shoulders to play a part in majestical matters." Philostrate urges that, although in rehearsal he laughed loudly and shed many merry tears, the entertainment is not suitable for the Duke, "Unless you can find sport in their intents,/ Extremely stretched and conned with cruel pain,/ To do you service." He assumes that it would be heartless to laugh publicly at such pathetic sincerity. But Theseus takes a much more magnanimous attitude. Nothing can be amiss ''when simpleness and duty tender it.'' In part he is mistaken, of course, because he himself cannot resist a few barbs at the expense of the players. But the point he makes involves the same ideas that occur frequently in Shakespeare's sonnets, and as I remarked in my opening chapter, his prologues and epilogues suggest that this is the response Shakespeare hoped for in the theater: he wanted a loving audience to look for the intended meaning, to search for the spirit not the letter, not to pass a strict judgment upon details of performance. Theseus had often seen great clerks recite prepared speeches of welcome, and they were so nervous that they made stupid mistakes and finally stood dumbly aside. Out of that he picked a welcome, more impressed by tongue-tied simplicity, for "Love . . . in least speaks most."

Theseus' remarks, coming before the little play, are not only instructions to his guests and his wife; they also tell actors how the roles of Bottom, Quince, and the rest ought to be played, and they tell us in the theater how we should take them. If actors can suggest, as they did in the Peter Hall production, the earnest intentions of the players, how painfully the Wall (Bill Travers) tries to live his role even though he can barely form the words of his speech, how majestic Bottom (played by Paul Rogers) thinks himself to be when he expresses Pyramus' hideous grief:

> Oh spite!
> But mark, poor knight,
> What dreadful dole is here!
> Eyes, do you see?
> How can it be?

99

Jonson and Elizabethan Comedy

O dainty. duck. O dear! . . .
 O Fates. come. come.
 Cut thread and thrum.
Quail. crush. conclude. and quell!

(V.i.274-85)

If they can imply to the audience how deadly serious they are about the whole difficult performance and that perhaps they see it as something marvelous even to be allowed in the presence of the Duke and his high-born company, then the audience can do the rest. Our imaginations will penetrate appearances, even though we are excruciatingly tickled by the silliness of the acting. This is what Shakespeare's comedy of admiration demands, that ability to get to the fore-conceit of characters, see how they feel about themselves, and finally to recover, if we can, the playwright's fore-conceit.

That conceit is related to, but distinct from, Shakespeare's expression of it, for the play is about the magic and folly of love, although imagination, play acting, and courtesy are means by which we come to understand love. Ordinary mortals probably never know the mysteries of mutual affection, whether it is sexual or mental or transcendant, and the course of true love seldom runs smooth, but sometimes by good luck or a gift of the gods, these bonds are blessed. Because of our ignorance, we should extend charity toward lovers of all kinds, but sometimes we cannot help but laugh.

An instance of this discord in concord occurs when Theseus reacts with amused superiority to the strange tales of Lysander, Hermia, Helena, and Demetrius. Although he later shows insight into the hearts of the simple, hard-handed Athenians, he is blithely indifferent to the sufferings of the four lovers. Their tales are just the sort of fancies that lovers, lunatics, and poets conceive. While he scoffs at their foolishness he inadvertently scoffs at the poet who wrote *A Midsummer Night's Dream*, and although a stern realist might observe that the play is "more strange than true" the audience is not inclined at the moment to settle for that description. We have seen the lovers' delusions and we know the causes behind them. Furthermore, Theseus, a hero himself and subject of antique fables, has little reason to dismiss them as fairy toys. Certainly the play "bodies forth the forms of things unknown" giving "to airy nothing a local habitation and a name," but more correctly speaking we know there were airy somethings involved, and those creatures will return to bless Theseus' own wedding. Shadows and visions though they be, their effects are palpable, sometimes even gross. The reality of love and concord, therefore, rests upon these seeming follies that the audience can understand are rooted in nature's mysteries, behind the apparent jesting of Theseus' speech. Hence because Shakespeare has done so much, we can go farther than the intents of the speaker, speculating on the deeper intents of the poet himself.

The play is nothing if not "imagination all compact," and certainly the lovers, including Titania, have been all as frantic, seeing Helen's beauty in the brow of Egypt. Certainly the play is a great deal more, but if we had to settle for one brief description during the onrush of stage action, this is adequate for the entertainment. After the drama is finished, when we have a chance to ruminate on the memorable lines, we find more penetrating turns of thought. Dramatic action has so interplayed with unnatural perspectives that the known and the strange unknown became entangled. Theseus is making a good joke that betrays his foolish wisdom, and in a glimmer of thought, his wise folly; so Shakespeare makes a self-deprecating joke about his play, also very much in character.

Unlike the stolid, "administrative" attitude of Theseus, Hippolyta expresses a vague feeling that there may be more to it all — "something of great constancy" in the story. It seems odd to her that all the lovers' minds are "transfigured together" — although the mystery is wonderful, "strange and admirable," she admits, the constancy of their testimony witnesses "more than fancy's images."[17] Constancy, we should remember from the sonnets (numbers 92, 93, 105, 116, and 117), means certainty, steadfastness, and truth. A true mind and a constant love are ever-fixéd marks; constancy is the sign of the best kind of love — beyond dotage and above family pride and foolishness, in the very motives of our hearts. It begins with natural affection and ends in a contemplation of a wonderful, indwelling spirit, the Idea curiously but powerfully known in the low and natural man, the mystery of love and poetry that is real yet "strange and admirable." Both Theseus and Hippolyta are aware of part of the mystery, but in the eyes of the audience the two views are as married as their spokesman. This union of dream and reality, play and practicality, is the ultimate charm of *A Midsummer Night's Dream*.

4.

The Wonder of Comic Satire

Long after he abandoned comic satire on the stage, Jonson remembered its potent blend of jest and earnest, learned from his predecessors as far back as Sidney. He reminds us of the debt, in his playful, self-mocking apology for falling in love, at the beginning of "A Celebration of Charis":

> Let it not your wonder move,
> Less your laughter, that I love.

His first encounter with Charis made more of that combination of feelings, for the "glory" of her beauty not only disarmed Cupid of his bow and arrows; her "lightning" also took away Ben's sight and motion.

> So that there I stood a stone,
> Mocked of all, and called of one
> (Which with grief and wrath I heard)
> Cupid's statue with a beard,
> Or else one that played his ape,
> In a Hercules his shape.
>
> (*Underwood*, iii, 2, 27-32)

The two familiar points of view are presented, one recognizing the ridiculous fifty-year-old poet, wanting a young lover's trim figure, smooth cheek, and chin merely "woolly as a peach"; the other acknowledging his and her substantial power — he has truth and

103

language, ardor and passion that give "weight"; she, seen in the lover's ideal vision, is a triumph of grace and purity. Cupid's statue with a beard or Ben acting the part of comic Hercules in love are the right emblems of admiration.[1]

Comic admiration became something distinct in the hands of Jonson, between 1598 and 1601, as he adapted Elizabethan forms of court entertainment for both the public and private stages. Delight and instructive ridicule remained the general goals, but the fine balance that Lyly maintained and that Shakespeare tipped toward delight in his early comedies was tipped back toward edification in Jonson. Shakespeare asked us to laugh and admire strange encounters of divine and human purposes, as if in a dream but enacted before us like a play of fancy in a literal world. His was an ideal actual, and in the end, Shakespeare seemed to celebrate human vitality with all the force of imagination. Jonson kept the ideal actual only provisionally, since he instituted a more thoroughgoing Platonic rhetoric than any major Elizabethan dramatist had used, by which an audience was encouraged to laugh at false imitations while admiring the potential ideas behind them. In Jonson's reuse of the rhetoric of praise, great human figures are admired for their reference to others of a more perfect pattern; fools are ridiculed for their shallowness and obsession with opinion, like people fabricated in images for modern politics and advertising.

That duality in drama resembles the theater itself, where players and spectators are distinguished. A passage in *Discoveries* (lines 1093-1109) makes the same analogy:

> I have considered, our whole life is like a play, wherein every man, forgetful of himself, is in travail with expression of another. Nay, we so insist in imitating others, as we cannot (when it is necessary) return to ourselves; like children that imitate the vices of stammerers so long till at last they become such and make the habit to another nature, as it is never forgotten. Good men are the stars, the planets of the ages wherein they live and illustrate the times. God did never let them be wanting to the world: as Abel for an example of innocency, Enoch of purity, Noah of trust in God's mercies. . . . These, sensual men thought mad, because they would not be partakers or practicers of their madness. But they, placed high on the top of all virtue, looked down

on the stage of the world and condemned the Play of Fortune. For though the most be players, some must be spectators.

The true reference point of the drama, therefore, is the virtuous spectator, alone, among sensual men.

The ostensible purpose of a comedy within this theater is both punitive and edifying, to bring the blameworthy to feel shame for their foolishness or ignorance, to repent, and to be reconciled with the good society, all the while that the really upright folks shine like stars in the firmament. Part of the play is a mirror of custom, and another part is a visionary glass: by one operation it produces shame, by the other, repentance and reconciliation with the good. The ideal figures found in life or history interpret for the audience, like the witness in a Renaissance painting, and they invent in their perfect minds some of the instruments that hasten the curative action. In other words, being the truest pupil of Sidney, Jonson made explicit what Lyly and Shakespeare had left implicit in the figure of Hercules, a fond prisoner of love: the amazing potential of a heroic ideal and the degrading entanglements of human passion, envy, and scorn.

Lyly and Shakespeare extended the audiences' feelings so that they could wonder at both Alexander and Apelles, Bottom and Titania, even while they laughed. In Jonson feelings are more often polarized or, by contraries "embattled," and he transposes the distressed gods and heroes of earlier comedies into the misunderstood intellectuals and the slandered poets of the comical satires. A pretentious ass or ignorant upstart who had his minor role in Lyly and Shakespeare now intrudes upon the holy of holies and has to be shown his place. To achieve Jonson's special dramatic effects, the cards are stacked from the beginning in favor of the "correct" point of view, and much of the play's energy is directed in a compelling movement to an overwhelming conclusion. Thus the endings that were more or less formalities or sport in prior comedies become extraordinarily important in Jonson's early comedies. The duality of feeling arising from an opposition of virtues and vices, and the movement toward a perfecting resolution have been insufficiently understood, however, because of the label "comical satire."

Fig. 2. *Hercules among Women,*
by Francesco Bassano,
Omphale in the lion's skin and
with his club

Some interpreters have contented themselves with tracing the connections between Jonson's comical satire, Elizabethan satire and morality plays. C. R. Baskervill pioneered this work in his *English Elements in Jonson's Early Comedy*[2] prompted by the interest among scholars of his day to find indigenous sources, sturdy English origins that subverted claims for European or classical sources of major English writers. Thus Shakespeare was "explained" by reference to the mystery plays, Milton by reference to Spenser, and Restoration comedy was really nothing but Caroline comedy smartened up to fit the later social milieu. This historicism was part of the effort, after the turn of the century, to legitimize English studies, to free them from classical philology; so the evolutionary analysis of native writing seemed to put English literature on a scientific

footing. Baskervill went so far as to suggest that the allusion to *vetus comedia (EMOH,* Induction, 231-32) may refer to the morality drama, not to Aristophanic comedy, and he was confident that English types and allegorical methods demonstrated Jonson's essentially Anglo-Saxon temper. Oscar Campbell engaged in a worse kind of nothing-buttery when he tried to show that the form of *Troilus and Cressida* was nothing but comical satire, and comical satire nothing but dramatized ridicule of social types, explainable as a variation of verse satire of the 1590s. Campbell's discussion of Jonson sometimes escapes from this critical cage, especially in his remarks on *Cynthia's Revels,* but his readings of *Poetaster* and *Every Man out of His Humor* are coarse-grained. Alvin Kernan's more sophisticated study of satire is not as reductive as Campbell's, although it suffers from a limited conception of the satirical persona, a paradigm made out of Marston and lesser satirists (with little relevance to Jonson's own verse satire); and when it appears that *Cynthia's Revels* and *Poetaster* will not fit the paradigm, Kernan pronounces them mistakes.[3] But in keeping with their their historical interpretations, these studies have enlarged our understanding of part of the literary scene in which Jonson began his career, and their many keen observations on social satire and vituperation in these plays have made it unnecessary for me to say more.

Nor has the "War of the Theaters" provided a completely satisfactory context for the comical satires, since for historians of the drama the plays were little else than archeological "digs" where they could search for references to real persons. Even the careful work of conservative scholars like Roscoe Small and J. H. Penniman did not come up with conclusions that reflected significantly on the drama. Muriel Bradbrook offers the most important suggestion about the matter when she says that the War is better understood as a struggle between the poets and actors about the question, What is a poet in the theater? Thereupon Mrs. Bradbrook engages in her own nothing-buttery; the plays of Marston, Dekker, and Jonson in this period are "only a rival set of definitions, constituting a set of rival claims, and set forth by means of a common stock of images."[4] She ignores that simplification in her useful comments on Jonson's independent manipulation of popular devices and traditional theory.

In what follows, I attempt to discriminate Jonson's work in comic satire from his predecessors and contemporaries, and to see how much he reshapes his dramatic forms. I assume that his most immediate courtly models in Lyly and Shakespeare were more attractive to him than popular and undramatic ones, and that his interest in making true poetry for the theater was a guiding, if not a dictating, principle. He did a great deal more with authority in comedy than others did, and he wished to impose authority on his audiences in a special way, hoping not just to reform the drama but the spectators as well. In effect he was shaping his audience to make the theater a safe place for high-minded poets. The magic of rhetoric and contemplation of virtue should transform their minds beyond mundane laughter into a finer consciousness, to make them under-standers, not just lookers. In three years he experimented with admiration as an effect of satirical comedy, only to abandon it, along with most of his half-formed theory of humors, once he had done his best in *Poetaster*. Perhaps reform of the audience proved to be as much a will o' the wisp as Puck himself, and admiration, although not a weak and idle theme, yet no more yielding than a dream.

At the outset, we should keep in mind that for Jonson satire never was simply vituperation or ridicule. A careful study of his epigrams (normally understood as satiric poems) will bear out his contention that both praise and blame are essential to his art.[5] The epigrams, more often than not, present men as models for approval, figures by which the rest of the world is judged. He praises "many great and good names," honoring them to posterity for their unswerving integrity and their commitment to high standards. He has less concern for Shakespeare's ideal actual, although the epi-gram to Pembroke comes close to that living idea; Jonson at least pretends not to worry about his credibility. Shakespeare (in Sonnet 17) said he was afraid readers would not believe his praise of the young friend unless they saw his real offspring. But Jonson proc-laims that if he remains faithful to truth and liberty and constant to his good intentions, his poems will be vindicated. Therefore, "if I have praised unfortunately, anyone that doth not deserve, or if all answer not in all numbers the pictures I have made of them, I hope it will be forgiven me that they are no ill pieces, though they be not like the persons."[6] Therefore, the laudatory poems represent the Idea, although men are the sometimes imperfect approach to that Idea; the poet's fore-conceit governed his creation, for "The con-ceits of the mind are pictures of things, and the tongue is the interpreter of those pictures" (*Discoveries*, 2128-29). It is that prior conception that readers must respond to, but if some will not grasp the essential idea, that will be a judgment on them as much as the poems are a judgment on men and women they praise. We shall see that Jonson expected the rhetoric of admiration to work this way for audiences of his comical satires as much as it does for readers of his epigrams.

Since his interest in admiration shows well in his endings, we can recognize a development of this aspect of his art most quickly by an inspection of the last act conversions. The dramatic problem was how to bring about a comic reconciliation in keeping with his severe disapproval of the greater part of mankind. More earnestness in the first part of a comedy tends to strain the fragile mechanism of a closure, because an audience is not so easily disposed toward mere wish-fulfillment in a serious comedy as it would be for, say, *As You Like It*. Although Lyly and Shakespeare used queens and dukes prominently, Jonson made more of an authority figure, a judge or law giver, and in contriving richer endings he solved his other problems better and better in successive plays.

1. *Every Man out of His Humor*

At the height of confusion in *Every Man in His Humor* (acted 1598 but not published till 1601), when everyone distrusts or feels injured by another, the characters resort to the magistrate, shouting accusations. Dr. Clement questions them assiduously, looking for the "devise" behind their mix-ups, and he finds it in Musco's witty disguises. As Clement drinks to Musco's merry inventions, he declares them "*Pro superi! ingenium magnum.*" "I admire thee, I honor thee, and if thy master or any man here be angry with thee, I shall suspect his wit" (V.iii.210-13).[7] Clement reconciles Prospero with his brother and Lorenzo Junior with his father by simply asking them to pardon each other. But when he works on the would-be soldier and the would-be poet, Clement's devices are highly dramatic, for he mocks them as he searches for any possible "conceit" in their behavior. He puts on armor and threatens Bobadilla with a duel; after all, if Bobadilla is a soldier he should act like a true soldier. He calls for a torch so they can see the conceit in Matheo's plagiarized poems — they are too "dark" — but when the light comes, he burns the paper. These are cues for the audience, too, aiming them toward better things and advising that the kind of poetry fit to burn was stolen verse, patched up ballads, and translations — mere stuff.

When Lorenzo's father remarks that this proves how low
poetry is ranked in "general opinion," his son replies heatedly that
gross opinion may sink as low as it pleases.[8] If his father wishes to
know what poetry really is, young Lorenzo can refute opinion and
demonstrate the worth of poetry's true estate, which is blessed,
eternal, and divine:

> Indeed if you will look on poesy
> As she appears in many, poor and lame,
> Patched up in remnants and old worn rags,
> Half starved for want of her peculiar food,
> Sacred invention, then I must confirm
> Both your conceit and censure of her merit.

It is a problem of one and many, for the Idea of poetry exists beyond
its worst imitation, self-sufficient, with divine right like a queen.

> But view her in her glorious ornaments,
> Attired in the majesty of art,
> Set high in spirit with the precious taste
> Of sweet philosophy, and which is most,
> Crowned with the rich traditions of a soul
> That hates to have her dignity profaned
> With any relish of an earthly thought.

Eyes of only a special kind can view her glory, and she judges her
imitators and inferiors.

> Oh then how proud a presence doth she bear,
> Then is she like herself, fit to be seen
> Of none but grave and consecrated eyes:
> Nor is it any blemish to her fame,
> That such lean, ignorant, and blasted wits,
> Such brainless gulls, should utter their stol'n wares
> With such applauses in our vulgar ears . . .

The trouble, therefore, is in the audience, the fat judgments of the
multitude who in this "barren and infected age" cannot tell the
difference between such "empty spirits" and the true poet, "than
which reverend name:/ Nothing can more adorn humanity" (V.iii.
318-43).

Clement agrees that these are "holy flames that should direct

111

and light the soul to eternity'' not popular choices governed wholly by humors. False poetry stifles the soul, since it hurls forth "nothing but smoke and congested vapors.'' This exalted position of poetry *vis à vis* the multitude is analogous to the ethical standards in *Every Man in His Humor*. A person who is influenced by his humor — "a monster bred in a man by self-love, and affectation, and fed by folly"[9] — is unable to be reasonable, unable to love virtue enough. Thorello's horns are apparently in his mind, just as Lorenzo Senior's false opinion of his son was bred by a misleading tendency to anger (and an error of the postal service). But the analogy between bad poetry and self-love is not worked into the main action of the comedy, just as models of Lorenzo Junior's true poetry are not presented effectively enough to contrast with Matheo's rubbish. Nothing positive is done in the body of the play to make Lorenzo Senior love true poetry or to make Giuliano love true virtue. Clement's little devices have to suffice: he orders the two imposters to do penance in the public square, and the rest can come to his house for an evening of happiness, a carouse to the health of Musco's "heroic spirit.'' Musco will wear the magistrate's robes, like a Christmas Lord, and be waited on by his real-life masters, Lorenzo Senior and Giuliano. "Composed spirits'' now can do this, free of discontent and putting a fair construction on the mirth. This formal close was Jonson's modest start in his attempts to bring high morals and true poetry into comedy — to devise an intellectual and curative comedy that used "allowed'' revels to seal the bond between men and the best in the social order.

The main force of *Every Man out of His Humor* (1600) is more distinctly corrective than its predecessor, and it betrays the roughness that often accompanies an artistic experiment. It, rather than *Every Man in His Humor,* was Jonson's big early success, if the three quarto editions in one year and a gaggle of allusions mean anything.[10] And it deserves a limited esteem for its innovations: the clever little character sketches in the *dramatis personae* started the vogue of English character writing; the induction is more elaborate and replete with dramatic theory than any before; the two-man chorus on stage makes sustained critical remarks through the entire play (Jonson's attempts to domesticate the classical chorus); the intrigue operates to de-humor various characters in a more explicit way than any comedy before Jonson; and the original ending written for court performance exploits the comic authority figure more effectively than did Dr. Clement. Even if the induction and the choruses were not acted but added for literary purposes to the published text (as I suspect), we can see here that Jonson was changing from a hack writer and play doctor to an artist determined to demand much more from his audience.[11] And when some critics did not like his bold conclusion, he blasted them for "rebelling ignorance" and assured his better critics that they were "right-eyed" and "solid," judicious fellows — the beginning of Jonson's courtship of the more intelligent public. Still his instincts as a dramatist enabled him to depict the satirist-playwright on stage with a certain wry objectivity.

Asper, the presentor, has written a play that goes beyond former, servile, imitating attempts at ridicule. He does not mean simply to unmask and expose folly, for he yearns to punish by vexation, to strip, whip, flay, and anatomize vice or various diseases of the mind. Cordatus, who, as a sort of stand-in for the audience, is on stage throughout with his friend Mitis, objects to Asper's aggressiveness; "Unless your breath had power/ To melt the world and mold it new again,/ It is in vain to spend it in these moods" (Induction, 48-50). Apparently that is what Asper hopes to do, as he proceeds to explain his theory of true humor in contrast to the abused (or affected) humor of the times. He leaves the impression that his insights, from moralized psychology, help him to know the real nature of man; they provide a philosophic basis for his art, and so he pontificates. A true humor, in medicine, is a quality of moisture and "fluxure" found in bodily fluid — the old yellow bile, black bile, phlegm, and blood. In describing character, he uses these "by metaphor" with reference to the basic emotional disposi-tions:

> And when some one peculiar quality
> Doth so possess a man, that it doth draw
> All his affects, his spirits, and his powers,

In their confluctions, all to run one way,
This may be truly said to be a humor.

(105-09)

But a pretended humor, an affectation of a humor, is an abuse Asper will not tolerate.

There is much historical evidence to suggest that Asper was talking of actual conduct among well-traveled literati and gentlemen of the time who returned from a tour of Italy with a fashionable case of melancholy, and others who imitated them.[12] Those are "more than most ridiculous," says Asper; and Cordatus agrees — "apish or fantastic strain," like wearing a pied feather, a three-piled ruff, or a yard of shoestring. These are the apes that Asper would scourge. Jonson probably had in mind people who at least imagined they had melancholy, like that from which Dudley North says he suffered after his tour of Italy, as well as those, like young John Donne, who posed as the melancholy man in his poems and had himself painted with the broad-brimmed hat, dark complexion, folded arms, and his whole figure "in shadows." England offered few public offices to ambitious young men, no military service to speak of, and no pleasure in a decayed court under an aging queen. Malcontent, therefore, spread quickly through the Inns of Court and along Paul's Walk, manifesting itself in peculiarities or affectations. It would also appear that the English comic tradition was helped on by that other English institution in its infancy, the eccentric gentleman.

As Asper rages on, he blurs the distinction between true and false humors that he so carefully made, for both affected and true humors become his targets.[13] But his method of dealing with them is more important than their classification, and it is his method that inaugurates Jonson's corrective comedy. Like a good Neoplatonist or a wise preacher, Asper knows the "souls" of men for whom he writes and whose minds he will minister to. So he says that he will use his play to give "physic to the mind," seizing on follies and vices that men should feel shame to act, and he will "squeeze out the humor of such spongy natures as lick up every idle vanity" (145-46). He suggests that there is a new mold that he would give to the minds of those he squeezed (''crushed'' is the word in the quarto version), and the process of squeezing and remolding is similar to what he will do to his audience as well. The stage will be a wide mirror to show the times' deformity anatomized ''in every nerve and sinew.'' The highest response will be from his better audience, which Asper describes in exalted language:

> Good men and virtuous spirits that loath their vices,
> Will cherish my free labors, love my lines,
> And with the fervor of their shining grace,
> Make my brain fruitful to bring forth more objects,
> Worthy of their serious and intentive eyes.

(134-38)

And if any person chances to behold himself, he will be shamed into silence, then squeezed out of his humor. This adapts the traditional Galenic theory of medicine, curing a disease by opposing or inhibiting medicines. In this case the medicine causes a guilty identification with ''true'' images on stage, their sufferings, followed by shame or fear of ridicule.

If this analysis is correct, the new mold to be formed for all characters and their counterparts in the gallery is a function of admiration, too, a healthy mind, a rectified spirit, or as Jonson so often called it, an erected confidence. With erected wit a poet makes good plays, and with erected confidence, a good opinion of himself, a spectator takes in the pleasure of a good comedy, no offense. Asper may be mad, but his madness is that Platonic *Furor Poeticus* that Cordatus praises him for (147). One striking example is given to the audience, as the play is about to begin, when Asper assures the ''attentive'' audience who have come to feed their minds that he will make superhuman efforts on their behalf.

> For these I'll prodigally spend myself
> And speak away my spirit into air,
> For these I'll melt my brain into invention,
> Coin new conceits and hang my richest words
> As polished jewels in their bounteous ears.

(204-08)

In order to melt the world he must melt his brains in a high rapture,

115

so that his rich words can fly to the ears of the right auditors. This is what Jonson's comical satire is aiming for, its ultimate delight, not just the ridiculous exposure of a humor.

For the diseased minds of others he offers shame, and shame is a complex emotion, involving awareness of faults, as well as a sense of what we ought to be. Sordido's repentance, after hearing the rustics curse the man who saved his life, illustrates that double power with brutal simplicity. Sordido carries his malignancy from life even to death, for his reliance on false and selfish prophecy led to his despair, and he thinks his very death will withhold benefits of his wealth from others. But when a pitying fellow cuts him down from the gibbet and he and his friends discover that the wretch is only Sordido, the caterpillar, they are revolted. "How cursed are the poor that the viper was blest with this good fortune!" (III.viii. 27-28). Sordido sees how monstrous he is in others' eyes — that he has lived like an unsavory muck-hill to himself. "Oh how deeply/ The bitter curses of the poor do pierce!/ I am by wonder changed." His new idea of life will prove "No life is blest, that is not grac't with love" (III.viii. 49-57).

As the victim's feelings have two sides, so there are two sides to the reformer, implied by the differences between Asper and Macilente — the truth-teller and the scourge. Asper himself encompasses righteous indignation, not just anger, and Jonson's sketch of him as the unselfish critic should be taken as a guide to an actor:

> He is of an ingenious and free spirit, eager and constant in reproof, without fear controlling the world's abuses. One whom no servile hope of gain or frosty apprehension of danger can make to be a parasite either in time, place, or opinion. ("Names of the Actors," 1-6)

But Macilente, his alter ego, whose role he plays in the drama proper, is described as a man of good parts and a sufficient scholar, who, because he has found no preferment or place in society equal to his merit, suffers from envy. "His judgment is so dazzled and distasted that he grows violently impatient of any opposite happiness in another" (11-13). Therefore the inventor and his dramatic instrument have the capacities of knowledge of the right and a hatred of wrong. Spite keeps Macilente from a proper view of right and good fortune, but it spurs him to action.

Macilente tricks men out of their humors in Acts IV and V, and spite, vexation, and shame play their appropriate parts. The chorus tells the audience in advance, "you shall see the very torrent of his envy break forth like a land flood" (IV.viii.155-56), and another torrent will come after: "you shall see the true picture of spite anon" (V.viii.79).[14] He sends a jealous husband to find his wife with her lover, he poisons Puntarvolo's favorite dog, he induces Carlo Buffone to vex the vainglorious knight, who in turn seals Carlo's mouth with hard wax — an early example of Jonson's dramatic efficiency.

But his best device, imitated from *The Courtier,* Book II, is an ingenious put-down that detects false perception and snobbery, applying one of those tests that snobs themselves use on others. It has been said, for instance, about the novelist Howard Sturgis, who always praised things "very neatly" and who liked a small, exclusive circle of intimate friends, that he once showed a new guest in his home (young E. M. Forster) some fine embroidery; next to it was a cheap, cloth pot-holder. Since the guest hestitated for a moment, not knowing which was which, he was never invited back. Macilente's scheme might work very well to expose Sturgis' kind of snob, as it works on the great courtly lady, Saviolina, who has too much "self-conceit." Her admirers say that she is "celestial and full of wonder and delight," her voice angelic, making a man feel "all quintessence and flame," and no spirit in the world is able to withstand her facetious and acute wit (IV.viii.16-32, 49-50). With the help of Puntarvolo, Fastidious, and the other sports, Macilente invents the device that will reduce her conceit. If so, they declare, it will make them "laugh with judgment," and they will applaud and admire him. According to the plan, they tell Saviolina that she is about to meet a brilliant gentleman at court who has such extraordinary facility at language or accent "that it breeds astonishment." His wit is exuberant and his marvelous ability is in mimicry. He can imitate a country fellow so well that "it is not possible for the sharpest-sighted wit . . . to discern any sparks of the gentleman in him, when he does it.'' It is, therefore, a test of fine perception, and of course Saviolina, having too good an opinion of her insight, takes the bait. Although she is introduced to a real rustic, she sees a true gentleman beneath. ''They were very blear-witted i'faith that could not discern the gentleman in him. . . . The carriage of his eye, and that inward power that forms his countenance'' convince her (V.ii.72-83). Her friends milk her vanity with a series of flattering speeches, drawing out more assurances of her miraculous perspicuity in deciphering him, but when they show by his rough hands that he has recently been plowing, the blushing lady is shamed.

This device is good for the stage because there is the extra pleasure for the audience, who scrutinize the actor playing the clod, who the lady thinks is a gentleman playing the clod. The audience can feel safe in their perceptions, while the lady is revealed to the world as a fraud, a false wonder. The trick reflects upon Puntarvolo and Fastidious, too, even while they help take away her self-conceit because, after all, they had falsely admired her. Macilente's methods, therefore, anticipate the art of Mosca and Face, those masters of efficiency and wizards of the confidence game. Here the trick depends on Macilente's confiding with his foolish helpers to undo her as well as themselves and playing upon the lady's trust in their story as well as her divine insight. But the trick's dramatic function extends beyond this episode since it offers a contrast between the false wonder and the true wonder of the queen who resolves the comedy at the end of the fifth act. The monarch's presence there is ''discovered'' and her ''figure'' like a clear glass makes Macilente ''see'' the true way to virtue. Her vatic power transforms the spiteful soul.

In the process Macilente is brought out of his humor, not by a Galenic method of vexation, but by something more like the Paracelsian method, first allowing the ''disease'' to follow its own course and then the application of ''spiritual'' and purifying medicine, medicine that goes to the cause, not just treating the symptoms. Thus during the earlier part of the play Macilente is not crushed or squeezed like the other humorists, and no shame inhibits his envious drive to vex the world. After his last dirty trick, he continues to gloat over the pain he has caused, turning the knife in Brisk's wounds, reminding him of all his faults, without mercy. Macilente concludes, "Now monsieur, you see the plague that treads o' the heels of your foppery: well, go your way in, remove yourself to the two-penny ward quickly, to save charges, and there set up your rest to spend Sir Puntar's hundred pound for him" (V.xi. 49-53). At this point, or perhaps even earlier (we cannot be sure because Jonson's note on the original ending is vague about which lines were rewritten later), Macilente "not only persisted in his humor but was now come to the court with a purposed resolution (his soul as it were new drest in Envy) to malign at anything that should front him; when suddenly, against expectation, and all steel of his malice, the very wonder of [the queen's] presence strikes him to the earth dumb and astonished." It is like the transformation scene in a court masque, when the actors suddenly "discover" the great person among the spectators.

Possibly the original version of the play had another scene at court, following the idea tossed out but forgotten in the previous court scene (V.ii.132) — that the gentlemen should go after Saviolina and "make her blush in the presence." In any case, Macilente's "opposed" spirit was struck down by the very wonder of the "figure" of the sovereign.[15] Like most other fits of admiration, the magic of this one makes him speechless for a moment, but when he rises, his eloquence pours forth:

> Blessed, divine, unblemished, sacred, pure,
> Glorious, immortal, and indeed immense.

Seeing something greater than himself, he becomes aware that he lacks appropriate words of praise to "lend or add" to her high majesty, but he knows that she has changed him profoundly.

> . . . in her graces
> All my malicious powers have lost their stings.
> Envy is fled my soul, at sight of her,
> And she hath chased all black thoughts from my bosom
> Like as the sun doth darkness from the world.
> My stream of humor is run out of me.

119

As London sewage runs into the Thames and is purified by the "strength" and "clearness" of the river, so are his corrupt passions drowned in the "ample and unreasoned flood of her perfections." Now that his spirit is sweet and clear "as the most rarified and subtle air," he is moved by a pure heart to offer a prayer for the queen's admired and happy government.

Jonson justified this moral and mysterious use of the queen because Macilente's envy so strongly possessed him that "it must be no slight common object that should effect sudden and strange cure upon him, as putting him clean out of his humor." Nevertheless, because of objections to the ending, Jonson was obliged to rewrite the transformation scene for later performance, putting in its place a somewhat undramatic declaration, lines 54-66 of scene xi, which contains the similar two-part process. First he finds himself empty of all envy as his victims are empty of merit to be envied. He has consumed his feelings as well as the cause of his feelings, since his melancholy fed on the follies of others, who are now repentant. Then he wistfully hopes for even further changes in the afflicted people, carrying his ideas into charitable desire:

> I am so far from malicing their states,
> That I begin to pity 'em. It grieves me
> To think they have a being. I could wish
> They might turn wise upon it, and be saved now,
> So heaven were pleased: but let them vanish vapors.

Either the original or the revised ending fulfills the expectations that the comedy aroused. We have seen Macilente soaking up everyone's frothy humors "like a dry crust," and his vision has been lifted to the wonder of a free spirit. Carlo Buffone had expressed that hope for Macilente in a moment of wry approval (V.iv.28-32): could he but "hold up his eyes at other men's happiness, in any reasonable proportion: S'lid, the slave were to be loved next heaven, above honor, wealth, rich fare, apparel, wenches, all the delights of the belly, and the groin, whatever."

II. *Cynthia's Revels*

If regeneration by the grace of majesty comes more or less by chance at the end of *Every Man out of His Humor* and it does not extend to anyone except Macilente, Jonson's next play brought about a more thorough reform by political magic. *Cynthia's Revels* is not just an expansion of the last act of *Every Man Out,* for enough new things are attempted to make this an important, though unsuccessful, play. The playwright adapts Lyly's humanized gods — Cupid, Mercury, and Cynthia — to teach the world about proper manners. It makes Shakespeare's play within the play more immediately functional for its sophisticated stage audience. Like Lyly and Shakespeare, Jonson seriously tried to evoke the excitement of admiration and to articulate it with the basic strategy of the comedy, but he "embattles" admiration more distinctly than they by pitting it against its cheap imitation.

Two contrasting forces operate in the play, one moving toward a contemplation of an exalted ideal, love of an almost unearthly perfection, the other force attacking self-love, showing up the triviality and pretense of sophisticated life. In the end the first force draws the second into its field, reconciling self-love to its subordinate place. So there are two fountains, as the dedication makes clear, the fountain of self-love and the true fountain of manners, an ideal court. In a proper kingdom, the court is a bountiful, brave spring, which, like the Plotinian Idea, bubbles up and overflows to water all the noble plants on the island. It is also the magic mirror where the whole kingdom "dresseth itself," thus teaching everyone to "hate their deformities" and to love their "forms." In other words, the court should influence royal subjects in the same way that Jonson's comical satire affects theater audiences. The lesson to be learned is that true manners (i.e. character) get their grace from reverence, not from powdering and perfuming and not every day "smelling of the tailor." The mind shining through any suit of clothes needs no "false light either of riches or honors to help it."[16]

The alternate titles of the play and Jonson's change of mind about which title should go first suggest the dual operations of the plot. It was entered in the Stationers' Register as "Narcissus the Fountain of Self-Love": the title page of the quarto (1601) was "The Fountain of Selfe-Love, or Cynthia's Revels" (but the head and running titles were "Cynthia's Revels"). The folio (1616) settled on "Cynthia's Revels, or The Fountain of Self-Love," giving top billing to the masque in the fifth act.

At the beginning of the comedy after the playful warnings of the induction, the audience sees the negative forces, as the Fountain of Self-Love sits on stage and Amorphus comes to drink from it. And the first three acts present mostly the trivia and pretense, for Crites holds himself aloof from the self-conceited fools, and unlike Macilente, he does not want to bother to punish others. He has his "erected confidence," his faith in truth and knowledge of the right, so his mind is composed and uncontaminated by envy.[17] But gradually, under the gracious influence of Arete (active virtue), he is convinced that he can assist the queen and he will cleanse her court. His method is to use her borrowed power to make the fools repent themselves and to rejoin the luminous court of Cynthia. By an emanation of virtue, the spirit of Cynthia must penetrate the hearts of everyone through the mediation of Arete, Crites, and Mercury. Like the courtiers, the audience at the end of the masque is presumed to feel the same rapture for Cynthia, now a definite character in the drama, not the queen in the audience or some "figure" brought on at the last minute. This technique of presenting the grotesque negative behavior before the beautiful positive action is probably another version of the double mirror that first shows things as they are, then as they should be, like the use of contrary "figures" in royal entertainments.[18]

Her masque at the end is the most interesting and I will say more of it below, but the rest of the comedy deserves some attention. Granted, most of it is overwritten, and Jonson shows a singular unwillingness to make the fools witty or attractive in any way. Carlo and Puntarvolo had their moments in his last play, but here Jonson goes to extremes in demonstrating the false courtiers' utter banality, an art which he learned to handle differently in his later comedies like *Bartholomew Fair* and *Tale of a Tub*. His technique here is to use games and comic routines so that the pseudosophisticates seem to turn on themselves unwittingly and, by reflex almost, reveal themselves to the audience pitilessly.

The action depends on the idea of self-love, all carried out very deliberately, too deliberately. Since self-love is based on ignorance and appetite, doting on painted vanities, conceited fools are unaware of their triviality. They cannot invent as witty men would do, they can only mimic each other (symbolized by the love between Echo and Narcissus). In their self-love they praise themselves in others, making their talk mere flattery,[19] like a teacher's inflated letter of recommendation, when the writer describes his own supposed abilities under the guise of praising his student. Echo complains of Narcissus' debility, helplessly:

> Oh Narcissus,
> Thou that wast once (and yet are) my Narcissus;
> Had Echo but been private with thy thoughts,
> She would have dropped away herself in tears,
> Till she had all turned water, that on her
> (As in a truer glass) thou mightest have gazed,
> And seen thy beauties by more kind reflection:
> But self-love never yet could look on truth,
> But with bleared beams; sleek flattery and she
> Art twin-born sisters and so mix their eyes
> As if you sever one, the other dies.
>
> (I.ii.29-39)

After drinking from the fountain, the courtiers cannot feel even Cupid's arrows, so isolated are they from human contact. Even before drinking they play games and routines, completely circular and independent of each other. They come as close to being puppets (or "motions" in Jonson's language) as a man can be. Crites emphasizes their lack of self-awareness when they contemplate levity rather than truth. They banish sense and act their

> mimic tricks with that free license,
> That lust, that pleasure, that security,
> As if [they] practiced in a pasteboard case,
> And no one saw the motion, but the motion.
>
> (I.v.61-64)

Jonson and Elizabethan Comedy

From every scene emerges the puppetlike behavior of all the conceited courtiers. Constantly they rehearse speeches, prepare little gestures and stupid replies, and plan brainless subterfuges to keep up their pretenses, as Anaides and Hedon practice their oaths, "by the tip of your ear, sweet lady" or "by the white valley that lies between the Alpine hills of your bosom" (II.ii.23-24). Amorphus' absurd instructions to Asotus take up a half-dozen scenes, teaching him the mysteries of fashion, such as how to enter a room and how to flatter a lady. Some of these routines could be funny on the stage, too, such as the catalog of the various faces that a man can wear — a tour de force for an Elizabethan clown (II.iii.11-50). The clown probably mimicked each face as he described it, and, in mock schoolmaster form, he proved that the face need not be an index of the mind. The speech ends with an elaborate pedantic analysis of the courtier's face — elementary, practic, and theoretic. Jonson composed mock instructions like this as early as *Every Man in His Humor,* I.iii, with Bobadilla's fencing lesson, and, in *The Case is Altered,* IV.iii, with Onion's lesson in compliment. This routine became a staple of later social comedy, like *The Man of Mode,* as when Harriet instructs Young Bellair in the gestures of amorous courtship.

Each courtier is a fake of some kind, using a disguise, a device to project his image to others. In place of personal worth Amorphus uses his talk to promote himself at ordinaries where he is hired to keep up the conversation. Asotus, the prodigal, can do nothing but spend money in an effort to buy self-esteem. Nothing comes from within, so they all must imitate each other, an act of mere envy. Asotus, ascending the social scale, first imitates Amorphus, then Hedon and Anaides, and when he reaches the top — receiving ladies' favors — he patronizes those he had imitated. Their behavior is like a dream of a court pageant, "so painted, pied, and full of rainbow strains" (III.iv.4-6).

Their parlor games are completely without magic, a significant matter for the design of the play, because they present the obverse of the two masques in Act V, like the trick upon the false court lady contrasted with the queen's wonder in *Every Man Out.* Incidentally,

124

the gimmick, like some episodes in *Every Man Out,* comes from Castiglione's *Courtier,* a sign of Jonson's early scorn of urbane life and a suggestion of the distance he had to go before he wrote *Epicoene* and the ten lyric pieces on Charis. While the courtiers wait for water to come from the fountain of self-love, they are at their wits' end. They have run out of talk, so they ask each other banal questions to get the game of court talk going. Who is the properest man in court? Who would you be if you could choose whatever happy estate you wished? And each person replies with his mean little ideas, like the table conversation of academics who have nothing to say to each other. The game of substantives and adjectives, anticipating the game of vapors in *Bartholomew Fair,* exactly represents the minds of the courtiers. They can mouth the attributes — *odoriferous, popular, humble, white-livered, barbarous,* and *changeable* — without understanding the substantives to which they belong. In the other game (added in the folio text), they speak of the circumstances of something — who did it, where, when, why, who would have done it better—all before they know *what* has been done. They actually enjoy not knowing what they speak of (IV.ii.160-263).[20]

The silly games here are supposed to contrast with chivalric combats, I suspect, like the Passage of Arms that took place in noble tournaments, which still survived in the French and English courts. Part of the dream of heroism, a tournament took place in an artificial scene with a romantic name like *La fontaine des pleurs.* At a fountain beside a pavilion, knights came each day to touch shields and pledge to follow the rules of combat. If a knight was unhorsed he had to wear something like a gold bracelet until he found the lady who held the key to it, whom he would serve.[21] The whole ceremony was suffused with an air of mystery and divine magic.

But the courtiers in *Cynthia's Revels* are unheroic and unmysterious, and they go through all these routines as if the light of the moon were not shining upon them, as if Crites, Cynthia, and the audience could not see through them like a transparent glass. This technique calls attention to the dramatic distance between the fools and the audience, encouraging us to see them as puppets, locked in their cubicles, self-defeating and finally shameful. The competition for courtly compliment (in only the folio text) brings them all to the point of embarrassment, when Mercury beats them at their own game, under the eyes of the false mistresses set up as judges: Folly, Self-love, and Fancy. Mercury thinks this should be enough to betray the servile flattery and naked conceit of the fools, but Crites insists that

> Though they may see it, yet the huge estate
> Fancy and form and sensual pride have gotten
> Will make them blush for anger not for shame;
> And turn shewn nakedness to impudence.
>
> (V.iv.625-28)

Seeing themselves is not enough, finally; other positive ideas must be instilled, some "worthier love" than these vain joys. They must study the inward comeliness of bounty, knowledge, and spirit before they are saved. To escape from mechanical routines, they must learn to admire "god's high figures" to which they must seek to conform. The final masques supply the model, and the ritual penance of the litany and public march seals their membership in a regenerated court.

Crites' references to Cynthia in the concluding masques establish her meaning in the language of the higher magic: she is the bearer of the Platonic "clear glass" of truth and perfection. Using the light of Jove she clears the heavens when "envious shades" would come in (V.vi.7-12), for she is a "clear spirit" (V.vii.9). She is "Heaven's purest light" (V.viii.36), a sphere of virtue in which people behold "themselves, more truly themselves, to live enthronized" (V.vii.11-12). The maskers present her a crystal globe, "a note of monarchy and symbol of perfection" (16-17). Jonson used this symbol again in *The Haddington Masque* (1608) to represent perfection, because it is made up of circles "in due proportion to the sphere of heaven" (that is, the crystalline sphere that contains all the zodiac, lines 276-79). The symbols of the zodiac and the circle imitate the eternal sphere of the heavens, so it is natural that Arete should praise Crites

Who (like a circle bounded in itself)
Contains as much, as man in fulness may.
Lo, here the man, who not of usual earth,
But of that nobler, and more precious mold,
Which Phoebus' self doth temper, is composed,
And who . . .
Stands fixed silent in [Cynthia's] glorious sight.

(V.viii.18-28)

Cynthia admits Crites to her favor, and she specifically likens him to the sphere in her hands: she finds an equal pleasure in looking at the sphere as in thinking of his learning and virtue. In rhapsody Crites affirms that Cynthia's grace, heaven's "purest light," her beauty, is his chiefest light "by whose propitious beams my powers are raised" (V.viii.29-43).

In this way, although Crites begins as a mere human, he achieves a special status on earth, immune from the darts of Cupid, because he aspires to the favor of the gods, Cynthia and Apollo, the children of Jove (V.x.105). The false courtiers who seek only social position and the opinion of others cannot be wounded either, but the presence of Cynthia where Crites and Arete walk protects them against wounds of baser human passion. There "thorns lie in garrison about the roses," for Cupid's darts are enchanted by her power (V.x.58, 110-14). In Crites' prayer to Apollo he explains his thoughts: in the busy tumults of his mind his path has been illumined and his invention has thrived by the bounty and grace of the gods but also (according to the Jonsonian credo) by his "right," and he hopes that Cynthia will recognize that worth. Fortunately she does, in her admiration for the masques (again identifying the audience effects that Jonson sought):

Not without wonder, not without delight,
Mine eyes have viewed (in contemplation's depth)
This work of wit, divine and excellent.

(V.viii.1-3)

And she adopts him as her servant "the more thyself to be," distinguishing him from common folk.

Cynthia also tells us what her light does for the people; she

127

takes it out of "Jove's treasury" and places it in her sphere, in order to give mankind — "the mutinous kind of wanting men" — the "looked for light." Although ordinary men's desert is little, allowing them nothing "by right," Cynthia offers hope for what might be, the eventual enjoyment of her whole light, simply because the high and noble should do good for its own sake (V.vi.26-36). Other humans, therefore, aside from Crites, can profit from her influence, can be transformed and can improve themselves, because she functions as a clear mirror, the sinless soul that reflects the better side of humanity when they look on her. In her light external disorder is quieted and conflict reconciled, just as the flowing ocean (i.e. the troubled soul) is calmed by her presence. This is symbolized in court entertainment when the foolish courtiers, at the request of Arete and by the wit of Crites, are made to wear masks representing them as they might be, not as they were earlier in the play. In the guise of a "neighboring virtue" (illustrating the Augustinian principle that vice is a perverse imitation of virtue, proving that God is still imitated even in our worst actions), each folly is to be presented to the queen. Arete assures us that "What's done in Cynthia's sight is done secure," and Cynthia does not insist on knowing the details of the forthcoming masque. She holds with Duke Theseus that "Nothing which duty and desire to please/ Bears written in the forehead, comes amiss" (V.vi.79-80).[22]

And nothing emphasizes better the contrast between Shakespeare and Jonson's use of comic admiration than this parallel, for the surrounding circumstances in Jonson's play change the meaning substantially. In Shakespeare the stress was upon what really goes amiss, requiring the generous audience to mend the faults of actors who are well-intentioned louts. In Jonson the stress falls on the conceited motives of the courtiers, masked by the skillful art of Crites. The inventor of the masque, not the performer, has the good intentions, as does Arete who commissioned him to use the loathsome courtiers, but their whole purpose goes beyond entertaining the queen. It is a trap to embarrass the actors themselves while our admiration goes toward the poet. Only the poet's desires to please and to do his duty really matter.

The actors' reform does not come directly from taking the clothes and names of complementary virtues; that is not a sufficient force to bring out their potential goodness. But it is a beginning.[23] As Mercury warns Cupid, "it was ominous to take the name of Anteros upon you; you know not what charm or enchantment lies in the word." So in the first masque Philautia (self-love) puts on the costume of natural affection called Storge; Gelaia (laughter) puts on delectable and pleasant conversation, Aglaia; Phantaste (lightness) puts on a well-conceited wittiness, Euphantaste; and Moria (folly) puts on simplicity, Apheleia.[24] Each carries an impress with an appropriate motto. Together they represent the four cardinal virtues upon which the whole frame of the court is constructed. In the second masque the male courtiers, led by Mercury, represent the four cardinal properties serving the queen of perfection, and they are disguised in similar complementary symbolic costumes. Amorphus (deformed) becomes neat and elegant; Hedon (voluptuous) becomes variety without excess; Anaides (impudent) becomes good audacity; and Asotus (prodigal) becomes good-natured generosity.

The moral power of these disguises engaged Jonson's imagination seriously, for the idealized costumes seem to bring the affected fools at least to a potential merit, by showing the difference between what they are and what they pretend to be. Later in his career, disguises of Cutbeard and Otter work in the same way. Simply putting on clothes of their betters exalts their spirits, making them more presumptuous than ever. In *Epicoene* there is the added suggestion that people who judge them by appearance alone are equally foolish, but that point cannot be made in *Cynthia's Revels* since the queen herself is deceived.[25] However, because they fail to live up to the costumes that express their ideal forms, the forms mock instead of flattering them (similar to what Jonson said in his epigram to his muse, number lxv.) The next step, therefore, was to unmask them — they who boldly pressed too far, who like Actaeon had presumed to enter the sacred bowers and hallowed places with "unclean aspect" most lewdly to pollute. The courtiers' self-love beclouded their self-knowledge, but at the unmasking they can see how far they were from their potential Idea. To make them ashamed,

Cynthia seems shocked that Philautia should have usurped Storge's name or that the others grace themselves with titles not their own (V.xi.60-65). Their presence is a sign of disease at court, and she delegates Arete and Crites to prescribe remedies as they please, "th'incurable cut off, the rest reform" (l.97).

Crites invents a penitential cure that mixes ceremony and satire. The courtiers must first take off their robes, for "'tis virtue which they want, and wanting it,/ Honor no garment to their backs can fit" (117-18). In the following ritual they must proceed to a public crossroads and weep tears on Niobe's stone (for Niobe was swollen with presumption, too),[26] so as to change the stone to a weeping cross. Then they go to the well of knowledge, Helicon, and wash themselves, purging their minds of "present maladies." Knowledge is to be the basis of renewed spirits with clear souls, as Helicon counteracts the effect of the Fountain of Self-Love, fitting them to return and serve great Cynthia. The delightful mock litany they sing along the way is, presumably, the "wise mirth" that is to be bent toward the useful "fruit" (V.xi.160). They publicly exorcize their follies, praying that "Good Mercury defend us" from Spanish shrugs, fresh faces, smirks, irps, and all affected humors, from courting puppets, wearing bracelets of hair, shoe-ties, gloves, garters, and rings with posies, from rushing about to tiltyards, playhouses, pageants, and all such public places, from coining counterfeit employments, vainglorious taking to them other men's services, and all self-loving humors.

The public humiliation of such fools was not just a dramatic device, for it had its roots in Elizabethan conceptions of honor and justice. The decline of a real military basis of chivalry seems to have led to a corresponding rise in the importance of personal honor. And the Elizabethan gentleman became hypersensitive about his name, as one courtier proclaimed "My credit is more than my life," and another reminded the Earl of Essex "how much the reputation and honor of a man doth master every other affection." Lord Herbert of Cherbury filled his autobiography with little else than accounts of his fantastic quarrels to defend his honor, which he regarded with preternatural devotion. The courts punished gentlemen by public humiliation, the stocks, pillory, and the apology read aloud in a marketplace, on the theory that that shame was a more effective punishment than a stiff fine. (The lower classes were whipped or hanged, of course.) When the Star Chamber ordered Sir Henry Winston to confess publicly at the next assizes at Gloucester that he had struck a bailiff, he refused to do so, saying that ''he preferred to remain in prison than 'to receive open disgrace in my country.' ''[27] Ceremonial public disgrace and dramatic repentance were the heritage of medieval justice, when a king, or peer, or a member of the gentle class committed a wrong. Its purpose was reform and reconciliation, like that between the Holy Roman Emperor and Pope Gregory VII, or between Henry II and the Church after the murder of Thomas à Becket.

Jonson himself invoked the power of shame in his own reform after his ill-fated *Isle of Dogs* (1597); when writing to Lord Salisbury in 1605 he says that after his ''first error'' in satire he had carefully avoided personal attacks. That error, he says, is still ''punished in me more with my shame than it was then with my bondage.''[28] Is there an implication that he feels that he has risen enough in the world so that shame is an appropriate penal treatment, or perhaps that the poet has an aristocratic spirit if not the social position to go along with it? At any rate the assumption is the same in life as in comedy that shame has reforming power if the offender possesses an idea of his good name by which to judge himself. Humiliation, therefore, ceremonially exposes a false wonder and puts the offender into a right relation with the true ideal, and Elizabethan judges, like Jonson, were aiming for the reestablishment of a right social order based on sanctioned virtue.

Cynthia's treatment of the foolish courtiers is in this as in all her actions a model for the kingdom and for other princes, so as to draw by spiritual magnetism the whole world toward an idea. The court must be cleansed first because

> Princes, that would their people should do well,
> Must at themselves begin, as at the head:
> For men, by their example, pattern out
> Their imitations, and regard of laws:
> A virtuous Court a world to virtue draws.

> (V.xi.169-73)

Jonson's next play was to show how these authoritarian ideals could be used to cleanse poetry and to place it in an order comparable to Cynthia's court.

III. *Poetaster*

Poetaster or His Arraignment was Jonson's most ambitious play up to the time it was written (about the winter and spring of 1601). In dramatic quality it lacks the simple charms of *Every Man in His Humor* (I mean the early version), but it has as vigorous characterization as that play, it has the most expressive and dramatically potent dialogue he had written so far, and it has at least four well-managed scenes where some high spirits and strong feelings are developed. Underpinning the whole is an intellectual structure more formidable than anything he had formerly contrived, and after this he never again attempted such a subordination of comedy to thought. The political tragedies, *Sejanus* and *Catiline,* and the court masques were to become the proper receptacles of his ideological concerns, with proper objects for our wonder.

In spite of its originality *Poetaster* still remains in the tradition of "right comedy" after Lyly and Shakespeare. There is still the expanded range of comic characters: an emperor and his daughter, noble patrons, a heroic poet, a satirist, a love poet, and various poetasters; a soldier, spies, actors, a tradesman and his ambitious wife. There is still the enclosed performance, here a mock banquet and Virgil's ceremonial reading from the *Aeneid,* instead of a masque or play within the play. As in Lyly and Shakespeare, there is still the impossible, even dangerous, love affair between vastly unequal parties. The audience is still asked to judge the confusion and mixture of fortunes and to wonder at the transformation and deliverance in separation. The final affirmation comes in the unmasking of Lupus, with the aid of Virgil's magic, and corrective punishment comes from Horace's wit, sanctioned by Virgil's blessing. Laughter and wonder still pervade the scenes, sometimes too intimately for Caesar to distinguish them from blasphemy.

Nevertheless, Jonson's variations on right comedy are more radical in this play than in *Cynthia's Revels*.

Since the *Poetaster* is at once a personal attack on false poets and an affirmation of the right place in society for true poets, it combines a remarkable intensity of feeling with high principles. This combination is made possible by the use of objective material — historical persons in a remote time and place who act according to their characters. It is part of the humanist's search for authority in a better, earlier age, and Augustan Rome as the pinnacle of ancient civilization had the same meaning for humanists as primitive Christianity had for the Protestant reformers. Therefore the struggle of poets, Rome's "worthiest prophets," who were mistreated and misunderstood under a great emperor, afforded luminous examples for a later age, and it served Jonson as a stalking horse for the indictment of society's exaggerated esteem for Marston and Dekker, and of its misjudgment of better poets. Moreover, *Poetaster* seems less calculated to disperse the audiences' feelings and to polarize them than his two previous comedies, because of the detached air of the play. There are now degrees of excellence in various figures to capture our interest as it rises toward the ideal conception of a poet, and our righteous indignation is somewhat modified by circumstances when authority makes mistakes, for there is no perfect congruence between political power and literary power.

Historical accuracy adds to that detachment as well. *Every Man in His Humor* was set in Florence, but the playwright used every opportunity to associate it with London and the surrounding fields, walls, taverns, and other landmarks. *Every Man out of His Humor* and *Cynthia's Revels* were on the Fortunate Island and in Gargaphie — transparent veils for England, Westminster, the Thames, the Mitre Tavern, and Weeping Cross. But *Poetaster's* Rome has a greater solidity remote from the present, and it is distinctly "out there," with its Capitol, Forum, Caesar's Gardens, Holy Street; its lictors and sesterces. As Jonson fits actual poems by Virgil, Ovid, and Horace into the story, the events are an imaginative reconstruction out of historical records of what might have happened, and Horace, for instance, is not given any views that might not plausibly be attributed to the historical original. The comedy seldom breaks out of its time capsule, aside from the jeer at the Chamberlain's Men (III.iv) who act in "your Globes" on the other side of the Tiber and the parodies of old stock plays in their repertory. To lace an imaginative work with historical detail is a good way to achieve dramatic distance, and in its operation an historical drama looking backward to an ideal age reflects on the present as much as utopian fiction sees the present in a vision of the future. Arthur Miller's *Crucible* illustrates the power that a reconstruction like this still has in the theater, although his Salem is a kind of dystopia, imbedded in events of the past, yet relevant to the 1950s. We can now see Miller's drama beyond its topical concerns, as we must see *Poetaster,* too, since both are more than cautionary tales for a naughty age.

The best discussions of *Poetaster* have settled on the play as an explicit defense of poetry and the need for discriminating taste.[29] I think this view is essentially correct for part of the comedy; however, Jonson's special emphasis on the social position of the poet and his social function must be recognized before we can appreciate his dramatic achievement. The comedy postulates two hierarchies, that of the great and of the good; the great are known by social rank depending upon position and wealth, the good by merit depending upon ability and moral character. The admired poets Virgil, Horace, Ovid, Gallus, and Tibullus have merit but not always an assured rank. Poetry does not make money like law or the military, and in order to survive, the poets must rely upon patronage and their reputation. Certain other people, such as Tucca, Crispinus, Chloe, and Lupus, have a rank in society given by money or presumption (some are even gentle born), but they have no merit; yet they expect those below them to defer to their "betters," removing their hats, obeying commands, succumbing to threats. These unworthy people envy those above them, too, and they envy their social equals who have merit enough to receive greater recognition — Horace, Virgil, and Ovid. Out of envy comes false report and slander, endangering a good name, so in the face of misfortune the true poet may suffer greatly, even though he is a "free spirit." His soul may live eternal in his poetry, but his body suffers abuse and his personal inspiration may be clouded. Poetry, after all, is created in this world, and it needs a good society — one that rewards merit — in order to thrive. Distressed poets, therefore, can be as fit subject for comedy as distressed heroes.

The most authoritative statement of the positive idea comes from the top of the social hierarchy, as Caesar explains why merit should be rewarded; he tells his court that the ability to write poetry is the most perfect faculty of the mind, the greatest crown of gentry (echoing Petrarch's oration on his coronation). Like a Renaissance prince he describes poetry's value in aristocratic terms, insisting that it should be "true born" and nursed with all science; then it can mold Rome and all her monuments in the "liquid marble of her lines" so that poetry stands fresh and miraculous, even after the buildings turn to dust. Poetry is the servant of power and creator of glory, a lasting fame. Poetry provokes admiration, for

> In her sweet streams shall our brave Roman spirits
> Chase and swim after death with their choice deeds
> Shining on their white shoulders; and therein
> Shall Tiber and our famous rivers fall
> With such attraction that th'ambitious line
> Of the round world shall to her center shrink,
> To hear their music.
>
> (V.i.25-31)

This affective power over our spirits will make Rome the ideal model, the spiritual center of the round world. Within Rome, Caesar is the great model, the "precedent," who gives inspiration, kindling fire in the poets. In a similar way, the court is the abstract Rome, where great men and great pomp stir up our following hopes. Julia, the emperor's daughter, is the inspiration of Ovid, the law of his life to whom he dedicates his poetry. Her spirit has entered his ear, and the expression of his devotion survives in his poetry, in his "eternal fame" that "through the world shall ever chant [his] name" (IV.vii.18-19; ix.68-73; ix.105-07; I.i.48-50).

If merit is not acknowledged the good poet feels righteous indignation, an amazed anger, as Virgil explains it in Act V, suggesting that virtue can be driven to such indignation when it is

135

"oppressed with the license of the time," so, like Jove's thunder, it controls the pride of base persons (V.iii.368-76). Jonson also speaks of this anger in the apologetical dialogue at the end of *Poetaster*,[30] explaining his indignation at parcel poets who give vent to base filth and offal, or whose work is mere theft like piracy on the high seas. They tax crimes that are their own or what their "foul thoughts" suggested to them, so in attacking others they show their own shameless characters. In contemplation of this, what more should he say than "turn stone with wonder!" (lines 60-68), and when the multitude of readers admire such trash in preference to the "most abstracted work" of a "free mind," like Jonson's no doubt, then he wishes to destroy his poems unread, to be silent.

> This 'tis that strikes me silent, seals my lips
> And apts me rather to sleep out my time,
> Than I would waste it in contemned strifes,
> With these vile Ibides, these unclean birds
> That make their mouths their clysters, and still purge
> From their hot entrails.

(216-21)

Thus in high disdain Jonson can still scourge his opponents, but he decides to rise a step higher in the poetical hierarchy. His next work will be a tragedy; but significantly its emotional effects will be about the same as for comedy, since he hopes it will strike some men with wonder, some with spite, and others with despair to imitate. Yet, like the true aristocrat of poetry, he will sing "high and aloof,/ Safe from the wolf's black jaw and the dull ass's hoof" (238-39).

The play affirms several times the ethical doctrine that merit is as valuable as wealth or rank, and, as usual in the humanist theology, merit is synonymous with knowledge — which tells us a lot about humanist ethics.[31] The emperor's daughter says that although social distinction may exist between high and low birth, "our minds are even yet" (IV.ix.8-9). Horace addresses the emperor forthrightly on the same point; "for my soul, it is as free as Caesar's," because knowledge is what makes equality of mind (V.i.85-90), and Caesar agrees that he should make no more difference between "great and good," merely on account of money

(V.i.97-98). Ovid says the same early in the play, that if men knew
the true difference between good and bad poets, they would admire
knowledge and dread far more "To be thought ignorant than be
known poor" (I.ii.240-52). Not that there is a wish to abolish social
classes. On the contrary, class distinction is necessary for poets if
they wish to be above the multitude. The leaders of society are
important to the poets because the poets want acknowledgement
from them of the aristocracy of letters. So writers like Horace who
know their own worth do not envy an even greater poet like Virgil;
all they expect is recognition of their place and protection from
irresponsible attack. In return they dignify the virtues of noble men,
inspiring emulation and love.

But when Albius, Tucca, and the parcel poet Crispinus try to
rise in the social scale by money and bluff, they must be ridiculed,
gagged, or sent away in a coach; and Crispinus and Demetrius must
learn their places in the poetical ranks. Crispinus, who gets the
severest treatment, is forced to purge himself of presumption,
plagiarism, and his grotesque diction, and then to take his place
amongst the lower ranks. This is the literal poetic justice that obtains
when an emperor follows the wise advice of men of literary merit.
In the case of Ovid and Julia, Caesar did not take wise advice, for he
condemned on a false report, taking the word of a spy. The actors,
already suborned by Tucca to produce plays attacking Horace and
his friends, are involved in this treachery from the first since they
told Lupus that they lent costumes and props to the banqueters.
Lupus, a fellow with adulterate brains who smells sedition in every
wind, interprets Ovid and Julia's banqueting revels to be some sort
of profanation or treason. "A crown and a scepter? This is good:
rebellion now?" He gathers lictors, men with fasces, half-pikes and
halberds, and he runs to warn the emperor — all while congratulat-
ing himself on his acumen: thank Jupiter who made Lupus so much
a politician!

Some historical background clarifies the role of such an informer. Since *Poetaster* was probably acted in the late spring or
early fall of 1601, it may have glanced at the circumstances of
Essex's rebellion. Spies kept the Privy Council in touch with

Jonson and Elizabethan Comedy

Essex's plans all along, and the actor Augustine Philips, a shareholder in the Chamberlain's Men, gave evidence before the lord chief justice that his company was paid to act *Richard II* on the day before that ill-planned and desperate uprising.[32] But the Essex affair was real treason, and it is hard to imagine that an informer misrepresented the importance of a play about the abdication and killing of Richard II. The meaning was all too obvious to everyone, and that is probably why it was thought to be effective propaganda for Essex's side. Jonson's own misfortunes following the performance of *The Isle of the Dogs* (written in collaboration with Nashe) supply more striking analogues to *Poetaster,* and they help us imagine Jonson's intent in Ovid and Julia's mock banquet. A professional spy, Richard Topcliffe, wrote to Robert Cecil in 1597 that a certain unnamed man "discovered to me that seditious play called *The Isle of Dogs.*"[33] On Topcliffe's advice, the Privy Council described the play as "mutinous" and "seditious matter."[34] Jonson and two other actors were imprisoned while Thomas Nashe fled to Yarmouth. Later Nashe objected that malicious men tried to find a "deep politic state meaning" in what contained no such thing. "Talk of a bear. Oh it is such a man that emblazons him in his arms, or a wolf, a fox, or a chameleon, any lordling whom they do not affect it is meant by."[35] Nashe complained that he mentions a rush, and the interpreters make it a reference to the emperor of Russia. This sort of foolishness brings to mind Lupus' interpretation of the emblem of a vulture and a wolf, in Act V of *Poetaster.* Lupus found it in Horace's room, and he thinks it is an eagle (Caesar).

More suggestive still are the remarks about the affair by Francis Meres, using an analogy with Roman history and the banishment of Ovid as well as the counsel of Virgil.

> As Actaeon was worried of his own hounds, so is Tom Nashe of his *Isle of Dogs.* Dogs were the death of Euripides, but be not disconsolate gallant young Juvenal, Linus, the son of Apollo died the same death. Yet God forbid that so brave a wit should so basely perish, thine are but paper dogs, neither is thy banishment like Ovid's, eternally to converse with the barbarous Getes. Therefore comfort thy self sweet Tom, with Cicero's return to Rome and with the counsel Aeneas gives to his sea beaten soldier.[36]

138

At the least, Meres' comment may very well have suggested some of the material for Jonson's play. Moreover, Jonson's hatred of informers such as Topcliffe was memorialized in Epigram lix, "On Spies," and in "Inviting a Friend to Supper" (lines 36-42). At Jonson's feast the assembled wits will read Virgil, Anacreon, and Horace's verses, sup "freely" but moderately; and to avoid Ovid's fate, they will have no professional informers around:

> we will have no Pooly or Parrot by;
> Nor shall our cups make guilty men.
> But at our parting, we will be as when
> We innocently met. No simple word,
> That shall be utter'd at our mirthful board
> Shall make us sad next morning, or affright
> The liberty that we'll enjoy tonight.[37]

In *Poetaster*, after the spies leave the stage, the audience sees the liberty enjoyed on the night of Ovid and Julia's banquet, when everyone comes dressed as a god. It is like a saturnalia with licensed mockery of things sacred and profane. It functions as an inverted tribute — the opposite of Vives' fanciful banquet of the gods where actors dressed as gods became more and more like their originals (i.e. the pantheon gathered to watch the play).[38] In *Poetaster* the revelers in effect de-god the originals. At the beginning, Gallus, dressed as Apollo, declares all pleasure lawful under Jupiter's "licentious goodness." Even though they have the names of gods, they are licensed to "speak no wiser than persons of baser titles, and to be nothing better than common men or women." In other words the costumes function differently from those in the masques at Cynthia's revels: there the assumed identity of a virtue enforced better behavior and symbolized potential good in the courtiers. Here the man under the mask asserts his character by a travesty of the god he represents. Apollo makes a special point about sexual license as well. No god has to keep himself more strictly to his goddess than an ordinary man does to his wife, and every lover can break loving oaths "as the heat of every ones blood, and the spirit of our nectar shall inspire."

Although that entertainment is a burlesque, it should be emphasized that it is largely "innocent mirth, and harmless pleasures bred of noble wit," as Horace describes it later. Jupiter is a lord of misrule, like the Prince of Purpool at the Inns of Court during the Christmas revels, or like the mock king who reigns over the country summer festivals. Suetonius tells that Augustus himself was rumored to have acted in such a saturnalia playing the role of Apollo. There is little reason to think the banquet in *Poetaster* is substantially different from Augustus' dinner of the twelve gods or the liberty of Jonson's poetical supper at the Mermaid. But Jonson has a difficult dramatic problem. On the one hand he must develop the social indecorum enough to give some justification for Caesar's wrath; his entry at the most embarrassing moment lends that plausibility. On the other hand Jonson must show the feast's essential moral innocence, so that Lupus' vile misinterpretation will be obvious. The liberty of a mock feast of the gods gives the playwright a chance to present both aspects at the same time, and burlesque which Homer found proper enough for the *Iliad* ought to be satisfactory for the court of Augustus. The charm of this sort of festivity is that it should always seem to be on the verge of overstepping the bounds of revelry, like Jonson's coarse but delightful Blessing of the King's Senses that so tickled old King James.[39]

Although multiple functions in a scene are the very life of drama, most critics of *Poetaster* see only one exaggerated aspect of the banquet scene — its "sacrilege" or sin and wantonness. Eugene Waith, for instance, finds the episode to be clear evidence of Ovid's bad morals and a justification of his banishment.[40] I do not discount this interpretation as if it were invented by Lupus himself, because the point at issue is one of emphasis, some elements to be given weight and others less. Since Caesar speaks judiciously about poets in the last act and is praised as the best emperor, most readers find it hard to see him mistaken earlier, especially since he refuses to admit his error or to forgive Ovid and Julia.

But we should pause to consider the special difficulties Jonson faced. The playwright's freedom was limited once he chose to dramatize Ovid's banishment. Historical fact was too well known for Caesar to relent or Ovid not to be exiled, and a major theme of the play is that poets are often judged falsely by the world. It is important that Ovid be recognized as a better poet than Crispinus and that he and Julia should be victims of false rumor. Neither the Elizabethans nor we know exactly why the historical Caesar banished Ovid; scholarly opinion in the Renaissance was divided and uncertain about the matter — perhaps Augustus misinterpreted some of Ovid's works, perhaps it was the licentiousness of *The Art of Love,* perhaps Ovid observed or took part in something embarrassing to Julia.[41] At any rate, the banquet scene represents Jonson's imaginative view of what might have happened if there had been love between Ovid and Julia. We must gather our impressions of the case from the play itself, for as a rule, external evidence in matters of interpretation shows the range of possible meanings, but it seldom, in itself, provides a discriminating reading of the text. If we can perceive the banquet as a delightful, licensed indiscretion fit for a private dinner, we may feel some of its dramatic force, and we can respond to the social injustice of Caesar's mistake. I think more attention to the text will show that Jonson took pains to suggest the basic innocence of the banquet itself and to control its potential blasphemy without removing it entirely. The scene lives in license and innocence.

After the opening declaration by Apollo, Tibullus underlines the liberty of their feast, remarking in jest "so, now we may play the fools by authority." Each part of the succeeding entertainment plays with the real-life implications of their words, as usual with such festivals, but the serious consequences are brushed off with a joke. Through the first section of dialogue the revelers laugh at the foolishness of Chloe and Albius, who hardly understand their parts of Venus and Vulcan, but they also restrain Tucca, playing Mars, from acting his part with Venus too literally. Julia and Ovid burlesque Juno and Jupiter wrangling like husband and wife; Juno chides the king of the gods turned into king of good fellows, much as Hal chides Falstaff in their mock king-and-prince play. She says Jupiter is a cuckold maker who has no fellow in wickedness.

This makes our poets, that know our profaneness, live as profane as we. By my god-head, Jupiter, I will join with all the other gods here,

bind thee hand and foot, throw thee down into earth, and make a poor
poet of thee, if thou abuse me thus. (IV.v.96-103)

Julia flirts with serious ideas about poetic theory: that poets look to
the gods for their models; poor poets like Ovid and Homer have
always known the awful truth of misconduct among kings and gods.
But in the topsy-turvy fun the revelers obscure any deeper meanings, as Jupiter says he will shake her out of Olympus into an oyster
boat for her scolding. She downs him with a joke about his nose,
playing on Ovidius Naso. When their mirth goes flat for a moment,
wine and song revive them, calling them

> To celebrate this feast of sense,
> As free from scandal as offense
> Here is beauty for the eye,
> For the ear sweet melody,
> Ambrosiac odors for the smell,
> Delicious nectar for the taste
> For the touch a lady's waist,
> Which doth all the rest excel.

(IV.v.192-99)

Not vicious debauchery, but a merry banquet of sense. Jupiter
continues the spoof with some waggish comments on the emperor's
beautiful and wanton daughter, to which Juno replies that her father
should not "suffer her to love the well-nosed poet." Rather he
should whip Ovid about the capitol "for soothing her in her
follies." At this moment Caesar bursts in with the rest of the court
and the informers.

Caesar's diatribe shows him not in full control of his feelings,
misled by false spies into a distorted view of the revels. This is the
first time he appears on stage, so we have no other impression save
his words and our memory of the historical Augustus. "Oh impious
sight," he cries, as he averts his eyes from the mock gods kneeling
to him. "The very thought [overturns] my soul with passion." He is
so wrought up that he would strike his daughter dead for the
supposed offense; she might as well be a strumpet for playing the
pageant, a degenerate monster in this company. As he interrogates
the others, his rage turns on the disgrace, the unseemly company for

Julia — a poet, a jeweler's wife, a citizen, and a captain; he knows the rest and he hates them all. He restates Julia's earlier jest, in a solemn form; that they profane the gods' dignities by thus counterfeiting those who should be images of virtue. People should understand virtue, "her unseen being and her excellence," and when they teach, they should "eternize her." Of course this is true, but it is not an appropriate response to the tone of the festivities. Since they were private, he cannot fairly say that the maskers suggest to the world by their mocking that the gods are but feigned, or that virtue is a painted thing.

As King Henry IV might have done to Falstaff if he had broken in on Hal and Jack's little play at the Boar's Head, Caesar in solemn exaggeration banishes "licentious" Naso from the court, for the "violent wrong" of "soothing the declined affections of our base daughter," and Caesar orders Julia locked in her chamber. The wise men around Caesar, Mecaenas and Horace, try to intervene on Ovid's behalf, asking Caesar to "forgive, be like the gods." "Let royal bounty . . . mediate." Later Caesar forgives Gallus and Tibullus, and he admits that Lupus is a "turbulent informer" (V.iii.17), but he argues that Ovid and Julia are without a shred of real goodness which could be redeemed by grace. The audience is in a position to disagree here, having seen that Julia and Ovid did not worship the "idol vice" and that they nowhere committed immoral acts. Neither did they do anything so serious as to rob travelers at Gadshill nor misuse the king's press. Moreover, Caesar insists on moral strictures that he has not followed himself, when he says

> I will prefer for knowledge none but such
> As rule their lives by it, and can becalm
> All sea of humor with the marble trident
> Of their strong spirits: others fight below
> With gnats and shadows, others nothing know.
>
> (IV.vi.74-78)

Clearly he has not ruled his humors with the trident of knowledge, and just as clearly Julia and Ovid are not devoid of virtue. Even though we do not like it, it is easier to justify King Hal's banishment of Falstaff than Caesar's exile of Ovid.[42]

143

Jonson and Elizabethan Comedy

The following three scenes emphasize the point for the audience. In scene vii Horace vehemently rebukes Lupus — an unworthy groom, the moth and scarab of the state, the bane of an empire, the dregs of a court. Is this the treason, this the dangerous plot that his "clamorous tongue so bellowed through the court"? Is this the way he and his wolvish train

> prey upon the life of innocent mirth
> And harmless pleasures bred of noble wit?
>
> (41-42)

Horace accuses Lupus of attempting to profit by blasting the fame of better men, for under the hypocritical mask of love for the sovereign, Lupus has endangered innocent lives,

> and pretending
> To be the props and columns of his safety,
> The guards unto his peace and his place,
> Disturb it most with . . . false lapwing cries.
>
> (50-53)

Mecaenas criticizes the spy just as severely, and glances at Caesar too:

> Princes that will but hear or give access
> To such officious spies can ne'r be safe:
> They take in poison with an open ear
> And free from danger become slaves to fear.
>
> (57-60)

These forthright accusations cannot be put aside as demonstrations of mere "disinterestedness and concern for the general welfare," nor do Horace and the other poets publicly disown Ovid as a reprobate. Jonson goes to great lengths to show the audience in the next two scenes that Ovid is not a "moral weakling," as one reader has described him.[43]

At the beginning of scene viii, it appears that Ovid might plunge into a melancholy decline, like Propertius when his beloved died. Both poets are "understanding" spirits (as Tibullus said of Propertius), but they feel excessive grief at "the common work of fate" (I.iii.65-66). Ovid, exiled from Julia and the court, almost

144

goes to pieces, but in the stress of parting he applies the principles of
true love and true poetry. By the end of scene ix he resolves that his
body may suffer but his soul will enjoy Julia, for he finds her image
in his heart. He will worship her there, and he regrets his dotage on
the follies of the flesh (IV.ix.107-09). As in his poetry his "name
shall live" and his "best part aspire" above death and poverty
(I.i.73-84), so his idealism in love gives him patience to persevere
against bad fortune. The social differences between him and the
emperor's daughter (represented by Julia on the balcony, Ovid
down in the garden) are too great to overcome, but the lovers can
maintain a spiritual love that lifts them above time and place. Their
whole debate amounts to an interpretation of Ovid's later poetry in
terms of the magic of Platonic theology, and since it has been
misunderstood, I will trace the thought in some detail.

Ovid enters the garden (scene viii) below Julia's window,
despondent, hoping to speak with her, to raise his "fainting
spirits." In soliloquy he doubts that he can live away from her and
the court. His love, although intensely sincere, is partly bound to the
flesh. Although her sacred sphere seems to comprehend all the
empire, it also restricts him like a conjurer of black spirits:

> As in a circle, a magician then
> Is safe against the spirit he excites,
> But out of it is subject to his rage,
> And loseth all the virtue of his art:
> So I, exil'd the circle of the court,
> Lose all the good gifts that in it I joy'd.

> (IV.viii.10-15)

He is scarcely more than a "heartless ghost" out of her physical
presence, and apparently he is not an entirely free spirit. His love is
like magic, but, at the moment, more like the lower magic of an
earthbound spirit than the higher magic compatible with a
philosophic mind.

Julia at first proposes to kill herself, since their fortunes are
insuperably divided although their "selves" are one, because she is
too high and he too low, although their "minds are even" (scene
ix). No place, duty, or power can come between them in death. The

145

form she holds in her soul will be made one substance, and the union of their spirits will prove that parents do not rule children's souls after death. In eternity there is no child nor father for they are freed from any temporal aspect. Ovid warns that after death her love would fade because a perfect soul has no affections: "we pour out our affections with our blood" when we die. Like the speaker in Donne's "Ecstacy," he recognizes that flesh and blood, whose quintessence is sense, in beauty, enables pure spirit to act in life. Love after death will exist only insubstantially as it does in dreams when the senses are locked up. Therefore, if Julia wants love, she must continue to live, in her high estate if necessary, and he will bear his low fortune patiently, rejoicing in her majesty. His is no mean-spirited argument.

Although now persuaded to live, Julia still complains of ugly necessity, and it is significant that she uses the same image of a swallow that Caesar used in his condemnation earlier — when he said that Ovid and Julia had no virtue in them (IV.vi.65-78).[44] She regrets that virtuous men must descend from their rightful, lofty sphere, into the common world where they must feed on what food is available in order to exist. Properly, they should fly high like eagles, and "with every stroke, blow stars in burning heaven," but necessity requires them to fly like swallows

> and with an eager plume,
> Pursue those objects, which none else can see,
> But seem to all the world the empty air.
> Thus thou (poor Ovid) and all virtuous men
> Must prey like swallows on invisible food;
> Pursuing flies or nothing.

(51-56)

In other words, poets without the support of Caesar's power or Mecaenas' money cannot fly high and aloof above the wolf's black jaw and the dull ass's hoof. They must find sustenance then in the invisible things of this world, just above the sordid earth. In the same way love itself must suffer under the oppression of existence, as Julia points out:

and thus love,
And every worldly fancy is transpos'd,
By worldly tyranny, to what plight it list.
Oh father, since thou gav'st me not my mind,
Strive not to rule it.

(56-60)

Because she must feel her own griefs, Julia ought to be allowed to enjoy her own pleasure; indeed, "virtuous love" was never disgraceful to a goddess. To symbolize their equality, she declares that although Ovid is exiled from the "officious court," he will enjoy her amply. She pours her breath, that is, her spirit, into his ears; and in spiritual ecstacy her soul kneels "beneath" him in her "prostrate love," kisses the earth that kisses his feet, even though her body stands on the balcony at its "proud height." Surely the audience is expected to recognize her exalted state of mind, but although Julia has reached a spiritual resolution, Ovid still struggles through the elaborate farewells, hesitations, and warnings of Caesar's approach. He knows they will die if Caesar finds them together, and he knows they must stay alive if only to enjoy the feelings of love. Yet the sight of her is enchanting — just as he was enchanted by poetry — and he admits its non-rational side.

I am mad with love.
There is no spirit under heaven that works
With such illusion: yet such witchcraft kill me,
Ere a sound mind without it save my life.

(99-102)

In his devotion he, too, worships the blessed place that holds his Julia and the loving air that encloses her body in its silken arms. But at this moment he pulls himself up, chiding his shallowness, as he transposes his feelings to the higher magic of an ideal love, a marriage of true minds.

Vain Ovid! kneel not to the place nor air;
She's in thy heart: rise then and worship there.
The truest wisdom silly men can have
Is dotage on the follies of their flesh.

(106-09)

147

And presumably he means this as sincerely as Astrophel does when he looks into his heart to find the idea of Stella, his true inspiration. Ovid's resolution establishes his high-mindedness, equal to Julia's, in the face of impossible social barriers. He knows that his proper place as a love poet would be in the court near his beloved, but failing that, even in exile he can maintain his integrity — his mind devoted to a wonderful idea.

Horace insists on a similar vigorous high-mindedness in his apology (added to the folio text, adapted from the original Horace's first satire, Book II). He realizes that there are loftier kinds of poetry than satire, praising Caesar's deeds for instance, but he cannot write that kind as well. He is a satirist by nature, and when his good name is attacked he will defend himself with his own weapons. The wolf uses his teeth, the bull his horns, the satiric poet his sharp verses. He is stoic about his fortune, even if exile might be brought upon him for his art:

> if to age I destined be,
> Or that quick death's black wings environ me;
> If rich or poor; at Rome, or fate command
> I shall be banish'd to some other land;
> What hue soever my whole state shall bear,
> I will write satires still in spite of fear.

(III.v.95-100)

Horace maintains this fearless integrity in the scene immediately following Ovid's farewell to Julia (V.i), when Caesar makes a slighting distinction between the social ranks of the poets, saying that Tibullus, Gallus, and Mecaenas, although they are higher ranked, are of the same profession as Virgil and may give an opinion of his work. Horace, who is poorest and likeliest to envy or detraction, may speak, too. Horace courteously but firmly replies that Caesar is less than wise in this remark, speaking in the manner of common men: as if poverty could sink as deep into a "knowing" soul as riches do in an ignorant one! A barren mind is made rotten by the "dung of damned riches" and it may sink beneath any villainous temptation. But "knowledge is the nectar" that keeps a perfect soul sweet in this world.

And for my soul, it is as free as Caesar's:
For what I know is due, I'll give to all.
He that detracts or envies virtuous merit,
Is still the covetous and the ignorant spirit.

(V.i.90-93)

The difference between Ovid and Horace, therefore, is a difference
of degree, not kind. Ovid has not quite the full confidence and
audacity of Horace; perhaps he has been indiscreet, and he has not
Horace's satirical weapons to fight his slanderers, but he knows
what is true poetry, his love is virtuous, and he comes to a resolution
worthy of a free spirit, devoted to his source of inspiration. Both
Horace and Ovid must practice their art like swallows winging just
over the earth, flying at invisible food, for their passions are
intimately involved in the kind of poetry they write. Virgil is the
only poet who rises like an eagle, far above the earth, invulnerable.

Virgil's admirers praise his merits in such glorious terms that
he stands as the Idea, and the qualities for which they value him are
those of Ovid and Horace made heroic. In his person he is a pure
spirit, refined from the tartarous moods of common men; he is as
clear and confident as Jove. His conception of perfection in poetry is
so high that he is dissatisfied with even his best writing — as if
fleshly pencils could never rightly depict his "mind's piece," his
fore-conceit. Nevertheless, his poems breathe the spirit of all useful
things, for he has labored with such judgment and distilled all
serious matters into his verse, truly "rammed with life." Consequently we can find passages in his poems applicable to all
circumstances. In Scaliger's terms, Virgil supplies us with all the
wisdom of Nature, distilled if not methodized. He is the very
Hercules of poets and his writings are the Idea of poetic art. One of
Jonson's other heroes, Francis Bacon, acknowledged the traditional
authority of Virgil, too, if grudgingly, "as certain critics are used to
say hyperbolically that if all sciences were lost they might be found
in Virgil."[45] Act V, scenes ii and iii, depict the importance of poets
by calling attention to this wisdom of Virgil.

It had been common practice since ancient times to consult the
Aeneid as an oracle for relevant passages on serious points, like the

149

custom of randomly opening the Bible in search of advice. God or Destiny chooses which divine words should apply to the occasion. This *Sortes Virgilianae* was still practiced in the seventeenth century, for instance, when Charles I looked in the Virgilian oracle in the Bodleian Library. In *Poetaster,* Virgil himself as well as his works betokens the higher magic, disclosing the guiding principles of life, commenting on the present, and divining the right path into the future. He represents the vatic power of poetry that Sidney had rated its highest function. Among Jonson's magicians Virgil is the ideal counterpart of Subtle, the fake alchemist. Subtle knows nothing but *Verba,* Virgil knows *Res;* Subtle deceives, Virgil enlightens; Subtle is after money, Virgil pursues the spirit.

From the first Caesar greets Virgil as an equal (although he would not allow his daughter to be equal to another poet).[46] He places Virgil on a chair higher than the imperial throne to read from the *Aeneid;* for virtue "without presumption" may take a place above the best of kings. Virgil objects that it is indecorous because "Poor virtue raised, high birth and wealth set under,/ Crosseth heav'ns courses and makes worldlings wonder" (33-34). But Caesar has the will to cross fortune in this matter, being endowed with reason which rectifies all disharmonies of fortune. Virgil therefore consents to sit in the elevated chair since by this symbolic act Caesar means to make unused goodness "shine proportioned to her worth."

The passage he reads from the *Aeneid,* although found where Caesar just chanced to open the book, turns out to be wisely prophetic, the episode in Book IV where Aeneas and Dido are driven by a storm into a cave. Here the prototype of Augustus succumbs to the charms of Dido, and from this encounter springs the multitude of false rumors about the lovers. Presumptuous rumor or fame

> dares attempt the skies, and stalking proud
> With feet on ground, her head doth pierce a cloud!
>
> (78-79)

Aroused by spite, with many eyes, ears, and mouths, rumor flies through the world.

> As covetous she is of tales and lies
> As prodigal of truth, this monster —
>
> (96-97)

At this moment Lupus and his crowd force their way into the presence chamber, crying treason — a striking parallel with the banquet scene when Lupus led Caesar in to discover supposed treason and impiety. Now by poetic divination Virgil has identified Lupus as a monster of false report, and this time Caesar understands, calling Lupus a "turbulent informer."

Horace and Mecaenas successfully expose this false report, and they mete out punishment in proportion to social status. The player Aesop needs must be whipped for his slanderous tongue in misrepresenting an emblem that Horace composed. What Lupus thought was an eagle is revealed to be a vulture, along with a wolf preying on an ass; hence Caesar decrees that his "fierce credulity" should be punished by making him wear ass's ears. Tucca, the jabbering captain, is simply gagged. In the momentary silence Virgil takes the opportunity to point the lesson, explaining the place of satire in the kingdom: it is not the sharp and wholesome morality or modest anger of satire that hurts the state,

> But the sinister application
> Of the malicious, ignorant, and base
> Interpreter, who will distort and strain
> The general scope and purpose of an author
> To his particular and private spleen.
>
> (140-44)

Once again, moral, intellectual, and social concerns appear together — malice, ignorance, and baseness define the enemies of poetry; just as virtue, knowledge, and noble wit belong to the true poets. The occasion has been spoiled for further appreciation of Virgil's prophetic lines, but Caesar allows some satirical "sports" to be played, some "noble mirth" in a mock trial, analogous to the mock feast of the gods.

The dramatic effectiveness of the final scene, the mock trial and punishment of Crispinus and Demetrius, along with the disposal of Tucca, Lupus, and Aesop, lies in its symbolic power and its economy. The scene has that specific pressure so typical of good dramatic writing, because it does several things at once: characterizing Crispinus' poetry as a "deal of filth" and crudities, exposing the envious motives of Demetrius, showing the appropriate poetic judgment that combines the social and literary modes, and all the while managing to be extremely funny. This is one of the few times to date that Jonson has succeeded in maintaining comic and didactic interests through an entire scene. Earlier plays had single speeches, like Thorello's address to Piso or characters such as Bobadilla in *Every Man in His Humor,* that were brilliantly made, and earlier plays had an occasional episode like Carlo Buffone's private drinking dialogue and the demystifying of the court lady in *Every Man out of His Humor,* that were well contrived, but Jonson's power to sustain significant laughter in his comedy of wonder came of age in *Poetaster.*

The witty purging of Crispinus reflects well upon Jonson's literary talents in another way, especially important because part of the play's artistic motive is Jonson's personal defense. The comedy as a whole neatly justifies his particular kind of imitation of classical models: it is a bold adaptation of pieces from Ovid and Horace (as well as from their lives), making them his own. He does indeed emulate the ancients, but is not enslaved by them, for he converts their "substance or riches . . . to his own use," imitating an excellent man, Horace, above the rest and following him until Jonson seems to grow the "very he," or so like him that the copy may be mistaken for the original.[47] Since he had been maligned for his translation and plagiarism, his defense openly uses some of the choicest flowers of Latin poets, drawing forth the best, turning it into honey and working it into one relish and savor. Whether or not the understanding audience was expected to know the sources, we now, with the aid of scholarly annotations, can see how remarkably faithful yet free he is in his treatment.

The final episode (V.iii) then seizes a device from Lucian's *Lexiphanes* and adapts it to this case by selecting dozens of ugly words from Marston's satires and interlacing the groups of regurgi-

tated words with coy little observations that intensify the vulgarity
but distance it just enough.

> Oh — *glibery* — *lubrical* — *defunct* — oh — . . .
> Oh, they came up easy. . . .
> Oh, I shall cast up my — *spurious* — *snotteries* — . . .
>   *chilblained* — oh — oh — *clumsy* —
> That *clumsy* stuck terribly.

The last heave of Crispinus' stomach produces the climactic
crudities:

> *Snarling gusts — quaking custard . . . oh — obstupefact.*

That is all the purgation necessary. leaving Horace the occasion to
prescribe a beneficial medication to follow: a strict and wholesome
diet of good conservative stylists. After a dinner of Cato's principles, he should suck Terence's phrases. He should avoid obscure
writers and foreign terms; the good, plain style allows the sense to
run before the words. If he follows this fair abstinence his verse will
be sound and clear, wearing the robe appropriate to his station.
Meanwhile Demetrius must don the fool's cap and coat. In short, as
their oath of good behavior declares, they will know their places and
not attack men whose merit transcends theirs.

Purgation and reform of poetasters allow the true poets to live
free of discord and scandal, above the flat groveling souls of the
multitude, being truly themselves. No doubt "Envy will dwell
where there is want of merit/ Though the deserving man should
crack his spirit" (624-25), but it is finally recognized that love and
respect among equal minds should always be renowned. What really
matters is the capacity to distinguish a free, noble mind from a low,
enslaved one. The end of *Poetaster,* therefore, fulfills Ovid's dream
expressed in the first act of the play, although by malice and
mischance Ovid himself cannot enjoy it in the court:

> When, would men learn but to distinguish spirits,
> And set true difference twixt those jaded wits
> That run a broken pace for common hire,
> And the high raptures of a happy Muse,

153

Borne on the wings of her immortal thought,
That kicks at earth with a disdainful heel
And beats at heaven's gates with her bright hooves;
They would not then with such distorted faces
And desperate censures stab at poesy.
They would admire bright knowledge and their minds
Should ne'r descend on so unworthy objects,
As gold or titles: they would dread far more
To be thought ignorant than be known poor.

(I.ii.240-56)

Admiration for poetical merit is expressed in aristocratic images that reveal social implications. A good poet shows his contempt for the jaded multitude by the curvets of his winged horse, smiting the earth with disdainful heel and aspiring to beat his hooves against the gates of heaven. But mounting higher he rejects the outward symbols of the social order — gold and titles — as well, in favor of the inward reward of transcendant thought. The aristocratic social order, therefore, is only less worthy of a writers's disdain than a democratic one. High rapture of bright knowledge seizes and claims as its own the man in his entirety.

In *Poetaster* Jonson had come a long way from his first experiments with comic wonder. He began by adapting the new theories of mixed comedy in his program for reform of manners, imitating the delightful and satiric methods of Lyly. *Every Man out of His Humor* was mainly a collection of sophisticated "jests," some out of Castiglione, ending with a sudden transformation under quasi-divine influence. In *Cynthia's Revels* he controlled his material better to define and extend the opposed forces, bringing the positive or admirable powers into the body of the play in scenes of instruction, rehearsal, and games, again out of Castiglione to some extent. For this reason *Cynthia's Revels* seems most like Elizabethan court comedy, with the mixture of gods, kings, and commoners learning their lessons under a wise monarch in earnest play. *Poetaster* still embattles the vices and virtues and still asks for our admiration of the highest conceptions, the Idea of a poet in Virgil, but Jonson modulated and differentiated the degrees of emanation from that Idea, as poets must modify their art to confront the actual world. Turning away from urbane jests and manuals for courtesy, he found new sources in the more problematic Latin poets as he mixed revelry and love and abused art in the social realities of Augustan Rome; and his use of Lucian in the luminously funny conclusion looks forward to his imaginative use of vulgarity in later comedies. It is no wonder that he was ready to try other things in the drama, for he had already outgrown the delicate instability of the Elizabethan mode. From now on, admiration would have its place mainly in his court masques, but that is another story.[48]

A new synthesis of his art was necessary when Jonson returned to comedy five years later. He had to shift comedy's focus from the court to the city and to reduce the social range of the cast, excluding the very top of the hierarchy. He needed actual places and the suggestion of actual language to represent men's appetites and illusions in a social milieu. He needed an integrated plot, generating from internal forces, to vex and sport with men's acquisitive motives. As the prologues to the revised *Every Man in His Humor* and *Volpone* make clear, admiration would not be relevant to this new urban comedy. Henceforth the audience is not so much to be wooed by embattled vices and virtues as to be laughed heartily out of their folly lest it turn into crime. The dramatist will present no marvels in his demystified comic world, and if the audience will confess their errors to themselves, he hopes they will be pleased not with monsters but with men. So the relationship between the play and the spectators will be less direct or rhetorical, without simple choices between contrasting moral figures; instead the "image of the times" will be equivocal, asking us to develop our powers of judgment with much less help from the playwright, as he entertains us with "quick comedy."

5.

Comic Language in "Volpone"

Good dramatic speech differs from ordinary talk when it has a certain economy, a packed intensity that exerts pressure in several ways at once to increase the audience's awareness of the drama. For example, an expository speech is essentially dead if it simply conveys information, but it comes alive in the play when it also suggests the character of the speaker, when it is delivered in a context that leads us to anticipate the reaction of the person spoken to, or when it thrusts the action forward into the future at the same time it fills in the past. This is the way Shakespeare creates the dramatic situation so quickly in the first forty lines of *Twelfth Night*. The information about Olivia's vow in grief at the death of her brother comes to the audience right after we have seen Orsino's self-indulgent "feeding" of his passion, and the facts are made lively and interesting because they contribute to the characterization and events at the moment they are explained. They function in that moment to augment Orsino's self-pity, encouraging his humor more than the music or the proposed hunt. In his love-melancholy he almost enjoys the bad news that Olivia will not see him or his messenger. His love thoughts are deliciously provoked by the news, for he plucks out its special meaning for himself.

> O, she that hath a heart of that fine frame
> To pay this debt of love but to a brother,
> How will she love, when the rich golden shaft

Hath killed the flock of all affections else
That live in her; when liver, brain, and heart,
These sovereign thrones, are all supplied and filled,
Her sweet perfections, with one self king!
Away before me to sweet beds of flowers;
Love-thoughts lie rich when canopied with bowers.

(I.i.34-42)

He thus meanders off stage, doing something, at least, that the proposed music and promised hunt could not make him do, even if it is only to lie in a bower of sweet flowers. The scene sets up a stereotype to be recalled and varied in later scenes: the dialogue culminates in the image of an enervated man in Illyria, the languishing world of lovers, a world that the witty, level-headed Viola enters.

A dramatist must create this sense of movement whereby each speech not only begets the next, but by repetition the next seems to look back upon and even out of the situation. It must fairly bristle with possibilities, causing us to expect future answers to present questions. Is the duke wooing Olivia in the best way? Does he deserve her? Is she perhaps a good deal like him, indulging her grief as he indulges his melancholy? In *Twelfth Night* the first speeches of the next scene pick up questions in a different but parallel situation, to suggest further questions. Although Viola has lost a brother, too, in the shipwreck, she sustains herself by a serene mind, unlike Olivia. The information about her brother's drowning and about the dangers in Illyria begets patience in her, equanimity that comes from stoic resolution, and she reaches an immediate, practical decision to serve the duke in disguise until the right time to reveal her identity. With the aid of another reference to music, the audience is encouraged, perhaps without being fully aware of it, to contrast her speech with Orsino's at the end of the previous scene. Instead of going to lie in a bower, Viola acts decisively, as she says,

For I can sing,
And speak to him in many sorts of music,
That will allow me very worth his service.
What else may hap to time I will commit,
Only shape thou thy silence to my wit.   (I.ii.56-60)

157

She can meet chance or ill fortune with a clear head and a bit of hope. Until she learns otherwise, she accepts things as they appear, so she believes the captain has an honest nature that corresponds to his fair face. She knows that often appearances are deceiving, but she takes his "fair behavior" on face value. In the same way she hopes for a fair chance to save her brother, but she knows that only chance saved her. There is a nice balance here of a bleak outlook and a resolute spirit that leads to productive action in a way that Orsino's speech did not. New questions then arise that must be dealt with in later scenes. Good dramatic speeches are the most immediately important parts of a play as they build the larger structure brick by brick. The way separate speeches are written so as to do things with people, emotions, and events is what gives them their essential dramatic quality.

The pressure of good dialogue becomes greater as a play develops complications, climaxes, revelations, and deliverance, but the same impulses are involved — those that thrust the action forward, generate double and triple functions, and repeat elements. Whether in comedy or tragedy, these mark the dialogue of a dramatic craftsman. In comedy, however, repetition is more important than the others. Kenneth Burke says that we perceive all artistic forms in the tissue of repetitions, but explicit repetition, taken to excess, is especially comic. What would happen in *Riders to the Sea,* an unremittingly gloomy play, if several of the sons' deaths were represented, the coffin carried on time after time, Moira and the girls keening time after time?[1] Comic effects would be hard to control if Hamlet ruminated on suicide every time he was left alone, because by the third or fourth soliloquy the audience would begin suspecting some added irony; they would become aware of the artificial pattern of each speech at the expense of the serious thought. Pattern is important for all dialogue, especially poetic dialogue, but as it approaches a predictable repetition, we feel crossed responses, and to reconcile them we search for other meanings. But of course, as Freud observed, repetition seemingly beyond funny coincidences can become frightening, and these uncanny happenings are common in the experience of obsessional neurotics.[2]

Language in "Volpone"

Our reaction to Molière's brilliant use of polite compliment illustrates the principle of comic repetition. If the *Misanthrope* is well acted, it does not take the audience long to get behind the social masks of Célimène, Philinte, Acaste, Clitandre, and the other polished talkers and to see that they use compliment to manipulate people and to allow them to say some true and witty things without permitting their listeners to take offense. Graceful compliment delivered properly is a supple instrument. Its almost predictable occurrence, finally, makes the slightly ludicrous and artificial vehicle especially delightful, for the fragile forms of polite society are made to express or at least partially contain "brittle malice," and impish, self-serving ends. Because Alceste will not play this game of society, he is too rude for polite company. This says something about society because Alceste has some high ideals, but it also casts an amusing light on him, for he cannot separate the sign from the thing signified. In fact, he is as preoccupied with the means of expression as Célimène, and Célimène is as frank as Alceste, in her way. Even though her manners are typical of the artificial society she lives in, we can enjoy her witty elevation above it. Alceste, however, lacks her self-awareness, and his pride in his sincerity is obsessional.

Moreover, in his most sincere speeches, in high dudgeon, there is a wisp of comedy that comes from habitual repetitions, a redundancy that Richard Wilbur manages to catch in his brilliant translation. For example,

> Did not truth, honor, decency, and the laws
> Oppose my enemy and approve my cause?
> My claims were justified in all men's sight;
> I put my trust in equity and right;
> Yet, to my horror and the world's disgrace,
> Justice is mocked, and I have lost my case![3]

It is the second line of a couplet that most often contains the repetition, and the closer it comes to the rime word, the funnier it seems: "rectitude and decency applaud!" "because I properly refused/ To flatter him, or see the truth abused."

Ben Jonson was especially skillful in his verbal repetitions, and his work offers many illustrations of their possibilities. Jonson exploits them to such an extent that speeches often seem prolix to readers, yet they are economical in their dramatic uses. Only a few examples are necessary to suggest their pervasiveness. Corbaccio repeatedly mishears Mosca's remarks about "dying" Volpone, and Corbaccio's all-consuming fears condition his responses — "What mends he?" "Not I his heir?" "How, how? stronger than he was wont?" (*Volpone,* I.iv). Kastril repeatedly uses terms from quarreling, even when he is ignorant of their meaning (*Alchemist,* IV.vii). Morose repeats orders to his servant — "Answer me not by speech but by silence, unless it be otherwise." Morose's constant, overblown exclamations are roared at the audience: "Oh! what villain! What prodigy of mankind is that?" "Oh, shut the door, shut the door." (*Epicoene,* II.ii). Justice Overdo reiterates his judgments of the "enormities" at Bartholomew Fair, as relentlessly as any outraged judge in a Victorian farce. To the end of his career, Jonson exploited opportunities for comic repetition, and his use of that device is probably one reason why Charles Dickens was interested in his plays.[4] Jonson has that same metonymy of character that Dickens achieved by depending on the reader's recollection of a repeated detail. For example, in *Our Mutual Friend* (chap. 4), after we have seen the beauteous Miss Bella Wilfer and her lovely shoulders a few times, Dickens can get a delicious effect with "in the Wilfer household, where a monotonous appearance of Dutch-cheese at ten o'clock in the evening has been rather frequently commented on by the dimpled shoulders of Miss Bella . . . ." Bobadill, Tucca, and Ananias receive this kind of reduction, too, in a single trick of speech. By the last act of *Alchemist* Jonson is sure to get a laugh, and perhaps some appreciation for his skill, from a series of mere fragments of speech, each absolutely perfect in its power to recall the speaker's whole dramatic and compulsive self.

> *Lovewit.* Gentlemen, what is the matter? Whom do you seek?
> *Mammon.* The chemical cozener.
> *Surly.*   And the captain pandar.
> *Kastril.* The nun my suster.
> *Mammon.*   Madam Rabbi.

Ananias.   Scorpions,
          And caterpillars.

Each is so imprisoned in his mode of speech that together the accusations sound ridiculously inconsistent. Again the repetition works in several ways, and almost formulaic speech does much of it.

An instructive test of this technique may be given to potentially painful and serious situations that Jonson renders comic, and *Volpone* lends itself to this test particularly well because many critics have doubted that it is really a comedy. Others come to its defense by suggesting that it is black comedy or comedy turning into satire or tragedy. I find both opinions misleading for they are based on too narrow a reading of certain speeches.

I. CORVINO'S COMIC ITERATIONS

The most intensely obsessed character in the play, Corvino, reacts in violent language to Celia's innocent glance out the window when she drops her handkerchief to Scoto. Meanwhile the audience sees the action in a larger frame of reference, knowing that there will be important consequences of her apparently harmless act, entangling her in Volpone's web of desire and provoking him more. In II.iv we have seen Volpone back at his palace, fresh from his masquerade as Scoto, crying out to Mosca that he has been wounded, devastatingly wounded, by Celia's eyes. He is possessed, too, and will do something about it more effectively than Corvino. But within the immediate scene that follows (II.v), given only what Corvino and Celia know, her husband reacts strangely. Should the audience consider his speeches with complete seriousness? His hideous jealousy, his moral degradation, loss of reasonable control, and almost fiendish cruelty could make him bestial in this bestial world. But Jonson takes pains here to insure that Corvino is as ludicrous as he is savage.

Corvino's reaction is ridiculously incompatible with what he saw happen. Celia simply stepped to the window, looked out, and tossed her handkerchief with some money to buy the medicine (she innocently thought). In return she was to be given a beauty powder. In Corvino's twisted imagination Scoto and his crew enacted a sexual intrigue, like Signor Flaminio trying to seduce Franciscina in the *commedia dell' arte*. The evidence before him clearly does not support his sudden, paranoiac conclusion, nor does our opinion of his wisdom rise because we know for a fact that he is accidentally correct in this case. His response is no more the sensible one than Sir Politic Would-be's predictable interpretation of the episode. In answer to the question, ''What should this mean, Sir Pol?'' he says, ''Some trick of state, believe it,'' and he will go home to protect himself from the design upon him. Pol thinks that all his letters may have been intercepted — his automatic response, his metonymic association.

Alone with Celia, Corvino raves like a madman, magnifying the details of the encounter. Hers are ''itching ears,'' Peregrine and Pol were ''old, unmarried, noted lechers,'' leering satyrs. She ''fanned her favors forth'' to give the ''hot spectators satisfaction.'' He imagines that she loves Scoto's copper rings, his saffron jewel ''with the toadstone in't.'' Surely he has a fixation on his approaching cuckoldry, for he repeatedly invites his simple wife to entertain the idea of ''mounting.''

> well, you shall have him, yes!
> He shall come home, and minister unto you
> The fricace for the mother. Or, let me see,
> I think you'd rather mount; would you not mount?
> Why, if you'll mount, you may; yes truly, you may.

He continues another twenty lines, speculating on how she will receive her lover, how Corvino will get revenge, killing her father, mother, brother, and all her family, and he imagines in remarkable detail and heavy accentual, alliterative verse how he will kill Celia. All because of a few glances.

> I should strike
> This steel into thee, with as many stabs
> As thou wert gazed upon with goatish eyes.

Celia repeatedly points out the absurdity of his judgment, but he lunges to more preposterous extremes.

Up to this moment, an actor could treat Corvino's jealousy seriously, uncomplicated by any other mood, but the next long speech must cause jealousy to topple into mad foolishness when he specifies the new restraints he will put on her. By comparison with his new decrees his earlier restraints seem liberal, and the repetition is obviously funny to us but not to him.

> First. I will have this bawdy light dammed up:
> And till't be done. some two or three yards off.
> I'll chalk a line. o'er which. if thou but chance
> To set thy desp'rate foot. more hell. more horror.
> More wild remorseless rage shall seize on thee.
> Than on a conjurer. that had heedless left
> His circle's safety ere his devil was laid.

He will lock a chastity belt on her, and he will keep her standing backwards.

> Thy lodging shall be backwards, thy walks backwards,
> Thy prospect — all be backwards, and no pleasure
> That thou shalt know, but backwards.
>
> (II.v.1-61)

She cannot even "snuff the air" of the "rank and sweaty" passerby, and if she so much as looks at the window, he will tear her apart — make an anatomy of her, dissect her body himself, and read a lecture on it "to the city and in public."

The effect of his exaggerated threats and prescriptions must be ridiculous, and Jonson has clearly signaled this to the actor and audience with absurd details like the "bawdy light" and her "desp'rate foot" over the asinine chalk line. As her offense was in showing her face, he insists on the nonsense of her lodging backwards, walking backwards, looking backwards, and enjoying her pleasures backwards. There may be a perverse suggestion in the last, that Corvino might enjoy his goatish pleasures backwards with her. At any rate, the grotesque image that caps the speech — his revenge for a glance — combines the comic and grotesque sadism of the man in an indissoluble union. He is impelled toward a public anatomy of his shame in an effort to save his honor and reputation!

Corvino habitually tries to persuade by threats so grotesque that they rebound upon him, exposing his ridiculous compulsions. Flaying and anatomizing her in public is not his only threat and exhibition; the most extreme comes later when he tries to push her into bed with Volpone.

> Be damned!
> Heart, I will drag thee hence home by the hair,
> Cry thee a strumpet through the streets; rip up
> Thy mouth, unto thine ears, and slit thy nose
> Like a raw rotchet. . . . Death! I will buy some slave,
> Whom I will kill, and bind thee to him alive,
> And at my window hang you forth, devising
> Some monstrous crime, which I, in capital letters,
> Will eat into thy flesh with aquafortis
> And burning corrosives, on this stubborn breast.
>
> (III.vii.95-105)

It is as if Corvino has designed an emblem or impress for himself here (as Volpone designed one for himself, "a fox/ Stretched on the earth with fine delusive sleights,/ Mocking a gaping crow" I.ii.94-96). In fact Corvino is the slave about to commit a monstrous crime, dramatically printed in capital letters with burning corrosive for us all to see. His favorite phrase is, suitably, "Be damned!"

The dramatic force of his speeches lies not just in the moment. They have built toward such an outrageous passion in order to make Mosca's interview with him (II.vi) more impressive. Mosca moves this man by doubly persuasive rhetoric to offer his beautiful young wife to Volpone, proving that Corvino's greed must be truly out of this world. Within the next hundred lines Mosca must turn Corvino's mind completely over and leave him prepared to urge his wife to do what he most feared she would do. The powerful words and feelings that cause this flip-flop surely reduce Corvino to a caricature, an instrument of Mosca's sport. The focal points of laughter in scene vi are precisely those details that recall Corvino's obsessive speeches a few minutes earlier, and they are punctuated by his exclamations and the "uncanny" repetitions. Scoto's oil is said to have brought Volpone to consciousness ("Death! that damned mountebank!"), his fricace helped the process ("Pox o' that fricace"), a group of physicians plan to use a young woman for a medical experiment ("Death to my hopes!"). A few minutes ago he declared that his wife's meddling with a quack was "Death of my honor," but now it is a "point of honor" to show that he is not jealous, and of course, he hopes to outwit the "covetous wretch," Doctor Lupo, who offered his virgin daughter for the experiment.[5]

Repetition of other details heightens our perception of Corvino's compulsion to act even though he contradicts himself. He had wanted to hang a chastity belt on Celia to make a circle of safety like the conjurer who tries to deal with the devil; now he will use his wife's body to conjure heat in Volpone, albeit Mosca assures him that the patient is so sick and so impotent that no "incantation can raise his spirit" in that long unused part. Whereas before, Corvino would stab everyone of Celia's relatives, now he will use her to "cut all the throats" of Volpone's clients. In a deeper sense, he is the compulsive husband as much now as before, when he directs Celia to put on her best clothes and choicest jewels:

> We are invited to a solemn feast
> At old Volpone's, where it shall appear
> How far I am free from jealousy or fear.

(II.vii.16-18)

His neurotic fear makes him vulnerable to precisely Mosca's kind of appeal, so he plays the clown, pretending to show his liberty when we know his bondage.

II. EXUBERANT SPEECH

Comic dialogue has other values aside from dramatic pressure and repetition, that are more independent of their representational use. They are intrinsic values especially important to comedy because individual speeches need to keep up a liveliness, a high-spirited sense of pleasure that is not expected in serious drama. Lyly, Congreve, and Oscar Wilde sustained that delicate excitement by a fusillade of wit. "It's a question that would puzzle an arithmetician . . . whether the Bible saves more souls in Westminster Abbey, or damns more in Westminster Hall," says Valentine in *Love for Love,* and no one is expected to answer; simply a clever observation, reflecting upon the interchangeable uses of religion, that leads to nothing else. In this sense the quip represents, vaguely, Valentine's pretended madness, a kind of extreme religious melancholy, used as a stalking horse from behind which he launches his witticisms, though the immediate pleasure of a clever antithesis like this outweighs its small dramatic function.

Some comic playwrights like George Bernard Shaw and Jonson, though they were witty men themselves, used formal repartee or facetious jests sparingly in their plays. Dryden considered this a defect of Jonson's art, for repartee, the very soul of conversation, is the "greatest grace of comedy." There may be "much acuteness in a thing well said; but there is more in a quick reply." [6] Dryden notwithstanding, it is possible to maintain a gayety in dialogue, at the same time avoiding the studied artificiality of wit, by exaggeration, mock pretentiousness, flattery, self-praise, brilliant over-simplifications, and all the tricks of the monologist. Verbal excitement in Shaw and Jonson does just that, without neat, balanced phrases or fine little ironies and arch whimsies that we associate with silvery laughter. Instead, they rely upon a flood of words, an energy of expression that seems to come from strong convictions. Since they do not write genteel comedy, the lack of wit should be no surprise; their more vital comedy needs greater force of expression.

In some characters like Zeal of the Land Busy, Ananias, Wasp, and Captain Tucca or like Shaw's Sergius, Ferrovius, Alfred Doolittle, and Mrs. Hushabye the flow of words is so impelled with energy that it suggests demonic possession. But more intelligent characters like Face, Mosca, and Truewit or Jack Tanner, Andrew Undershaft, and Captain Bluntschli use vigorous language as an instrument of power and assurance. Their dialogue has its appropriateness therefore, since it helps to depict the characters of confidence men, mockers, rogues, and supermen, who are above or outside conventional morality.[7] But its intrinsic vitality is its immediate force, its surplus value, which bribes the audience to accept their meaning for more than it may be really worth.

When Jonson spoke in his own voice, he habitually avoided high-flown style, preferring the astringent tone and precision of the plain style. He was different from Shaw, for in this mode Jonson usually steered away from superlatives or sweeping generalizations. But when he praised a great beauty or a great virtue, he could be more expansive, and when he depicted zany comic figures he gave freer play to his powers. It has long been recognized, for example, that Jonson was particularly disposed toward hyperbole in his middle comedies, with his ability to out-Marlowe Marlowe. After all, he coined the phrase "Marlowe's mighty line," and later in the century it was reported of "Mr. Marlowe . . . whose mighty lines Mr. Benjamin Johnson (a man sensible enough of his own abilities) was often heard to say, that they were examples fitter for admiration than for parallel."[8] Jonson did not try to equal Marlowe, but to turn his extravagance to comic use in such memorable passages as Sir Epicure Mammon's description of his sexual fantasies, making a parody of the heroic imagination. Indeed, hyperbole is generally pervasive in Jonson's plays and not confined to isolated examples.[9] It is especially interesting to see how, in terms of poetic theory, his comic style was related to the language of praise.

Jonson practiced formal praise seriously in his masques and poems, and there he distinguished praise from flattery, especially in the poems. Honest commendation called for the utmost scrupulousness on the part of the poet: 1) the contemplation of an ideal type, the idea of his subject that a man should live up to; 2) the establishment of the poet's true relation to the object of praise, his sincere feelings, and his lack of ulterior motives; 3) expression in restrained but dignified language, appropriate to the thing praised and accompanied by little unspoken compliments and apt analogies; 4) appeal to the literal truth, the actual subject, or the man himself. In the masques Jonson especially liked to insist on this last point, that the true perfection of someone's virtues was finally inexpressible; we must go beyond art to the real thing. In the presence of the king and queen all rhetoric seemed pale, all other loves to be imitations, as in *Love's Welcome at Bolsover*.

Conversely, flattery was for Jonson the worst poetic sin, and when a poet praised someone who was later revealed to be unworthy, he felt that he had betrayed his art. That is probably what disturbed him about the Essex-Somerset-Overbury affair, as much as his personal connection with Sir Thomas Overbury. His masque, *Hymenaei,* had praised the young earl and his wife for their "auspicious" marriage in 1606, but in 1612-13 the couple was involved in a scandal including divorce, adultery, and finally murder.[10] His only consolation was that such praise survives as a libel on the subject more than on the poet.[11] In the words of the epigram "To My Muse," the poet commits "fierce idolatry" to a great image when he praises a worthless lord. In contrition he expects his new muse will instruct him to write things "manly and not smelling parasite." Yet, a higher understanding of his art allows him to affirm the double-edged principle of laudatory poetry: "Who e'er is raised,/ For worth he has not, he is tax'd not praised" (Epigr. lxv). Flattery belongs to the parasite, praise and blame to the true poet.

The language of praise in *Volpone* has important connections with this poetic strategy, for the play shows how double-edged flattery and self-approbation can become the tissue of comic dialogue. The play smells of the parasite and things unmanly, as most audiences agree, but the playful use of flattery goes beyond Jonson's practice in the epigrams or masques.

In the early scenes, inflated dialogue generates rising expectations, and these thrust the action forward, as Volpone and Mosca reach for ever more daring achievements. They first seek only presents from the clients; then they lust for the most prized possession from two clients — Corbaccio's whole estate (getting him to disinherit his son) and Corvino's beautiful wife. After an unforeseen setback, they recover all by use of Voltore's talent for legal oratory. More daring than ever, they outdo themselves by the mock death of Volpone and by their delight in vexation of the disappointed heirs.

In this expanding scheme, the play's last act cannot be considered as tacked on so much as a culmination, a final outrageous yearning toward the ultimate practical joke. What started as a game of flattery and false hopes ends in a self-contained fantasy of vexation, the flatterers subverted by their own ruse and imprisoned by the self-serving and corrupt instruments of justice.

Skillful use of flattery moves this action forward, especially in the early scenes where the atmosphere is almost gay. We are first treated to an exhibition of hyperbolic congratulation in the exchanges between Mosca and Volpone. They are so terribly pleased with themselves and their clever fun that they fairly burst with exuberance in language abounding with words that suggest pleasure beyond ordinary experience. Volpone's favorite superlatives — *all, every, all things, any* — are set against the sweeping negatives — *no* and *nothing*. (Puttenham's *Art of English Poesy* describes such hyperbole as the "over-reacher" or "loud liar," and recommends it for praise, although still a figure of dissimulation that may have a false bottom.)[12] Volpone praises his possessions as "far transcending/ *All* style of joy in children, parents, friends,/ Or *any* other waking dream on earth." Money is a dumb god who "gives *all* men tongues," it can do nothing, "yet mak'st men do *all things*." It levels all distinctions, is an amalgam of all good — "virtue, fame, / Honor, and *all things* else," and whoever gets money has unlimited *virtus*, "He shall be noble, valiant, honest, wise . . . what he will." It is possible to read these speeches as profane prayer because of the sprinkling of religious images, but that interpretation emphasizes a moral tone that is not yet as prominent as the exuberant boasting. (Anyway, the rhetoric of praise always tended to use religious imagery.) What matters is the emphasis here on "delights" in free invention of one's conceit.

Volpone goes on to commend his sport in getting money, and his great negative catalogues help to build an impression of extraordinary vanity. He gains in

> No common way: I use *no* trade, *no* venture;
> I wound *no* earth with plough shares, fat *no* beasts

To feed the shambles; have *no* mills for iron,
Oil, corn, or men, to grind 'em into powder . . .

After a dozen more lines in the same vein by Mosca, Volpone
agrees that he "strikes truth in all." and so they proceed to set their
actions above the common way, leading them to a high gratification
of "all delights" (I.i.15-73).

In nearly every scene of the play, these two rogues puff each
other with repeated interjections like "my beloved Mosca," "right
Mosca," "thanks, kind Mosca," "good rascal," "loving Mosca,"
"excellent Mosca," "my divine Mosca," "exquisite Mosca,"
"Oh my fine devil," and "excellent varlet." "Thou art mine
honor, Mosca, and my pride. My joy, my tickling, my delight!"
(III.vii.68-69). Mosca returns the compliments with similar but
more modest praise of "your sweet nature," "sharp sir," along
with his corresponding self-denigrations. He tells his master that he
hopes to see Volpone lord of thousands more rich presents, and
when "I am lost in blended dust, and hundred such as I am, in
succession . . . You shall live still to delude these harpies." "My
patron" he says in mock gratitude.[13]

Their extravagant expressions of joy make indiscriminate use
of verbal formulas for praise, such a thicket of comparatives and
superlatives as *more than, better than, best, even brighter than,
most,* and *too.*

> More glad than is
> The teeming earth to see the longed for sun
> Peep through the horns of the celestial Ram,
> Am I to view thy splendor, darkening his.
>
> (I.i.3-6)

"Even hell, with thee to boot,/ Is made worth heaven." "Riches are
in fortune a greater good than wisdom is in nature." But in order to
outdo his praise of riches, Volpone goes one better:

> Yet, I glory
> More in the cunning purchase of my wealth
> Than in the glad possession.
>
> (I.i.30-32)

Subsequent speeches continue these intensifiers, as the confidence men jump from one success to an even more ambitious attempt.

> The Turk is not more sensual in his pleasures
> Than will Volpone. . .
> Why, this is better than rob churches, yet.
>
> (I.v.88-91)

All these exaggerations, like their preposterous games with the clients, tend to elevate the speakers' spirits, for "Good wits are greatest in extremities" (V.ii.6).

The verbal energies of Volpone and Mosca are powerful enough to carry them and the audience away so that we do not think very much about the moral implications. Flattering language therefore is one of the means by which Volpone "cockers up" both his genius and our pleasure in order to "live free to all delights" that fortune calls one to (I.i.71-72). It is typical, at the departure of each client, that Volpone should leave his restraint and confinement, to let himself go.

> Oh I shall burst:
> Let out my sides, let out my sides — . . .
> I cannot hold; good rascal, let me kiss thee:
> I never knew thee in so rare a humor.
>
> (I.iv.132-38)

These are cues to the audience as much as expressions of his gladness. "Thou hast today outgone thyself" (I.v.85), he exclaims. And at the moment before the last climax of the play, Mosca says nearly the same thing: "We cannot think to go beyond this," while Volpone exults,

> Oh more than if I had enjoyed the wench:
> The pleasure of all woman-kind's not like it.
>
> (V.ii.10-11)

So pleasure in tricks is a surrogate, superior indeed to normal sex, but not without homosexual implications.

Sometimes Volpone's alternating moods are signaled by language that hints at his helplessness without his "sweet" Mosca. Alone, he is quickly bored or depressed without the stimulation that

Mosca's tongue usually supplies. As he awaits his servant's return
with news of Celia, he is restless at the "wretched" long time it
takes (III.iii.1-2), and Lady Would-be's talk depresses him even
more. But as Mosca disposes of her, his "hopes" burst forth anew.

> My spirits are returned: I am alive
> And like your wanton gamester at primero
> Whose thought has whispered to him, "Not go less,"
> Methinks I lie and draw — for an encounter.
>
> (III.v.35-39)

Thus cockered up, he will not go for less than everything. When a
deeper depression comes upon him after the first trial, recalling that
he had a cramp while trying to lie still on the stretcher in court, he
imagines that some supernatural power struck him with a "dead"
palsy. His language picks up life, however, with a series of
intensifying words.

> Well, I must be merry
> And shake it off. A many of these fears
> Would put me into some villainous disease,
> Should they come thick upon me: I'll prevent 'em.
> Give me a bowl of lusty wine, to fright
> This humor from my heart. (*He drinks*) Hum, hum, hum.
> 'Tis almost gone already: I shall conquer.
> Any device, now, of rare, ingenious knavery
> That would possess me with a violent laughter,
> Would make me up again! (*Drinks again*) So, so, so, so.
> This heat is life; 'tis blood, by this time: Mosca!
>
> (V.i.8-17)

Wine, like words, sex, and ingenious knavery, brings a new
vitality.

Exuberant language also works on the willing victims, as
flattery raises their hopes, like pouring oil in their ears; so Mosca
says, "You know this hope is such a bait, it covers any hook"
(I.iv.134-35). By grand lists of things and by verbal bait, he creates
their ridiculous desires for greater and greater exclusive benefits. To
Voltore, he says "Only you of all the rest are [the one who]
commands his love" (I.iii.1-2). "All my hopes depend upon your

worship'' (I.ii.35-36). He lists the things he has done for Voltore, emphasizing *your* in each case.

> I am a man that have not done your love
> All the worst offices: here I wear your keys,
> See all your coffers and your caskets locked,
> Keep the poor inventory of your jewels,
> Your plate and monies, am your steward, sir,
> Husband your goods here.
>
> (I.ii.39-44)

A few minutes later he assures Corbaccio of his future success, in the same flurry of pronouns.

> Your cares, your watchings, and your many prayers,
> Your more than many gifts, your this day's present,
> And last produce your will.
>
> (I.iv.100-02)

Corbaccio is especially excited by the signs of decay in Volpone's flesh, and each item has its familiar intensifier: "his face drawn longer," "His mouth is ever gaping, and his eyelids hang," "A freezing numbness stiffens all his joints and makes the color of his flesh like lead," "a cold sweat with a continual rheum." Corbaccio responds with rising enthusiasm: "Good . . . tis good . . . good . . . excellent, excellent. Sure I shall outlast him. This makes me young again, a score of years" (I.iv.41-56). He fastens on the delusion of restored youth, but Volpone describes a moment later the real Corbaccio, by contrast, a man beyond all cares, maladies, and fear attending old age — no teeth, wracked with palsy and gout. He

> flatters his age,
> With confident belying it, hopes he may
> With charms, like Aeson, have his youth restored:
> And with these thoughts so battens, as if fate
> Would be as easily cheated on, as he,
> And all turns air.
>
> (I.iv.154-59)

We should take this remark in its context as pleasant ridicule of Corbaccio; it applies to Volpone himself only when the action becomes more serious.

Corvino is cockered up with similar promises, as Mosca tells him he is "most wished for," "How happy were you, if you knew it now!" (I.v.1-2), "He still calls on you, nothing but your name is in his mouth" (I.v.8-9). And in response to Mosca's assurances, Corvino is properly appreciative, again in pronouns.

> Grateful Mosca!
> Thou art my friend, my fellow, my companion,
> My partner, and thou shalt share in all my fortunes.
>
> (I.v.79-81)

Mosca's favorite linguistic device is the stupendous heap of words, an accumulation appropriate for a play about greed. In his use of this figure Jonson's cumulative style clearly emerges. It works by asymmetrical parallelism, repetition, climax, and a singular lack of subordination or connectives, aside from *and, but, or,* and *as.* Mosca has little desire to twist his way through a periodic sentence or to pause and suspend his thought long enough to make balanced phrases, in the manner of Lyly or Congreve's characters. Logical subordination and a sense of orderly deduction from premises seem foreign to this style, because the main impression must be of the restless energy and boundless high spirits that Mosca shares with his master and their victims. His description of Voltore's dreams of success illustrates the connection between exuberant style and high expectations. Voltore's thoughts, as he waits outside the bedroom, are depicted by an accumulation, sprinkled with the ultimate intensifiers, *last, all,* and *naught.*

> That this might be the last gift he should give;
> That this would fetch you; if you died today
> And gave him all, what he should be tomorrow;
> What large return would come of all his ventures;
> How he should worshiped be and reverenced;
> Ride with his furs and foot-cloths, waited on
> By herds of fools and clients; have clear way
> Made for his mule, as lettered as himself;
> Be called the great and learned advocate:
> And then concludes there's naught impossible.
>
> (I.ii.100-09)

Emphasis on his hopes comes from the frequent *would*'s and *should*'s and *might*'s. It builds with repeated *this*'s and *what*'s, along with palpable verbs, the reality almost in Voltore's grasp — *worshiped, reverenced, waited on,* and *have clear way made* — and it climaxes with the grand deification that naught's impossible.

Even when Mosca talks to himself (in his only soliloquy, III.i.1-32), he is carried away by enthusiasm and flattered by his opinion of his own cleverness, for success has made him wanton and his "prosperous parts . . . so spring and burgeon" that he imagines he can feel the whimsy in his blood. He is so limber that he feels like skipping out of his skin, as a snake does in spring. Like Corbaccio and Volpone, therefore, when he thinks of his cleverness he feels reborn. In the long speech that follows, Mosca praises himself as the ideal parasite, the divine, Neoplatonic model of the flatterer and self-server, and the anti-Virgilian artist, opposed to the archetype of the true poet that we saw in *The Poetaster*. The style of the passage displays all the features of the figure of accumulation, or the heaping figure, as Puttenham calls it, and it stands as a counterpart of Volpone's opening praise of gold and his cunning purchase of his wealth.

As in many laudatory poems, Mosca begins with his heavenly genealogy. The perfect parasite is "dropped from above, / Not bred 'mongst clods and clodpoles here on earth." Then he proceeds to a demonstration of the universal practice of his professional art, worthy to be a "science" — and this is surely the comic puff — "All the wise world is little else . . ./ But parasites or sub-parasites." Next he makes a long, negative catalog of the inferior kinds of parasites, which he is not: not men who have the "bare town art" with no house, no family, no care, and who make up scandal to "bait" the ears of their host; not men who bow and flatter, "echo my lord" and lick away the vermin on his jacket. Mosca caps his vainglorious hymn with the inflated definition of the true flatterer. Since his exuberant metaphors were usually associated with descriptions of the whimsical imagination that controlled the melancholy aberrations of men, we are expected to see his ideal parasite as imagination personified — moreover, imagination uncontrolled by judgment. It is the faculty that can rise and stoop almost at the same time (like Volpone's spirits, and Mosca's flattery that seems humble as it is self-serving), like an arrow shot through the air, nimble as a star, able to make sharp turns like a swallow in flight,

> and be here,
> And there, and here, and yonder, all at once;
> Present to any humor, all occasion;
> And change a visor swifter than a thought!
>
> (III.i.26-29)

He does not have to learn such deception, for he was born with the art, and he practices it "out of most excellent nature."

Mosca's self-praise is, of course, just, because he has extraordinary charm and ability to create illusion. But at the same time it is caricature, for there can be no doubt that his monologue delineates the great vice of praising, as Jonson calls it in *Discoveries* (lines 1586-1635). There Jonson describes flatterers in terms identical with Mosca's ideal parasite. The parasite with the "town art" flatters for his bread, praising all that "my oraculous Lord does or says, be it true or false." Jonson says that the flatterer invents tales that will please, "makes baits for his Lordship's ears," he shifts to any point of the compass, affirms and denies the same statement, fitting discourse to persons and occasions. (We should note how dangerously close this attribute of the flatterers comes to Jonson's favorite theory of decorum in language, that required fitting language to the audience and the subject.) Flatterers "praise my Lord's wine and the sauce he likes; observe the cook and bottle man, while they stand in my Lord's favor, speak for a pension for them, but pound them to dust upon my Lord's least distaste or change of his palate." The basic metaphor in Jonson's account suggests appetite — the flatterers and calumniators gather scraps of discourse and devour them at one table, utter them at another. They are like magpies or swallows who "picking up filth of the house . . . carry it to their nest (the Lord's ears) and oftentimes report the lies they have fained for what they have seen and heard."[14] Jonson concludes, "I know not truly which is worse, he that maligns all or that praises all. There is as great a vice in praising and as frequent as in detracting.'' Parasites specialize in lies and flattery, precisely Mosca's talents. Mosca's soliloquy praises those qualities which Jonson dispraises, and both use the same device, an accumulation. Mosca's speech, however, is different from the solemn pronouncements in *Discoveries*. It is especially lively because of his high spirits, and he tells us, in effect, that he thinks he can do anything now. The impression that the play has created suggests that this assurance is not far from the truth.

III. GORGEOUS SPEECH

Exuberant speech contributes to the play's force and high spirits, aiding characterization, moving the plot, raising a laugh at the right moment, and at times shadowing a lickerish and voracious undertone. But finally, I am less concerned with these internal functions of dramatic speech than with speech that affects the audience more than the actors — language more presentational than representational. Assuming as we do that style is the man, we have trouble getting the tone of certain passages in Elizabethan plays because we look for reflections of character in every passage, and when they cannot be found, we search for larger meanings in the subtext or in other concealed implications. The eager critic forgets that when a dramatist wishes the audience to glide over the depths, he can dazzle them with surface impressions. I think T. S. Eliot goes wrong when he pronounces Volpone's first five hundred lines to be "forced and flagitious bombast," although he admits that we do not know that it is vicious rhetoric "until we are able to review the whole play."[15] L. C. Knights and Edward Partridge come dangerously close to spoiling the gayety of the first scene when they "place" the dialogue in its full moral context, and their solemn and overserious thematic interpretations make the drama into almost a renovated morality play.[16] It is more appropriate to describe Jonson's method at the start as a way of provoking an audience, not necessarily with inverted rituals, stern morality, or "shocking and terrifying directness" (Eliot's phrase), but with pleasure, temptations, and charm mixed with various amounts of implied disapproval. As in much good comic writing, every passage need not fit the grand design of total meaning, for comedy needs a more relaxed, playful air, tempting spectators to enjoy and perhaps to give tacit assent to decadent but delightful release of inhibitions. In this way the audience tends to be implicated as it is drawn more into the fun, if only because sympathies have nowhere else to rest but with the exulting rogues and scoundrels.

These sustained effects come from comedies as different as Machiavelli's *Mandragola,* Molière's *Don Juan,* or Shaw's *Major Barbara,* but in Jonson's play high spirits at first predominate, and after the crisis we begin to feel more powerfully the disease of it all. Yet even to the end of the play, Jonson never entirely drops the superficial cleverness and the little absurdities — bits like the arbitrary but comically "just" punishments that are meted out by the court and the little touches like Corvino's thankfulness for his punishment: it is good to have his eyes beaten out with stinking fish and bruised fruit, for then he will not see his shame.[17] At the same time I acknowledge the presence of a dark undercurrent of feeling from the very beginning of the play. But how does Jonson modulate these responses in various parts of the play? A single-minded interest in moral or social themes will not answer the question.

Since drama is a temporal art and since the whole is never experienced directly at one moment, and especially in the theater since we cannot turn back to earlier episodes as the action pushes forward, an interpretation presupposing a stern and unremitting control of every part has considerable difficulty. If it is pressed too hard it is likely to distort our impressions of individual moments or of entire scenes. In parts of the play, Volpone's dialogue makes us take in the pleasure in a rush of words and inflated expectations, whose main appeal is superficial but real. Comedy especially needs many of these "surplus values" (to borrow Elder Olson's term), and the dangerous undertones must be controlled to get the right mixture in a system of developing responses. I have no intention of reverting to the study of isolated beauties of literature; I am just calling for a more sensitive concern for the distinct tone of scenes and of their potentially mixed effects on an audience.

The most brilliant and controversial example of this development of responses in *Volpone* is the scene of attempted rape. For critics cannot agree about the effects of its major passages. One critic admires the "splendors" of Volpone's speech to Celia, beginning "See, behold,/ What thou art queen of" (III.vii.188-89), as he shows her his collection of jewels.[18] But another thinks the song "Come my Celia, let us prove,/ While we can the sports of love" (lines 166-67) is too exquisite for lecherous Volpone, a breach of artistic decorum; the base use of the delicate song profaned the word "love."[19] A third critic urges that profanation is indeed what Jonson tried to get across: "If the song were less exquisite, the ironic effect would be that much less sharp."[20] He makes the most of the moral inversions in the episode, the obverse of true love and purity, although he denies that such emphasis detracts from the comedy. "Vile as Volpone's room is, it has its appeal. . . . [Volpone's] allusions to nature and mythology, taken alone, give the scene a glow of the sensuous, the dreamt-of, the impossible. Spoken to an unwilling young girl by a lecher, they bring the scene close to pathos. But however sensuously romantic and latently pathetic the scene seems to be, it remains comic." I agree, but we want to know how Jonson manages to do this in the face of his supposed moral earnestness. And I do not for a moment think the ironic elements here are especially sharp.

At the grossest extreme some readers find the whole seduction merely farcical, because otherwise they are overwhelmed by the moral implications. "How else is one to take the rape scene . . . and to endure Volpone's song to Celia at the moment when she is supposed to be in terror for what is to her dearer than life, unless one sees it as Harpo Marx in pursuit of the too simply innocent female?"[21] I want to discriminate better than that and to try to say why the scene remains comic and why the ironies are blurred amidst our developing responses. My method is to compare similar episodes involving the unwanted suitor, a familiar figure on the

179

Elizabethan stage, for Jonson's contemporaries made some of their best scenes out of unsuccessful wooing.

It appears to have been especially delightful to see a clod or a cad use all of his persuasive powers, including beautiful songs, only to be turned down by the innocent maiden. Apparently there were implicit in such scenes certain interesting conflicts between artful speech and natural feelings, suggesting the limits of a seducer's skill when the girl's heart is not naturally affected. Possibly the theater audience should be persuaded by the apparent richness of language, even though the maid is not. At any rate, the variety of ways in which the scenes were handled will show the choices that a dramatist had in the matter. No iron hand of convention ruled the stage; on the contrary, playwrights exercised their characteristic freedom in reshaping conventional material for their ends. First the convention of the "inappropriate" song.

In *Cymbeline,* Shakespeare uses one of his most exquisite songs in a ludicrous context, where none of the poetry rubs off on the wooer. The oafish Cloten woos Imogen in a morning serenade of "Hark, hark, the lark" (II.iii.19-27). In this case Shakespeare made the irony genuinely sharp, for the song is distinctly different from the man. Cloten has just come from an all-night gambling spree; he woos coldly and with vulgar innuendos: "If I could get this foolish Imogen, I should have gold enough" (ll. 7-9). He follows instructions to the letter: "I am advised to give her music o'mornings; they say it will penetrate. [*Enter Musicians*] Come on, tune. If you can penetrate her with your fingering, so; we'll try with tongue too. If none will do, let her remain; but I'll never give o'er." He obviously has little to do with the music except that he pays the piper, and he calls the tune in a calculating way, revealing what the song should be: "First, a very excellent good-conceited thing; after, a wonderful sweet air, with admirable rich words to it; and then let her consider." After the lyric, he dismisses the musicians peremptorily — and the ludicrous note is unquestionably here: "So, get you gone. If this penetrate, I will consider your music the better; if it do not, it is a vice in her ears, which horse-hairs and calf's-guts, nor the voice of unpaved eunuch to boot, can never amend." Bernard Shaw admired this passage as an example of the gayety of genius — that Shakespeare could see the ridiculous side of such a situation.[22]

The song is still beautiful, Imogen is still pure, although Cloten cannot appreciate either. His wooing is funny but still a menace to Imogen's safety, just as Iachimo's lovely description of Imogen and her chamber (in the scene just before the song) enchants us but menaces Imogen and Posthumous. Apparently, like the great Renaissance painters, Shakespeare did not hesitate to mix beauty with fear and folly in the same experience. (Rembrandt's *Rape of Ganymede* is an astonishing example of what I have in mind.) Going beyond mere irony, Cloten's song evokes a sense of how true passions should be expressed to Imogen, just as Caliban's description of Ariel's music tells less about Caliban than about the beauty of the music, since even this monster can be affected by it.

A more exaggerated and less bittersweet scene is found in Beaumont and Fletcher's *The Captain* (ca.1612), where the widow Lelia tries to seduce her father, who is disguised as a gallant. Meanwhile the basically good and noble Angelo watches from above, feeding his desiring eyes (IV.iv). Angelo illustrates a typical double response to the drama; he knows Lelia is a whore, but as he watches he is moved by her irresistible beauty. "I am made to be thus catched, past any redresss, with a thing I condemn too. I have read *Epictetus* twice over against the desire of these outward things, and still her face runs in my mind" (IV.iv.10-13).[23] Like Bonario, he breaks in at the critical moment, although as with Celia there is never any question that Lelia's old father will succumb. Her father is there to trap and to shame her, and only at the last minute Angelo prevents him from killing her. In this respect the scene outdoes Volpone's attempted rape of Celia, and the authors may very well have had something like Jonson's play in mind. The play emphasizes Lelia's power of enchantment and her degradation. Lelia presents a banquet of sense beginning with a table of sweetmeats; she follows with a delicate song "Come hither you that love, and hear me sing . . . with the power of my enchanting song." She offers the old man a strong drink to raise his blood, and when she still thinks he is her lover, she speaks ardently:

181

Then mouth to mouth will we walk up to bed,
And undress one another as we go;
Where both my treasures, body, and my soul
Are yours to be disposed of. . . .
And bring a thousand kisses on thy lips,
And I will rob thee of 'em, and yet leave
Thy lips as wealthy as they were before.

(IV.iv.117-20, 143-45)

Later, when she knows he is her father, she wants to take him anyway, but her language now is much less appealing and more matter-of-fact. "Though I know him now/ To be my father, never let me live/ If my lust do abate." This distinction of two styles possibly suggests that a fully moral awareness was not supposed to be in the forefront during her earlier passionate speeches. They were sensuously exciting and neurotically interesting, but after the discovery, spectators can feel all their degradation.

In *Two Gentlemen of Verona,* IV.ii, the cad Proteus addresses Sylvia in words that are enmeshed in an even more complicated and stagey situation. Sylvia knows Proteus is a false gentleman, and she remains wholly unmoved by his sweet song, "Who is Sylvia?" Coming from him, the song seems mere flattery, since Proteus not only has been unfaithful to his true and gentle friend, Valentine, he has deceived Julia as well. Sylvia says,

Return, return, and make thy love amends:
For me — by this pale queen of night I swear!
I am so far from granting thy request,
That I despise thee for thy wrongful suit.

(IV.ii.95-98)

Proteus is definitely not a true gentleman, but he loves something, perhaps the idea of a woman, when he contemplates Sylvia's picture. The implication is that this shadow of a woman in the picture corresponds to the spirit of his wronged Julia (see IV.iii), for Julia herself is another complicating figure in the presentation of the song. In disguise as a page, she hears everything, but the musician displeases her, he plays false, he grieves her very heartstring. Presumably the lyric enthralls only the audience. As in *Volpone* and

182

The Captain, a beautiful song, comes from the mouth of a seriously corrupt person, is addressed to an innocent, and is overheard by an injured third party. Something compellingly formal and theatrical derives from this use of song, and part of it seems to be its power to fetch an audience.

The second convention behind the scene in *Volpone* is the catalog of delights spoken by a rapturous but repulsive lover, probably a version of Beauty and the Beast.[24] It originated, for Elizabethans anyway, in two frequently imitated models from classical literature: Theocritus' Eleventh Idyl and the thirteenth book of Ovid's *Metamorphoses*. In his unfinished pastoral drama, *The Sad Shepherd,* Jonson patterned his rustic swineherd, Lorrell, directly upon Theocritus' Polyphemus, evoking the earthiness of the monster in love with a nymph. Lorrell praises the innocent girl he has imprisoned in a tree — "Deft mistress! Whiter than the cheese, new prest!/ Smoother than cream! and softer than the curds!" (II.ii.2-3). He brags of his wealth, what rent he gets, his large herds and pastures, swine, and cattle. Like Polyphemus he makes some explicit mention of his ugly face: "And though my na'se be camus'd, my lips thick,/ And my chin bristled! Pan, great Pan, was such!" (II.ii.7-8). His cows have a hundred udders for the pail; he has twenty swarms of bees, an aged oak, a broad beech, a chestnut, a swine "Whose skins I weare, to fend me fra the cold." At morning he puts his feet in the cool water, looks at himself to clear his pleasant eyes and plays his pipe; and still he wonders why she scorns him — for he has a badger's cub, two hedge hogs, and a ferret. But alas the maid rejects the swineherd in spite of his quaint and strangely ugly-beautiful appeal, devoid of moral inversions or sharp irony. It is finally alive because Lorrell's speech has an irreducible dramatic substance: it represents the swineherd almost lifted out of himself yet still imprisoned within his idiom. I think that is why Jonson so effectively transposes Theocritus' sweet-sour naiveté from Arcadian simplicity to the immediacy of English rural talk. The most obvious stylistic feature here, aside from the northern dialect, is its catalog of delights — Puttenham's "heaping figure." Rhetoric books especially recommended it to show earnestness; so in a dramatic character it signified intense feeling. But in this dramatic situation it also emerges as virtually an inventory of the wealth he offers the girl.

Christopher Marlowe imitated the Ovidian model, of course, in his catalog of delights for the "Passionate Shepherd to His Love," but more sensuously Ovidian and more pertinent to our scene is Ithamore's speech to the prostitute in *The Jew of Malta* (ca.1589-90). At first Ithamore sees himself as a poor Turk, a nobody, hardly a gentleman or one worthy of love. A few flattering comments by the pimp make him suspicious, but the sweet courtesan Bellamira need only say, "Welcome, sweet love" to open his flood of passion and words: "Sweet Bellamira, would I had my master's wealth for thy sake" (IV.ii.55), and again there is a connection between love and money.[25] When Ithamore lies in her lap, completely subjugated and hoodwinked, he cries out eloquently, imagining the delightful roles they will play together, not unlike Volpone's appeal to Celia to possess her in many disguises and fictional persons:

> I'll be thy Jason, thou my golden fleece.
> Where painted carpets o'er the meads are hurled,
> And Bacchus' vineyards overspread the world,
> Where woods and forests go in goodly green,
> I'll be Adonis; thou shalt be Love's queen.
> The meads, the orchards, and the primrose lanes,
> Instead of sedge and reed, bear sugar canes.
> Thou in those groves, by Dis above,
> Shalt live with me, and be my love.
>
> (IV.ii.90-98)

And as they go off to a banquet and to bed, Ithamore extends his mind to the ultimate Marlovian ecstasy:

> O, that ten thousand nights were put in one,
> That we might sleep seven years together afore we wake.
>
> (IV.ii.130-31)

As with Ovid's Cyclops, these speeches garnish the ugly situation with gorgeous words, but unlike Ovid's they have even less moral tinge. Marlowe was confident enough of the general impression of the scene between the whore and a bloody villain that he could set this rapture in the middle. In effect, he tempts the audience to participate in the licentious pleasure when we know full well what it means. Marlowe presents lechery, theft, and poisoning frankly for what they are, but who can resist the dream of ten thousand nights' joys compressed into one? It is as if Marlowe flaunts the aspect of drama that Plato most disliked — excitation of dangerous passions in the audience — and at the same time he gives them their correct names.

Perhaps it can be objected that *The Jew of Malta* is a freak — a savage farce T. S. Eliot called it — but a similar effect comes from Faustus' famous speech to the specter of Helen of Troy — "Is this the face that launched a thousand ships" — addressed to a demon. During his magnificent praise of Helen, Faustus kisses her, and in ecstatic language he describes his soul going out of him, a gorgeous foretaste of the suffering he will soon undergo. Examples like these abound in Elizabethan literature — for instance the hairy wild man, Bremo, woos the beautiful Amadine in the anonymous play *Mucedorus* (ca.1590), and Bremo suddenly breaks out with similar Ovidian language to express his feeling. Amidst the typical catalog of delights he sounds like a rural Volpone:

> Thou shalt be fed with quails and partridges,
> With blackbirds, larks, thrushes and nightingales.
> Thy drink shall be goats milk and crystal water,
> Distilled from the fountains and the clearest springs.
> And all the dainties that the woods afford,
> I'll freely give thee to obtain thy love.
>
> (IV.iii.32-37)[26]

In Book I of *The Faerie Queene* Satyrane shows that he is at least temporarily ennobled by the magic of a woman whose power mysteriously overcomes him; Comus expresses his wonder gorgeously when he first beholds the lady, in Milton's masque, and Satan outdoes himself when he first sees Eve. In other words, this is a stock situation for Elizabethans: whenever a male creature — be he natural, simple, or good, be he ugly, lustful, or absolutely evil — whenever he speaks passionately to a supremely beautiful woman, he must pull out all the stops and speak gorgeously, often in a catalog of delights.

To return to the example of Faustus, I assume that Marlowe expected his audience to appreciate the sensuous beauties in such passages, partly for their own sake, partly as a display of his poetic talents; but finally his method is more dramatic and is necessary for poetic drama. The way he does it, spectators can feel some emotional counterweight for what is said and done. Intense emotion is projected in words, and for the moment it blots out almost everything else and has its own claim on our attention. W. B. Yeats probably refers to this quality of dramatic art in his essay on "Emotion of Multitude."[27] And I think good dramatic speech, like this, has to convey feeling more or less solidly, without much intervention of moral judgment. An example of the distinctly undramatic use of seductive language may be seen clearly in Andrew Marvell's "Upon Appelton House": the smooth-tongued nun's tempting speech to Isabel Thwaites, asking her to renounce her lover in favor of the cloister. It is a lurid piece of writing, completely fraudulent because Marvell seems afraid that the speech might convince his readers, as it did Isabel, and he insists that readers see the ill counsel and false enchantment exactly as William Fairfax saw it. In drama, on the other hand, gorgeous, seductive speech usually depicts the response to a woman's magic beauty, and it invites the audience to enjoy, tempting us to be emotionally implicated.

If this conclusion is correct, I can return to *Volpone* with a little more confidence. Jonson would have blundered indeed had Volpone spoken anything less than gorgeously, and what would we think if the magnifico who can play the dying man or the mountebank cannot play the lover as well? In a drama where just about everyone has been "gaping" — gaping and hungering for delights — the audience must not be cheated from some contemplation of exotic and stolen pleasures.[28] The main appeal must be to our gratifications:

> Thy baths shall be the juice of July-flowers,
> Spirit of roses and of violets,
> The milk of unicorns and panther's breath
> Gathered in bags and mixed with Cretan wines.

(III.vii.213-16)

186

Celia's pious but helpless interjections, like Amadine's in *Mucedorus* and like the Father's in *The Captain,* seem to stir Volpone's blood, but at the same time they prevent an audience from exculpating themselves from unknowingly enjoying these pleasures. They know that Celia is innocent, but they will not forego the vicarious enjoyment, and the way Jonson has set up the emotional appeal, the better poetry and passion is on the side of the ravisher, not the maiden.

By his imagined mythical roles, Volpone indulges his fantasy, as he rivals the desires of exuberant rakes of Restoration comedy — Dorimant, Wildblood, and Horner — although he is denied their gratifications and he gets his pleasure only in contemplation of it. He thinks about artful masquerades designed to heighten his jaded taste. He will first take her in roles of ancient gods and heroes, but also in "more modern forms".

> Attired like some sprightly dame of France,
> Brave Tuscan lady, or proud Spanish beauty;
> Sometimes unto the Persian Sophy's wife
> Or the Grand Signor's mistress; and, for change,
> To one of our most artful courtesans
> Or some quick Negro or cold Russian;
> And I will meet thee in as many shapes.
>
> (III.vii.226-33)

He imagines the effect experienced by such lovers, whose very souls go out of their bodies in an ecstasy. Here, unlike Faustus, he uses ecstasy probably as a metaphor for orgasm, but he still keeps up the appearance of high-flying idealism:

> we may so transfuse our wandring souls,
> Out at our lips and score up sums of pleasures,
> That the curious shall not know, [Sings]
> How to tell them, as they flow;
> And the envious, when they find
> What their number is, be pined.
>
> (III.vii.234-39)

His catalog of delights apparently unending, Volpone varies the asymmetrical but parallel phrases, and culminates with one periodic sentence, intensified by the grammatical pattern *so . . . that*: "We may *so* transfuse our . . . souls . . . *that* the curious shall not." The whole speech is finally rolled into one hyperbolic ball, one compressed, momentary effect in the song, typical of the play, as Volpone promises that curious people could not count the pleasures and the envious would pine. The emphasis on "counting" and on "pining" of course has overtones associated with the longing, yearning, acquisitive desires that are never satisfied in the play, but let us not substitute the overtones for the melody itself.

As I have tried to suggest, Volpone's appeal to Celia exploits the rhetoric of praise, and by this time in the play he has convinced the audience that he and Mosca can do just about anything with their Protean rhetoric, because they have succeeded so well before and because this language overwhelms. We have complete confidence in Volpone's, as we must in Richard III's, power of persuasion. And Richard expressed the same supreme assurance.

> I'll play the orator as well as Nestor,
> Deceive more slyly than Ulysses could,
> And, like a Sinon, take another Troy.
> I can add colors to the chameleon,
> Change shapes with Proteus for advantages,
> And set the murderous Machiavel to school.
>
> (*3 Henry VI,* III.ii.188-93)

The dialogue between Volpone and Celia develops by debater's arguments and rejoinders, as Volpone plays the orator and treats her to his entire repertoire, always responding chameleonlike to her innocent appeals. When she deplores her husband's shamelessness in selling his honor for money (III.vii.134-38), he twists that to his advantage, for it shows how low a mind Corvino has — that he would sell "his part of paradise/ For ready money." Then Volpone flatters her beauty, that it transforms him from a sick to a vigorous man — "thy beauty's miracle" and "thy great work" that has raised him in several shapes, only this morning as a mountebank. In tribute to her beauty he would contend with blue Proteus of the horned flood by varying his "figures." Thus ends the puff of the lady's worth.

He takes her instinctive recoil as a sign that she questions his sexual potency (line 154), so next he praises his own virility, describing how hot, high, and jovial he can be, as when in earlier years he had acted young Antinous in a play and attracted the eyes and ears of the ladies present. That self-flattering appeal leads directly to the invitation itself, conveyed by the first part of the song from Catullus: "Come my Celia, let us prove,/ While we can, the sports of love." As Jonson adapts it, it is an elegant, beguiling defense of stolen love, secret passion, and sweet thefts; distinct from the wistful transience in Catullus.

Her response is to accuse herself, her beauty that caused such lust to break out; "Some serene blast me or dire lightning strike/ This my offending face" (184-85). Either Volpone does not hear her or he misinterprets her assumption of guilt as more discontent with Corvino, for he replies with a long speech to buoy up her spirits, showing how "worthy" a lover he will be instead of her base husband. Behold the wealth that she will be queen of and the rich pleasures it will buy! When she rejects the implied bribe, saying that her pleasure is in her innocence, Volpone still thinks he can move her with words. Conscience is a beggar's virtue, but if she has wisdom she should listen to him. And he promises her the most fantastic and exquisite sensual pleasures.

He is ready to drop the rhetoric and turn to direct action, however, after Celia innocently offers to pray for him and to report him publicly to be virtuous. The outrage! That anyone should think him impotent! He has played with opportunity too long, when he should have raped her at the start and parleyed after. As he leaps on her, Bonario leaps from his hiding place to save her from the foul ravisher.

The titillation of the preceding speeches may result from the delays themselves, holding the audience's expectation in abeyance while Volpone talks of love rather than acts, but the words substitute for acts that could not be performed on stage. The gorgeous speeches are surrogates for supposed pleasure, all a heap of fantastic metaphors and masks for Volpone's yearnings in the presence of innocent, helpless beauty. They are a bribe to the audience to accept less than the real thing. They lack the simple desperation of the gentleman of Verona; they are completely different from the vulgar ineptness of Cloten, or from the heavy moral placing in the speech by Marvell's nun. The innocent monster, Polyphemus, never dreamed like this, and the hungry Ithamore did not defer his gratification by unnecessary play. In the largest sense, therefore, the surplus values have a use in Jonson's drama, for Volpone is taken in by his own rhetoric, by the conceits that flatter him to talk of incredible delights and personal attractions when he should be enjoying things at hand.

The use of exotic metaphor, simile, and masquerade go together in these speeches, ostensibly to insinuate into the mind of Celia:

> Whilst we, in changed shapes, act Ovid's tales,
> Thou like Europa now and I like Jove,
> Then I like Mars, and thou like Erycine.

(III.vii.221-23)

Having a resolved soul, Celia resists the blandishment, but perhaps he and the auditors do not. This effect of distorted or deceiving metaphor apparently interested Jonson more than most playwrights, and its importance has been overlooked. It may be the most original part of Jonson's handling of the conventional appeal by the loathsome lover. The curious allegorical character Miles Metaphor in *A Tale of a Tub* (1633) suggests some primitive connections between metaphor and disguise, just as metaphorical language was thought of as lying or deceptive language. Miles "insinuates" with a court official to "fetch" him off with rhetoric and to steal his uniform (I.v.49-51). Then in stolen disguise Miles tries "by metaphor" to steal the girl everyone wants. When he fails, he is "beaten to an allegory," and he returns to his master to lead him "by the nose with . . . new promises/ And fatted with supposes of fine hopes" (III.vii.78-79) — precisely the method of Mosca and Volpone, although they are much more skillful than poor Miles. "By metaphor" therefore means by pretense, by disguises, or in Elizabethan English by suppose. And if the suppose is "untrue," it deceives the mind.

Language in "Volpone"

Implying the neoclassic distinction between true and false metaphor, Jonson alludes to this process of the transformation of a person's mind when he describes Carlo Buffone in *Every Man out of His Humor* as a "public, scurrilous, and profane jester, that more swift than Circe, with absurd similes will transform any person into deformity" (Dramatis Personae, ll. 25-27). Whatever comes within the reach of his eye "is turned into all manner of variety by his adulterate similes" (Induction, ll. 362-64). He confounds with his similes (II.i.10), his "stabbing similes" (IV.iv.114). Moreover, Jonson illustrates how the humorous man's overactive imagination can be "poisoned with a simile," if he is susceptible as is Master Kitely, causing him to have "extreme conceits" (*Every Man in His Humor,* IV.viii.31-35). All Kitely hears is a "suppose" that the "good warm clothes" he is wearing "might be poison'd for anything he knows." Consequently, either the speaker of the distorted supposes or the hearer may change nature by extreme conceits.

I am suggesting that much of Volpone's game is a bundle of extreme conceits and that he and Mosca are poisoning the minds of their already susceptible victims with "supposes" and "fine hopes." Then, at the first major crisis of the play, self-deception begins to get the upper hand as Volpone's vainglorious words and the images of his fantastic hopes increase near the end of the seduction scene. He seems to strain for more powerful means of persuasion, counteracting the vitality of the temptation itself. And surely most members of the audience agree with Bonario's final assessment of the situation, conventional though it may be: Volpone is a "foul ravisher" and "libidinous swine"; the gold and jewels he offers Celia are his idol; the house is a den of villainy. It seemed for a few splendid moments to be something more, but now Volpone has been "unmasked, unspirited, undone."

When art fails, force and chance take over, throwing events into the lap of providence and starting the machinery of a formal close. Jonson's play probably seems more serious at the end than others of this kind mainly because he dared to start the wheels of comic justice much earlier, having confidence that he could, with

191

turns and counterturns and with more exuberant rhetoric, revive the spirit of mirth again before an inexorable catastrophe. The rogue and the comic artist make a seemingly self-contained and self-generating world of tempting fantasy that we must participate in, although we may finally acknowledge its essential ugliness.

At first we may not see Mosca and Volpone's exuberant style in its true light, and by the end (or as Eliot said, when we can "review the whole play") we may recognize to some degree its vicious rhetoric, when the speakers begin to cramp and sweat (V.i.5; ii.37,98). In Jonson's words from *Discoveries*, "vicious language is vast and gaping, swelling and irregular" (ll. 2047-48); when it lacks well-joining and cementing it is "rough, wrinkled, gaping, or chapt" (l. 2071). Like flattery from false counselors, it prostitutes the mind (l. 1090). The man who uses it dishonors himself (l. 1607), and the man who responds to it demonstrates his impotency and marks his weakness (l. 1622). But had Jonson followed his moral theory of style literally, he would never have given us perpetual delight in his comedy of *Volpone*.

6.

The Illusion of Completeness

It is hard to explain the characteristic design of Jonson's four best plays — *Volpone* (1606), *Epicoene* (1609), *The Alchemist* (1610), and *Bartholomew Fair* (1614) — because they are not only very different from each other but they are so complex that no single pattern accounts for their form. Nevertheless we feel that something about the way that *Epicoene* and *The Alchemist* unfold distinguishes them and casts light on the incipient form of the first and the residual form of the last. Some great motive generates their plots; some daemon controls their design. Apparently Jonson discovered a better way of writing comedies as he worked on *Volpone,* and part of it may be related to that primitive sense of metaphor mentioned in the last chapter, whereby cunning men use language to disguise thought or put on a "suppose." Their insinuating speeches deceive impressionable people by playing upon base impulses, but they delight the rest of us. Certainly Jonson has his characters use such two-valued persuasive speech again and again in the plays that followed *Volpone,* speech that praises what it secretly disparages (like Truewit in praise of cosmetics, *Epicoene* I.i, or Face transparently praising Dapper and Drugger, *Alchemist* I.ii, iii, or Busy hypocritically urging a sanctified consumption of pig, *B.F.* I.vi), and speech that dispraises while it entertains us with the whole subject, (Truewit against marriage, II.ii, and Overdo against bottle ale and tobacco, II.vi). Certainly tricksters use language like this, so it

193

would be natural for dialogue in plays about confidence games, but, as we saw, this way of using dramatic speech is not peculiar to Jonson. In any case, such two-valued dialogue creates local more often than general effects.

Another motive toward design, also found in dialogue, has more than local effects. It is the impulse to amplify or expatiate on a subject to the limits of endurance. At first it takes root in scenes of vexation — for instance when Lady Would-be visits Volpone (III.iv). Finding him ill, in bed, a captive audience, she drowns him in a flood of words, in "a very torrent," as she prescribes medicine and discourses on all the arts of a modern educated woman. Like the noise of bells in time of plague, her everlasting voice inflicts real pain on Volpone when he pretends to be in pain for other reasons. So they talk at cross purposes, he complaining of her and she commiserating with him for the very pain that she gives. It is one of those comic ironies that Jonson liked so much, when the cozener is accidentally cozened and the pretense is suddenly very real. It is odd but true that amplitude of speech turns out to be highly efficient, because the audience sees its operation from a wider perspective than the speakers do. The energy of this prolific talk is present in greater and greater quantities as Jonson worked on his next comedies, and it seems to press the episodes to their limits of fullness, so much as to take over the design of the plays themselves. Speech, scene, and play take on the form of an anatomy, which exhausts as it examines serially all the parts of a limited subject.

The discussion that follows will focus briefly on the meaning and rhetoric of the anatomy that aimed to give the impression of completeness and literal exhaustion. Examples of that kind of completeness will be drawn mainly from the two central plays, *Epicoene* and *The Alchemist,* to show how their design is different from the copiousness of Elizabethan comedies. I will finally try to suggest what might have been Jonson's and his audience's attitudes toward the device. Since I have already said much about speech and scene in *Volpone* and since Jonson did not amplify as relentlessly in that play as in those that followed, there is less need to say more about it. I will not comment on *Bartholomew Fair* here, because, although it has some of the signs of serial development that I see in *The Alchemist* and *Epicoene,* its impact is so different as to require a separate consideration, which will take up the next chapter.

I. THE RHETORIC OF COMPLETENESS

Renaissance writers had valued copiousness highly for a long time, copious style as well as copious invention and organization. Erasmus recommended that school boys learn to take a statement like "Good morning" or "Your letter has delighted me very much," and amplify it two, three, four, even a hundred and fifty ways, and teachers set students to exercises in dilation of a pithy saying — expanding it to four times its size. Nowadays most composition teachers loathe verbosity and love Strunk and White's rule thirteen, "Omit needless words." Then, a teacher wanted verbal exuberance that called for maximum use of figures, synonyms, puns, and mannered phrases. Copious matter for argument was found by searching the places of invention; so one learned to amplify a subject by thinking of all that might be said about it under sixteen or more headings, of definition, cause, effect, contraries, contradictories, comparison, and so forth. Good composition, moreover, had to be fully fleshed with varied examples, heaped and enlarged with detail.[1]

Copiousness worked well because it persuaded better, not necessarily informing but moving auditors. Again, Erasmus demonstrated effective writing in a famous passage (from Quintilian) where he showed how to amplify a simple statement:

> If someone should say that a city was captured he doubtless comprehends in that general statement everything that attends such fortune, but if you develop what is implicit in the one word, flames will appear pouring through homes and temples; the crash of falling buildings will be heard, and one indefinable sound of diverse outcries; some will be seen in bewildered flight, others clinging in the last embrace of their relatives; there will be the wailing of infants and women, old people cruelly preserved by fate till that day, the pillaging of profane and sacred objects, the running about of those carrying off booty and those seeking it, the prisoners in chains before their captors,

195

and the mother struggling to keep her infant and fighting among the victors wherever there is greater plunder.[2]

None of these details is a fact; all are "fained" for effects upon an audience as a story teller or dramatist might do it.

As we should expect, these assumptions about writing fostered a sense of literary design somewhat different from our conception of organic form. Selectivity and economy rated lower than fluency and variety. Originality gave way to conventionality and to received moral truths that were appropriate for a subject. In fact the age was characterized by inclusive forms, encyclopedic works, sonnet sequences, collections like *Mirror for Magistrates, The Book of Martyrs,* and Shakespeare's cycle of history plays. The desire was to see how much could be compassed within a work by copious invention and variation, and ancient texts seemed to offer authority for such a purpose. Commentators on Homer and Virgil found all the world's learning somehow implicit in the epics; Macrobius did the same with only the *Dream of Scipio*; so why should not Spenser try to comprehend as much as possible in his major poem, to represent the full range of experience, moral, political, and divine? Shakespeare was similarly broad, depicting in his history plays the entire social spectrum from Mistress Quickly to Lady Percy, from Nym to Prince Hal, with suitable gradations between.

In fact, traditional rhetoric had not offered many rules for the composition of whole poems, so that quantitative or accretive development could easily occur,[3] and Renaissance dramatic theory also lacked a satisfactory account of unity of action. Most theoretical statements went little beyond the traditional quantitative parts of a play: the protasis, epitasis, and catastrophe, or the setting forth of the first action, tying the knot, and unraveling. As Madeleine Doran has noticed, since this is an inadequate plan on which to develop a plot, the Elizabethans searched for ways of achieving more careful design. Some writers relied upon a titanic hero such as Tamburlaine to supply a kind of biographical link between parts. Other writers were satisfied with a narrative sequence of scenes that was frankly episodic. Shakespeare and many of his contemporaries most often tried to satisfy the English taste for variety by means of a double and triple plot in order to create a more-or-less thematic harmony. "Multiple unity" (Miss Doran's term) was therefore possible within a theme that combined disparate and often contrasting elements.[4]

Jonson solved the problem in quite a different way, it seems to me, because in his middle comedies he rejected not only episodic or narrative form but subplot, overplot, and parallel plot. The last subplot he wrote was in *Volpone,* and already he tried to make it co-present with the rest of the action more than was usual with his contemporaries. After that he placed stricter limits on time, place, and event, composing with more crowded scenes, and he called attention to the gradations of tone and meaning. Miss Doran may have meant this in her comments on Jonson's "remorseless and ironic logic" in the unraveling of his plots, which has a "perfect rationality of cause and consequence in Jonson's closed world" (pp. 329-31); "he creates a wholly logical world in which the interplay of the interests of his characters moves the plot towards a necessary conclusion. Though there may be a plentiful use of coincidence in the plot, it is part of the data the author makes his characters manipulate in solving their problems." On the other hand, Shakespeare lets "happy chance" determine the outcome (p. 339). These differences may be caused by Jonson's greater dependence on one main intrigue, but the remorseless logic also seems to me less rational and more illusory as the play works out an elaborate pattern, the repetition of a basic motive with seemingly infinite gradations and variations of application. How often, for instance, he relies on a situation where a foolishly wise fellow gulls himself; how perfectly circular and infinitely various is the plot that eventually brings the cleverest manipulator to out-do himself. The logic of such a plot derives not so much from strict application of cause and effect as from the accumulated expectations of the audience, the illusion of perpetual irony and the sense of graduated intensity, inversion built upon inversion, until the final self-laceration or renunciation must be enacted.

An analogy with mathematics helps to clarify the point. Bertrand Russell, in *Our Knowledge of the External World,* distinguishes two kinds of infinity. He illustrates one kind by the progression from zero to 1, 2, 3, 4, 5, and so on to infinity; he calls this an infinite progression, and it is unlimited. The other is illustrated by the division of an interval between, say, one and two; first divide it into halves, then divide one of those into halves, and so on infinitely. This is a compact series or infinite class, and it is limited. The infinite progression and the infinite class involve quite different sequences of thought and have different implications.

The old cosmology offers a similar distinction between two sorts of plenitude. Of course Renaissance writers did not always mean to imply mathematical infinity when they spoke of plenitude; the common synonyms were completeness or fullness, and before the seventeenth century the familiar model for fullness was the world itself. The plenum of species, the gradation of levels of being, and the continuity of existence from the lowest specks of dust to the highest angels all went together to make the grand scheme of the world, a great model for comprehensive literary works. A. O. Lovejoy traced the genealogy of this cluster of ideas in *The Great Chain of Being,* and a generation of scholars has shown its relevance to the works of Dante, Chaucer, Spenser, and Shakespeare. But we have not paid enough attention to another configuration that emerged most clearly in the seventeenth century, the notion of a "limited" completeness, a sort of compact series, not exactly a "little world" but just a segment of the world.

The philosophical uses of limited fullness are most clear in Bacon, who openly scoffed at the idea of correspondences between man and nature, between the earth and the heavens. To think that man is a microcosm, says Bacon, is a treacherous analogy that leads man to measure all things by the standards of his mind, an idol of the tribe. Instead of vast intellectual systems, Bacon insists, we should look for middle axioms; we should anatomize the world, break it into small parts, segment knowledge and gather all the data we can within each category. If you want to know the winds, do not look for anthropomorphic or teleological explanations, but rather collect all you can about the behavior of wind itself. If this method eventually led to the disastrous separation of science from religion, of morals from psychology, and of man from nature, it was nevertheless fruitful for science.

Something like Bacon's *Novum Organum* occurred in literary composition too, as Jonson along with more advanced writers of the century chose to be less cosmic than their predecessors and less quantitative, more selective and exhaustive. This attitude was often accompanied by a preference for the plain style, as in Bacon, Burton, and Hobbes, or in essayists like Cornwallis and Feltham. During the second and third quarters of the century fullness within narrowing limits became a more obvious formal principle in the drama too, in comedy, tragi-comedy, and the heroic play. From the pen of Dryden, for instance, a heroic play developed in a graduated series of moral dilemmas within a carefully defined situation.

Passages in *Discoveries* and in "To the Reader" of *The Alchemist* suggest that Jonson had a due respect for lively invention and full expression, but disliked excess in style and in things. He had an abiding interest in fitness that demanded that there be conscious limits to everything. Since brevity and restraint and propriety made good prose, he criticized those who judge style "wholly by the bulk, think rude things greater than polished; and scattered more numerous than composed." He scorned those who turn over books and write out "what they presently find or meet, without choice" and those who "speak all they can (however unfitly)"; whereas he admired "composition," "election," "wisdom in dividing." Limits come up again in his comments (after Heinsius) on magnitude of plot. The plot should seek its "utmost bound," and "every bound, for the nature of the subject, is esteemed the best that is largest till it can increase no more: so it behooves the action in a tragedy or comedy to be let grow, till the necessity ask a conclusion" (VIII, lines 640-42, 720-21, 768-69, 770, 787-88, 2735-45 and with variations in "To the Reader," lines 30-35). There is not a mean-spirited narrowness here, but a concern for increase and for boundaries. These pronouncements do not add up to very much of a theory of form, and they are woefully inadequate to describe Jonson's art, for his practice is almost always better than his theory.

Another bit of advice in contemporary rhetoric adds a twist to the art of anatomizing. Bacon explained the traditional topic of division (and added a little simulation to enhance the representation of things): "So when a great monied man hath divided his chests and coins and bags, he seemeth to himself richer than he was, and therefore a way to amplify anything is to break it and to make an anatomy of it in several parts and to examine it according to several circumstances. And this maketh the greater show if it be done without order, for confusion maketh things muster more, and besides what is set down by order and division doth demonstrate that nothing is left out or omitted, but all is there; whereas if it be without order, both the mind comprehendeth less that which is set down, and besides it leaveth a suspicion, as if more might be said than is expressed."[5] John Hoskins, a friend of Jonson's and teacher of prose style to Jacobean gentlemen at the inns of court, copied part of this passage into his *Directions for Speech and Style* under the heading "Division."[6] He added some hints about specifying parts: "So in saying a *fair tree* you may divide it into the *roots, body, branches,* and *fruit;* and *fairness* into *tallness, straightness, fresh color,* and such things as are fair in a tree." "This in some sort used is more properly called dilation than amplification; and being after practiced will enable you to discourse almost of anything wherein you are not precisely tied to the exact manner of division with use, but you have the liberty of seeking all things compassed within the sense of your general theme" (p.24).

II. THE DESIGN OF *The Alchemist* AND *Epicoene*

The plots of *The Alchemist* and *Epicoene* are like the working out of a series of permutations with a fixed number of constants and one variable. What are the maximum number of combinations of character and situation that can be represented onstage within the limits of the subject without repeating? The resultant form of the plays in Jonson's middle period seems curiously tight, but the actions are less well knit than were the best popular or courtly comedies of his age. We can easily follow the development of two or three threads of action in a typical comedy, such as *Twelfth Night, The Shoemaker's Holiday,* or *Friar Bacon and Friar Bungay,* whereas in *The Alchemist* and *Epicoene* when Jonson seems to have found his métier in English settings, there appear a welter of characters and episodes, whirling within a central situation. The unity of these plays has been variously explained in terms of image clusters, of a central extravagant conceit, and most recently of an adaptation of the technique of the morality play.[7] We should appreciate the insights in such interpretations, and I think it is reasonable to believe that Jonson was partly indebted to the late moralities and that he was interested in the art of old Greek comedy, but for the moment I want to follow the impulse toward a kind of controlled completeness, to see if it will bring us a little closer to Jonson's design. *The Alchemist* (1610) offers a clear example of this triumph of artifice, so I will comment on it first.

One reason for the play's power is the way Jonson has fashioned the material into something like a compact series. Let us imagine the difficulties that he had to overcome. Assume that he began with the idea for a play about a confidence game — the fake alchemy game — for which he needed at least three principal rogues — an inside man, some bait, and a "rope" or outside man (Subtle, Dol Common, and Face). Once he was committed to his confidence men, he needed a large number of victims or "fish," for the sake of variety and surprise and to enhance the audience's sense of the power of the "cunning man" and his colleagues. It would be dull to play with only one or two fish, so Jonson chose a representative group, seven people who display a limited range of the social spectrum of a city (and two country folk), from a knight down to a tobacconist, from a shrewd fellow like Surly to an utter fool like Dapper.

But Jonson's choice of numerous and carefully discriminated clients immediately created new problems of unity, because the play was likely to break up into episodes. As early as *Every Man out of His Humor* (1599) he recognized the danger of episodic actions when he allowed the choral character Cordatus to comment on the suggestion of Mitis that characters be presented in single scenes,

201

one for each: "That had been single indeed: why? be they not the same persons in this [one crowded scene] as they would have been in those? and is it not an object of more state to behold the scene full and reliev'd with variety of speakers to the end than to see a vast empty stage and the actors come in (one by one) as if they were dropped down with a feather into the eye of the spectators?" (II.iii.295-301). But in *The Alchemist* the interviews with the victims had to be kept as separate as possible for the confidence game to work; consequently Jonson made this need a major part of the tension. He has the second visitor come right on the heels of the first, the third on the heels of the second, so that Face and Subtle always have too little time, and they have to hustle Dapper offstage (put him "on the send," to get his money, as con men say), in order to make room for Drugger. At first the transitions between episodes are leisurely, later they are quickened. This illusion is suggested to the audience by little remarks such as "Pray god, I ha' not stayed too long" (II.vi.95), "O, no, not yet this hour" (III.iii.76), "God's lid, we never thought of him till now. Where is he?" (III.v.51-52). By the middle of Act III the crowding has become so dense and so absurd that something has to break. The stupidest gulls — Dapper, Drugger, and Kastril — are dealt with simultaneously, efficiently making the advice to Drugger serve as an example to Dapper. Mammon has come too soon, so Dapper must be pushed into the privy with gingerbread in his mouth. This is the first serious muddle due to overlapping clients.

By the middle of Act IV, the first crisis of the play, the overlap becomes more threatening, with two clients, Mammon and the Spanish nobleman, asking for the services of Dol Common, so that a new exchange must be made. Typical of Face's genius for improvisation, Dame Pliant is given to the Spaniard. Then the first major triumph occurs when Mammon has been gulled and success-fully "brushed off." Immediately (IV.vi) there follows a second crisis, a nearly complete disaster, for Surly has told Dame Pliant how she has been cheated, Subtle collapses, but Face counter-reverses and saves the day by turning the other victims upon their would-be deliverer. Economy is the watchword. If more and more clients are going to fill the stage, Face will put them to use as ingeniously as possible and employ them in all possible combinations. Composing the scene artistically, using subordinate characters as his tools, he induces Kastril to try out his new technique of arguing; Ananias is shown the papist in his Spanish slops and cries against the "profane, lewd, superstitious, and idolatrous breeches." So they drive Surly offstage. The rogues breathe a sigh of relief, just as a new disaster comes to their door — Lovewit has returned without warning.

The rest of the plot is built in the same way, forming a compact series with repeated turns and counterturns, with successively greater crises and more and more people crowding onstage.[8] Face's wit is always equal to each crisis, only to be surprised by a greater challenge. At each maneuver the situation becomes funnier, and at each turn the characters are drained of some of their humanity. The mess of brass, pewter, and iron in the basement is a leitmotif that recurs through the whole play, a proof of Face's power of intrigue. Like the furnace in the next room that will eventually blow up; the metal hoard is never seen by the audience, but it figures prominently in the dialogue, and Face rings changes on it wondrously. The iron was contributed by Mammon, sold to Ananias and Tribulation as widows' and orphans' goods, sold again to Kastril to furnish his house, and finally given to Lovewit as an inducement to protect Face's secret. Everything except the metal that we never see dissolves into nothing, an insubstantial show. Such art is the epitome of Jonson's skill — to vary, to press a matter to its greatest potential, to please us at the same time that we stand admiring the subtle means by which our feelings are manipulated.

To keep the material within the bounds of his subject, Jonson has endowed the victims of the confidence game with various degrees of credulity — from Mammon, who will believe almost anything he conceives, to Surly, who believes nothing — so that the fools in their quest for money or position provide a witty anatomy of credulity. At the top of the scale is Mammon, who was normally a "grave" sir, a rich man who had no need, but who, once he was bitten by the alchemical bug, lost all power of judgment. His imagination is distended; like Volpone he is flattered by his own arguments and his grandiose schemes. He will be a patron of the arts and a benefactor of mankind. His appetite for sensual pleasure is the most monstrous of all, for he imagines a dozen crude means he will use to stimulate his lust, and ultimately he wishes to play the part of Jove, coming in a shower of gold to every mistress; he will drink the elixir and enjoy a perpetuity of lust. This strongly developed character, therefore, stands as an emblem of the other clients, all who lack reason and judgment; their desires have control over their imaginations and their imaginations over their actions. All the customers are variations on Mammon, and their common deficiency of judgment is often distinguished by their language. In the words of Jonson's address to the reader, their speech is a "simple mocking of the terms when they understand not the things" (12-13). Several characters who identify themselves by empty affectations of speech are Ananias (by the words of Old Testament prophets), Kastril (by the terms of conducting an argument), Mammon (by the high-flown alliterative diction of Marlovian tragedy). It seems appropriate, therefore, that they should be cozened by Subtle's fancy alchemical terms and Dol Common's ridiculous raving in phrases from Hugh Broughton's learned controversy. The variety of language both separates them and joins them as common victims.

It must have been a delight to find that a writer could imitate the fullness of the world in an exhaustive order and gradation, if not correspondence of all parts. The key to it was the arbitrary limitation of the situation and the rules for a confidence game. In other words, a restricted field, a set number of persons, and some simple principles for the game. Modern writers, such as Joyce, Beckett, and Ionesco, have rediscovered the uses of these principles in literature — when Joyce chooses to allude to only actual places in Dublin, or to restrict events to only a certain day, or to use words from only a certain list. The art of such writing seems to involve our sense that the fullness of life (or the emptiness of life for that matter) is being represented in one intense moment.[9] The difference, however, between Jonson and the moderns is that he is much more schematic about it, and he gives us more of the gradations within limits.

The plan of *Epicoene* unfolds in a way similar to *The Alchemist*. Although at first it seems like a miscellany of portraits and bravura passages, by the time it gets halfway through the performance we can see the movement toward an "excellent comedy of afflictions," generated from a tissue of vexations visited upon social monsters. It is a game of vexation copiously filled with variety but carefully limited. Instead of the open-ended design of an Elizabethan comedy, this play effortlessly directs every speech, character, and episode into a single stream of experience.[10]

Jonson chooses a little society, represented by a large but circumscribed cast. They are Londoners who might come in contact with the fashionable gentry, a step below the court and a step above the city. All are afflicted with a similar social disease. Jonson marks the gradations clearly between servants, pretenders, and collegiates; between womanish men, mannish women, lusty men, insatiable women, and an impotent old man. He has strictly limited the time — one crucial day during the plague when Morose, although he lives in his chamber sound-proofed against tolling of the passing bells and all other noise, has determined to marry. Typical of Jonson's neat adaptation to the moment, the play was one of the first offerings of the re-formed children's company at the Whitefriars Theatre, when the plague had diminished enough to permit public gatherings. He has limited the place: the fashionable district between Westminster and the City near the Strand, the Law Courts, and the Thames, in short, near the Whitefriars Theatre. He has controlled the plot, allowing it to rise by gradual degrees of complication and furor, developed by a series of reciprocities. At first it is like an expandable filing system in which a large number of set speeches, characters, and episodes can be inserted, as long as the cross references are complete. At first only two or three characters come together to irritate each other by their speech; then four, five, and soon the stage is filled. At first, Truewit seems to upset Dauphine's whole plan when he visits Morose and declaims against marriage, but in an unforeseen reverse, it merely hardens the uncle's resolve to marry instantly. At first La Foole's invitation to a feast seems like an accident, having nothing to do with Morose and

Dauphine, but in the next turn of the plot in Act III, Truewit directs the dinner guests over to celebrate Morose's wedding, and the mob washes over the stage in waves. In separate episodes, Mr. Otter begins on Mrs. Otter and in the same action he belittles the knights for their timid drinking. The ladies work on Morose's melancholy, in a parody of learned dispute over ancient versus modern writers. Finally Daw is set at odds with La Foole once more.

This second series is linked in two ways: by the noise each creates to irritate Morose and by the rising challenge to Truewit's ingenuity. Can he make the ladies dote on Dauphine before the night is over? Efficiency becomes the watchword again, as in *The Alchemist*. He improvises brilliantly and makes the play within the play, the tragicomedy of Daw and La Foole, serve as entertainment to the Collegiate Ladies, but he allows the credit to go to Dauphine. In the third series Cutbeard and Otter double as canon lawyer and divine, who will presumably help Morose find a legal way out of his marriage. Along the way, Truewit exploits the linguistic pretensions of Otter and Cutbeard, showing that a garment and a few "terms" are enough to make a disputant. All of this vexes Morose further, in some elaborate casuistic disputation that seems overdone in the reading, but it works on the stage. The vexations have become "waking dreams" (IV.vii.42) and at the pitch of the excitement Morose exclaims, "Oh, the variety and changes of my torment!" (V.iv.9).

Jonson apparently believed that he needed something bigger than the charade of the fourth act, something with suspense, to precede the final surprise. With the entire cast assembled for the first time, in Truewit's highest moment, he maneuvers Morose into his lacerating confession: "I am no man, ladies." It is Clerimont's finest moment too when he forces Daw and La Foole to brag about their intimacies with Epicoene, but in their final unmasking Dauphine exposes everyone's limitations.

The limited subject of the play is, as Edward Partridge has shown,[11] a distortion or loss of sexuality, symbolized by Epicoene herself, the boy actor dressed as a woman who turns out to be a boy in the play world as well as in the actual world. This transvestism is obviously associated with the varieties of sexual metamorphosis that were railed at in the age. Puritans attacked players for wearing women's garments, just as they attacked learned ladies and prostitutes dressed as roaring boys with pistol and sword. Men who played badminton or submitted to the governance of mannish women became womanish men. Thus the Collegiates in the play live away from their husbands, pretend to learning, "cry down or up what they like or dislike in a brain or a fashion with most masculine or rather hermaphroditical authority," and they call each other by their last names as men do. La Foole is a "precious mannikin," a "wind fucker," who claims to have served Epicoene and suffers a ritual castration. Daw, who also serves Epicoene, is a "mere talking mole!" Otter, an amphibian (i.e. of indeterminate sex) "is his wife's subject; he calls her princess." Mrs. Otter, a Gorgon's head, an Amazon with a brazen throat, "takes herself asunder still when she goes to bed, into some twenty boxes, and about next day noon is put together again, like a great German clock." After her tongue loosens, Epicoene is full of "Amazonian impudence," she snores like a porpoise, and she too would rule her husband with her "masculine and loud commanding." Morose exclaims the minute he is married, "She is my regent already!" To escape from this trap, Morose would geld himself, and he unmans himself, at least in word, becoming a bridegroom uncarnate. Finally he even thanks the knights for proving him a cuckold in advance of his wedding.

Although each of these characters puts up a facade of sensibility, courage, sexual prowess, fashion, family, language, or learning, trying to impress the world, it only makes us question what is behind their act. The job of Truewit is to expand every action by inspiring wit in the others and to penetrate appearances, to vex the fool and hypocrite until they reveal their essential hollowness. "Why, all their actions are governed by crude opinion, without reason or cause." Appropriately, Truewit enjoys putting words in other people's mouths. Although comedy usually aims to "cure" the blocking characters (to use Northrop Frye's terms) or to cast them out of the comic society, that is not possible here, for although beneath their bad poetry, false fashion, and affected language, the fools are shown to be empty, there are so many of them and they are so incurably ignorant that all cannot be cast out. Daw and La Foole go, displaced by Dauphine and Clerimont, but the rest must be tolerated, manipulated, and "taken." Therefore a limited inclusiveness is reaffirmed at the end.

Morose is a special case, however, and he must be cast out for many reasons. He is a sadist, a tyrant, a man afraid of life, and it is clear that he too distorts his character, when he steps out of his retiring humor and tries to marry and beget an heir. His fantasies about his sexual potency make him an obvious target for humiliation and a victim of unsexing.

III. Satire and Play

Dryden, who preferred it before all other plays, thought that the intrigue of *Epicoene* was "the greatest and most noble of any pure unmixed comedy in any language," as the whole comedy, he thought, was a pattern of a perfect play, according to French rules, but superior to the French, having more variety of design and lively representation of human nature.[12] The comments above are to a great extent merely footnotes to Dryden; yet something still disturbs us about the tone and affective power of the play. How is it supposed to strike us, finally, when Dauphine sends his uncle off to die? "I'll not trouble you till you trouble me with your funeral, which I care not how soon it come" (V.iv.215-17). Earlier he says he would like to cut off Daw's arm or tweak off La Foole's nose, except that Truewit restrains him: "How! Maim a man forever for a jest? What a conscience hast thou?" (IV.v.135). In Act I.ii.15-49, Truewit talks just as violently when he imagines how he might draw Morose out of his chambers on coronation day to the Tower Wharf and kill him with the noise of cannons. "Thou art bound in conscience, when [Morose] suspects thee without cause, to torment him." He also recommends suicide by hanging or drowning. Apparently going all the way with their practical jokes means going beyond the limits of sport and lacking charity. Similar rough treatment of simple folk is found in *The Alchemist,* like the manipulation of Dame Pliant, and some people wonder about Lovewit's crassness at the end, which puts him on the level with Face and Subtle.

The design that I've described also has a hardness and rigor, so that by the end of each play some may think that there is little reason to endure the barrage of words. In *Epicoene,* particularly, the series of brilliant set speeches so thoroughly attack polite learning, feminine beauty, art, marriage, and fashion that urbane life seems not worth the effort to live it. Furthermore (as in *The Alchemist* too), when each of the fools vies with himself to aid in his public humiliation, we see Jonson trying for maximum irony, to have a character convinced that he will personally profit by some degrading act, only to fall deeper into self-deception and frustration. Such turns, although expertly carried off, finally drain a character of his last ounce of humanity. We can laugh callously and cast him aside, but the net effect may leave us troubled.

It is easy to imagine that this is the way Jonson wanted us to feel, for in fact he might have felt that way, at least when he was younger and his comedies exhibited that polarity that he identified with comical satire, the embattled images of right and wrong. Evidence suggests that he did not approve of variety and novelty in manners. Good taste and good morals were inseparable for him, and he constantly set the plain old virtues and the plain style in contrast with the luxurious, vulgar, and dishonest in contemporary life. If mere luxuriousness and variety were at stake in the design of these plays, we might wonder whether some of the art of his great London comedies may have been an attempt to please the very same people he was satirizing. Are these plays, so packed with modern grossness, so full of surprising new twists of plot and unusual characters, made to appeal to the very popular taste that the author deplored? Only if we mean the kind of people who would overlook the fine decorum that the poet observes, the controlling limits of design within which he works. We do not mean those auditors who shared the poet's view that he could have written the play differently if he had chosen to. In other words, there is a deliberate strategy and a special pleasure that the better people are supposed to recognize.

The two prologues of *Epicoene* imply that he aims to delight his audiences more than before, to administer "sweet" remedies to the grossness and folly bred in his contemporaries.[13] It is possible but not necessary to infer that the sweet remedies cover a bitter pill and that the plays approach the very condition that they satirized, as they turn on themselves, exposing the taste for variety in the fools, in the rogues who vex the fools, and in the "artists" who serve them both.

It may be significant that the "contriving" men in these plays are themselves lovers of the various: Face in all his disguises seems more himself. Truewit likes a scene that is "full and twanging." And there are contrivers in later plays, like Littlewit and Medlay who get their variety by savoring pretty little conceits, quips, and puns or who, with little knowledge of design, can vary it to *infinito*. Surely the latter two are mocked at, although rather affectionately.

In *Cynthia's Revels* Jonson exposed the taste for mere variety in the portrait of Phantaste. Her long explanation of her desire to assume the identity of "all manner of creatures," to live in a whirl of pleasure, to be at the center of "all lines of love," and prove "all manner of suitors, of all humors and of all complexions" (IV.i.171-214, new in the folio text), reads like an attack on sophisticated London women. It may be significant for the comedies because she concludes her speech by dreaming that, after all these infinitely various affairs with men, she would have a book made of this, which she would call the book of humors, and every night she would read a little piece and laugh at it. Here is the typical Jonsonian inversion, where self-portraiture turns into self-parody (that was remarked on in chapter one, above). The insatiable woman delights in the spectacle of her folly when she sees it preserved in a book — part of the psychology of audience response that may be postulated for the comedies we are talking about.

However, there must be more to the tone than these odd satirical turns, if we are to account for the plays' gayety and their continued appeal. What finally appeals to me is the gusto and the fascination with an absorbing game played by the poet and the witty characters. We are invited to enjoy the competition between Face and Subtle that amounts to an alternative drama going on while they cozen others.[14] After the truce and bargain at the beginning of Act I it becomes a matter of who will take in more money that day. Who can steal the other fellow's customer, and who can have the favors of Dame Pliant without Dol Common knowing it? Crossfire between cheerful antagonists goes on even as they bamboozle the customers. And no small pleasure with *Epicoene* depends on our recognition that some characters know very little about what is going on, others know more, and a few know most. Even Truewit's proud assumption comes to grief, the assumption that he holds all the cards and that Clerimont and Dauphine are doing his bidding. These levels of discrepant awareness are elaborately exploited in the next comedy, *Bartholomew Fair*.

The final charade in *Epicoene* of Cutbeard and Otter has a special pleasure when they remorselessly go through every one of the twelve possibilities of divorce. Morose has been driven so far by female babble that he has fairly asked for this final, excruciating inquisition. The situation is perfect for the master of ceremonies, the director of the game, and his subordinates. The Collegiate Ladies have so played the game into their hands that every reaction can be controlled. Truewit stations himself at one door, Dauphine at the other, and Clerimont in the midst so that Morose cannot escape when the disputants "grow hot once." Even after he confesses his impotence the agony continues with new and funnier turns, for the ladies insist that they will inspect him to verify his claims. Epicoene cuts that short by declaring that she will take him as a husband with all his faults, and the experts agree that in that case it is no divorce. So Morose plunges into worse despair. As a counterturn, the effeminate little men, Daw and La Foole, are led to tell their tale of carnal knowledge of the bride. Morose exults again; he worships his deliverers and pays money to the men who supposedly cuckolded him. But he is crushed more completely by some legal technicalities: the alleged intercourse occurred before marriage, and the bride had not sworn in the presence of witnesses that she was a virgin. Morose cries weakly, "Oh my heart! Wilt thou break? Wilt thou break? This is the worst of all worst worsts that hell could have devised! Marry a whore and so much noise!'' By now the variety of his vexation has made him a mere reflex, a tool for Dauphine's use, what he had been waiting for all along. But it has been a tremendous lot of fun getting to this point. After all, the whole jest and day's mirth has been staged as a charivari, a mock bride-ale that was given for incongruous marriages. It requires an ingenious playfulness that must be sustained throughout the comedy.[15]

As the play becomes one great jest, it even includes a joke on the audience, with what must have been a shopworn device of the boy disguised as a woman. The convention in the sources for the story, by Plautus and Aretino, involved a male slave disguised as a woman who was married to an old man, but neither of the plays kept the secret from the audience. Writing for a children's company to boot, Jonson made the most of a confining situation, for the audience could hardly miss the fact that a boy had to be playing the woman's part, and they probably had accepted the convention of a "squeeking Cleopatra boying her greatness" on the stage. The convention is taken up into the plot of *Epicoene* ingeniously, toyed with, manipulated (even Truewit does not know she is a boy), and just when the audience has entered the illusion that this unnatural silent woman has turned into the other extreme, a jabbering woman and a collegiate lady, when we have seen her reputation sullied by tales of promiscuity, and have accepted that she is an image of the aggressive modern woman, a mannish creature, a very hermaphrodite, it is suddenly revealed that the illusion is the reality. Or more precisely theatrical necessity is metamorphosed into dramatic life. The game is earnest, and the poet is the master of the game.

In the early seventeenth century, when verisimilitude had not yet fastened its restraints on the drama, Shakespeare also worked such an effect in *The Winter's Tale*; the actor playing Hermione had to play the statue of herself in order for the illusion of Act V, scene ii, to come off, so the natural *coup de théâtre* was to bring the statue to life. It is the ultimate game of pre-illusionist staging, to draw the pretense up into the plot, calling attention to the artifice and transcending it. Hence the popularity of the play within the play. But Jonson's is an especially neat self-conscious trick, since the unmasking of Epicoene pulls many things in the play together in a surprising knot of fancy, reminding us of the rich sport of word, whimsy, and action on which we have been feasted.

At the end of both *The Alchemist* and *Epicoene* we have reached the substratum of comic form, that rests on farce. When a play develops with such perfect, dreamlike mechanism, when all the coincidences work so consistently to one end and all the talk has been drained of its sense and many of the characters drained of their humanity, we experience the essential development of farce. I do not mean that *The Alchemist* and *Epicoene* are nothing but farces, for they are a great deal more. I mean only that the design of their plots corresponds most to that fantasy of logic and coincidence that makes farce. All comedy is, as Eric Bentley says, basically farce, but it is farce plus something else.[16] Jonson's accomplishment in these plays is to keep the something else although he contrives the dazzling artifice of the action that brings us to the very wellsprings of laughter.

7.

The Real Presence of Vulgarity in "Bartholomew Fair"

"What can you expect from a hog but a grunt?" says the proverb, and most audiences or readers probably remember *Bartholomew Fair* more for its grunts than anything else. The play is, as C. H. Herford remarks, a picture of "unadulterated English roguery and vagabondage" (II.37) depicted in vulgar language and evoking its foul smells, its vomit, urine, and cursing; human degradation in all its action. As the denizens of the Fair are corrupt, so they corrupt or exacerbate the silliness and fraud of those who visit it. Nothing is sacred, whether in body or soul, as all submit to the processes of consuming and evacuation. Consequently, most of the good criticism of the play has emphasized the squalor of this world turned upside down, and the inversion suggests the author's implied contempt for the failure of justice in an unhealthy society, an immoral order, symbolized by chaos at Ursula's booth while Justice sits in the stocks.[1]

Much of the power of the play comes, indeed, from inversions in the scenes of vulgarity, but it must be understood that Jonson treats them less harshly than is usually supposed. He allows vulgar characters to be themselves, to jabber on with little restraint and to enjoy their verbal eruptions, since noise, drink, and excrement are the elements in which they live. Asses and rogues suffer only nominally for their weaknesses, and at the end of the play there prevails an almost happy air of release by good fortune, when chance discovery of his frailty permits Overdo to drown all memory of the spectacle he witnessed. The natural inference has been drawn by other commentators, that Jonson reveals here his newer tolerance of human folly, his judgments more mature, more sportive and provisional. Jonson seems to cast his lot with the entertainers in defense of pleasure, albeit foolish pleasure of puppet shows, joining ranks with the rogues against the censurers.[2]

If we acknowledge, as I do, the play's special defense of idle pleasure, its tentative affirmation of life and acceptance of our humanity in a more generous spirit than Jonson was able to conjure up earlier in his career, we still cannot forget the coarseness of that life, present in every scene. To the very end, its filth impinges upon our senses, as Mistress Overdo vomits at the foot of her husband, he transfixed in the moment of righteous indignation. There is some intrinsic power that emanates from the crudity depicted with such obvious relish, even zest, as much as from everyone's pretentious inanity, and we must not shrink from its immediacy. This play is not a moral tract, nor does it end with a feast of forgiveness and reconciliation, for enormities are simply forgotten, not forgiven. Moreover, the demotic life of *Bartholomew Fair* is presented so strongly and frankly, if not objectively, that even though the players forget it, the audience cannot. We should do better to experience the vulgar side of the play, along with its silliness, grasp the nettle and not ignore the money grubbing of Quarlous nor forget that foul-mouthed, sweaty Ursula, Punk Alice, and the rest, although unrepentant, are included in the general amnesty of Overdo's supper and bowl of wine. If talented acting can project with sufficient force the earthy vigor of the words and can depict the too-human people vividly enough, our laughter may blend scorn with sport and foul-smelling reality with delight in the vagaries of man's wit, even as we recognize The Beast.

The greater part of the play's achievement rests in the causes of this laughter, which can accurately be described as a mixture of impressions, loosely related by travesties. Although it is true that the play has a careful design, like the compact series in *The Alchemist* and *Epicoene* discussed in the previous chapter, and that it has the same crowded scenes, nevertheless, its hidden symmetries and witty reciprocities are not enough to unify *Bartholomew Fair*.[3]

There is simply too much energy in the individual parts to be held together for a theater audience. Our mixed impressions may at best attain a fairly consistent mood associated with burlesque or travesty. Various episodes include a wide range of opposites without reconciling them — high and low, learned and stupid, pretentious and mean. At first the travesty is only hinted at, but it comes nearly to dominate the comedy by the middle of the fourth act. And the whole never jells into a single experience, that unified response so favored by modern criticism, nor should we expect it to jell. As each person goes into the Fair he finds himself caught up by routines that seem to celebrate something, as they caricature sophisticated life. Foolish games or other verbal contests reflect, in their ugly fun, the larger concerns of the established order. Nevertheless the interface of vulgar game and fondly earnest society does not simply deflate the great institutions of civilization, nor does Jonson's ridicule of low life simply denigrate it. He plays with the two together, in vigorous discord, one allowed to mock the other while each keeps a shred of self-respect in a jumbled world. In this way, because travesty undermines most attempts at determinate form, cacophony strikes the ears of the audience with full force while the mind plays with the echoes of sweeter harmonies.

Because the play has so much in it, tumbled about and overlapping, there is no way to go through it scene by scene showing its real development clearly enough. I am obliged to take four somewhat different tacks in the argument to reveal the important elements of its dramatic power. First, I will comment on its use of travesty mainly in the game of vapors; second, its mock heroics in earlier scenes; third, the implications of its swinish characters and the impact of Lucianic comedy. Finally, I will try to understand the play's more general meaning and its humanizing energies.

I use travesty in a primitive sense, suggested by its etymology, as it comes through French, *travesti* to take on another person's clothes, and Italian, *travestire* to disguise. Thus a travesty is a transvestite composition, and to change the dressing of a thing may be to dress it up or down. The word entered English about the middle of the seventeenth century, but there were various kinds of travesties written long before Scarron (1648) and Charles Cotton (1664) travestied Virgil in ridiculous style. A mocking way could trivialize a great subject like Falstaff's mocking honor or Chaucer's *Tale of Sir Thopas,* or it could aggrandize a trivial subject like Nashe's praise of the red herring in his *Lenten Stuff* (one of the antecedents of Jonson's Hero and Leander travesty in *Bartholomew Fair*). The ancient rhetorical tradition also passed down the mock encomium, taken up by Erasmus' *In Praise of Folly* (one of the acknowledged sources of *Volpone*), where the line between seriousness and play is indeed hard to draw.[4] All these mocking compositions mixed parody with exaggeration and low matter with high manner so thoroughly that there seems to be little point in distinguishing too sharply between burlesque or travesty.[5] Suffice it to say that Peele's *Old Wives' Tale* (ca. 1590) and Beaumont's *Knight of the Burning Pestle* (ca.1607-10) showed Jonson and his contemporaries what delightful fun there could be in a dramatic spoof. But typically, Jonson's mockery affects us with greater seriousness than Beaumont's play because its crude parts have such curious and gross elaborations that at times they seem grotesque, and the playful episodes always reveal a deeper concern. The asinine game of vapors illustrates these qualities especially well.

I. TRAVESTY OF DISPUTATION

It is probably true, as often said, that the game of vapors in Act IV, scene iv, has implications for the whole of *Bartholomew Fair* and that the events in the puppet booth later develop this significance. However, we have not discovered exactly what were the contemporary implications of the game. Jonson's marginal note is misleading when he explains the game as simply "nonsense. Every man to oppose the last man that spoke: whether it concerned him or no." From this evidence we can imagine that "vapors" means almost nothing, aside from noise, and since Knockum also uses the word variously, it seems to be just a counter word, the way college students recently used "thing" or "fantastic." But "vapors" is more accurately described as omnific in the comedy, because it finds added meaning in various contexts.[6] After all, words in living speech have a controlling context that selects meaning from the store of possible ones. Thus we have no doubt that "vapor" literally means sweat when Ursula enters "dropping," as Knockum says, "How? how? Urs, vapors! motion breed vapors?" (II.iii.45). By metaphor, vapors as the fumes of error and ignorance can cause misjudgment and leave men victims of compulsive urges; their brains have been "smoked like the backside of the Pigwoman's booth" (II.vi.42-43), and their vanity is "smoke of tobacco to keep [them] in mist and error" (III.vi.32-33).

We should not equate vapors and humors, either, since in application to characters in the play, vapors have different effects from humors. As Jonson applies the terms, a humor arises from a person's self-conceit, whereas a vapor springs from natural ignorance. A humor isolates one from other men, a vapor brings people together in abrasive dispute. Thus the common braggart or street brawler who shoots off his mouth is vaporing, in this case the word being a synonym for "roaring." For instance, Knockum makes peace with Ursula, saying, "Let's drink it out, good Urs, and no vapors" (II.iii.23-24). Ursula reinforces that sense when she reprimands Mooncalf for trying to quiet an argument, "and they have a mind to be i'their vapors, must you hinder 'em? . . . must you be drawing the air of pacification" (II.v.59-61). So a vaporer was a roaring boy, a riotous ruffian, spendthrift, giver of the lie. Milton implies such unrestrained impudence, commonly noticed in Jacobean London, when he said of a disputant, "his design was, if he could not refute [his opponents] yet at least with quips and snapping adages to vapor them out" (*Apology for Smectymnuus,* paragr. 7, 1642). The game itself is best understood in the last meaning, for it is a formalized quarrel.

The game functions in the story of Cokes and Grace Wellborn (or what we might call the "little plot") like a coney-catching device; it was invented to divert Wasp's attention while a pickpocket steals the marriage license. So IV.iv begins with Knockum's order to his accomplices, ''continue the vapors for a lift, Whit, for a lift.'' But as in so many other episodes in the play the ruse grows into something larger than mere comic intrigue, into an excuse for sottishness, an explosion of words, and in every way the reverse of a convivium. Jonson's own convivium, a sociable drink with his friends in the Apollo room of the Devil Tavern, offers a nice contrast; instead of witty talk by learned, civil, and merry men, we see dunces, rogues, and sordid guzzlers — all in vain quarrels.[7] Moreover, the game is a travesty, and contemporaries would surely have recognized its mocking at academic disputation.

To appreciate the implications, we need to remember the scholastic routines that prevailed at universities, where a question was debated by calling forth all possible doubts and objections and isolating every contradiction for discussion and resolution. By the early seventeenth century this worthy educational instrument had solidified into an academic ritual, required for undergraduates. Sometimes a dispute was put on as a full-dress show for visiting dignitaries, like those that Nashe satirized when Jack Wilton saw the Duke of Saxony's entertainment at Wittenberg.[8] Published summaries of similar official proceedings at English universities help us imagine how the disputes went; manuscript records supplement these, revealing the more informal exercises at Cambridge.

Normally a moderator presented questions for dispute, some quite serious, such as ''Whether the often taking of tobacco be wholesome for people as are sound in health,'' ''Whether Justice depends upon law only and not upon Nature,'' ''Whether imagination may produce real effects,'' or ''Whether gold can be made by Art from baser metals.''[9] Some questions were deliberately trivial or playful to foster invention, such as ''Whether a dog can make syllogisms'' or like Milton's prolusion ''That day is more excellent than night.'' The performance was divided into three separate stages. First a respondent or answerer gave his brief interpretation of a question, along with his reasons. Second, an opponent (or several opponents — there were seven in some of the Oxford disputes of 1605) stated contradictory propositions and attacked flaws in the respondent's case. Then the respondent replied to each objection.

The final act was the determination by the moderator, who summarized arguments for and against, pointed out fallacies, and reconciled differences where possible. Afterwards, the respondent treated everyone to a supper.[10]

Of course there were variations on the routine, in the heat of debate. Whimsical attacks and parodies by a "prevaricator" also had their place in Cambridge disputes, and sometimes the participants or spectators broke the rules. King James frequently interrupted the 1605 Oxford performances, asking questions and injecting royal opinions, and he turned the 1615 Cambridge disputes into chaos. The question was *Can a dog syllogize?* One debater said that a hound in the chase has a major premise in his head when he comes to a turn in the track, "namely, *the hare is gone either this way or that way*. He smells out the minor premise with his nose, namely, *she is not gone that way*, and there follows the conclusion, ergo, *this way with open mouth*." The King disliked the moderator's biased handling of the occasion and openly advocated the affirmative side, declaring that a hound had more reasoning power in him than was imagined, and he desired that the moderator either would think better of his dogs or not so highly of himself. In the Oxford disputes, the moderator, Dr. Gentilis, began ahead of his usual time to interpose his judgment, answering arguments that had been urged. An opponent, Dr. Martin, "not liking well of Doctor Gentilis his answer which he made to his argument, did upon a sudden rise up and began to dispute again, saying that he might as well dispute out of order, as Doctor Gentilis might moderate out of order. Wherewith the King was wonderfully moved to laughter" (sig.B4v-C1v). It is easy to imagine how mere wrangling could soon dominate and how comic possibilities were inherent to disputation.[11]

The forms of academic dispute are fairly obvious in the game of vapors. At Ursula's booth, Knockum takes the role of *moderator,* announcing the first seemingly innocent proposition "Thou'lt never tire I see." Thus begins the first line of dispute. Like the moderator he pronounces upon the justness of the arguments, saying who is in the right and who utters a sufficient vapor: it is "a gross vapor,"

Fig. 3. *Six Learned Men Disputing,* woodcut by Hans Burgkmair

"That vapor is too lofty," "I think you may [say so], and 'tis true; and I allow it for a resolute vapor." Val Cutting as *respondent,* Whit as *opposer,* draw Wasp into the dispute later as another opposer. If we look at the development of the squabble we can see that after a few sallies they seem to shift Wasp into the position of *respondent.* Certainly they use various strategies of opposers to make him contradict himself. Also the civilities of academic disputation are especially evident in the talk of these men who normally utter only the crudest imprecations, but here their replies are sprinkled with little proprieties like "Sir," "Pardon me," "Prithee," "By your leave," and "Will you mind?"[12] The actors could also bow to the moderator and to opponents and visitors, the booth arranged with a table in the center, the moderator's chair between the respondent on the one side and opposers on the other side. (See the woodcut, figure

221

3.) In the course of their arguing, we see other signs of debater's methods: *The flat denial of a proposition,* "nay, . . . I deny that" and "there you are in the wrong." *The claim of irrelevancy,* "That was not my question," "no matter so long as he know." *The call for explanation,* "Who told you so?" "How can it not?" "To what do you say nay, Sir?" *Concession,* "I grant you" and "Let him mistake." *Making a distinction* (the most common method in academic disputes), "in some sort he may allow," "pardon me, can allow"; "in some sort, sir, he may neither laugh nor hope"; "in some sense you may have reason," "in some sense I care not if I grant you."

The favorite device of academic dispute was the distinction, following the scholastic rule, "When you find a difficulty make a distinction." Repetition of phrases from an opponent's propositions, with those all-important distinctions, occurs in every part of the game of vapors. For instance: "I do not like it"/ "dou musht like it a little"/ "He must not like it at all"/ "He musht not like it indeed"/ "He both must and will like it, Sir, for all you"/ "If he have reason, he may like it, Sir." Another series ends with a general categorical proposition: "It is a sweet vapor"/ "It may be a sweet vapor"/ "It is no sweet vapor neither, Sir, it stinks, and I'll stand to't."/ "Yes, I tinke it dosh shtink, Captain. All vapor dosh shtink." This is followed by a flat denial: "Nay, then it does not stink, Sir, and it shall not stink," and the argument dissolves into mock politeness and another distinction: "By your leave, it may, Sir"/ "Aye, by my leave, it may stink, I know that." The climaxes given to Wasp punctuate the confusion of cries, when he declares unwitting truths about himself with terrible emphasis: "I have no reason, nor I will hear of no reason, nor I will look for no reason, and he is an ass that either knows any or looks for't from me." "I am not i'the right, nor never was i'the right, nor never will be i'the right, while I am in my right mind." The game ends with a real brawl instead of the ceremonial determination, for nothing can be adjudicated when the disputants use only the forms and not the matter of argument. Wasp's license having been stolen, he is left screaming, soon to be put in the stocks with the other clamorers, Overdo and

Busy. So the mock dispute evaporates into Wasp's habitual imprecations, "Shit in your hood" and his favorite "Turd in your teeth."
The latter expression is Wasp's only way of silencing opposition,
his earthy equivalent of "Shut up," "Be quiet," "You're wrong."
And his foul words were not without precedent in public dispute, for
Martin Luther, in his argumentative style, did not shrink from turd
and dunghill.[13]

If the audience has missed the nuances of an academic spoof in
the game of vapors, they cannot fail to discern the mock-religious
dispute in the puppet booth (V.v).[14] In the midst of the puppet
show, Busy enters, roaring at the heathenish idol, Dagon, the
profane performance that he classes with riming, morris dances, and
stage playing. We have seen that it is really a miserable travesty of
the tale of Hero and Leander, all confused with Damon and Pythias,
hardly a threat to anyone's sanctity unless it be Chapman and
Marlowe's. Lord save them from the Puritans! Leatherhead insists
that his shows are licensed "by authority" — an important defense
in a play about people lacking any authority — but that does not stop
Busy. Why should he recognize the authority of the Master of the
Revels? Like Wasp he simply has to silence that show with his
iterated commands, "Hold thy peace, thy scurrility, shut up thy
mouth" (V.v.20). To avoid a fight, they arrange a formal dispute,
although Leatherhead modestly declines to defend his profession in
the contest, pretending that he is "not well studied in these con-
troversies between the hypocrites and us." One of his pupil puppets, "the best scholar of them all," Cokes says, will venture forth
as his champion. And Busy, calling upon his zeal (i.e., the Holy
Spirit) to fill him, takes up the role of respondent.

It is worth keeping in mind that Busy has recently been inspired
after eating swine's flesh, and coming out of the pig booth he said,
"I was moved in spirit to be here this day . . . in my zeal and glory
to be thus exercised . . . 'tis a sanctified noise" (III.vi.86, 101,
104). In the stocks he prophesied the destruction of fairs and other
entertainments (IV.vi.90-92). It is natural, therefore, that he should
think his dispute against Dagon is guided by God's hand. Divinity
may have shaped his ends, yet we are ready to agree that he has

rough-hewed them badly up to this time. Our assessment is prompted by the choral comments, that Busy is a "desperate, profane wretch," ignorant and impudent "to call his zeal to fill him against a puppet" (V.v.47-49).

The roles settled, with Busy as *respondent*, the puppet Dionysus as *opponent*, and Leatherhead the *moderator*, the dispute follows the same course as the game of vapors, with its flat denials, repetition, and distinctions. But these fellows dispense with academic courtesies, and here they stick to the question with a semblance of reasoning. Step by step, the puppet rebuts Busy's arguments, in effect leveling differences between Puritan and puppet. Like the whimsical "prevaricator" at Cambridge the puppet establishes that he has a "calling" by applying the literal meaning — after all, he is called Dionysus. If he is an idol, as Busy says, it is as lawful a vocation as Busy's "calling of the spirit." If he is a profane idol, that is no worse than the profane Puritans who make their living by manufacture of vanities like feathers and bangles. Dionysus, like his adversary, speaks by inspiration, and his best inspiration comes in answering the standard Puritan objection to actors. Busy sets forth his supposedly best argument, saved for last, that the puppet is an abomination according to Scripture; "The male among you putteth on the apparel of the female, and the female of the male." (A transvesting indeed!) And Dionysus' reply wins the dispute with a neat distinction: Busy's argument will not apply to puppets for they are neither male nor female. By lifting his skirt, the puppet offers a "plain demonstration" of the irrelevance of Busy's charge, and the refutation adheres to a strict interpretation of the letter of the law, nicely in keeping with the Puritan controversy. The puppet thus declares by his action that he has "as little to do with learning" as Busy, and his inspiration scorns the help of reason as much as any Puritan. Devastatingly confuted, Busy consents to dwindle into an ordinary mortal, a silent observer in the audience of a show.

Wasp and Busy have been silenced by half-witted sports, gross imitations of important public rituals of Renaissance Europe, and in the eyes of the audience the games have leveled them to the lowest common denominator of Jacobean entertainment. The tutor of young Bartholomew Cokes must admit that he never is right, and his very utterance of that truth mocks an educational recitation. He has flunked out of the lowest school for quarreling in the land. In the corresponding scene Busy thought he would overturn the forces of the Devil, and, being more self-aware than Wasp, his presumption strikes us with greater force. Our perception of the ludicrousness of his dispute comes, of course, from our measure of the gap between this spectacle and a worthy subject for public controversy among learned divines. The only appropriateness of the confrontation is that the opponents are worthy of each other; yet even a puppet can overcome a Puritan.

So much of the travesty probably could not have been over-looked by playgoers and readers — John Selden for one, who said that the play "satirically expresses the vain disputes of divines by Inigo Lanthorne disputing with his puppet."[15] However, Jonson may also have had some less obvious intention behind the mock disputes; at the least, I think there are tantalizing possibilities that bring to light associations with other parts of the comedy. The best way to approach these speculations leads through Jonson's personal interest in disputes of the time. His notes in *Discoveries* include an opinion about a style of dispute, in a vigorous passage for which no source has been found:

> Some controverters in divinity are like swaggerers in a tavern, that catch that which stands next them, the candlestick or pots, turn everything into a weapon; oftimes they fight blindfold, and both beat the air. The one milks a he-goat, the other holds under a sieve. Their arguments are as fluxive as liquor spilt upon a table, which with your finger you may drain as you will. Such controversies or disputations (carried with more labor than profit) are odious; where most times the truth is lost in the midst, or left untouched. And the fruit of their fight is that they spit one upon another and are both defiled. These fencers in religion I like not. (ll. 1045-57)

Jonson also parodied the execrable style of Hugh Broughton in *The Alchemist*, when Dol Common comes on stage raving mad and reciting passages from Broughton's controversial works.

Broughton, who advocated translation of the New Testament into Hebrew, thought he could convert the Jews to Christianity by public dispute, in the same way that he hoped to overturn the Pope. It is more to the point, however, that the dramatist himself witnessed a typical squabble between Catholic and Protestant divines in Paris, September 1612, when he traveled as tutor to young Walter Raleigh. This was after Jonson had renounced Catholicism and returned to the Anglican fold, and less than a year before his completion of *Bartholomew Fair*. Several summaries of the proceedings were printed years later, and Jonson publicly vouched for the accuracy of the first Protestant account, entitled "The Summe and Substance of a Disputation between M. Dan. Featly, opponent, and D. Smith the younger, Respondent."

The spirit of contention governed nearly every aspect of that dispute, and we shall see that it took a distinctly carnal turn. The adversaries differed on who should be present, on how much notice should be given in advance of the scheduled day, on the limits of the question, and on the authority of the Oxford rules for dispute. After it was over they quarreled about who was the least honorable in negotiations for a rematch that never took place.[16] The dispute itself was on the Catholic doctrine of the Real Presence of the body and blood of Christ in the communion bread and wine — perhaps the most emotional issue between Anglican, Lutheran, Calvinist, and Catholic. The respondent, M. D. Smith, defended Catholic (and to some extent Lutheran) belief that Christ's flesh was miraculously present after the priest consecrated the bread, but he granted that it was there in a "veiled" form, "shrouded" under the accidents of the bread. The opponent, Daniel Featley (former tutor of young Raleigh and a student of the rhetorician John Rainolds at Oxford), argued for a divine, spiritual, and sacramental presence, but not a carnal one. St. Augustine had said, according to Featley, "If the scripture seem to command a sin or an horrible wickedness . . . the speech is figurative." The words of Christ are *Hoc est corpus meum,* and He told us to eat it; but that is "carnal eating of Christ with the mouth," and it is a horrible cannibalism to eat human flesh; therefore the words must be meant figuratively. Smith replied that we commit no sin when we eat mummy. But Featley pointed out that mummy is dead not live flesh. Smith insisted that the flesh is under another form. Featley then asked if it is not horrible to eat human flesh masked or disguised? This is a Capernaite literalism. Smith objected that the Capernaites meant that Christ's flesh should be cut in pieces and sold in the market. Featley replied that a man might eat flesh according to the letter though he neither buy it in the market nor cut it. "The horror of the sin of anthropophagy or eating man's flesh is not in buying man's flesh nor in cutting it but in eating it with the mouth and chamming it with the teeth." Christians should follow the spirit not the letter of the laws. To eat Christ's flesh according to this doctrine is to follow the killing letter of the law and to "urge the minds of the faithful to gross and carnal imaginations." As Quarlous said about the game of vapors, "this is such belching of quarrel as I never heard" (IV.iv.78-79).

A number of details concerning Jonson's comic Puritans and this dispute invite speculation. First, the dispute centers on literal versus figurative interpretations of scripture, like Busy's dispute with the puppet. And there is the anomaly that although extreme Puritans often insisted on the strictly literal meaning of the Bible, it was the Catholics who were accused of literalism in their defense of the Real Presence, and the Puritans would appear to a neutral observer as inconsistent in their advocacy of a figurative meaning of the command to eat Christ's flesh and blood. Second, Dame Purecraft's mock horror of the "unclean beast, pig," put before them by "the wicked Tempter," "a profane black thing," "the fleshly motion of pig . . . and its foul temptations, in these assaults whereby it broacheth flesh and blood . . . its carnal provocations" (I.vi.8-20), sounds suspiciously like Daniel Featley's "gross and carnal imaginations" and his "horror of the sin of anthropophagy . . . eating man's flesh . . . with the mouth, and chamming it with the teeth." Similar phrases often recur in Calvinist arguments against the Popish view of the Lord's Supper, so that an informed audience might pick up echoes from, say, Theodore Bèze, William Perkins, W. Fulke, and their fellow Protestants.[17] They objected that the Real Presence implied not spiritual but "carnal eating" of

Christ's flesh, and they were particularly distressed with Catholic concern that unused sanctified bread might be bitten by mice, spiders, and other brute beasts. They thought that the Catholic interpretation turned Christians into cannibals, encouraging "fleshly cogitations" of grinding teeth on the flesh of Our Lord, "teeth to be fastened into His flesh," at a veritable "devil's table."

More suggestive evidence comes a few lines after Purecraft's "carnal provocations" in the same scene of Act I before Busy's first entry, when Littlewit describes him for the audience. He has been seen cleaning his beard and was "fast by the teeth i'the cold turkey pie, i'the cupboard, with a great white loaf on his left hand and a glass of Malmsey on his right" (I.vi.33-36). Perhaps the bread and wine, here, and the teeth in the flesh are not significant, aside from their obvious signs of gluttony, but once Busy is on stage he proceeds to an analysis of the moral questions put to him. It is an effort to "raise . . . a scruple" and prove it lawful to yearn for pig, to eat a Bartholomew pig, and to eat it in the Fair. His two long speeches parody the notorious cases of conscience, which the leading Puritan spokesman, William Perkins (1592), called upon his brethren to examine. The Jesuits were making such a success with their new-found casuistry that Perkins wrote his own manual on the subject (editions 1604, 1607, 1608, and 1611) and encouraged its use to combat the spread of the Roman Church in England. In this respect the satire on casuistry may cut both ways, glancing at contemporary Protestants and Catholics. Moreover, the two-edged possibilities increase when we notice that Busy's argument parallels Popish reasoning about transubstantiation, sounding like Dr. Smith's analysis of eating Christ's flesh under the "veiled form" of the wafer. Pig may be longed for, that is natural. Pig may be eaten, but not "as Bartholomew pig," nor in the Fair. However those injunctions are subject to interpretation.

Busy marshals his ridiculous arguments in opposition to supposed objections. So, although the eating of pig in the Fair has the appearance of offense in the eyes of the weaker sort of believers, he construes it as a demonstration of faith by covering the ugly facts, for the offense is subject to construction, subject, and hath a face of offense, with the weak, a great face, a foul face, but that face may have a veil put over it, and be shadowed, as it were. It may be eaten, and in the fair, I take it, in a booth, the tents of the wicked: the place is not much, not very much, we may be religious in midst of the profane, so it be eaten with a reformed mouth, with sobriety, and humbleness, not gorged in with gluttony or greediness. There's the fear, for should she go there, as taking pride in the place or delight in the unclean dressing, to feed the vanity of the eye or the lust of the palate, it were not well, it were not fit, it were abominable and not good. (I.vi.67-79)

If there is blasphemy anywhere in Busy's dialogue, the odor rises from this passage, for not only do we have the literal-minded and highly suspicious veil over the face while the pig is eaten, but there is the Puritan idea that no place is sacred over another and there is the emphasis on pure motives. Moreover, the "reformed mouth" would probably smell bad, indeed, to even the least learned in the audience.[18]

The Calvinist controversialists cited above elaborated, like Featley, on the differences between spiritual and carnal eating, declaring that transubstantiation denied the glorified body of Christ in heaven, and made it inhabit impure, corruptible bread. Catholics imagined that communicants should "eat Christ's flesh by pieces . . . [and] that accidents [as] veils and curtains . . . cover the said flesh." On the other hand, a Christian should receive the sign of Christ's body, sanctified by faith not by "carnal copulation," hence the importance of preparation for Holy Communion and for the correct manner in taking bread, with a clear conscience and a "mouth of faith."[19] Anything else is an abomination. Again, "sharpen not the teeth," say the Puritans, "nor prepare our belly, but with sincere faith, we break the holy bread." A travesty of these attempts to avoid carnal temptations is acted out in front of Ursula's pig booth, of which I will say more below. We should observe in passing that Busy and his troop pretend that they are resisting evil sounds, sights, and smells — the bells of the beast, the vanity of the eye, and the titillation of the nose — as they plunge forward to their gluttonous feast in the tents of the unclean. The actor's business here is especially significant if he follows Jonson's stage direction, "Busy scents after it like a hound." The final blasphemous suggestion comes from Busy as he emerges from the booth, having gorged himself. Earlier he had said that he would eat pig "exceedingly" and prophesy (I.vi.93), so now he begins to preach against the idolatry that "peepeth out on every side" (III.vi.45-46).

As a further hint to the audience, Knockum remarks on that inspiration.

> An excellent right hypocrite! Now his belly is full, he falls a railing and kicking, the jade. A very good vapor! I'll in and joy Ursula, with telling how her pig works, two and a half he eat to his share. (III. vi.47-50)

Busy emphasizes the point again, saying, "The sin of the fair provokes me, I cannot be silent" (77-78), and "Hinder me not woman. I was moved in spirit to be here this day in this fair" (86-87) to make this "sanctified noise" (104). The implication is fairly clear that, for Busy at least, in his effort to enjoy the Fair and to rail against it, that is to have his pig and eat it too, the experience has been an inverted communion. Superstitious folk thought the communion wafer had magical properties, so in Busy's case the pig has "worked" like a magic prophetus on his tongue, causing him to vapor against the vanities of the Fair. In his carnal wisdom he declares that a drum is the broken belly of the Beast, gingerbread is a basket of Popery and a nest of images.

An ugly symmetry comes to mind, that Wasp's game of vapors degenerates into nothing but turd in the teeth as Busy's vapors seem nothing but pig in the unsanctified mouth. And if Jonson had not treated both travesties with a wonderfully light touch, often only hinting at the possibilities, we might have carried away nothing but grotesque debasements. As it is, the vulgar experience strikes the senses with all its vigor while the mirrored patterns of ritual in education and religion remain indistinct, tantalizingly in the shadows, suggested in the fun of drinking games, cases of non-conscience, and asinine debate. The atmosphere then is only lightly scented with derision and blasphemy.

II. JONSON'S INTEREST IN MOCK HEROICS

The playful possibilities of mock form came to Jonson early in his career, although he used it sparingly until his middle period. The unfortunate banquet of the gods in *Poetaster* (1601) illustrates how dangerous travesty can be, and the ritual cleansing of Crispinus in the same play is perhaps his most successful early use of mock form. In *Volpone* (1606) the entertainment written by Mosca and performed by the three monsters — the dwarf, hermaphrodite, and eunuch — travestied the Pythagorean transmigration of souls. The three monsters' song celebrates the progress of folly, its virtue and its ubiquity in their age. But mock form became prominent in Jonson's work after 1609, with the legal mumbo jumbo of Act V of *Epicoene,*[20] in the mockery of Hugh Broughton in *The Alchemist* (mentioned above), and in a practical joke on Thomas Coryat. Coryat wanted to publish an account of his travels on the continent,[21] notes that are now considered valuable sources of information for historians, but Jonson and his friends made the publication their chance for a spoof on Coryat's amiable self-importance and exhibitionism. Altogether the Mermaid wits garnered over seventy dedicatory poems to swell the volume (and to add to printing costs that Coryat paid). Many of the poems ridicule Coryat with mock encomium, Jonson's being conspicuous. There are also marginal notes sprinkled through the dedicatory verses that suggest Jonson, since they coyly deny improper puns and by that means call attention to excremental and bawdy meanings. The title itself, *Coryat's Crudities* (1611), implies undigested bits that the author has voided after five months' travel, and Jonson said in one of his poems that the jottings were Croyat's five months' crudities, the work of a man not "costive of acquaintance" (VIII,376).

Some time after 1610, that is after finishing *The Alchemist,* Jonson wrote the coarsest of all his poems, a brief mock epic entitled "The Famous Voyage" — patterned after Lucian's *Menippus* and echoing Ulysses' trip to Hades. Since Jonson printed it among his highly prized epigrams in 1616, he must have thought well of "The Famous Voyage." It memorializes another trip, this by two gentlemen in a rowboat, Shelton (presumably Sir Ralph Shelton) and a man known only as Heyden, taken up the Fleet Ditch, then a fetid sewer. The poems' heroic invocation places their action above the accomplishments of Hercules, Theseus, Orpheus, Ulysses, and Aeneas because what those old heroes conquered were "subtly distinguished" in various actions, but all were "confused" here. These two men in a dory were modern adventurers going into the bowels of the City to a sort of hell on earth, where "ghosts" of humans were heard "lashed by their consciences," laden with plague sores and confessing their sins, as if their mortal remains contained dead souls. The boat passed a number of perilous obstacles, as Ulysses' did, but these are smells from Hydra-like dung heaps, Cocytus-like sounds from privy outlets, and the like. Past the mythical rivers of Hades they found the Inferno — the ovens of London cooks (or "Furies") along Fleet Lane, a place with "still-scalding steam," that reeked of its dead flesh. Grease ran out of the sinks, "and hair of measled hogs, / The heads, houghs [i.e., hocks], entrails, and the hides of dogs." The voyagers met the Tiresias figure there, counterpart to the oracle that Menippus and Ulysses sought in their descent into the underworld.

The oracle of the Fleet Ditch was, however, not Tiresias but the soul of old Banks, the horsetrainer and juggler, a much-heralded showman at English inns and fairs.[22] Whereas the soul of Pythagoras in Lucian's *The Dream* inhabits the body of a cock, "our Pythagoras, grave tutor to the learned horse" lived in a cat's body, so this creature delivered the oracle's praise of the daring gentlemen. The travesty of a soothsayer's amazement at their heroic, nasal voyage to Pluto's hall (somewhere near the Holborn bridge) ends the poem.

> How dare
> Your dainty nostrils (in so hot a season,
> When every clerk eats artichokes and peason,
> Laxative lettuce, and such windy meat)
> Tempt such a passage? when each privy's seat
> Is filled with buttock? and the walls do sweat
> Urine and plasters? when the noise doth beat
> Upon your ears of discords so unsweet?   (164-71)

Others were frightened of the plague and by the tolling of St. Sepulchre's bell, but the two heroes acted without fear of deathly odors, contamination, disease, or sin. They laughed at Banks's fate, and after securing evidence of their accomplishment, they went home the way they came. There is more to say about the meaning of this famous voyage, but for the moment we should notice the elements that were to reappear in *Bartholomew Fair:* the mocking jumble of grand and vulgar, the smells, noise, and excrement, the hot fire tended by cooks in the steam and grease of hogs, the gentlemen voyagers laughing at it all like brave clowns before a paper tiger; yet they risk taint both moral and physical.

Jonson's mock-epic inclinations should also be understood in connection with Chapman's Homer. Jonson apparently worked on *Bartholomew Fair* in 1614 (acted October 31, 1614, at the Hope and at court November 1), and later on he may have revised the text (as was his habit) for the first edition of 1631. George Chapman was also completing his translation of the first twelve books of *The Odyssey* in 1614 (entered at the Stationers' Register November 2, 1614, and published in the same year). Chapman's *Iliad* had come out in installments beginning in 1598, completed in 1611, and his continuation of Marlowe's *Hero and Leander* had been done in 1598. In 1605 Jonson and Chapman were friends and collaborators on *Eastward Ho!,* but enmity came between them, possibly after Inigo Jones's production of Chapman's masque (February, 1613) for the marriage of Princess Elizabeth. At any rate Chapman complained in his commentary on *The Iliad* that a "great scholar" made "hot objection" to his free translation of Homer.[23] About twenty years later, Chapman disliked his old friend enough to compose a savage invective in reply to another Jonsonian mock poem, "An Execration Upon Vulcan" (1623). That poem is a *jeu d'esprit* on a serious personal loss, but Chapman saw it as just a Luciferous boast, a product of Jonson's "swinish itch," his forked tongue and sorcerous pen; a poet who ignores the "sound parts" of mankind and dwells on the sores; a gatherer of poisons who transforms all his "most wrathful fumes to jests."[24] Something swinish Jonson wrote must have lingered in Chapman's nostril, and it is hard to believe

233

that Chapman would have enjoyed Jonson's puppet show of Hero and Leander. Also suggestive to a writer interested in burlesque or travesty, Chapman's preface to the 1614 edition of the first twelve books of *The Odyssey* repeats some traditional observations on epic poetry (also found in Spondanus' Latin edition of 1605), that *The Odyssey* is greater than *The Iliad* because *The Iliad* has magnificence of persons and event to aid the poet's industry. *The Odyssey* however is based on a "jejune and fruitless" subject — a man's going home, which helps the poet little (as jejune perhaps as going to a fair). On this "poor plain groundwork," says Chapman, Homer erected a structure so elaborate and pompous that the topic seems a "naturally rich womb" that "produces it needfully."

We need only recall Thomas Nashe in praise of the red herring, Nashe's *Lenten Stuff* (1599), to suggest how this argument can also justify mock encomium. It is the difficult art of making molehills into mountains, says Nashe.

> Every man can . . . write in praise of virtue and the seven liberal sciences, thresh corn out of the full sheaves and fetch water out of the Thames; but out of dry stubble to make an after harvest, and a plentiful crop without sowing, and wring juice out of a flint, that's Pierce a God's name, and the right trick of a workman.[25]

A specific contrast with an earthy comedy like *Bartholomew Fair* comes to mind when Chapman says, in an unfortunate choice of words, that *The Odyssey* is a "digested confluence" of all nature, "where the most solid and grave is made as nimble and fluent as the most airy and fiery, the nimble and fluent as firm and well bounded as the most grave and solid." Finally, Chapman sneers at "popular vapors" like Lord Mayor's shows that are preferred to great literature, and he dedicates the translation to Robert Carr, earl of Somerset, as the most open and heroical condemner of "popular vapor."[26]

III. SWINISH VAPORS AND THE LEGEND OF CIRCE

So much for Jonson's growing interest in mock poetry and Chapman's annoyance at swinish vapors. The swinish part of

Bartholomew Fair, mainly in Acts II and III, conveys strong impressions of a tendency toward the mock heroic mode that turns to travesty in the last two acts. It begins with an absurd justice, a man costumed as a natural fool declaiming to us "in Justice name and the King's, and for the Commonwealth." He poses as the familiar stage figure, a rustic clown like Costard in *Love's Labor's Lost,* as distinct from the domestic fool in motley. He wears the long coat characteristic of children and idiots, but Mooncalf mistakes him for Mad Arthur of Bradley, a sort of Hyde Park orator. Overdo secretly sees himself in much loftier terms, modeling himself upon the Roman hero Junius Brutus, who, disguised as an idiot, concealed his opposition to the Tarquins until the right moment. A superpatriot, Brutus loved the state more than his children, and he subsequently killed two sons for conspiring to bring back the Tarquins.

But closer to London audiences, Overdo follows the example of Thomas Hayes, the lord mayor, "a worthy worshipful man," says Overdo, "sometime a capital member of this City" (II.i.13-14). Hayes zealously enforced the laws on prostitution, ale houses, bakeries, inns, and all those that sold food and drink in the byways. At least once Hayes disguised himself for a personal inspection of bawdy houses; otherwise he employed spies to report false pricing, short weights, and low-quality goods. An early Ralph Nader, we might think, but Overdo trivializes that "high wisdom" by measuring the length of puddings and taking the gauge of black pots.[27] He wants to do his own spying, for he distrusts any subordinate's reports, so he goes into the Fair to discover enormities for himself; he feels acutely the danger of judicial error by those who sit in "high places," where intelligence lies idle. In short, he is our familiar friend, the over-zealous administrator, euphemistically described as "over-exuberant."

At the beginning of Act II, the first scene at the Fair, Justice Overdo functions like the interpreter in a Renaissance painting, who stands to one side exclaiming at the wonder of the event and explaining it to the spectators. Overdo sees his first "enormity" in Joan Trash's gingerbread progeny, made with "stale bread, rotten eggs, musty ginger, and dead honey.'' But his second discovery is literally an enormous exemplar of Eve, all fire and fat, a roaster of pigs. She is so hot that she sweats profusely, watering the ground in knots (like Falstaff's larding the earth); ''I go like a great garden pot, you may follow me by the S's I make.'' She may even melt away into the first woman, a rib again, no doubt a pork rib. After Ursula drinks and gives instructions for various ways of cheating customers, Overdo cries out against this ''very womb and bed of enormity.'' But since he resolves to play the madman to the hilt, he joins the others for a drink — giving a reason strangely reminiscent of Busy's reason for eating pig: ''Let me drink, boy, with my love, thy aunt here, that I may be eloquent; but of thy best, lest it be bitter in my mouth and my words fall foul on the Fair'' (II.ii.130-31). He takes to the role eagerly to come off with a reputation that he would be ''a certain middling thing between a fool and a madman.''

That last remark is unwittingly a true description of himself, because in every episode from here to the end of the play Overdo misconceives himself as he misunderstands what he sees of others. He acts on heroic urges that get him deeper and deeper into folly. He wants to rescue the cleverest cutpurse from the supposed bad influence of his associates, a metamorphosis he thinks worthy of Ovid. His exhortation to the cutpurse in fact lures people to the pig booth while Edgeworth plies his trade. Overdo's speech turns into its own metamorphosis, an oration against bottle ale and tobacco: all of man's faults are consequences of bottle ale. ''Still the bottle ale slavereth, and the tobacco stinketh'' (II.vi.85-86). Wasp, however, identifies Overdo as a Patrico, an ass, a kin to his Cokes, and a roarer. When the Justice tries to quiet Wasp and Ursula, saying ''hold thy hand, child of wrath, and heir of anger, make it not Childermass day in thy fury or the feast of the French Bartholomew; parent of the Massacre'' (II.iv.146-47),[28] Wasp can only beat him into silence to stop his new fit of preaching. A real put-down for the preserver of Law and Order.

A sagacious critic has noticed that as the play goes on, Overdo assumes even more inflated judicial roles, finally emerging as a type of the Lord God Jehovah, Giver of the Law, who punishes in thunder and lightning.[29] And there are enough references to a forthcoming, almost divine retribution to help an audience see those godlike associations. Overdo speaks like a megalomaniac who enjoys the "terror of his name," and his discharged servant, Trouble-All, calls pathetically for the "name of names" to give every action its authority. "Take Adam Overdo in your mind and fear nothing" (IV.vi.161). There is certainly a suggestion of blasphemy here, as I suspect it in "eating pig," but we should not overdo it, any more than we should with Busy. Justice Overdo is a "Prospero figure," as has been suggested, in only a limited interpretation. A Don Quixote figure would be closer to the mark, but even Quixote grants him too much dignity, for the events on stage constantly represent in Overdo a bumbling ineffectuality akin to the rabble and babble of the Fair. He has a jumble of ideas about himself, not only as the severe enforcer of the letter of the law, but as a statesman, a noble Roman orator, an ancient stoic, patriot, friend of Ovid and Horace, a rescuer of wayward youths.

Overdo is carried away by his fancies, and we see that he belongs in the Fair, by the pig booth, vaporing. Although his role edges on the blasphemous, he is more obviously a special mixture of taunted clown and pompous master of ceremonies, a mockery of a Justice, whose disguise reveals his true nature, a fool playing a judge playing a fool.[30] The emphasis therefore is on both his exuberance and his deflation in every episode, inviting us to enjoy his delight in his vast political, heroic, and divine offices, even though we know he is just the keeper of Piepowders Court. His theories about justice bear no relation to actual crimes nor to his duty, just as his orations about tobacco, fortitude, and morality have nothing to do with Jehovah, but they create a tremendous amount of fun. A light-footed, mercurial actor can animate these different moods to heighten the zaniness of this figure (as the actor did in the Folger Library production of 1972). His role produces the most foolish and contradictory effects in the play world, showing what "bad events may peep out o'the tail of good purposes."

Ursula emanates more vitality than Overdo, a combination of

magnetic and repellent forces. Just as everyone who goes to the Fair must visit her booth — like an undigested "confluence of all nature" — and something must happen to him there, so every reader or theater goer has to come to terms with her. She first reveals herself vaguely, as we have seen, the prototype of a woman, a fat Eve tending the fires of Hell. The London cooks of Fleet Lane had struck Jonson in the same way in the Inferno of "The Famous Voyage." But we soon learn in the play that Ursula signifies other grand things, variously apprehended through her and Knockum's vapors: a she-bear, for instance, a rump-galled horse, a pillar of the Fair, and a witch. She may very well suggest the Old Testament and classical, blind fate in the image of Ate or Discord, with her torch, smoke, and lame leg (Cope, p. 144). In that sense she nicely complements a mad justice of the peace, while she rules over contentions in her booth. I can understand why other interpreters find in her the great earth mother,[31] since her "offspring" teem around her and her talk abounds with generative metaphors, especially in her verbal duel with Quarlous: "you dog's head you . . . you look as you were begotten atop of a cart in harvest time, when the whelp was hot and eager," or "Snotty nose? Good Lord! Are you snivelling? You were engendered on a she-beggar, in a barn, when the bald thrasher, your sire, was scarce warm" (II.v.123-25, 135-36).

But by frequent repetition the drama makes most of her fleshly, swinish, and hence gluttonous associations. She is "mother o'the pigs," people nearby are her "litter," and she was rumored to have died of a surfeit of ale and tripes or of cow's udders. Pig is the provocation and the cure for just about everything — as she says to Knockum "You angry? you are hungry: come a pig's head will stop your mouth and stay your stomach at all times" (II.iii.51-53). Moreover she seems in her very piggishness to be an earthy witch, with Mooncalf her "incubee." Her sign is "The pig's head speaks," "The pig's head says," and she is "the oracle of the pig's head" (III.ii.60-71).

In conjunction with the pigs are a number of mock-epic insinuations that enrich the atmosphere of her booth. Thus Leatherhead the ballad singer is dubbed "Orpheus among the beasts, with his fiddle and all," and Joan Trash is "Ceres selling her daughter's picture in ginger work"(II.v.8-12). Quarlous says of Knockum, "I'll see him and roar with him too, an' he roared as loud as Neptune" (II.v.27-28), and later on Edgeworth is "our Mercury" for his stealing (IV.iii.105). Knockum called the booth "old Ursula's mansion, how like you her bower?" and Mooncalf repeated, "my mistress' bower" (II.v. 40, 57). Specific heroic details from Books X and XII of *The Odyssey* emerge as Busy approaches, like Ulysses directing his sailors to stop their ears from the Sirens' song (although, typically, he gets the passage wrong). He warns his crew to pay no attention to the temptations around them; the trinkets in that grove of hobbyhorses are the wares of the Devil, this the shop of Satan. "Let not your eyes be drawn aside with vanity, nor your ear with noises." The wares are hooks to catch them by the gills and by the nose. "Therefore you must not look nor turn toward them — the heathen man could stop his ears with wax against the harlot o'the sea. Do you the like with your fingers against the bells of the Beast" (III.ii.31-48). Having escaped the Sirens, the party finds Ursula's booth, Busy "driving them to the pens." The booth is covered with boughs as in a grove; steam is in the air, like Ulysses' first view of Circe's Bower (Chapman translated it as a "bright vapor," line 191), and there are temptations of food and drink. Swinish transformations are bound to follow.

According to nearly all ancient and medieval commentators, Ulysses' voyagers were tested for temperance at Circe's Bower, just as Guyon had to face his ultimate test in the Bower of Bliss, also modeled on Circe's Bower. Those who failed were turned into bestial representations of their humors. The Circe episode was the most frequently moralized adventure in Homer, and it was blended in most readers' minds with Ovid's treatment of the same tale, making Circe the witch, soothsayer, and harlot. Jonson alludes to her corrupting power in describing Carlo Buffone's absurd similes that "more swift than Circe . . . will transform any person into deformity," an effect of his "scurrilous and profane" jests, his railing, and ribaldry (*EMOH,* character sketches) and Circe's incan-

239

tations and witch power, like Ate's, interested Jonson in *The Masque of Queens* (line 83, note 1. and lines 209-11). Aside from *The Odyssey* and *The Metamorphoses* a whole body of secondary narratives and dialogues surrounds Circe. most notably the delightful fragment by Plutarch usually known as *Gryllus*, a dialogue between Ulysses and a hog. where the hog proves that animal life is superior to human: our so-called reason makes us worse than beasts. who are naturally courageous and naturally drawn to the good. Lucian's animal dialogues also exploited the paradoxes of animal superiority. as did the popular dialogues of the Italian Giovanni Gelli. entitled *Circes*.

Interpretations of Circe usually saw her in terms of her pigs and what those creatures meant. For instance the standard reference work, Edward Topsell's *The History of Four Footed Beasts* (1607), says that Circe signifies unreasoning pleasure, Ulysses is the soul, "and his companions the inferior affections thereof, and so were the companions of Ulysses turned into swine by Circe, when unreasonable pleasures do overcome our affections and make us like swine in following our appetites . . . [Socrates] said in jest that Circe turned men into swine when as Ulysses, by his own abstinence and Mercury his counsel, was delivered and saved from the most savage transformation" (p. 675). A swine has a narrow forehead, thought to imply a "foolish unwise disposition"; a pig's curling lip about canine teeth betokens a "contumelious and clamorous railer."

> This beast is a most unpure and unclean beast, and ravening, and therefore we use (not improperly) to call obscene and filthy men or women by the name of swine or sows. [Those who] have foreheads, eyelids, lips, mouth, or neck like swine, are accounted foolish, wicked, and wrathful: all their senses (their smelling excepted) are dull. (p. 675)

> No beast [is] less profitable being alive than a hog, and yet at his latter end he payeth his master for his keeping. Cicero said . . . A hog hath nothing in him beside his meat, and that therefore the soul thereof was given to it instead of salt to keep it from stinking: for indeed in lions, dogs, bears, horses, and elephants, all their virtue lieth in their minds, and their flesh is unprofitable and good for nothing, but the swine has no gifts at all in the mind. (p. 677)[32]

Since swine dig in the earth they are emblems of earthbound spirits, as Thomas Nashe describes them, who cry "all bread and no drink," that love gold and naturally hate good wits. "If with their earth plowing snouts they can turn up a pearl out of a dunghill, it is all they desire. Witches have many of these spirits and kill kine with them. The giants and chieftains of those spirits are powerful sometimes to bring men to their ends, but not a jot of good can they do for their lives" *(Terrors of the Night,* I.352-53).[33] The prophetic aspects of Circe and her swine were connected with this earthly power, as many old commentators agree (Plutarch, Thucydides, Cicero). Vapors rising from the earth inspired ancient oracles, and pigs were thus often sacrificed. The most interesting treatment of Circe and prophecy is found in the work of an important Jacobean political figure (and enemy of Jonson's), Henry Howard, earl of Northampton.[34] Northampton's carefully researched and reasoned attack on false prophets begins with a Circe story. Circe was a great sorceress and known for wantonness, who transformed Ulysses' sailors "into sundry shapes of savage and wild beasts, according to diverse qualities and affections of their humors." But after Ulysses made a bargain with Circe, she allowed him to take his men back in human forms, if they wanted to be restored. Some men preferred to stay as animals, especially one Echinis, who had been a soothsayer in his former incarnation. As a pig Echinius feels more in tune with the wind and weather, more free of guile and treachery, and repentant of his former misdeeds. Northampton points the lesson:

> By which plain figure, represented for our better feeling of the falsehood of this slippery world, we may be moved to lament and pity the gross ignorance of those who, waxing weary of the toils and travails of this transitory life, were very willing to retire, but under-stood not whither for default of skillful guides, had a mind or inclination to change, though to the worse, and rather choose to drown and to depress themselves into the grossest element, than to advance their hearts and hopes to that Jerusalem which lies aloft, by the wing of immortality. (sig.A3)

Northampton elaborates on these ideas with quotations from the New Testament, proving that if we had no hope beyond this life we would be wretched amongst beasts, and none but mad fools who say in their hearts that there is no God will consent to the choice of these castaways (I.Corinthians 15.19, II.Peter 1.4). Disdain of human reason advances Dagon; this is "the cup of Circe, spiced with conceits and fancies" (sig.A3).

Giovanni Gelli's *Circes* (1549), the probable source of this tale of Ulysses, is not nearly as clear cut and moralistic as Northampton's version.[35] Gelli's animal dialogues, in fact, are highly contradictory and playful, with a skeptical, urbane Circe, a naive, philosophic Ulysses, and some canny beasts. Only Gelli's dedication resembles Northampton's serene confidence. The dedication says that of all creatures only man can "choose of himself a state and end after his own mind and walking in that path that most pleaseth him" according to his own free will, rather than being controlled by the inclination of nature. All things have natural limits except man. Gelli claims that Ulysses' dialogues with the beasts signify that man can transform himself like a new Prometheus into what he most wills, "taking like a Cameleon the color of all those things unto the which with th'affect he is most nigh." Men who fasten their eyes on earthly things become like brute beasts, wholly lacking reason. Those who look up achieve their true perfection in contemplation of divine things. The question is, therefore, What is man? Is it better to live according to nature or to respond to divine promptings from our reason? The dialogues themselves answer these questions less decisively than the dedication leads us to think, for they maintain a delicate balance between the beasts' tough experience and Ulysses' fine-drawn logic. And Ulysses cannot persuade his first nine interlocutors at all of the advantages of human form. He comes close to being dissuaded himself against human life, because so many barriers stand in the way of happiness. He is about to run back to his ship and return to Ithaca alone, when he meets an elephant, the only beast he finally persuades to change back to human shape. And the elephant accepts our life more for what it is not than for what it is. All goodness will come to us after we die, not in this life.[36] There seems to be a playful equivocation in that ending, and it resembles some of Jonson's favorite dissimulations. Similar ironic implications may be found in the ultimate source of the tale, Plutarch's *Gryllus,* but Gelli allowed the arguments to unfold much more according to their own laws, liberating the playful possibilities in a defense of lower levels of existence.

Assuming that these are representative traditional and contemporary readings of Circean tales, I see some of those themes in *Bartholomew Fair* but not others. I do not find Gelli's cultivated, witty arguments coming from Jonson's bestial men, nor do I find the new Promethean man rising above his natural inclinations. No clearly heroic leader like Ulysses emerges. But the earthy power of the Oracle of the Pig is often present in the play. Ursula and her brood certainly are not only gluttons but clamorous railers; her scolding at Knockum (II.iii) establishes this for the audience as something Ursula fattens on, and eating and drinking are for her the only alternatives to clamor. The analogy between Jonson's play and Gelli's *Circes* rests more on their authors' similar ironic reservations, their willingness to let the beasts justify their lives, be themselves, and win most of the arguments against the representatives of civilized humanity. And it is that tentativeness about the human condition that can begin to dawn upon the spectators as they witness the self-satisfaction of the clamorers and raveners.

Throughout the day, the roarers of the Fair, like Captain Whit and Val Cutting, make their obligatory stop at the booth, and they recognize other visitors as potential roarers. Edgeworth is a ravener not only after purses but after smocks, and he asks the pig woman if she will have a supply of "smocks" and whimsies that night for their party. Win and Mistress Overdo are recruited for Edgeworth's party, where they will learn the trade of prostitution. Cokes, we should remember, is a ravener after everything he sees, and as he contemplates each new object of his appetite, he loses a sign of his humanity — two purses go first, then his cloak, and finally his hat. "Sailing" all alone without his protector, Cokes has only some half-rotten fruit to feed on. While he scrambles for the pears on the ground, Nightingale comments: "His soul is half way out on's body at the game." But Edgeworth, in disagreeing, identifies Cokes with Cicero's saying about a pig's soul; "Talk of him to have a soul?

243

'Heart, if he have any more than a thing given him instead of salt, only to keep him from stinking, I'll be hanged'' (IV.ii.54-56). The principal censurers of the Fair, Overdo, Busy, and Wasp, also turn into common clamorers and must pay the price, sitting in the stocks, as do rogues and vagabonds who break order. There is a definite leveling of moral (if not social) differences between Circe's litter and the voyagers to the Fair, who must "grunt out" together the possibilities of life in "another Bartholomew Fair" (II.iii.1-3).

Some of these visitors, like Cokes and Littlewit, were natural fools before they left home, so the Fair is merely a fulfillment of their characters, promised to the audience in the first act. Littlewit's ridiculous pride in his wife, as in his art, marks him, as he savors his vacuous fancies, that he "ever had the fortune to win him such a Win" (I.i.31). His motive for visiting the Fair is to see his play enacted by the puppets, a work of his wit, inspired by beer, not Mermaid wine. The "hot coal" on his tongue (I.ii.40) is not Isaiah's gift of prophecy but the silly idea that his wife "play the hypocrite" and pretend that she wants pig. Cokes belongs in the same class from the start. His motive for visiting the Fair comes from his identity, his cherished name, so nothing Wasp says will dissuade him.

> Nay, never fidge up and down, Numps, and vex itself. I am resolute Bartholomew in this; I'll make no suit on't to you; 'twas all the end of my journey, indeed, to show Mistress Grace my Fair. I call't my Fair, because of Bartholomew. You know my name is Bartholomew, and Bartholomew Fair. (I.v.62-67)

Wasp picks up the journey idea, and as is natural for him in his rages, he makes a grotesque conceit, at first digestive then mental.

> Would the Fair and all the drums and rattles in't were i' your belly for me. They are already i' your brain. He that had the means to travel your head, now, should meet finer sights than any are i'the Fair; and make a finer voyage on't to see it all hung with cockle-shells, pebbles, fine wheat-straws, and here and there a chicken's feather and a cob web. (I.v.91-97)

His head contains a model of a booth at the Fair, and Cokes' going there will be a "ravening after fruit." Wasp foresees that his charge will "buy of everything to a baby there" and he will lose every-thing. Pray God he can bring Cokes home with at least one testicle. The "motion" comes upon Cokes like an "itch of the feet," it is so primitive, brainless, and compulsive. The rest of his group, Wasp and Mistress Overdo, follow him ostensibly to keep him from trouble. Grace goes because she must, and on their tail go Quarlous and Winwife, hoping to see those flies in a hot season "engen-der . . . excellent creeping sport." Nevertheless, they admit that it takes only a "spoonful of brain" to think so.

Once they are there, Quarlous, Winwife, and Grace are the only major characters who resist the degrading attractions of the Fair, and Quarlous at first seems to be a lively and perceptive fellow, maybe even the temperate man. At the least he is a reliable commentator. Even he has to agree that it is natural for the beasts to think that frequenters of the Fair are like them. In response to the vendor's cries, Winwife expresses surprise "That these people should be so ignorant to think us chapmen for 'em! Do we look as if we would buy gingerbread or hobby-horses?" Quarlous sets him straight, saying, "Why, they know no better ware than they have, nor better customers than come. And our very being here makes us fit to be demanded as well as others" (II.v.13-19). He wishes that Cokes would come, for he is a "true" customer.

A few moments later Quarlous himself behaves like any other visitor who comes to mock and stays to quarrel. At first sight of Ursula, he calls her some highly refined names. "Body o'the Fair! What's this? Mother o'the Bawds?" Knockum corrects him, "No, she's mother o'the pigs, Sir, mother o'the pigs!" Winwife thinks she is "Mother o'the Furies, . . . by her firebrand." "Nay she is too fat to be a Fury, sure, some walking sow of tallow!" replies Quarlous. And Winwife adds, "An inspired vessel of kitchen stuff!" (II.v.73-84).

Ursula returns their volleys with slightly stronger language and implies that they are not men enough to take on a juicy and wholesome "plain plump soft wench of the suburbs." They need some "thin pinched ware, pent up i'the compass of a dog collar." The scolding contest begins in earnest when Quarlous draws Knockum into the fun by asking if she is his personal quagmire, his bog where he stands his horses (an improper suggestion here, too). Now, the heroic metaphors mix with billingsgate, as Quarlous declares that any man who ventures onto that great quagmire might sink into her and be drowned for a week before his body be found. Intercourse with her would be like falling into a whole shire of butter. A remark that sets Ursula into a sputtering fury, and her invective becomes greasier and more anatomical the more she scolds. Her railing recalls the ancient magic of a shrew's curse. As the Gauls were said to raise welts on the skin with their imprecations, so Quarlous fears that maybe she is able to give a man the sweating sickness by looking at her. Finally, unable to scald any more with her tongue and having run out of metaphors, Ursula tries to scald her attackers, literally, to drive them from the battle with a pan of grease. It misses aim and falls on her leg. "I ha' lost a limb in the service," she cries. As the horse dealer tends her combat wounds, he delivers the heroic prophecy of her final transformation into the heavens. "I'll tend thy booth and look to thy affairs the while; thou shalt sit i'thy chair and give directions and shine Ursa Major" (II.v.188-90), just as the North Star gives directions to voyagers in the greater seas of the world.

Quarlous and Winwife escape from that encounter unmarked, but the temptations continue for them. So, in the second scene of Act II, they witness the arrival of Busy's troupe at the pig booth, Purecraft in their midst, an attractive, rich widow whom Winwife has had his eye on. Quarlous advises his friend that this is the opportunity to assault her and board her, like a buccaneer, rush at her and carry off the prize. Winwife hesitates and the moment is lost. In the ballad-singing scene (III.v) they not only witness the heroic purse snatching accompanied by the Orphic minstrel, Nightingale, but they spot another opportunity. Why not use Edgeworth to steal the marriage license from Wasp? This starts as a joke on the severe moralist and governor of Cokes, and it generates the main event of Act IV, the game of vapors, again witnessed by Quarlous. This involves them further, for his intimacies with Edgeworth cause him further solicitation. He is offered a "wife" worth forty marks

246

(III.ii.9), and he must refuse disdainfully to take a share of the prostitutes available at Ursula's place.

> Keep it for your companions in beastliness, I am none of 'em, sir. . . .
> I am sorry I employed this fellow, for he thinks me such. . . . But, it
> was for sport. And would I make it serious, the getting of the license is
> nothing to me, without other circumstances concur. (IV.vi.22-32)

And he quotes Lucan against himself: *"Facinus quos inquinat, aequat";* crime levels those whom it pollutes.

Getting the license may have been done for jest, but once Quarlous has it he makes it useful in earnest. His encounters with Dame Purecraft illustrate, in little, the same kind of development from the proud, playful observer to the serious opportunist, perhaps like Dauphine in *Epicoene,* another ravener, although still an inventive one. But like other episodes in *Bartholomew Fair,* it is possible to judge him and Purecraft too sternly. We need to pay close attention to the mood of the scene, for Jonson's treatment of them places their behavior in a benign context, and it hints at a resolution we can expect in the muddled world of the play.

Purecraft is shaken by the presence of Trouble-All, the madman, perhaps the one she is destined to marry, according to the prophet who examined her urine. Trouble-All has "dropped in" on her like an agent of Fortune (IV.vi.123), and by chance his fight with the officers allows the prisoners to escape from the stocks. Busy interprets the event as "this madness was of the spirit" (IV.vi.167), so they must not refuse the divine opportunity to fly. Purecraft stays behind because she thinks she loves the madman, and she interprets her passion by mocking a passage from I Corinthians on Christian wisdom and the world's folly:

> Mad do they call him! the world is mad in error; but he is mad in truth:
> I love him o'the sudden . . . and shall love him more and more. How
> well it becomes a man to be mad in truth! Oh that I might be his
> yoke-fellow and be mad with him, what a many should we draw to
> madness in truth with us. (IV.vi.169-74)

Her literal interpretation of the cunning man's prophesy leads her to pursue a real madman, but she is "saved" (and deceived as well) by

247

the figurative interpretation of the mad gallant, for she drops her pretense of sanctity as Quarlous drops his false pride. He marries her in the disguise of a madman in order to have her money, but that impulsive act, by the event redeems her.

Trouble-All had trivialized the legal warrant, and Purecraft trivialized the biblical warrant — an absurd use of law and scripture (IV.i.109-13), but Quarlous seizes these opportunities, and he acts boldly. Nor does he have to stoop the whole way down to compromise with a dirty world, because his dissimulation enables him to take a happy chance. When Purecraft first offers herself to him, he rebukes her, as he had rebuffed the vulgar crowd three times before. "Away, you are a herd of hypocritical, proud ignorants, rather wild than mad. Fitter for woods and the society of beasts than houses and the congregation of men. You are the second part of the society of canters, outlaws to order and discipline and the only privileged church robbers of Christendom" (V.ii.41-46). As severe an attack on Puritans as any in the play. But since he finally admits to himself that it is money he wants, he might as well marry money when it is offered (V.ii.80-82). He had been unwilling to confess his venality earlier in the comedy, and this admission amounts to self-denigration, a consciousness that his worth is not far different from the folk he sneers at.

Dame Purecraft's confession is more startling, for her faults are grievous. She had posed as a willful, holy widow only to inveigle gifts and feasts from suitors, as in Volpone's confidence game. Monstrously, she devoured charity that should have gone to the poor. And thinking she confesses to a madman, Trouble-All, she puts herself into the hands of a "sane" man, and perhaps she becomes more gentle, more human.

> And thus having eased my conscience and uttered my heart, with the tongue of my love, enjoy all my deceits together [i.e., her six thousand pounds], I beseech you. I should not have revealed this to you, but that in time I think you are mad, and I hope you'll think me so, too, Sir! (V.ii.70-74)

Chance has arranged the opportunity "in time" for her mistaken confidence, and there is no playing with one's fortune, Quarlous and

Purecraft seem to agree; "follow me an' you will be mad, I'll show you a warrant!" Quarlous has no sooner said this than chance acts once more and drops in Justice Overdo. Overdo wants to salve his conscience about his former clerk, and Quarlous is ready to take money where he finds it. So Justice disguised as a fool gives his warrant, in effect a blank check, to prudent Opportunism disguised as a madman — an equivocal emblem of wise folly, indeed.

Even the most indistinct characters of Winwife and Grace are touched by the folly of a day at the Fair, and although their handful of unmemorable remarks shows their scorn of the proceedings, they are, like Quarlous, tempted to seize an opportunity for instant marriage. They accept the chance medlay of a spouse discovered by lottery, under the strangest of circumstances. In her sweet simplicity, Grace knows that Cokes is impossible, but she refuses to choose between two better young gentlemen, Quarlous and Winwife, lest she seem to forsake her modesty. She, therefore, proposes the lottery, because "destiny has a high hand in business of this nature," letting the next man who comes their way choose which name he prefers. When Trouble-All wanders by, they press him into service as a soothsayer, but, alas, recognizing no name except Overdo, he marks Grace's book at random. For all Grace's caution, it is clear that no prudence or reason determines her choice, and she needs the offices of a madman—for all we know, a fortunate folly.

IV. HUMANIZING POWERS

The mockery and hence the vulgarity of their experiences stimulated the visitors at the Fair. Contact with the chances of low life seems to have released something, exaggerating their inanities, making them clamor with the rest of the crowd. But some have come, finally, to a new, provisional awareness. This development is particularly clear in the minds of the three censurers. Wasp has, at least for the moment, lost his tyrannical power over Cokes, when Cokes learns of the faults in his governor, who has been disgraced in the stocks. Wasp then declares, "He that will correct another must want fault in himself" (V.iv.99-100). The bluster has gone out of him, so he resigns his government. Justice Overdo, thereafter, finds the frailty of his authority, as his "enormities" reveal their true nature. She whom he thought a whore is his own wife. What he thought was his atonement for Trouble-All is a swindle of Grace. As these people are visibly taken down, they come to understand something about their condition. They are humanized insofar as they achieve a consciousness of themselves, and possibly they are in the way of knowing what is "better."

Certainly Overdo is shamed. like Busy and Wasp, and Quarlous persuades him not to prosecute the cutpurse (lest his magistrate's wit be shown). It is better to recover the goods and save his estimation of himself and the thief. Shame, therefore, helps to change a justice into a slightly more civilized one, similar to the way shame worked in Jonson's comical satires. Quarlous, who now knows his own worth and has outwitted everyone else, can now be generous with his advice; he shows Overdo how knowledge of his frailty makes him tolerant. That he is Adam, flesh and blood, prompts Overdo to invite everyone to a supper (as was done after an academic dispute), to "drown the memory of all enormity in [his] biggest bowl" of wine. Having been convinced by Quarlous and moved by his own chagrin, Overdo advises Wasp to practice the virtue of patience, too. He recognizes even Punk Alice as a person who can care for a "sick friend," his wife. He no longer cherishes their fear of him, so his intention is to correct not to destroy, to build up not to tear down. His convivium will be the symbolic opposite of the game of vapors, supporting life rather than stifling it in forms and rage, and together they will drown not people, but the memory of their faults. Unlike Jonson's earlier comedies, no one is banished; everyone, even Punk Alice and Ursula and the puppets, is included.

Contact with the squalor of the Fair in disguise as a fool apparently helped Overdo to know his weaknesses and his possibilities as a man. And in a similar disguise, as we have seen, Quarlous eventually accepts a less than perfect marriage. It is worth noting that Ulysses' best argument in Gelli's *Circes* comes after he has failed to persuade nine different animals of the advantages of reason and free will. The animals have almost convinced him that nature and brute experience surpass reason, but Ulysses converts the tenth creature by an affirmation of the greatest gift to man — his consciousness of his own worth, his potential virtue, no matter how bad his condition may be. Jonson's epigram on the hero of "The Famous Voyage," Sir Ralph Shelton (cxix), suggests the same kind of moral outlook, praising Shelton's way of living in a vulgar world. Jonson admires Shelton for his judgment and his daring, courage in the face of disease, bad air, and the plague. Other men avoid the press of crowds on account of the pox, some avoid court because they have no fancy clothes, some cry out against cock fights because they have no money to bet. But Shelton refuses to play the hypocrite; he takes or leaves these entertainments according to judgment. He dares to breathe "any air," and although he looks for virtue, he will choose the least evil. He can associate with "the vulgar" while "treading a better path, not contrary." In the maze of errors he can know his way, "which is to live to conscience [i.e., consciousness of right], not to show." In other words, Shelton represents the autonomous man, like Quarlous perhaps, who lives among people, breathing the stench he finds around him, and although he may perform ethically impure acts, by choosing the least evil, he escapes infection of his mind because he knows and pursues the good. The epigram is important because it makes something of moral action in a corrupt world. Amid the stench and clamor we who maintain a consciousness of the best can know our way, even if we die in the course of treading it, and

> He that, but living half his age, dies such,
> Makes the whole longer than 'twas given him, much.

Jonson approves of Shelton and disapproves of stoic passivity because people should not shrink from experience of common life and squeamishly withdraw into some specious purity. Morose's aversion to noise has the same implications, and Dauphine's often brutal jests are appropriate reactions to it. We should be willing to choose a risky course of action, in search of the better way that we hold in our mind's eye.[37]

The same advice applied to the audience at the Hope theater.

Jonson told them they would enjoy a merry play, made for the delight of everyone "and to offend none. Provided they have either the wit or the honesty to think well of themselves" (Induction, lines 83-84). If they are conscious of their worth and think well of their potential good, they can relish whatever fare is put before them, without offense. For such auditors, Jonson would extend the same praise he gave to Shelton,

> That to the vulgar canst thy self apply,
>   Treading a better path not contrary,
>   And in their errors maze, thine own way know.
>   Which is to live to conscience not to show.

The comic world of Lucian's dialogues also seems relevant to *Bartholomew Fair,* in addition to the specific connections with a journey into Hades and dialogues with the beasts, mentioned earlier. The ethical implications of Overdo's desire to enforce an ideal code of behavior, in contrast with Quarlous' willingness to settle for the least evil in common life, are commented upon by Lucian. Menippus adventured into Hades to resolve the contradictions between authorities of the world and their prescriptions for a good life. Some philosophers advised hard work for a successful career, others said money does not matter, only duty, and others advocated (or at least implied by their actions) that pleasure is the end of life. The oracle Tiresias told Menippus not to worry about such doctrines; "The life of the common sort is best, and you will act more wisely if you stop speculating about heavenly bodies and discussing final causes and first causes. Spit your scorn at those clever syllogisms and, counting all that sort of thing nonsense, make it always your sole object to put the present to good use and to hasten on your way, laughing a great deal and taking nothing seriously."[38] Such anti-utopian advice might be given to Justice Overdo, Zeal of the Land Busy, and Wasp, who have aimed for moral absolutes, purity of spirit, and strict enforcement of every jot and tittle of the law. They certainly need to learn how to laugh. But instead of Menippus' earnest desire for ultimate answers, Overdo and Busy had developed an enormous fanaticism. According to Lucian, such people (along with rich men) do not go to Hades right away. They must first suffer 250,000 years on earth as jackasses. The mature comedian of *Bartholomew Fair* treats them more gently.

Jonson's, like Lucian's, is a chance world where ideals of man must be held only tentatively. Common life, symbolized by humble dress and the company of rogues and fools, is not to be avoided. The madman's garments prove "very fortunate" when a ragged robe produces the effects of wisdom and wealth that cunning failed to accomplish for Quarlous. The low garment over fine clothes amounts to an acknowledgment of personal traits shared with the rest of humanity, like Prince Hal in an Eastcheap tavern and Henry V disguised as a common soldier. I think the ragged robe suggests the most important function of vulgarity and travesty in the play. Encounters with potent representatives of the earthy world, facilitated by such disguises, cause most of the visitors to trans-vest themselves, just as the romantic tale of Hero and Leander is travestied into the low life of the suburbs. Contact with the Fair humanizes these people — with all the ambiguity involved in being human. That ambiguity is reflected in common speech, for instance, in the words of Karl Kraus, "When a man is treated like a beast, he says, 'After all, I'm only human.' When he behaves like a beast, he says, 'After all, I'm only human.' "

The basic ambiguity is latent in other parts of the play, too, as we observe the variety of human consequences amidst the characters' shared experiences. After Win Littlewit and Mistress Overdo are willing to admit that they must urinate and they learn that only a broken pot will serve, they soon discover their flesh and blood. Henceforth, they wear prostitutes' clothes like Punk Alice's. When his wife needs to vomit, it emphasizes the humble meaning of Overdo's pretentious discoveries, his need to be gentle as he returns to judicial power. After all, weakness has been uncovered in his own family. When Cokes is stripped to his shirt and left, pig-like, with a bunch of rotten pears, he has been flayed like St. Bartholomew. And Jonson calls the audience's attention to the parallel with the martyr:

Would I might lose my doublet and hose too . . . Bartholomew Fair,

253

quoth he: an ever any Bartholomew had that luckin't that I have had.
I'll be martyred for him and in Smithfield. too.[39]

The most ambiguous instance of human covering and uncovering is
Trouble-All, who ceases to call for a warrant when his madman's
garment is taken away. He enters for the last time, as mysterious as
ever, a poor, bare, forked creature, covering his nakedness with
only a dripping pan, shouting "be uncovered" (V.vi.49). Ursula's
dripping pan as a substitute for his gown (lines 57-60) may be
intended as a visual comment on the family resemblances between
the other humans and the Sow of Enormity; as the pan is the least
covering, so our piggishness, like that creature with the least soul, is
the most basic human trait. Whatever it means, Trouble-All's final
entrance is an arresting moment, puzzling and terribly funny.

At best, the Fair confers a provisional blessing upon everyone,
not exactly divine grace. Something more distinctly playful, vis-
ceral, and alive to animal existence, a life-enhancing laughter, is
involved. The close of the play leaves us with only a tentative
feeling about human possibilities. Whereas Puritans separated the
realms of nature and grace, or separated carnal wisdom and inspiration, Jonson finds life inescapably impure, a mixture of prudence
and foolishness, of chance and clamor. The play suggests that we
need a bit of the profane, the irrational, a streak of madness in the
face of ignorance and fortune. And it is a blessing to be able to
laugh, as Edgeworth does when Ursula rushes into the fight with a
pan of hot grease. He says, "God bless the woman" (II.v.156).
Wasp's laughter has a similar tone when he says of the cutpurses
who robbed his pupil, "Bless 'em with all my heart. . . . Now as I
am no infidel, that I know of, I am glad on't" (II.vi.106-08). No
matter how he is treated by others, Trouble-All gives the sweet
benediction, Overdo (i.e. God) "quit you, and so multiply you."
Purecraft accepts the madman who is offered her, saying, "heaven
increase his madness and bless it and thank it" (IV.i.104-05). A
blessing is the gift of fortune for which we pray and give thanks;
Leatherhead implies as much when at the opening of his puppet
booth he prays for "luck and Saint Bartholomew."[40] A whimsical

destiny has a hand in the great and small actions of life; not everything is rational and planned and sweet-smelling. Trouble-All may pray for us, but Jonson shows us our fuller humanity, helping us to laugh.

8.

Romance in a Diminished Mode

If *Epicoene* and *The Alchemist* aimed at exhaustion of dramatic possibilities and resulted in draining men of their humanity, Jonson's later comic ventures, beginning with *Bartholomew Fair,* tried to put humanity back into comedy. He became more interested in the possibilities of a tarnished but audacious hero, already suggested in Dauphine, Truewit, and Quarlous. He had long had an inclination toward dramatic conversions, as we saw in the denouements of *Every Man out of His Humor* and *Cynthia's Revels;* and in *Bartholomew Fair* he developed a playful tolerance, even a vulgar sort of gayety. After Justice Overdo has exhausted his desire to uncover enormities, only to find that his behavior was the greatest enormity of all, he discovers that he is only Adam, and Quarlous admonishes him on the point. The appeal obviously touches Overdo, for he turns to angry Humphrey Wasp and says, "Nay, Humphrey, if I be patient, you must be so too; this pleasant conceited gentleman hath wrought upon my judgment and prevailed." As the crowd skips off to supper at his house, he delivers what amounts to an epilogue to the theater, assuring everyone that none should fear to go along, for his intentions are for correction not destruction, building up not tearing down. It is this impulse toward a tentative reconstruction of human relations by patient effort that is reasserted in *The Devil is an Ass, The Staple of News, The New Inn, Tale of a Tub,* and *The Sad Shepherd.* Trying to show that he is not exhausted, Jonson made

256

more agreeable yet probationary comedies, intended to strengthen and lift the hearts of his sullen auditors. *The New Inn* and *The Sad Shepherd,* moreover, seem to return to the old comic matter of love and admiration, adapted from romance material — separated families, obscure motives, wonderful discoveries of identity, festive celebrations, and long rhetorical speeches. Nevertheless, since they were partly a response to the Caroline vogue for French romances, they are not mouldy tales like *Pericles,* and they maintain a close touch with low-life, actual places and practical human choices in a diminished world.

I. THE OLD MIRTH AND *The New Inn*

The New Inn (1629) was justifiably unsuccessful on the stage, but the author's artistic purposes come through the text clearly enough for us to feel some of its mood. Few students of Jonson are willing to dismiss this play as a mere dotage any longer, although its defects are obvious enough. Jonson's faults as he got older became magnified, so that here every character talks too much, about ten lines more than each speech requires. We must hold too many relationships in our minds too long before things start to happen, and the vigorous, carefully wrought language presents insuperable difficulties for actors and audiences. Jonson never seems to have had much faith in his audiences; yet he wanted to please them, and he wanted them to understand. In the face of a failure, like *Cynthia's Revels* or *Poetaster,* he told everyone that the fault lay not in the cook but in the taste of the banqueters. Consequently, when in disappointment he revised the plays for publication, he expanded their didactic parts, trying to explain how stupid the spectators were and what the real point was that they had missed. Presumably, once they understood, the judicious readers would hold the plays in high esteem. Something like this may have happened to the text of *The New Inn,* for we know that certain changes were made. At least "Cis" had her name changed to "Prue," and not all the other alterations were made in printer's proof for the first edition (1631). But in spite of the deficiencies of the script, *The New Inn* has considerable vitality. Its freshness and its artistic daring make it an interesting specimen for study, because frequently the rough surfaces of dramatic failures reveal more for analysis than the smooth and well-joined structures of the best plays. Tendencies that have been only partly understood in Jonson's later work emerge here with particular clarity.

Most discussion of *The New Inn* concentrates on the clothes symbolism and the theatrical metaphor — how the inn is a stage whereon all the world's a play. The Host has a seat there in his own inn, "To see the comedy, and laugh, and chuck / At the variety and throng of humors." Clothes disguise men from themselves and reveal to others what they are; Nick Stuff and his wife, naturally, epitomize such follies. Mr. C. G. Thayer and Miss Harriett Hawkins give the best accounts of these themes, and their remarks about particular episodes are genuinely perceptive.[1] But after a good beginning their essays expand in scope from episodes to the play as a whole, concluding that the drama is ironic, that it is attacking court Platonism, or that it is unified by the theme of appearance and reality. However, since all drama deals with appearance and reality, I do not think that this interpretation tells us much more about *The New Inn* than about *Love's Labor's Lost, Oedipus the King,* or *Charley's Aunt.* And any discourse upon modern ideas of role playing and the uncertain line between dream and experience makes contact with Jonson's play at only a few points. Moreover, Jonson handles the court Platonism in *The New Inn* with such sympathy and consideration that it can hardly be satirized, in the usual sense of that word. In any case, I find the play to be the comic romance that it seems to be, and I see little reason to recycle it into a satiric comedy, albeit the romance is modified by the importance of practical action following upon a vision of the ideal. A study of the tone and dramatic development will elucidate Jonson's sustained and not exactly ironic treatment of the themes of love and virtuous action.

The play's subtitle "The Light Heart" suggests what Jonson meant to be our emotional response. Since the phrase occurs dozens of times and in almost every scene, more frequently than the theatrical image and the clothes metaphor, Jonson obviously wanted to remind the players and audience that light-hearted mirth should prevail. At the outset, the Host calls attention to his sign for the inn, an emblem of a heart weighed down with a feather, and "outweighed too: a brain child of my own." The sign probably is the judicial balances familiar in many emblems of the time; on one side is a playing card, the ace of hearts, lifted by a feather that weighs down the other pan. (The Host refers to it again this way at II.v.46-47.) He swears that he will maintain this rebus against all humors and all complexions in the body of man, because he is an innkeeper, and he must have "jovial guests" to drive his ploughs and "whistling boys" to bring the harvest home, or he will "hear no flails thwack." His professed motive is commercial as the motto under his emblem suggests: "A heavy purse makes a light heart," but his temperament also requires a gay atmosphere, and Lovel's melancholy bothers him so much because it is the obverse of his own.

The inn at Barnet, a place outside of London notorious as a resort for city and courtly folk, should be ringing with pleasant shouts; guests should drink healths and eat heartily. Between 1600 and 1640 outlying inns, such as the Saracen's Head at Ware with its famous bed eleven feet by eleven, were proverbially sites of unrestrained revels. Sir John Daw and Sir Amorous La Foole bragged that they had sported in that great bed with noble ladies and afterwards their bath cost fifteen pounds. Tottenham Court was within walking distance for a lower-class rendezvous, but the wealthier gamester hired a coach to carry him and his "countess" to Rumford, Croyden, Hounslow, or Barnet — "the next bawdy road" *(New Inn,* IV.iii.71). Massinger celebrates them too, where

> . . . pleasures stol'n being sweetest. apprehend
> The raptures of being hurried in a coach
> To Brainford, Staines, or Barnet.
> > . . . in all these places
> I have had my several pagans [whores] billeted
> For my own tooth, and after ten-pound suppers,
> The curtains drawn, my fiddlers playing all night

259

"The Shaking of the Sheets," which I danc'd
. . . with my cockatrice.
                              (*City Madam,* ca.1632, ed. Hoy, II.i.106-14)

So far the problem that suggests itself to a contemporary audience is whether the inn can be merry without being debauched.

Lovel poses this question to the Host when he wonders how a man of his sagacity and clear nostril can keep an inn, for innkeepers are usually rogues, bawds, and cheaters. The Host replies, a bit sharply, that he is not that kind of person and that anyone who says the contrary is a rogue. Rumor may say that he talks bawdy, and Lovel may believe it at his peril. There follows a characteristic Jonsonian defense of the honorable man as victim of slander:

No slander strikes, less hurts, the innocent.
If I be honest, and that all the cheat
Be of myself in keeping this Light Heart,
Where I imagine all the world's a play,
The state and men's affairs all passages
Of life to spring new scenes, come in, go out,
And shift and vanish; and if I have got
A seat to sit at ease here i' mine Inn,
To see the comedy and laugh and chuck
At the variety and throng of humors
And dispositions that come justling in
And out still, as they one drove hence another,
Why, will you envy me my happiness?

                                            (I.iii.125-37)

The theatrical metaphor, in this context, is part of the Host's justification of his essentially innocent house in contrast to others. In personal terms, the speech justifies his integrity and his capacity to enjoy life. The only "cheat" he perpetrates is in his own imagination — his capacity to transform the behavior of other men into his entertainment. By superior knowledge and a detached point of view, secure in the center of himself, he can laugh at the variety of humors, and in his happiness, sustained by his serene confidence in virtue, he professes not to care about vulgar opinion.[2] This is the ethical importance of the theatrical metaphor — emblem of a life of detached amusement, by a spectator like Montaigne.

Diminished Mode

It is what Lovel does with his imagination that so disturbs the Host. He prefers not to take part in any "cheerful chirping charm" with Fly, the inn's resident spirit and more or less its social director. Lovel would not find joy alive in his cups, as he would not find a fly there, for he spends his time reviving dead flies with crumbs, drawing fleas out of a mattress, impounding them in cages, poring over them with magnifying glasses. He dissects crab lice and cheese mites with a "neat Spanish needle," he measures ants' eggs with some fantastic instruments (the Host observed all this through a keyhole). Like virtuoso gentlemen of the time, who withdrew from society to collect specimens of natural history or a variety of curious art — John Tradescant for instance, under the patronage of the duke of Buckingham, amassed the most famous collection of oddities — Lovel idles away his time in a melancholy fit. Life has lost its savor for this "complete gentleman," soldier, and scholar; he has no employment in the commonwealth nor under the king, and even his scholarly or scientific investigations lack a purpose. He is caught in an eddy of Jacobean and Caroline society, where a number of well-educated and sensitive young gentlemen floated, since they found no preferment at court — or, as in the case of Sir Kenelm Digby, they were on bad terms with the duke of Buckingham, who controlled patronage. They retired to their country houses (suffering from melancholy and disgust, no doubt) where they dabbled in various arts and sciences, collecting sculpture like the earl of Arundel or coins like Thomas, Lord Windsor. Digby went in for books and manuscripts at an early age; Robert Burton gathered lore on melancholy itself. The whole cultural impulse was toward the useless, curious, and ornamental use of knowledge, like the renaissance courtier turned into an eccentric scholar.[3]

Lovel is also typical of his age in his fascination with Platonic love. As a youth he had been tutor to his patron's son and had instilled the old-fashioned aristocratic values, along with good language, self-defense, and horsemanship. But after he fell in love with one of the new-style ladies, the Platonic Lady Frances Frampul, he lost ambition and zest for the world. Like the hero of John Ford's *The Lover's Melancholy,* when he tried to dissemble his

261

passion, it oppressed him severely. Lovel must be silent, "As the tame lover should be, and as foolish" (I.iv.20), because his former pupil, Lord Beaufort, once "affected" Lady Frances; therefore, he must not presume to offer his suit. Lovel simply ruminates on his Idea of a mistress in her perfect, unattainable beauty. Later in the play, his speech in praise of love reminds one of the speech in defense of love that Sir Kenelm Digby included in his memoirs: essentially it is the coupling of two souls in spiritual union, with no accompanying, unworthy thought or loose appetite, because it rests on immovable minds. The holy fathers of this religion of love are Plato, Heliodorus, Ficino, Sidney, and D'Urfé (as Digby would agree too), but it still allows for sex or "increase." It is an honorable and chaste passion, entirely sincere and not given to control by appetites, but appetite has its place. Like Digby, too, Lovel has had a vision of perfect beauty, which he memorializes for us in one of Jonson's most perfect songs:

> It was a beauty that I saw
> So pure, so perfect, as the frame
> Of all the universe was lame
> To that one figure, could I draw
> Or give least line of it a law!
>
> A skein of silk without a knot!
> A fair march made without a halt!
> A curious form without a fault!
> A printed book without a blot.
> All beauty and without a spot.

Digby's vision came to him with the aid of a magician in a Spanish garden, where he saw the spirit of his Lady Venitia Stanley; Lovel's comes in a meditation.[4] But as the Host recognizes from the start, this love is ineffectual and debilitating, no matter how wonderful its conception or how sincere its motives.

In other words Lovel and the Host complement each other: the one idle, melancholy, noble, and Platonic; the other energetic, jovial, consorting with people of doubtful morals, and practical. They criticize each other justly, and as the play proceeds, both make important discoveries.

The Host's main effort in the first half of the play is to draw Lovel out of his depression, just as Prue's effort is to draw Lady Frampul out of her affectations of a cold, courtly mistress, and Fly's effort is to draw out (in another sense) Sir Glorious Tipto. Although they use masks and role playing as their tools, the whole atmosphere of forced gayety, happiness put on for the occasion, seems important. For instance, the Host constantly exhorts Lovel to "be jovial"; Lovel's food and drink are a scandal on the inn's reputation. It is against his "free hold," his Magna Carta of the light heart "to drink such balderdash" as clarified whey. "Gi'me good wine, or Catholic or Christian, Wine is the word that glads the heart of man," a paraphrase of the glowing celebration of God's bounty to man in Psalm 104: we bless the Lord for all his gifts, "wine that maketh glad the heart of man . . . and bread which strengtheneth man's heart." The Host's poetry is "Be merry and drink sherry," for he will never be happy with a light heart as long as he has a single sullen guest (I.ii.22-32). He is trying to foster an atmosphere of recreation, of temporary withdrawal from a corrupt society, possibly a place of spiritual renewal like Duke Senior's Forest of Arden.

Beneath the forced gayety and studied melancholy each man has a secret, another life that he tries to keep out of sight. Lovel's is his secret love. The Host's is a guilty past, his noble birth, and his abuse of his wife. Apparently some unspoken bond exists between them, some inexplicable attraction that they have for each other. The Host wonders why the melancholy gentleman came to the Light Heart, the seat of noise and mirth, and Lovel wonders how such an educated man could choose to run this inn and bring up such a cultivated son as Frank. When new guests arrive, Lovel prepares a hasty departure, even though he has just begun to "taste and love" the Host. The bond becomes stronger as the Host pleads eloquently for Lovel to stay, urging him with vigorous expressions of personal loss. The Host must "take hold" of Lovel's heart, and he does this by insisting that they must live together, because they cannot survive separately. If Lovel goes, he will break up house, fire his bush (i.e., his ivy hung out as a vintner's sign), turn country bankrupt, break his heart. All his fresh guests will stink.

263

Jonson and Elizabethan Comedy

> I'll pull my sign down,
> Convert mine inn to an alms-house! or a spittle
> For lazers or switch-sellers! Turn it to
> An Academy o' rogues! or gi' it away
> For a free-school to breed up beggars in
> And send 'em to the canting universities,
> Before you leave me.

(I.v.34-40)

In effect, this is what the New Inn would be if it could not hold people like Lovel, and by analogy with a play, we might say this is what comedy would be if it could not appeal to "sullen" men, thoughtful, well born, but corrupted by the times. The analogy suggests an overtone of the speech, slightly hinted at by the mention that Lord Frampul had been a puppet master and had lived with gypsies for half a year. But since the audience does not yet know that the Host is mad old Lord Frampul, the implication could not be prominent on the stage.

The young Lady Frances Frampul imitates her father's former ways; as cock-brained as he, she takes all lordly, conspicuous ways to consume her estate, "if clothes and feasting/ And the authorized means of riot will do it." The word "authorized" is important to distinguish her revels from unrestrained licentiousness, just as a court jester is authorized to say sharp things that other attendants cannot say to the prince. Since the Host recognizes this noble essence, he blesses her with the remark that she shows her lineage "and I honor her for it." We are probably supposed to think, by hindsight, that the Host wants Lovel to stay as much for his daughter's benefit as his own. At any rate, Lovel seems affected by this displeasure at his leaving, and he resolves to stay — the first step in his rehabilitation.

Jonson may have tried to suggest, in this relationship of the two men, not only that they complement each other, but that the rehabilitation of the one satisfies some unspoken need in the other. Certainly, the Host's subsequent emphasis on Lovel's personal involvement has a passionate note. Having been recognized at the inn, Lovel is asked to take part in his lady's sports. It has been proposed that Prue shall be the queen of misrule and hold a court of love for everyone's mirth. Lovel again declines, but Prue persuades him at least to attend the festivities if not to play in them, because as authorized mistress of the revels she promises to hold a mirror up to her lady's error (like the presentor of an earlier Jonsonian comedy). This promise transports Lovel, for the moment, to contemplate "fancied treasure," his love, although the Host undercuts him by asking whether, according to his name he is *Love-ill* or *Love-well* (I.vi.95). Lovel does not know except that he has loved long and impotently, with desire enough but no success. He has never had the nerve to overcome his noble self-denial and to declare his passion to the lady. Because of Beaufort's prior claim, his piety or stoic sense of duty holds him back.

The Host urges him nevertheless to ignore these scruples; he must be himself, "be still that rage of love,"[5] burn on, and if Prue can strike some spark in Lady Frampul, it may beget bonfires of love. You can never tell what might happen, "What light may be forced out and from what darkness" (I.vi.163-66). That last phrase contains the basic idea of the Host's whole program of action. Chance, a cheerful throw of the dice, and hope for some unexpected pleasures seem to sustain him. His job is to nurture this hope in Lovel, to give him the courage to act in the face of possible failure. And as the first big scene of make-believe proceeds (II.vi), Lovel is gradually drawn in. By command of the sovereign of the revels, Lady Frampul must kiss Lovel, which she does, but so grudgingly that her poor lover feels a mixed pleasure. "Was there ever kiss/ That relished thus! or had a sting like this." A social form has permitted Prue to order her lady to do this; she does it by form only, but out of the mere form Lovel can extract an ideal motive. Although aware of her actual feelings, he convinces himself that the experience means a great deal more. The better part of her kiss has drowned the bitter part; his imagination now activated, he yearns for another kiss. "The distillation of another soul/ Was not so sweet," and until he kisses her again, he would as soon die as have a similar "relish and this taste."[6]

According to Prue's next sovereign decree, the lady must grant

Jonson and Elizabethan Comedy

Lovel two hours of gentle courtship with a kiss each hour but never again to have such converse. The Host now intervenes to convince Lovel that he must accept the role. He should not be afraid of the assembly's scorn: ''Bear up master Lovel./ And take your hours and kisses: they are a fortune'' (196-97). These are two hours of hope, but the fond lover answers in the style of melancholy idealists in D'Urfé, a beggar's pleasure lies in not knowing what he lacks, so if he sees treasure for only a moment, his misery is increased rather than mitigated. Two hours of hope will give years of despair. ''Better be never happy than to feel/ A little of it, and then lose it ever.''

The Host's ultimately persuasive argument amounts to his credo of the power of hope in a good life. Who knows what will happen two hours from now if we have hope? The wind shifts often, three times a day sometimes, and perhaps Prue will change her decree. She may be wise in the law ''yet not sour''; she may be sweet, smooth, debonair, and amiable, as well as rough and stern. ''Try but one hour first and as you like/ The loose [i.e., the upshot, as in discharging a bow] o' that, draw home and prove the other.'' Perhaps he will die in the blessed moment with Lady Frampul.

> I marry, there were happiness indeed;
> Transcendent to the melancholy . . .
> A death
> For emperors to enjoy! And the kings
> Of the rich East to pawn their regions for,
> To show their treasure, open all their mines,
> Spend all their spices to embalm their corpse
> And wrap inches up in sheets of gold,
> That fell by such a noble destiny.
>
> (II.vi.233-42)

Since the Jonson who wrote *Volpone* seldom used such hyperbole without ironic overtones, we might suspect that the Host has a twinkle in his eyes during this piece of enthusiasm, but his intent is apparently serious. He is trying to instill hope in the irresolute heart, encouraging Lovel to play the game of life, draw his lots, be daring. The daring but virtuous short life is praised in equally enthusiastic

266

terms in Jonson's Cary-Morison Ode, and here the suggestion is that chance is an expression of God's gifts to man. The actor Edward Alleyn had a similar faith in chance when he founded his College of God's Gift, where officers were to be chosen by lot and the winning lot to carry the inscription "God's Gift."[7] There is a difference in tone, therefore, between this hyperbolic oratory and that in Jonson's great middle comedies, just as there is a difference in the function of disguise. The former deceptions are here converted to benevolent opportunities.[8]

Nobody ever died of love, the Host may be thinking, in the manner of Rosalind. The basic idea of the speech, however, accords with what he said earlier about his integrity. Because the Host knows he is a good man at the center of his being, he does not fear other people's scorn of his role as innkeeper. So Lovel should bear up in his knowledge of the right, no matter what kind of trivial sport or disappointment may come. Chance and fortune cast us about in many ways, but integrity gives us the ability to grasp the few moments of happiness available. Light-hearted sport is one of those moments. The same chances emerge at the end of Lovel's first hour when it appears that Lady Frampul mocks him. The audience has reason to believe that all is not mockery, and she might be genuinely moved by Lovel's lofty devotion. In an aside she admits, "I could begin to be in love with him," but she will postpone an open declaration "because I hope/ T'enjoy the other hour with more delight,/ And prove him farther" (III.ii.233-36). Latimer suspects that she is serious, but since Prue and the others judge that she pretends, Prue warns Lady Frampul that she may be conjuring a spirit that she cannot lay quiet again. Lovel, as usual, thinks the worst: "she dissembles! All is personated,/ And counterfeit [that] comes from her!" If she were sincere, he grants, all the Spanish monarchy and both the Indies could not "buy off the treasure of this kiss." That supposition is enough for the Host to work on, as he urges Lovel to cheer up, for we cannot guess what might come of this.

> Why, as it is yet, it glads my light heart
> To see you roused thus from a sleepy humor,

Of drowsy, accidental melancholy;
And all those brave parts of your soul awake,
That did before seem drowned and buried in you!
That you express your self, as you had backed
The Muses horse! or got Bellerophon's arms.

(II.ii.264-70)

However, the arrival of the fraudulent or anti-queen of love, Pinnacia Stuff, breaks up their revels, and apparently the chance is lost.

In a moment of confusion when the below-stairs roisterers offend the bogus Lady Stuff (she poses as a countess), Lovel leaps into action — his first impulsive act of the play — he draws his sword and chases the cowardly rogues back to where they belong. Like a knight having saved a lady in distress, he is buoyed up with new confidence, and Lady Frances notes how calmly he speaks after the noise and tumult,

With that serenity of countenance,
As if his thoughts did acquiesce in that
Which is the object of the second hour [courage]
And nothing else.

(IV.iv.20-23)

The Host had been right to make Lovel join the festivities, for unexpected benefits came from them. It seemed for a moment that the arrival of the absurd countess would tear down all the castles in the air that they had built, but by chance it provided the foundation under all. It has given Lovel renewed courage to act regardless of consequences, and now he is ready for his second perilous hour, thinking of nothing else in his erected confidence.

The interlude shows the audience how chance and mistaken identity, along with Lovel's illusions, actually generate real effects. High imaginings, even when they encounter deception, can produce good consequences, but it takes the Host and Prue's game to prepare for the opportunities, and Lovel is still unaware of these truths.

Lovel's discourse on true valor, coming next (IV.iv), relates to the action, as his discourse on true love related to his condition; it is a beautiful lie, an impotent wish. Beaufort, his former pupil, had earlier shown the difference between idealistic love and direct action. He needed no court of love to press his suit to the fair Laetitia, and in this scene he rightly challenges Lovel's theories. Courage does not depend wholly upon knowledge, reason, justice, and honor. We come to see that Lovel's only impulsive act was done in ignorance of the true identity of Pinnacia Stuff. And Beaufort is at first incredulous that Lovel should ignore the danger-ous power of pride, personal reputation, and passion. Not entirely a vice, anger has "profitable" uses, Beaufort says, for it makes us fierce and fit to undertake chances. Lovel insists that reason, not anger or chance, motivates true valor (IV.iv.128); otherwise we might as well use the "poor helps" of drink or frenzy to make us valiant. Hence Lovel's intellectual system, although beautiful and true in the eyes of heaven, allows no place for the accidents of life, nor does it recognize the imperfect nature of man and the unpredict-able side of our passion or courage. But he espouses his idealism so manfully — as if Achilles had the chair of valor and Hercules were but a lecturer — that Lady Frances is moved; "Who would not hang upon those lips forever/ That strike such music" (IV. iv. 138-42). And Lovel's clinching arguments, that the valiant man should be above private quarrels over personal slights, convince Latimer, Beaufort, and the rest; "Truth, and right!" exclaims Beaufort. However, Lovel still lacks audacity to break out of the rules of the court of love. He kisses Lady Frances for the prescribed seconds, and as the game ends he turns bitterly on the charade, for Lady Frances still hesitates to declare her love openly to him. And since Lovel thinks it was all play acting, especially by the lady, he returns to his bed to dream away the vapor of love — if the house and the drunkards of the place will let him.

Although the other participants in the court of love finally seem convinced that Lovel is right, their conviction is of a special order, like the seventeenth-century fideist who believed in a divine order and yet was skeptical about the possibility of realizing it in this world. Sir Thomas Browne, for instance, had faith in the mysteries of the trinity and he delighted in the apparent impossibilities of grace, yet he doubted, hedged, and accommodated his principles to fit the wisdom of this world. It is almost *because* one has faith in the unknowable that one can survive in a world of contingencies. Similarly the people at the New Inn, although converted to an ideal, rational virtue, act upon impulse that breeds unexpected results. In the outcome, audacious behavior, above and below stairs, delivers them from an unresolvable opposition of ideal and action. With the help of Fly (the Puckish figure in the comedy), Beaufort dares to marry Laetitia — in the stable no less, a distinctly unideal place for a noble wedding — and he marries her in ignorance of her identity, for Beaufort's lusty instincts are enough to carry him forward. It looks as if we are going to be entertained by another of Jonson's practical jokes, another Epicoene or a vexation of spirit to shame some young pretender, but what happens is a measure of the distance between this play and the earlier ones. The scene of new mirth on stage, when everyone except Beaufort thinks Laetitia is a boy, expresses this high-spirited energy with vivid delight. While the wiseacres think they are taunting, he boldly prepares for his wedding night.

> Get our bed ready, Chamberlain,
> And Host, a Bride-cup,you have rare conceits
> And good ingredients, ever an old Host
> Upo' the road, has his provocative drinks.

(V.iv.28-31)

In the genial bed tonight, he will cast his dice for a brace of boys. As Fly goaded Tipto on, so Prue draws out Beaufort even more and plays upon his superb confidence by asking for the laces in his codpiece. Like a bride throwing her bouquet, he takes off his doublet, rips out the codpiece points, and hands them to his friends. "I ha' clasps, my Laetice's arms, here take 'em boys."[9] His instincts were right, after all, for the maiden is transformed before his eyes, first into a boy, then discovered to be truly a girl, and finally an heiress of noble blood.

The compounded error has given him more than his wildest dreams, and without his high-spirited audacity, he might never have had her. One revelation begets another in a chain reaction, unmasking old Lady Frampul and the Host, bringing together Lovel and

Frances Frampul, Latimer and Prue. Although Lovel went to bed to dream himself out of love, he has awakened into the wonderful world of fulfilled wishes. All these fancies were made in the light heart by careless daring to act and to enjoy what seemed possible in the moment.[10] Lovel's vision of beauty may be there in everyone's heart to admire, but the realists see the need for sport and mirth in a contingent world. The Host, for instance, confesses that long ago because of his guilt, he too withdrew from society, roamed the country, lived among tumblers, pipers, fiddlers, puppet masters, jugglers, and gypsies — showmen and cheaters all, like the frequenters of Bartholomew Fair. He wanted to "search their natures and make odd discoveries." What he learned from these, apparently, enabled him to survive at his inn, although "coffined" alive, somehow living out his penance. For indeed, all his family have been, in a larger sense, gypsies, tapsters, ostlers, chamberlains — "reduced vessels of civility." Consequently, the hints of a wistful tone that we noticed earlier beneath his mirth are confirmed by the Host's final speeches. He saw what to make of a diminished thing, like Robert Frost's "Oven Bird," a loud, mid-summer bird, who sings a somewhat forced song:

> He says that leaves are old and that for flowers
> Mid-summer is to spring as one to ten.
> He says the early petal fall is past
> When pear and cherry bloom went down in showers
> On sunny days a moment overcast;
> And comes that other fall we name the fall.
> He says the highway dust is over all.
> The bird would cease and be as other birds
> But that he knows in singing not to sing.
> The question that he frames in all but words
> Is what to make of a diminished thing.

In this spirit, the Host goes off with his aged wife to woo afresh, and, like Mecaenas "having but one wife," he will marry her every hour hereafter. He is no longer just a spectator in the theater of life.

Nor is it that Lovel's dream of beauty has come true, any more than the Host's wife has turned young, for Frances Frampul is obviously not the perfect beauty that Lovel envisioned. But Lovel's

271

dream of beauty, of which he sings again at the close of the play, brings them all joy to light their way to bed or to air the sheets with a sweet odor; that relationship symbolizes how his grand ideals have taken a less dominant position in his life, at least for the moment. Now the idea of perfect beauty is a happy and necessary adjunct to lusty pleasure. The dream is in their light hearts, making them careless of fortune's consequences in a diminished world. Mirth operates as a kind of saving remnant, an artificial means of sustaining our courage to be. The courage to wonder, to pretend, to make merry in the face of ridicule, disgrace, or shame, seems to carry one through. It is like a song or bowl of wine to drown the memory of enormities. I do not mean to suggest that this view is the same as the alcoholic dreams of old Cavaliers looking back at the lost cause; the Host and Lovel and Beaufort are not frozen grasshoppers or old warriors musing before a winter fire. In varying degrees, they are audacious men even though they are contemplative, and they know how large is the gap between perfection and the chances of life. This is the dualism that *The New Inn* ends with.

If we understand the main action in this way, the roisterers below stairs have an important function. In fact, they support the spirit of the light heart with less self-denigrating artifice than those above the stairs (partly because they have less of the higher magic of contemplation). Their heartiness, appetite, and thirst, and their capacity for whimsies as well as roguery all go together. Since they are the representatives of life that must be touched in order to give strength and hope, we should not exaggerate the differences between the goings-on at the court of love above stairs and of the roaring boys below. Their baiting each other may be overdone, but the vitality of it outweighs its weakness. The gusto, for instance, with which they catalog Peck's tricks in the stable and Tipto's fancies about duels and proper Spanish forms goes beyond mere ridicule. It has a kind of animal energy, no matter how foolish the men sound. They drink, brag, and fight even though they have little martial courage. But Tipto has the courage to make merry and to demean himself in the presence of his social inferiors. His announcement as he walks out of the less virile court of love suggests this analogy with Beaufort. Tipto tried in his preposterous way to appraise Fly for his true value, the professor of the inn, its true inheritor at the end, the true fly who can problemize, syllogize, elenchize; a bird of the arts, who chirps better below stairs perhaps, but Tipto will "dare to drink and with a fly" in spite of everyone's scorn. In the diminished world of the kitchen these men have known they are mortal, but they have their visions too (III.i.129-30).

Even Pinnacia Stuff and her pitiful husband, the tailor, have a real value (but diminished) in their sad charade. We need not adopt a solemn moral tone about their sexual aberrations, although we recognize their satiric importance in the play. Granted, they stand for the fraudulent new nobility that the Host and Lovel disapprove of so strongly, enormities who have nothing but clothes to speak well of them. Nevertheless, their pleasures are enhanced by their little fantasy — she disguised as a countess, he her page, going to a wicked inn (that really is not wicked), for an assignation (that is really legitimate married love). As Beaufort notices, it is a fine species of fornication with one's own wife, a new kind of authorized riot. The Host sees the amusement of it all, for the brave little tailor, Stuff, and his wife "preoccupy" all his customers' clothes (according to Edward Partridge it was a common sexual pun to "occupy" a woman), and Latimer sees the symbolic satire on them all, as Stuff "lies with his own succuba," in all the ladies' names (IV.iii.76-81). Pinnacia and her husband give a good deal of mirth not only to themselves but to the company who toss them in a blanket — hardly a severe punishment for a vicious behavior. Beaufort cannot help complimenting Stuff at the last moment; "Go thy ways, Nick Stuff, thou hast nicked it [scored well] for a fashioner of venery!" Through the perspective glass of the play, then, the Stuffs have some of the life-giving vitality of mirth that involves hope beyond ridicule.

If this interpretation is sufficiently close to Jonson's purpose, it suggests how much his comic values had changed. No doubt his respect for the ideals of Platonic art, like Platonic love, remained firm to the end of his career, as we can see from his poetry and his masques. The centered self, the man with erected confidence, still

273

won Jonson's highest praise. In his poems he continued to extol ideal virtues, but his awareness that life cannot always be lived by these ideals grew stronger as he matured. Knowledge without action is not enough, contemplation without active virtue leaves man isolated and ineffectual. We will be disappointed if we hope for perfect results, but we must have hope. Also chance is not enough to make a man good, although it might make him great. It is by vision and patient striving that men arrive at good. The distance between the ideal and actual widens, and a good man's effort to cope with the world becomes more difficult. Nevertheless, Jonson seems to feel an obligation to try, and mirth was one of the few points of intersection between the mighty opposites.

The Caroline audience that a comic dramatist had to please was much taken with French romances, like D'Urfé's *Astrée* (London, 1620) and Jean Pierre Camus' *Iphigène* (Paris, 1625), which contain most of the idealism and romance in *The New Inn* (as well as skeptical men of action like Beaufort). Therefore a playwright must at the outset accommodate his art to their interests. A skeptical and critical spirit will, nevertheless, do something to this audience's thoughts and try to remold them as he goes along. I think Jonson tried to do this in *The New Inn*. It must have been a blow when they were not moved; yet he went on, even though he had suffered a stroke and was more or less a forgotten man in London. He flamed into righteous indignation for a moment in his "Ode to Himself," and that rage out of him, he went back to his pastoral about Robin Hood and to his even more playful *Tale of a Tub*. A tough old poet with a lot of energy and insight left was able to throw the dice once more, to take his chance in an uncertain world, while he maintained consciousness of right. A light heart probably helped.

II. *A Tale of a Tub*

As *The New Inn* was a modern version of the old mirth transposing the Forest of Arden to Barnet where love, chance, and fortitude delivered men from their bondage, so Jonson's last play, *A*

Tale of a Tub (ca.1633) seems to toy with the material of other old rural comedies, such as *The Merry Devil of Edmunton* (1602), *John a Kent* (1589), and *Two Angry Women of Abington* (ca.1588-98). With deliberate archaism *A Tale of a Tub* is set in the time of Queen Mary, and the world is seen in a diminished image of country folks — displaced into simple concerns of crops, cattle, constables, and weddings — where the comedy becomes genial. The prologue sets the tone, for it is truly a "ridiculous play," a trifle, a toy — almost solely for pleasure. Although it seems to spoof gently at romance, it operates like many pastorals, glancing at courtly concerns, casting the affairs of ladies and gentlemen into a different mold, not only to "show what different things/ The cots of clowns are from the courts of kings," but to hint at similarities among all men. In effect, Jonson has dramatized one of the themes of *The New Inn,* what to do with a diminished thing, here giving us a literally diminished world, where simple folk try to master their destinies while they reflect general human values.

Herford and Simpson, following C. R. Baskervill and prior theater historians, believed that the play was mainly an early work, perhaps for the Admiral's Men in the 1590s, and that Jonson later touched it up and adapted it to a satire on Inigo Jones. But since this opinion has been effectively refuted by W. W. Greg, E. K. Chambers, and G. E. Bentley,[11] we may conclude that *A Tale of a Tub* is almost entirely the work of Jonson's later years and that whatever rough or seemingly primitive dialogue still remains in the text comprises only a small fraction of the whole. No matter what its date of original conception, for better or worse, Jonson rewrote the play later in his life and apparently rethought it as well. The satire on Inigo Jones, surely from a later time, is found in acts one and two as well as in later scenes, and the elaborate playing with names, pseudolearning, and history that would naturally accompany the composite figure of Vitruvius Hoop-Medlay occupies much of the dialogue. Moreover, the technique, design, and tone of the play hold together sufficiently to justify our interest in it as it stands.

The play's method is reductive, almost trivializing in every respect, but not quite a burlesque. It is a kind of "aping" or miniaturizing that comes from imitating in little, as Nano praises dwarfism in *Volpone* (III.iii.9-14):

> First, for your dwarf, he's little and witty,
>   And everything, as it is little, is pretty;
> Else, why do men say to a creature of my shape,
>   So soon as they see him, "It's a pretty little ape?"
> And why a pretty ape? but for pleasing imitation
>   Of greater men's action, in a ridiculous fashion.

Some of the same charm could be felt in watching the antics of Queen Henrietta Maria's dwarf, Jeffrey Hudson, or in admiring the curious artifacts in John Tradescant's museum — for example, half a hazel nut containing seventy pieces of household furniture. The quaint effect is like seeing a landscape in a small reflecting glass, much simplified and encapsuled in a harmless plaything. Jonson writes of clowns and constables, illuminating the whole with a cooper's wit. His story is drawn from old records, Whitson Lords, and "their authorities at Wakes and Ales," "country precedents and old wives' tales" stuffed out with "antique proverbs."

Encapsulation of place is perhaps most obvious. Instead of Tempe or Arcadia, the setting is a rural Middlesex that was barely rural in 1633; and the familiar names that crop up in the day's adventure — Totten Court, Finsbury, Marylebone, St. Johns Wood, and St. Pancras — were on the edges of urban sprawl. Moreover, other contemporary plays emphasized the sophisticated people and the bustle of suburban events in these places, like James Shirley's *Hyde Park* (1632), Thomas Nabbes' *Covent Garden* (1632-33), and the same author's *Tottenham Court* (1633), as well as the "place" comedies of Richard Brome. *(Bartholomew Fair* started the vogue for place comedy, so in a sense Jonson is following himself, too.) In 1633, city people went to Totten Court to drink, wench, and roister; it was becoming a resort of ill repute, as Barnet was for *The New Inn,* and an area infested with rogues. St. Pancras church was used for hasty and irregular marriages, just as a Pancridge knight was somehow bogus, a knight in dress alone, and Jonson said of Inigo Jones that he will have to content himself to be a Pancridge Earl —

"An Earl for show."[12] I also suspect that the environs of London offered few examples of country dialect by 1633; for instance, the rustic who sings Suckling's "Ballad upon a Wedding" (1638) is presented in some texts as not a local yokel but a "west country man," with his quaint "vorty" and "volk," as he describes a fashionable wedding at St. Giles-in-the-Fields and around the Hay Market, like Constable Turfe and his men who say "vive," "vace," and "veet."[13] Thus Jonson's rural Middlesex of about 1550 contrasts with a more citified present.

Historical references also removed the play from the present to a time shortly after the death of "our late liege and sovereign lord" King Edward. King Harry's doctor is fondly remembered along with the poet laureate Skelton; the priest reads the service in Latin, old John Heywood still lives, and her majesty is frequently mentioned. The livery from Queen Mary's coronation is still recognizable to serve as a disguise for Hilts. These were simpler times, therefore, presumably remote from a money- and status-ridden culture, before the nobleman's pursuit of a rich heiress, before the memory of greedy Buckingham or the murders of inconvenient courtiers or the deposing of Bacon and Lionel Cranfield, before Wat Montague's preposterous *The Shepherd's Paradise* (that took seven to eight hours for the Queen and her ladies to perform), and before the ignominious subordination of poets to the fantastic court architect.

Inanity is the dominant note of the play, but tender inanity. Jonson indulges the audience's wistful sympathy for country clowns while he emphasizes their meager abilities, so characters repeatedly show a combination of humility and pretension. They have the heart to take chances with fortune, trusting nature, but at the same time they attempt little intrigues that might control the outcome. Finding a mate for Awdrey occupies the main action, and it is reduced to a lottery in which a husband is "pricked out" as in a folk game on Valentine's eve. Each man wants Awdrey, honestly or dishonestly, and each makes his little attempt at an opportune moment, but finally the inane polecat, Pol-Marten, gets his chance. In his unsuitable role as usher to Lady Tub and newly endowed with his euphuistic speech (see I.vi.7-12), he cuts a ludicrous figure, but he knows a good thing when he sees it:

> I smile to think after so many proffers
> This maid hath had, she now should fall to me,
> That I should have her in my custody;
> 'Twere but a mad trick to make the essay,
> And jump a match with her immediately;
> She's fair and handsome, and she's rich enough;
> Both time and place minister fair occasion;
> Have at it then.
>
> (IV.v.65-72)

All the others before him have tried their hand at it — often with the dice players' refrain "have at it" — and now it is his hazard. When he learns that the girl does not know the meaning of the word *love* (although if it is a toy she wants to play with it), he goes about his wooing with no nonsense. By analogy with Beaufort in *The New Inn,* chance and the light heart win the maid.

When he sees that she wants to "prove it," he cuts short to an immediate declaration, "Will you have me Awdrey?" And her decision takes no longer than a moment of unromantic reflection. She thinks John Clay has too rough hands and besides he is a thief; Justice Bramble would catch her; Squire Tub would make her a lady. Can Pol make her a lady? He offers a silken gown, a rich petticoat, and a French hood — enough to persuade any sensible girl. So Pol is indeed a "groom was never dreamt of," and the "happy error" of his marriage gives "heart's ease" to everyone except the tearful John Clay. In a parallel development that emphasizes the anti-romantic strategy of the play, the itchy waiting woman, Wisp, takes impudent Puppy as her valentine — with less than minimum courtship. Yet she set out that morning to find the ideal husband of her dreams, as she had described him to her mistress, Lady Tub: "The bravest, richest, and the properest man/ A tailor could make up, or all the poets/ With the perfumers" (I.vii.26-28). The double wedding provides them an excuse to use the provisions of a marriage feast; consequently even the meanest urges of an opportunist bring some mirth and content into this diminished world.

Similarly the priest, Sir Hugh, cheerfully takes money from the Squire, from Preamble, and presumably from Pol, while he plots against his benefactors. Yet he finally performs a bona fide marriage and is forgiven. The testy clown, Basket Hilts, roars about the stage "like middle March," but he is also a tender clown "melting as the weather in a thaw." He weeps like April, is mellow and tipsy like October, and grave like the frost in January — "as rigid as he is rustic" (I.i. 77-83), while he helps and hinders the progress of his master's suit.

The diminished mode approaches travesty in Jonson's handling of lofty allusions in the play. Each low character travels under a pretentious name (and we know how important names were for Jonson) that suggests a heroic original reduced to mean circumstances — like *Bartholomew Fair's* Busy as a modern Ulysses or Nightingale as Orpheus among the beasts. Diogenes, the philosopher famed for his challenge of Alexander and memorialized in Lyly's *Campaspe,* is now Diogenes Scribben, a country scribe, a clerk who may "face down" the Constable Turf. He disputes of law and poetry in terms of mouldy old records, like Fabian's Chronicles and Finsbury books.[14] Saucy Hannibal Puppy, who later marries Dido Wispe, feels that law and poetry are "all but writing and reading," and anything more is mere cheating (I.ii.41-43). His mock-heroic style sets the mood for him and the ensuing action when he comments on the epic portents of Awdrey's ill wedding day. This bride-ale could not hope for a better fortune because

> the night before today
> (Which is within man's memory, I take it)
> At the report of it an Ox did speak,
> Who died soon after, a cow lost her calf,
> The belwether was flayed for't . . .
> The Ducks they quacked
> The hens too cackled at the noise whereof.

(III.ix.54-74)

If anyone misses the point, Puppy makes it clear that he is talking about the wedding feast, for he closes with the observation that the pig cried his eyes out while he was roasted on a spit. All is reduced to Puppy's interest in food. Hannibal Puppy proves what his courage is made of, too, when he meets the "legion" of spirits in Turf's barn, for he sees every straw as a devil. Since he feels sure that only Friar Bacon or Faustus' conjuring stick can control the devils, he refuses to go back to investigate. And while Tub goes alone to find only poor John Clay hiding out, Hannibal imagines demonic horrors:

> Now, now, even now they are tearing him in pieces:
> Now are they tossing off his legs and arms
> Like loggets at a pear tree.

(IV.vi.67-69)

When Clay comes in, Puppy makes a typical joke to cover his cowardice; had Clay been crawling in barley straw rather than wheat straw, Puppy had taken him for the drunken Devil, the spirit of the bride-ale. But as it is, he is only tame John of Clay "that sticks about the bung hole." Thus even Robin Goodfellow, presumably the spirit of the bride-ale, is replaced by a clay spirit.[15]

Medlay, the godson of a weaver and a dramatic relative of Bottom, starts out as a joiner and cooper (although before censoring of the play perhaps he was just a joiner, and Vitruvius Hoop was the cooper), but he wants to be styled an architect. Rasi Clench, the godson of a famous Arabian doctor, is now a horse leech. To-Pan the tinker finds his identity by reference to some "merry Greek," his version of the Great God Pan, who beat a drum in Julius Caesar's army at the invasion of Britain. The original Hoop no doubt found meaning in his role as a diminished Vitruvius, the Roman architect turned into a tub maker. In the eyes of these clowns the world becomes literally a reduced thing, and sometimes a considerably more real thing. As their master is Turf, so they level everyone to the soil. They see that Clay may "cover"Awdrey Turf, and a "fine silken" or even a salt peter tub (i.e., Squire Tub) is inappropriate for her, but a polecat is most appropriate of all to lie on her. Lady Tub is "dried earth" in the Canon's estimation, as Justice Preamble rightly becomes Bramble, by folk etymology. They understand a dictator only as a person, Dick Tater.

Saint Valentine offers them the opportunity to diminish the

central mystery of the holiday, as they variously transpose the mythical patron of love into their own terms.[16] Lady Tub and Canon Hugh see him as "Bishop Valentine," a man of position (I.vii.8, I.i.1). He gives her an excuse to go out and play Lady Bountiful and perhaps *be* somebody's valentine. The Canon rejoices in that day's patron because of the chance for more marriages; the more lovers who get out of their beds early on this day to sing in the woods, the more clinking coins in his purse. Clench thinks that the saint must be a "zin," perhaps a deadly "zin," who once dwelt at Highgate, "a woundy, brag young fellow" or maybe a matchmaker. Pan thinks he must have been a stately "zin" of the church who kept a brave house. Puppy thinks he could have been a giant, for all he knows. Meanwhile, Diogenes Scribben vainly searches his county records for a former resident named Sim Valentine (I.ii.1-28). Tobias Turf resolves the mystery, however, in terms of his and the play's overriding concern — Saint Valentine surely signifies Son Valentine, since this day John Clay will play Son Valentine, marry Awdrey and get a son. Clay will leap his daughter ere night and "spring a new Turf to the old house" (I.iv.16).

The style of the plain folk's dialogue itself suggests a calculated reduction of the level of discourse because of the frequent use of proverbs. For instance, the first thirteen lines of Act II are virtually all proverbs: "cheer up, the better leg avore . . . This is a feat once done and no more. And then 'til done vor ever, as they say . . . vor a man ha' his hour, and a dog his day . . . keep still on his old gate[way] . . . wedding and hanging both go at a rate . . . hit the nail on the head . . . my own flesh and blood." The rest of the scene is sprinkled with common expressions like "It would lick salt," "Dear meat's a thief," and "True as a gun." Jonson normally avoided proverbs in his plays, as unfit for good style, and when he used them in his earlier plays, at least, they suggest a speaker's limited intelligence. In this he was unlike Shakespeare, who delighted in proverbs and used them in some of his most serious writing.[17] But in *A Tale of a Tub* Jonson achieves a special homely mood by familiar sayings, and there are so many of these old saws that can be found in John Heywood's collection of proverbs (1546) that Jonson must have had a copy of that book before him as he wrote.[18] Moreover, he calls our attention to the penny wisdom of his characters by adding little tags like *as they say;* "I love no trains o'Kent/ Or Christendom, as they say." "Your wedding dinner/ Is starved without music. [Medlay replies,] If the Pies/ Come not in piping hot, you ha' lost that proverb." Other sayings do not need identifying because they are too familiar, like "Tell the troth and shame the Divel," "All is not gold that glisters," and "as guilty . . . as the child was born this very morning."

Better-spoken characters, like Squire Tub, offer pretentious styles that suggest pure inanity. For example a passage that Simpson believed was "early" writing, appears rather to be pompous, copy-book wooing, when Tub addresses Awdrey.

> Hath the proud Tiran, Frost, usurped the seat
> Of former beauty in my love's fair cheek,
> Staining the roseate tincture of her blood,
> With the dull die of blue-congealing cold?
> No, sure the weather dares not so presume
> To hurt an object of her brightness. Yet,
> The more I view her, she but looks so, so.
> Ha? gi'me leave to search this mystery!
> Oh now I have it. Bride, I know your grief;
> The last night's cold, hath bred in you such horror
> Of the assigned bride-groom's constitution,
> The Kilborn Clay-pit, that frost-bitten marl,
> That lump in courage, melting cake of ice;
> That the conceit thereof hath almost killed thee.

(II.iv.52-65)

Awdrey's equivalent of this farrago is her simple remark a few minutes earlier: "I am a cold." Old Turf's style, however, is the most vigorous, when he lets his feelings come out with full enthusiasm, in the manner of Simon Eyre, for example, in the scene where everyone is in low spirits because he has lost something valuable, and Turf feels depressed for he has lost two interchangeable things, "My money is my daughter, and my daughter/ She is my money, Madam." But John Clay walks in, and Turf's mood changes to unmitigated delight.

> John Clay age'n! nay then — set cock a hoop;
> I ha' lost no daughter nor no money, Justice.
> John Clay shall pay. I'll look to you now John
> Vaith out it must, as good at night, as morning.
> I am e'n as vul as a piper's bag with joy,
> Or a great gun upon carnation day!
> I could weep lion's tears to see you John.

> (V.iii.51-57)

Style like this almost redeems his greed, and for the moment we may not notice that he rejoices to have saved money, no matter about his daughter.

The "masque" at the end of the play reveals Jonson's intent most clearly, for it is the culmination of his genial inanity. Since the comedy was presented as a toy and a foolish device in archaic form, so the wedding masque is a childish toy to entertain the guests at Totten Court. It is an emblem of the Tub family, a little dumb-show mounted on a tub, and it is very dumb, indeed. Exactly how this show was staged remains uncertain, but it was probably some variation on a puppet show. One passage has stumped several commentators:

> this tub, I will have capt with paper,
> A fine oiled lantern-paper, that we use. . . .
> Which in it doth contain the light to the business.
> And shall with the very vapor of the candle
> Drive all the motions of our matter about,
> As we present 'hem.

> (V.vii.30-36)

E. K. Chambers, Simpson, and Miss Snell thought that the show was a shadow play, in which images of mute actors were cast on the lantern paper from behind. But shadow plays apparently originated in the eighteenth century. W. W. Greg supposed that the story was drawn on paper, and the tub turned around (in imitation of Inigo Jones' famous revolving sets) showing each episode. But if anything revolved it had to be on the top of the tub, that is exposed when the curtain is drawn. A more plausible interpretation is that there were some projections of images on a screen, as from a magic lantern placed on the tub.

Jonson and Elizabethan Comedy

In 1618, Cornelius Drebble, the engineer and inventor of a perpetual motion machine — that Jonson alluded to in *Epicoene* — put on a magic lantern show at court. In it he "projected images of himself in different costumes from a beggar to a king, one figure metamorphosing into the next through the social scale."[19] This may have been a late version of the *camera obscura,* like what G. B. della Porta describes in his *Magia naturalis* (Naples, 1589). Porta entertained great men, scholars, and ingenious persons with scenes of huntings, banquets, armies of enemies, plays, and "all things else that one desireth," by use of mirrors and lenses, projecting from a light chamber into a dark one through a narrow aperture. He would assemble wooden figures, trees, animals, and the like in the light chamber, having them move in and out like puppets, accompanied by the blowing of horns and music.[20] But Drebble's device sounds even closer to the magic lanterns that Athanasius Kircher describes in his *Ars magna lucis et umbrae* (Rome, 1646). Kircher had colored pictures on a drum that could be turned to various images, reflected in a mirror onto a wall or ceiling. The presence in Kircher's illustrations of an artificial light from candles and images drawn on paper corresponds to the light within the lantern paper that Medlay uses. At any rate, it would have been natural for Drebble and Jones to have worked together on such a light show, a fit production of the cooper and architect, In-and-in Medlay.

The candle driving all the "motions" of the matter around would normally have suggested a puppet show for Jonson, and we know from *Bartholomew Fair* and allusions in his earlier comedies that he had a low opinion of those motions. The close association of Inigo Jones' "lantern-lerry" arts and a puppet play appears again in Jonson's verses, written about 1633, "An Expostulation with Inigo Jones."

> Henceforth I do mean
> To pity him, as smiling at his feat
> Of lantern-lerry, with fuliginous heat
> Whirling his whimsies by a subtlety
> Sucked from the veins of shop-philosophy.
> What would he do now, gi'ng his mind that way
> In presentation of some puppet play!

(VIII, p. 405, ll. 70-76)

Lanthorn Leatherhead, by his very name, suggests some connection with the figure of Medlay and his lantern show. And puppets could still have been used by Medlay, even though they do not speak — simply as dolls that move silently as an interpreter tells the story and points to various figures.[21] Medlay's five motions, then, were possibly five pictures or little skits with dumb figures, and Medlay, with a pointer in his hand, "his verge t'interpret, tipped with silver," tells each part of the story.

The puppet show in *Bartholomew Fair* was a travesty of two beautiful stories reduced "to a more familiar strain of our people," but Medlay's lantern show seems even more pathetic and poverty stricken. The fable he tells is no more than a bare recapitulation of the events of the day: so the guests are treated to a representation of themselves doing what they just finished doing. The trick lies only in the eyes of the theater audience who view the masque as an illusionist device, an imitation of an imitation, much like the seventeenth-century painter's wit in occasional portraits, to show the subject not just as himself, but as he is having his portrait drawn. So the first four acts of *A Tale of a Tub* represent the subject of his masque in all its earthiness: then Medlay tries to draw the portrait of the action, an inadequate rendering by an incompetent artist. Like Thomas Randolph's aim in *The Muse's Looking Glass* (1630), "it is the end we meant:/ Yourselves unto yourselves still to present."[22] The device reappears with a new twist in Jonson's last masque and his parting shot at Inigo Jones, *Love's Welcome at Bolsover* (1634). There Jones' attempt to depict the love of the king and queen is inadequate and pretentious. By geometry, dance, and mechanical means, Jones's art becomes a part of the antimasque, grotesque by comparison with the real thing present in his audience. Real mutual love embodied in the persons of Charles and Henrietta Maria outshines the artifice of an inventor like Jones.[23]

In *A Tale of a Tub* the lantern show finally diminishes human affairs to the ultimate banality. Seen through the understanding of a cooper, what happened that day is not totally meaningless, but his five motions exactly correspond to the five acts of the play, and Tub's epilogue simply recapitulates the plot again—at the bidding of the poet who invented the whole *Tale of a Tub* "for your sport."

He tells the audience his vacuous purpose — to show the fortune of "empty tubs rolling in love," in a masque "that you be pleased, who come to see a play./With those that hear and mark not what we say" — a typical Jonsonian slur at the least of his spectators, and hence a reflection upon his and Medlay's art. The joyous wedding, thus, is transposed into a banal dumbshow, more stupid than the tedious brief scene of "Pyramus and Thisbe" or the procession of the Nine Worthies in *Love's Labor Lost*. This show is suitable for a play of proverbs, clowns and constables, and old wives' tales, because it is even lower in the artistic scale. We can imagine Jonson's dramatic problem, just as "The Murder of Gonzago" must be dramatically simpler and more stylized than *Hamlet*, so a play on a reduced level of artifice must be capped with a masque even more reduced. The method of reduced recapitulation has been used in a similar way by Samuel Beckett in part two of *Waiting for Godot* and at the end of *Endgame*. So a conspicuous restriction of scope, language, and invention shows what he can do differently from courtly art of the time. When a man rides a bicycle with no hands we do not expect many fancy maneuvers.

Yet, even in its ultimate banality, the motion of the tub has a possible saving grace, a touch of charity. It memorializes in ceremony the events of the great day when, after all, something really happened. Each participant is duly honored and given a little pat on the back, especially Medlay's friends, the "wise of Finsbury." Turf seems "like St. George" in his rescue of his money and daughter. Medlay kindly omits an episode embarrassing to Hilts — his fear of entering the barn infested with devils, and Hilts thanks him, saying "Well, In-and-in, I see thou canst discern!" Although the discernment is at an extremely low level, in the context of the play's gentle foolishness it amounts to a remnant of courtesy. At the end, the stage spectators freeze in a pose like their portrait in the mock masque, all a quaint miniature dignifying a dimished world.

III. THE CATALOGICAL IMPERATIVE

The iterated entertainment and the lottery of their St. Valen-

tine's Day festivities are worked out so simply and their effects are so innocent in *A Tale of a Tub* that they tell us more about Jonson's comic art than we might at first suspect. In the same way, the formal Court of Honor and Love in *The New Inn* had a benign effect on the fortunes of everyone involved, even though the courtly game seems dramatically less interesting and more stilted and repetitious than the events below stairs. In *The Sad Shepherd,* too, the celebration of a sheep-shearing festival is highly formalized, and as in *The New Inn,* it is interrupted by the spoilsports who prevent observance of all the rites. Although we can only speculate about the ultimate consequences, they surely were intended to be benign. The melancholy lover Aeglamour acts like Lovel, to throw a damper on the fun, and had Jonson finished the play, presumably some game or gimmick would have turned the tide, changed Aeglamour's condition, and restored the playful mood. Earine had to be liberated from the tree, and Puck Hairy converted to the side of virtuous love. Douce, Maudlin, and perhaps Lorel should have been stripped of whatever power or delusions they share, and perhaps they would have joined the feast as well, if Jonson followed his precedent from *Bartholomew Fair.* From the three acts that Jonson drafted, we cannot be sure exactly how he meant to finish the story, and there are dozens of unanswered questions, but we can see that he was moving in ways similar to *A Tale of a Tub.*[24]

If *A Tale of a Tub* recalls English rural comedy of the 1580s and '90s, the closest Elizabethan analogy to *The Sad Shepherd* is *A Midsummer Night's Dream,* with its delicate beauty, magic illusions, and distraction of lovers, but in this case the supernatural forces are led by an evil witch, not aerial spirits; her curses seem to call powers from the depths, not from the stars, and Jonson's Puck Hairy is, at first anyway, potentially dangerous. His soliloquy at the beginning of Act II, however, hints that Puck is leading the witch by the nose. Her magic is really his illusionist trick, and he is her Devil who both deludes and protects her. Perhaps, when the chance or occasion is right, Puck Hairy will take the scales from her eyes and even bless the great feast. Robin Hood and Marian are an anglicized, jollier Duke Theseus and Hippolyta; the couples Aeglamour and Earine, Karol and Amie, bear faint resemblance to the confused couples in the dark wood. And Robin's promised celebration at the feast, with rustic dances, music, and games, may have been meant to correspond to the amateur theatricals of *A Midsummer Night's Dream*. But Jonson's different handling of this "old mirth" is more significant than the possible Elizabethan echoes.

The dialogue keeps within a limited decorum of an ideal but earthbound pastoral, and the talk is carefully and leisurely worked out in various styles according to character, the lowest style, of the witch and her family, suggesting actual Lincolnshire speech. Without much tension in any passage, Jonson elaborates a thought or mood with a remarkable cataloging of details. Apparently he meant to prove that a pastoral could have mirth (unlike the solemn pieces then in vogue at court, the "late heresy" mentioned in the prologue), and the multiplication of bits of experience was his way of doing it. Starting with Aeglamour's disruption of the celebration, the lover lists the things he will do to throw a pall over them, by inscribing everywhere his tale of his drowned mistress; with plenty of tears he will "alter the complexion of the spring," like the fog and floods of Shakespeare's Athens. Aeglamour's story is a virtual pastoral elegy expanded into a play,[25] and behind his grief, unbeknownst to him, stands the malignant witch, Maudlin. On the side of mirth are the merry men and their festival promised to us in lists of delights, fitting for the beatitude of Robin and Marian's love.

Lorel's address to Earine proceeds almost entirely by cataloging the material things he can give her, a badger's cub, a hedgehog, a ferret, milk and curds that make cheese, honey from twenty swarm of bees, acorns, chestnuts, pigskins, and the like — in the manner of the Cyclops' wooing of Galatea (II.ii.1-40 and see chapter 5 above). Maudlin's curse on the feast enumerates the ill effects that should follow from her "Devil's Paternoster." Wise old Alken's description of the witch's dell has the most horrific, earthy connotations, to suggest that her motives are malicious and thus her actions not just "merry pranks." The vigorous poetry here still develops the idea by itemization, and it is skillfully done, as the vision plunges down, down, down:

Within a gloomy dimble she doth dwell
Down in a pit, o'ergrown with brakes and briars,
Close by the ruins of a shaken abbey
Torn with an earthquake down unto the ground,
'Mongst graves and grots near an old charnel house,
Where you shall find her sitting in her form,
As fearful and melancholy as that
She is about; with caterpillars' kells
And knotty cobwebs, rounded in with spells;
Thence she steals forth to relief in the fogs
And rotten mists upon the fens and bogs,
Down to the drowned lands of Lincolnshire,
To make ewes cast their lambs! swine eat their farrow!
The housewives' tun not work! nor the milk churn!
Writhe children's wrists! and suck their breath in sleep!
Get vials of their blood!

(II.viii.15-30)

Alken goes on listing her favorite venomous plants and her choice insects. He contrasts her low "nocent" charms with those of "airy spirits" who play with falling stars and "mount the sphere of fire to kiss the moon," while she sits and reads by the glow worm's light, wounding puppets with the signs of her witchcraft.

The sad shepherd believes in a higher magic, of course, signified by the idea of Earine, whose soul hovers in the air above, "and doth haste/ To get up to the moon and Mercury" (III.ii.25-26). Eventually she will rise into the midst of Jupiter and Phoebus, tempering all the jarring spheres.

Oh what an age will here be of new concords!
Delightful harmony! to rock old sages
Twice infants, in the cradle o' speculation.

Only silence will be fit tribute to the wonder, as Nature herself will hush to hear "the changed chime of this eighth sphere" (III.ii.33-35, 42). The other shepherds think this is wild fantasy, reading a "music-lecture to the planets," but they acknowledge that there are hidden mysteries of love that cannot be understood by ordinary means. Some sort of anatomy lesson might help, opening a window into a lover's bosom to allow us to see all his parts. We could search

289

the liver, heart, and so forth, to see where the seat of love is, but apparently that will be insufficient, because the beloved finds love in lips and eyes, too. Some vast illusion takes charge of a lover's mind and accumulated details can only suggest the invisible power. An evocation like this may be Jonson's dramatic intention in using the iterative method or the apparent chance-medlay of a game, to suggest new concords, harmonies that rock old sages in the cradle of speculation.

From the beginning of his career, Jonson had been attracted to games and similar iterative dialogue more often than other comic writers, for in addition to the familiar ceremonies of courtship, troth-plight, weddings, dinners, or duels in popular comedies, he took a distinct pleasure in the detailed working out of minor forms like the parlor games of substantives and attributes in *Cynthia's Revels,* the mock trial in *Poetaster,* the mock dispute between divines in *Epicoene* with its astonishing repetitions, and the required alchemical steps that Subtle recites so joyously: putrefaction, solution, ablution, sublimation, cohabitation, calcination, ceration, and fixation, from thence to ascension, and to ultimate projection. The intent in each of these seems mainly derisive and belittling to the speakers or victims, and that purpose continues to a certain extent in the game of vapors as well as in the jeering games in *Staple of News.* His poetry also generates its patterns, often in step by step verbal formulas. The epigram "To Fine Grand" (lxxiii) begins with a conceit of the poet as a moneylender addressing a noble debtor who does not want to be seen with him, for the secret of the fellow's borrowed wit must not be known abroad. In the middle of the poem the lender of wit lists the debts, beginning with *In primus* and proceeding *item* by *item* as on a legal bill of particulars: a jest for a feast, a tale, a Babylonian song, a Greek posie for a ring, a charm to be inscribed on the nobleman's picture, a gulling impress or emblem for him to wear at titling, an anagram, an epitaph for my lord's cock "in most vile verses, and cost me more pain/ Than had I made 'em good, to fit your vein," and forty things more. The formal close is achieved by a one-line threat to prosecute or foreclose the loans for the which he should either pay the poet quickly or the poet will pay him. Presumably the "pay" would be another poem, indicting or convicting or sentencing, and we can imagine the innuendoes that Jonson might tease out of the words for those processes.

The brilliant inventory scene in *Volpone* (V.iii) demonstrates how funny and vexatious just a list of things can be if the spectators are aware of the human values that surround it. The audience sees the confrontation of the rivals for Volpone's estate who have come to his house gloating over their inheritance, each thinking that he is the sole heir. Meanwhile Mosca serenely checks off the items: "Turkey carpets, nine," "Two suites of bedding," and so forth. Voltore's indignant question "Is he come now to trouble us?" and Corbaccio's eager "Is it done Mosca?" and Corvino's "Is the hour come?" all get no reply, just "Eight chests of linen." At the same time Volpone hears it all behind the curtain and his asides urge Mosca on, "Excellent varlet." The scene works perfectly with fine articulation of its elements, and each discrete fragment is pregnant with meaning because it fulfills an expectation for character, theme, or action. We can anticipate how each remark by Mosca will strike each of the birds of prey and how it will tickle Volpone behind the curtain. (Incidentally, E. E. Stoll admired this scene and observed how similar Jonson's dramatic economy was to Molière's.[26] And is it not typical of Jonson that an inventory, potentially a monotonous rehearsal, should be the occasion for dramatic economy?) The scene does other things for the play, driving off the birds, vexing them to an extreme. Volpone comes forth wishing to continue their vexation, so they will curse him "till they burst." "How [he] would vex 'em still at every turn" if he put on some disguise and followed them into the streets. That wish allows Mosca to play his last double cross that begins their undoing. That Jonson needed to cut the inventory short and that he needed to suggest more and more vexation is again typical of his dramatic method in the great comedies. Whatever amazement this provokes in the spectators is a response to the apparent plentitude of vexations. Things could be invented indefinitely by these clever rogues.

His later plays, however, use iterative games and catalogs somewhat differently, as we have seen. They contain hidden blessings more often than not, as he exfoliates detail upon detail. Like the mysterious beauty of Charis that transfigures an old lover, turning him into Cupid's statue with a beard, "Or else one that played his ape/ In a Hercules-his shape." What he sees in his mind's eye can be depicted only by a collection of scattered impressions. She is white, soft, and sweet, to be sure, but

> Have you seen but a bright lily grow,
> Before rude hands have touched it?
> Have you marked but the fall o'the snow
> Before the soil hath smutched it?
> Have you felt the wool o'the beaver?
> Or swan's down ever?
> Or have smelt o'the bud o'the brier?
> Or the Nard i'the fire?
> Or have tasted the bag o'the bee?
> Oh so white! Oh so soft! Oh so sweet is she!
> (Charis, "Her Triumph," 21-30)

Sensuous details, imagined in their pristine state, suggest the incredible pleasure of an admiring lover. His beloved's beauty is suggested much like the Greek sculptors were said to have worked, picking out an arm from one model, a face of another, and hand of another, and composing in their minds the perfect figure, but Jonson does it with nonhuman comparisons, and he tosses in that tart and threatening "smutch."

Jonson's vision of paradise, when all the Digby family will be united in the presence of God, describes the almighty in another catalog, unmistakably like the praise of ideal beauty in Charis:

> Where He will be all Beauty to the sight;
> Wine or delicious fruits unto the taste;
> A music in the ears will ever last;
> Unto the scent, a spicerie or balm;
> And to the touch, a flower like soft as palm.
> ("Eupheme," no. 9, 122-26)

The passage suggests the ultimate source for Neoplatonic visions of beauty in the religious tradition, as Isaiah and St. Paul tried to evoke the wonders of heaven. Their catalogs promise wonders that eyes have not seen, ears have not heard, when we shall know God as a certain light, a voice, a sweet odor, a food, and an inward embrace.

The details are lower, more vulgar, in Jonson's distinctly comic writings, as we have seen, but the charm of his catalogs persist and seem to have a similar cumulative effect, although each detail has its intrinsic value. One final example, from a masque performed in 1621, two years before the estimated date of "A Celebration of Charis,"[27] shows the special force of Jonson's additive or formulaic method. It is the blessing of the King's senses in *The Gypsies Metamorphosed* (written especially for the final, Windsor version). After the transformation scene, the Patrico, a "cunning man" or roguish gypsy priest, who has acted as the impressario of the masque, brags that he has given everyone "his fill."[28] Among other miracles, Patrico has changed those gypsies we thought were offenders (that is courtiers) into true men. He further promises that before morning all clowns will be good knights, and the lasses, formerly disguised as pages, will behave according to their ages. It remains for him "to come off with a grace . . . some short kind of blessing." He "studies" out loud about his poetic assignment; the piece must be light, "faster than wishes can fly," and his art will work only if the hearts and voices of others standing by will join in the jocund mood, blessing the Sovereign and his senses.[29] If the piece is fanciful enough it might wish away all offenses. In other words, it is to be a willful delusion, like the masque itself, possibly a healing recreation. A large part of the blessing must be read to get the cumulative effect, as it moves through seeing, hearing, smelling, tasting, and touching.

> From a gypsy in the morning,
>   Or a pair of squint eyes torning,
> From the goblin and the specter,
>   Or a drunkard, though with nectar,
> From a woman true to no man
>   And is ugly beside common,
> A smock rampant and that itches
>   To be putting on the britches,
> Wheresoe'er they ha' their being,
> Bless the Sovereign and his seeing.

Jonson and Elizabethan Comedy

From a fool and serious toys,
  From a lawyer three parts noise,
From impertinence, like a drum
  Beat at dinner, in his room,
From a tongue without a file,
  Heaps of phrases and no style,
From a fiddle out of tune
  As the cuckoo is in June,
From the candlesticks of Lothbury
  And the loud pure wives of Banbury,
Or a long pretended fit
  Meant for mirth but is not it,
Only time and ears outwearing
Bless the Sovereign and his hearing.

From a strolling tinker's sheet
  And a pair of carrier's feet,
From a lady that doth breathe
  Worse above than underneath,
From the diet and the knowledge
  Of the students in Bears' College
From tobacco with the type
  Of the Devil's glister-pipe,
Or a stink all stinks excelling,
  A fishmonger's dwelling,
Bless the Sovereign and his smelling.

And so on through tastes like oysters, a suckling pig, or any portion of swine; touches like bird-lime, pitch, a doxie, and her itch, bristles of hog, ringworm, and gout. The piece ends with an afterthought.

Bless him too from all offenses
  In his sports, as in his senses;
From a boy to cross his way,
  From a fall or a foul day.

Bless him, oh bless him heav'n, and lend him long
  To be the sacred burden of all song,
The acts and years of all our kings t'outgo,
  And while he's mortal, we not think him so.

An obvious impression of the list of petitions strikes the mind immediately; this is neither light nor short, contrary to Patrico's

294

promise. The blessing is in danger of being what it professes to save the king from, a "long pretended fit/ Meant for mirth but is not it." Perhaps it was meant to be spoken as fast as a music hall comedian does, like Danny Kaye's bravura recitation of the names of fifty Russian composers or like the modern major general's song in *The Pirates of Penzance.* Since in that case the individual jokes would be lost, I suspect that a measured delivery worked better, to emphasize the anticlimaxes and to distinguish personal touches. Subtle's catalogs of alchemical terms, authentic as they are, would lend themselves to rapid speech, since they are essentially mumbo jumbo for the audience, but these items have a point. As normal for all masques, the king was the principal spectator; therefore, it was proper for the benediction to bring focus back on him after interest had been dispersed among the courtiers during the fortune-telling episodes. In design the blessing is both a benediction and, by implication, a magic charm for the king, and the most striking thing about the items is their triviality. In a formal benediction we might expect some divine face to shine upon him, to give him peace, and a blessing on the head of state should normally involve the great fortunes of the realm. The gypsy's restriction to James's senses helps reduce the grandeur, limiting the blessing to the king's animal functions. A human being possesses three souls — vegetal, animal, and rational, and as Pico said, if the vegetal soul is cultivated, a man tends to have plant-like characteristics; if the animal soul is developed, he resembles a beast; if the rational soul, he becomes angelic. In a travesty of a benediction, Patrico thus addresses his magic to the beastlike parts of his royal audience.

Jonson goes farther than the usual catalog of senses by sprinkling the list with ugly details so remote from a monarch as to seem silly, the smell of a carrier's dirty feet or a strolling tinker's sheet, the sound of a workman turning a brass candlestick, and the unlikely danger of his touching birdlime, pitch, or the bristles of a hog — in other words, a gypsy's idea of what an ordinary man needs protection from. Mixed with these vulgar details are others so close to King James that they might raise a royal eyebrow, even cause offense (while presumably removing offense).[30] It is doubtful that

295

even the Lord God Almighty could save James from drunkenness, and James was always in danger of falling from his horse, he sat in the saddle so badly. On the other hand, his well-known sexual preferences would suggest little risk of his getting an itch from a doxy. The king was deathly afraid of daemons, but he loved bearbaiting. He loathed lawyers, puritans (hence the loud wives of Banbury), boiled ling, tobacco, pig, and oysters. The king is reported to have said that he was a valiant man who first ate an oyster, and on one dreary occasion, James's courtiers played a trick on him — they thought it would cheer him up — by wrapping a piglet in a blanket and performing a mock baptism in his presence.[31] He was not amused. One puzzling detail in the blessing, the "unfiled tongue," is ambiguous since it implies that James was beset by people who, to the ears of a literary monarch, spoke and wrote in poor style, but the opposite, a "filed tongue" implies deceptiveness. Furthermore, James himself had tongue problems; his was so long that he could not keep it properly in his mouth, and he consequently drooled while he drank, and he talked with some difficulty. (The Prince of Wales had a stammer.) Altogether, the blessing's quaint but decorous vulgarity, indelicate compliments, and harmless but low familiarity evoke whatever lightness it has while threatening to become as serious as the form would imply. Yet the discrete and almost wholly disconnected items never come together in a steady, single impression, as the afterthought emphasized; in effect, Patrico says, "I had to bless his hunting, even though it doesn't fit the rest of the scheme." That is true unless the spectators and the poet have in their own hearts the wish to bless the king, in keeping with the sentiments of the last four lines. With a real desire of good will, everyone can enjoy the "allowed" profaneness of it all, the displacement from a grand and stately prayer that must be implied. So the king can, like Duke Theseus, pick a blessing out of the well-intentioned vulgarity.

W.W. Greg remarked that the coarseness of *The Gypsies Metamorphosed* misses the enormous *entrain* and gusto of Burns, and I think he is partly right because this masque maintains a distinctly gay and innocent tone, with its harmless rogues bursting out of the antimasque, so to speak, and taking over the whole show. It had to satisfy the formal criterion for such an entertainment, fitting a king's after-dinner sport, even for a king with as low taste as James. We need only remember *Bartholomew Fair* to know that with the restraint loosened somewhat, Jonson could match Burns's gusto at every point. It is probably no coincidence that for the 1631 printing of the play Jonson dedicated *Bartholomew Fair* to the king who loved his *Gypsies Metamorphosed* so well that he raised the poet's annual stipend from one hundred to two hundred pounds. The coarseness and attendant low life in *Bartholomew Fair* are important not only because we are invited to enjoy them, but because they seem to advance the comic spirit. In similar ways, mean and ugly things, iterated and played with, seem to enrich the life of his last few plays. His packed dialogue and his mocking sports often bless us, bringing a hazardous but real laughter and delight.

Epilogue

MEANINGS OF THE BROKEN COMPASS

Jonson sometimes invented personal devices or emblems with Latin mottoes for friends and noblemen to use in court ceremonies, but if he had not told Drummond that "his impresa was a compass with one foot in center, the other broken, the word, *Deest quod duceret orbem,*"[1] future readers could never have guessed that this symbol was one of his favorites. Apparently the broken compass had a special resonance for him, but he never mentions it in his surviving works. In recent years there has been recurrent speculation about its meaning, resting on partial evidence, justifying, perhaps, a more detailed survey of the relevant facts.

Because Jonson often invokes the circle as a potent symbol, interpretation of his impress has tended to follow the line of least resistance around the circumference. Allan Gilbert remarks in his notes on "Perfection" in *The Masque of Beauty,* that the impress "represented the compass as broken, leaving the circle incapable of completion. . . . Whatever its source, the idea of the compass [indicates] completion," as in the "Epistle to Master John Selden":

> You that have been
> Ever at home, yet have all countries seen,
> And like a compass keeping one foot still
> Upon your center, do your circle fill
> Of general knowledge.

Gilbert also points out passages elsewhere in Jonson containing images of the circle, but we are left to puzzle out the relationship between the complete circle and the broken compass.[2]

Edward Partridge is more explicit as he expands upon the same evidence in the closing paragraph of his last chapter entitled "The Broken Compass," after an eloquent summation of Jonson's ironic perspective. Jonson might be thought of as the Marlowe of low life, and his major comedies "seem now like antimasques to the Renaissance masque of the Golden Age — grotesque violations of the exalted vision."[3] Partridge concludes:

> One symbol of Jonson's sense of perverted values in an age that was a lamentable falling off from the Golden Age was his own impress. It represented a compass, which Jonson in *The Masque of Beauty* called one of the "known ensigns of *perfection.*" In this masque the allegorical figure "Perfectio" is described as having "In her hand a *Compasse* of golde, drawing a *circle.*" But in the impress — and this is the revealing part — the compass is broken, so that the circle is incapable of completion. The motto *"Deest quod duceret orbem"* was adapted from a passage in Ovid's *Metamorphoses* which goes *"altera pars staret, pars altera duceret orbem."* For Jonson (and perhaps for any comic writer) one part might stand fixed, but the other part could not describe a circle, for the compass was broken, the circle could never be complete, the perfection was eternally marred here below the moon.

This analysis implies that Jonson chose a device for himself that expressed the perverted values of the world. Although he may very well be the Marlowe of low life, an excellent way of describing some of his plays, I question whether the broken compass fits the theme in exactly that way. Like Gilbert's, this reading of the symbol makes more of the circle than of the two legs of the compass, "one foot in center, the other broken." And the contrast of perfection versus imperfection, like that of the Golden Age versus the Iron Age, has still not been related to the passage from Ovid, nor does it show the personal trenchancy that we expect from the author of the epigrams. I am most troubled by the symbol's vagueness, according to Partridge's interpretation, and that it denotes a metaphysical more than an ethical or an artistic statement. As I understand the later Jonson, his work persistently mixed morality and poetics, although as time passed various quantities in the recipe changed.

Thomas M. Greene examines the symbol in a much larger context, pursuing the images of the "centered self" in various circles, points, and compasses, suggesting that there were two tendencies in Jonson's art, one centripetal and the other centrifugal. The circle and center symbolize not so much harmony and completeness as stability, repose, fixation, and duration. The incompleted circle, uncentered and misshapen, "comes to symbolize a flux or mobility, grotesquely and dazzlingly fluid."[4] Greene is especially perceptive about the "homing" instincts that Jonson so often praised, relating them to moral integrity and unchanging values. The centrifugal forces of variety and rapid change are normally associated with stupid people, travelers like Sir Politic Would-be and vapid characters like Lady Would-be, who exude the "fatuousness of cosmopolitanism." Greene feels, as I do, that Jonson delights in Brainworm's metamorphoses (whereas he usually scorns rapid change in his poems). "Perhaps this early play [*Every Man in His Humor*] betrays a genuine tension in Jonson's moral sympathies which the 'authorized' morality of the verse and later plays tends to becloud. There is indeed scattered evidence to suggest a strain of half-repressed envy for the homeless and centrifugal spirit. *Volpone* seems to me the greatest, though not the only work to deal with that strain and make it into art" (p. 337). This seems to me to be an attractive conclusion, as I have tried to suggest in the pages of the present study, but the connection of the broken compass with Greene's main interpretation of the centered self does not immediately spring to mind, since the uncentered, centrifugal forces go astray, unable to make a circle, as Greene says, while Jonson's broken compass *has* one leg in the center. The two images, a circle about the centered self and the broken compass, are slightly incongruous. A look at other possible meanings of the poem mentioned earlier offers a few more clues.

The epistle to Selden is Jonson's most extensive treatment of an unbroken compass and since it was written for a 1614 edition of Selden's *Titles of Honor,* the poem comes within five years of the visit to Scotland and the poet's conversations with Drummond. The first twenty-eight lines establish the poet's personal connection with Selden, who trusted Jonson's judgment enough to ask for a commendatory poem from him, and the poet affirms that he knows of whom he writes. There will be no flattery here, although he concedes that even poets with good judgment are sometimes misled into false praise of a friend.

> Though I confess (as every muse hath err'd
> And mine not least) I have too oft preferr'd
> Men past their terms and praised some names too much,
> But 'twas with purpose to have made them such.

As in his masques, he hoped that by delineating the ideal the actual person would live up to the model. But he forsakes that strategy now that he has been deceived (an echo of his epigram "To my Muse"). He may have sensed that men's failure to live up to his ideal demanded a more circumspect rhetoric to protect his poem's integrity.

> Since, being deceived, I turn a sharper eye
> Upon myself and ask to whom? and why?
> And what I write? and vex it many days
> Before men get a verse, much less a praise;
> So that my reader is assured, I now
> Mean what I speak and still will keep that vow.

So he establishes a character for himself in order to praise Selden's circumspection. Jonson affirms that he tells the truth because he knows himself, his judgment is fit to assess Selden's achievement, and the poet calculates accurately with his sharp eye and discriminating mind to whom, what, and how he writes. Some of his poems were written with ulterior motives, the author knowing full well that the actual man did not live up to his description; here the man and the poem (and the poet) correspond exactly.

Now he addresses the object of his praise, using the compass image to suggest that Selden combines the two qualities that make a good scholar — thorough knowledge and judgment.

> Stand forth my object, then, you that have been
> Ever at home, yet have all countries seen,
> And like a compass keeping one foot still
> Upon your center, do your circle fill
> Of general knowledge.

So one leg's movement around the circle signifies traveling, in books or in foreign places, to gather information. The other leg in the center is that steady mind which examines and judges the material on the periphery, its judgment the point of reference which orders experience. In the rest of the poem Jonson singles out a number of qualities that show the exercise of choice and earnest labor toward good ends. Thus Selden has active intelligence, skill in "things" as much as a will "to instruct and teach"; he takes pains to gather and to pour out his knowledge. He scrutinizes fables severely and redeems truth; he purges errors and reforms times, manners, and customs. He seeks the sources of things as well as paths and byways. He digresses into stories but brings them back into the analysis properly to instruct. Selden's whole work is indeed rich but discriminating. Even his style is an appropriate measure of Selden's intelligence, as it avoids rough and rioting wit, while maintaining a sharpness "of all search, wisdom of choice,/ Newness of sense, antiquity of voice." The two qualities emerge in another form at the end of the poem, as Jonson praises his immense mind (his "wit") that "Nothing but the round/ Large clasp of Nature" can enclose, like a great monarch of letters. Yet Selden's moral center is signified by his innate modesty — as Selden dedicated so wonderful a book to no great name but to his learned chamber fellow, Edward Heyward. The plainest meaning of the circle and center in this poem, therefore, is labor and judgment: energetic, thorough searching, and keen analysis based on truth and virtue.

Iconographical evidence supports and extends that meaning in the various collections of emblems and figures published in the sixteenth and early seventeenth centuries. Perhaps the closest analogy to the compass in the Epistle to Selden, mentioned above, is the well-known device used by the notable, scholarly printer of Leyden and Antwerp, Christopher Plantin. On hundreds of title pages Jonson and his contemporaries could see the image of a hand coming down from the clouds, grasping a compass that draws a circle, distinctly not complete, not half complete in some versions. The motto *"Labore et Constantia"* is interpreted in many of Plantin's larger devices by figures on either side representing the twin virtues. Constancy, usually sitting on the side nearest the fixed leg of the compass, reads a book, has her foot on a globe, holds a

Fig. 4. Compasses Drawing a Circle

cross, or some other symbol of faith or wisdom. On the other side, a man holds a shovel, mallet, ax, hoe, or other instruments of work. The whole run of devices can be seen in Gustave Van Harve, *Les Marques Typographiques de L'imprimerie Plantinienne* (Antwerp, 1911), of which one from Lipsius' *de Cruce* (Antwerp, 1593), is reproduced in Figure 4, where Work carries a compass, square, mallet, bell, and staff.[5] Constancy, so praised by Lipsius (and published by the Plantin Press), is that firmness of mind associated with theory and contemplative virtue; Work is the exercise of practical wisdom.

Both theory and practice are associated with compasses, as Cesare Ripa's *Iconologia* (1603, 1625, 1630) shows them: Theory with compasses on her head, with the legs pointing upward, Practice with compasses drawing a circle on the ground.[6] And other figures in Ripa frequently hold compasses and are interpreted variously in his descriptions to signify measure, proportion, judgment, or simply instruments of action or work. Thus *Architettura* (p. 55) holds a compass and square, as instruments of geometry. *Astrologia* (p. 66) has a compass to measure with. *Bellezza* (p. 80) holds a compass because beauty consists in measure and proportion. *Corografia* (p. 149), i.e., topography, uses a compass to set limits on places. *Dissegno* (pp. 193-94) shows a man with a mirror and compass, the compass pointing upward; whereas the mirror signifies the interior mind where fancy makes a perfect image, the compass shows that design requires measure and proportion. *Economia* (p. 205), *Liberalita* (p. 441), and *Misura* (p. 483) use it to keep measure and proportion. *Inconsideratione* (p. 333) puts a compass under her foot to show how a humor oppresses judgment. *Operatione perfetta* (p. 532) holds a mirror, square, and compass — the glass is a resemblance of our intellect wherein we fancy many ideas of things that are not seen, but may be practiced by art with the help of material instruments. *Giuditio* or Judgment (p. 296) shows a man with a square, rule, and compasses, these instruments denoting discourse and choice, how ingenuity should make methods by which to understand and judge and measure anything.

Obviously there was no single meaning of the compass in Renaissance symbolism, and its significance depended upon the context. The most common explanations denoted measure and proportion, as we should expect, since the Latin *compassare* means to measure, but instruments of work rank second in frequency, according to Ripa. Among the students of Donne's ''A Valediction Forbidding Mourning'' who have scoured alchemical, astronomical, and philosophic imagery as well, the most brilliant and learned essay by John Freccero shows convincingly that Donne had in mind the spiral movement of a compass — moving along its radius at the same time turning around a center.[7] It is like the movement of the planets in the heavens as they seem to wander from tropic to tropic, although they still keep a center. Freccero also demonstrates the relevance of this symbol to the movements of the mind as the will remains fixed in its constancy while the reason moves out.[8] Similarly in Jonson's poem, Selden's compass has twin powers, one to move out and gather information, the other to judge it and exercise choice of various kinds, with intellectual *labore et constantia*.

Jonson's other reference to a compass, in *The Masque of Beauty*, describes Perfection: "In a vesture of pure gold, a wreath of gold upon her head. About her body the zodiac with the signs: in her hand a compass of gold drawing a circle." The marginal gloss says of the zodiac "both that and the compass are known ensigns of perfection." However, the gloss is a compressed statement referring to the compass drawing a circle, like the corresponding passage in Ripa, which implies that the circle is the main symbol of perfection; "The compass with which she describes the circle is a perfect figure among mathematicians, . . . and the circle of the zodiac is a symbol of reason, and is a fit and proper measure of perfect actions."[9] The compass, therefore, when it is identified with the circle, may be said to signify perfection of some sort, or more precisely it is the instrument for making or measuring various kinds of arcs and so by association has potential perfection.

The neglected clue to Jonson's meaning of the broken compass is his motto, adapted from Ovid: *Deest quod duceret orbem* (It fails or is missing that would draw the circle.)It refers to the story of Perdix (sometimes called Talos), a bright young man who was placed with his uncle Daedalus to learn "the teachings of his well-stored mind," but the boy threatened to surpass his teacher, as he "observed the backbone of a fish and, taking it as a model, cut a row of teeth in a thin strip of iron and thus invented the saw. He was also the first to bind two arms of iron together at a joint, so that the arms kept the same distance apart, that one might stand still while the other should trace a circle *(altera pars staret, pars altera duceret orbem)*. Daedalus envied the lad and threw him down headlong from the sacred citadel of Minerva, telling a lying tale that the boy had fallen. But Pallas, who favors the quick wit, caught him up and made him a bird and clothed him with feathers in mid-air. His old quickness of wit passed into his wings and legs, but he kept the name *(perdix,* partridge) which he had before. Still the bird does not lift her body high in flight nor build her nest in trees or on high points of rock; but she flutters along near the ground and lays her eggs in hedgerows; and, remembering that old fall, she is ever

305

fearful of lofty places.''[10] William Golding translates the last few lines with a little more pointed interpretation:

> Yet mounteth not this bird aloft ne seems to have a will
> To build her nest in tops of trees among the boughs on high
> But flecketh near the ground and lies her eggs in hedges dry
> And forbecause her former fall she ay in mind doth bear,
> She ever since all lofty things doth warely shun for fear.[11]

It is suggestive that the boy who invented the compass fell, and because his soul ever after fears to fly at lofty things, he skims along near the ground.

The motif reappears later in the same tale when Daedalus escapes from Crete; he makes wings for himself and his son, Icarus, warning Icarus to "fly a middle course, lest, if you go too low, the water may weight your wings; if you go too high, the fire may burn them. Fly between the two" (ll. 103-06). Icarus is too bold, however, and he falls to the sea. His father, "now no longer a father, called 'Icarus, where are you? Icarus,' . . . then he spied the wings floating on the deep, and cursed his skill [Golding: and curst his art that had so spited him]. As he was consigning the body of his ill-fated son to the tomb, a chattering partridge (an incarnation of Perdix) looked out from a muddy ditch and clapped her wings uttering a joyful note . . . 'a lasting reproach to you, Daedalus.' "

A plausible inference from these passages is that Jonson thought of the broken compass as a symbol of the failure of art, in the lives of Perdix and his parallel, Icarus, for whose fall Daedalus has two reasons to curse his art. Moreover, the failures are clearly on account of envy and striving to go too high — related sins of the father and the son. The phrase "his father now no longer a father" resonates with Jonson's cry at the death of his own son, "Oh could I lose all father now" in a poem that ends with a humble statement of his failed fatherhood and art: "here doth lie Ben Jonson his best piece of poetry." His sin had been "too much hope" for young Benjamin and God had taken him away.[12] By analogy with Daedalus and Icarus, then, the failure of art derives from a moral defect — pride, envy, ambition, flattery of a great name, pandering to inferior taste, just as failure of a father springs from corrupt motives in loving his son selfishly not generously.

I do not suggest that Jonson admired the fearful partridge (or lapwing) nor that he thought the fallen Icarus admirable, for indeed he identified the lapwing with a deceiver like Lupus (*Poetaster*, IV.vii.53), and he mourned the loss of his own Icarus. But he recognized that only very few poets could fly as high as Virgil, like an eagle; most poets (like Ovid and Horace) and "all virtuous men/ Must prey like swallows, on invisible food [near the ground],/ Pursuing flies, or nothing; and thus love,/ And every worldly fancy is transposed,/ By worldly tyranny to what plight it list" (*Poetaster*, IV.ix.54-58). It is the middle way between the water and the fire that most poets must fly, and many accidents can happen because, like all humans, they and their art (as it partakes of worldly fancies) are subject to fortune. Even the most ethical and high-minded poet, like Horace, is a victim of envy and detraction; his works are misunderstood and distorted. Consequently, he learns to use indirection and to dissimulate (like a lapwing) or to accommodate himself to the "fancy of the times" as Jonson told Drummond. If the poet must fly low to the ground feeding on invisible food that others cannot even see, it is no wonder that he fails to be understood by some of his public. If he flies higher he may fail even more disastrously.

Nevertheless, high, low, or middle flying, Jonson never stopped exerting himself, and like Selden (in the poem cited above) he continued to travel, moving out one leg of the compass through many regions of the mind. He wrote another motto in his personal books, *"Tanquam explorator,"* which he took from Seneca's *Epistles* (II.5): *"soleo enim et in aliena castra transire, non tanquam transfuga, sed tanquam explorator,"* (for I am wont to cross over even into the enemy's camp, not as a deserter, but as a scout.)[13] In the same epistle Seneca said that the primary indication of a well-ordered mind is a man's ability to remain in one place and linger in his own company. He thought we should read a limited number of standard authors for ideas that will have a firm hold in the mind. "When a person spends all his time in foreign travel he ends having many acquaintances, but no friends." But some variety is refreshing. "This is my own custom; from the many things which I have read, I claim some one part for myself." So it is the critical choice that matters, even when we scout in the enemy's camp.

That the broken compass signifies unsuccessful (or only partly successful) endeavor, which tends to wander when it should draw a circle, is explained, albeit rather negatively, by the only emblem on the subject (Figure 5). It appears in Gilles Corrozet's *Hecaton-graphie* (Paris, 1540, 1543, 1548, and 1550), the accompanying poems being in French. The heading is "To venture beyond one's power" (*Entreprendre par dessus la force*), with a picture of a compass in a partly complete circle; one leg stands firm on the ground, the other is broken. The verses beneath say that he who forces his mind and desires more than he is capable of is like one who wants to strive beyond his strength. Somewhat more helpful are the longer verses on the facing page that deal specifically with art. They begin by warning that in the art of speaking and writing we are seriously at fault if we waste time merely repeating what others have done. By sloth or cowardliness the artist will spoil his name if he does not dare. But he is more at fault who makes nothing of value for the opposite reason, presuming too much, in his great ignorance. "He resembles the compass which, opened up to make a circle, opens so far that it is broken and the circle begun is left imperfect." The fool intends to do things without judgment or discretion, but he deceives himself, for whatever he attempts lacks (or has in it no) purpose, order, and logic; the result is imperfect because he uses force for the enterprise. He will be criticized eventually when his obstinacy is recognized.[14] The broken compass thus signifies for Corrozet an artist's or writer's need, while daring to be original, not to attempt things beyond his capacity to execute. Corrozet's warnings about art may have been what Jonson meant by the impress, for they emphasize originality and its limits, and they certainly echo the Ovidian passages on the fall of Perdix and Icarus. But there is something still too narrow, too pinched about Corrozet's admonitions to satisfy Jonson's expansive energies.

308

Entreprendre par deſſus ſa force.

*Celluy qui ſon eſprit efforce
Et veult plus qu'il ne peult cōprendre,
C'eſt comme qui veult entreprendre
Oultre ſon pouoir & ſa force.

Fig. 5. Emblem of a Broken Compass

Jonson and Elizabethan Comedy

I suggest that Jonson felt that there were ethical reasons involved in poetry's failure, the defects implied by Daedalus' artifice and envy, for the dangers of a proud poet surely involve moral as well as intellectual difficulties. We need only read Jonson's notes on his travels through books — his *Discoveries* — to see how often ethical considerations come to the forefront. The best known of these is the precept that one cannot be a good poet unless he is first a good man, and we can imagine how many times Jonson had reason to feel culpable on that score. Moreover, he frequently liked to fly along the very bounds of his craft, going to the limits and sometimes going beyond, if only to scout where the outer limits should be drawn. In this sense he sometimes broke one of the legs of his compass, as in his novel treatments of comic form in *The New Inn* or *Cynthia's Revels*. On the other hand, if we interpret the traveling leg of the compass as the one that encounters the world of his readers and auditors, we might suppose that what is broken is the relation between the maker's conception and his execution, and the world sees only the execution. So the poet fails as an artist not because he cannot perceive coherence in his art; there is no defect in knowledge or intent. Rather he fails because his relationship with the world is contaminated, so the embodiment of his foreconceit may be faulty and misunderstood. The tyranny of worldly fancy will transpose what he intends into some monster of apprehension, and because of necessity the artist has left some gaps.

At any rate, I believe that we should be very circumspect in assigning too simple a meaning to Jonson's impress. As I fancy it, the broken compass probably carried a twofold message, one personal, the other social. He must keep his mind on the central purpose of his work, its ideal conception, choosing fit matter and using discretion where necessary, and in execution he should be courageous but not foolish, humble but not cringing, else he will fail. Secondly, he has to cope with potential misunderstanding of men in the world, and he must act and suffer the consequences of his inventive genius; circumspection, strategies, and dissimulation may be necessary. They may compromise him, but he has to dare to move out and meet the adversary. He has to risk drawing a line that is not a true circle or that in the eyes of the world seems to wander, it is so original, even eccentric. Good readers ought to be able to fill in the gaps, or see the true intent in the arc of the wandering or incomplete line. Yet he warns himself in advance that in any case the compass will probably break, not from presumption but from a great original conception.

We have come around to nearly the same point from which Edward Partridge began (no Perdix, he). The perverted values of the world are partly responsible for the imperfection of Jonson's comic art; that must be acknowledged. There are inherent defects in being inventive, moral as well as artistic, that are implied by the tale of Daedalus, Perdix, and Icarus, no doubt a measure of our decline since the Golden Age. Nevertheless, the poet's conception of his task may still be seen by some of his public, in spite of his imperfect expression. The gaps themselves may be a test of the audience's ability to be more than ordinary interpreters.

Notes

CHAPTER 1. JONSON, SHAKESPEARE, AND THE DIVIDED AUDIENCE

[1] A handy, short collection of documents and essays on conditions of playing is *The Seventeenth-Century Stage,* ed. G. E. Bentley (Chicago, 1968), with a current bibliography. The most complete reference works are E. K. Chambers, *The Elizabethan Stage* (Oxford, 1923) and G. E. Bentley, *The Jacobean and Caroline Stage* (Oxford, 1941-68).

Glynne Wickham's *Early English Stages 1300-1660* (London, 1959-72) stresses the continuity of medieval traditions of playing, accompanied by gradual differentiation of design and function. The most searching discussion of dramatic art with respect to classical and medieval origins is Madeleine Doran's *Endeavors of Art: A Study of Form in Elizabethan Drama* (Madison, 1954). Arthur Kirsch's recent study, *Jacobean Dramatic Perspectives* (Charlottesville, 1972), shows how important self-conscious theater was for the early seventeenth century. Changes in the late seventeenth-century drama that hastened the tendency toward more verisimilar or probable actions and away from self-conscious artifice in language and character are discussed by Moody Prior in "Poetic Drama: an Analysis and a Suggestion," *English Institute Essays 1949* (New York, 1950), pp. 3-32. Arthur Kirsch in *Dryden's Heroic Drama* (Princeton, 1965), pp. 152-54, remarks on the influence of Thomas Rymer's strictures, and how such a stern insistence on probability as Rymer advocated was fatal to the artifice of heroic plays. Rymer had insisted that the rapid changes of heart, as in confrontations between Melantius and Amintor, were not literally credible, for "once a sword is drawn in tragedy, the scabbard may be thrown away"; a soldier would complete the "probable" line of action he had begun. "No simple alteration of mind ought to produce or hinder any action in a tragedy." As Kirsch observes, this doctrine spoils the chances to have fine passionate speeches and sudden reversals; it alters the balance of detachment and engagement that prevailed in Fletcherean tragicomedy. The great shifts back and forth between artificial and natural acting continued periodically, down to our time, but in general there seems to have been a tendency toward the natural. Although comedy must have been less susceptible to these changes than serious drama, since artifice, improbability, and surprise were traditionally the stuff of comedy, it does not take much reading of eighteenth- and nineteenth-century plays to see the erosion of comic liberties. Even farces, like those of Pinero and Feydeau, seem much tamer and less playfully artificial than Elizabethan and Jacobean farce.

[2] "As a jig is called for when the play is done, even so let Monsieur go," *Jack Drum's Entertainment,* attributed to Marston (acted by Paul's Children, 1600), sig. C1v. Describing a man who is playing at being a suitor in a studied routine Carlo Buffone says, "it's a project, a designment of his own, a thing studied and rehearsed as ordinarily as his coming from hawking or hunting, as a jig afterplay," *EMOH,* II.ii.35-37 (acted at the Globe, 1599). All quotations of Jonson are from C. H. Herford and Percy and Evelyn Simpson's edition, *Ben Jonson* (Oxford, 1925-52), unless otherwise specified, and I have modernized spelling and punctuation. The following abbreviations have been used for Jonson's plays:

EMIH Every Man in His Humor
EMOH Every Man out of His Humor
CR Cynthia's Revels
BF Bartholomew Fair

Devil The Devil is an Ass
Staple The Staple of News
His other works go under their short titles.

[3]Bearbaiting occurred at the Hope Theater on certain days, fencing matches (called "prize fights") at various public and private theaters; Blackfriars had on two different occasions been rented for a fencing school, E. K. Chambers, II, 529 and I, 361; II, 413-14, 499. As the evidence suggests, fencing was common in the smaller private theaters, and bearbaiting, vaulting, etc. in an arena where the stage itself could be removed, as at the Hope.

[4]*Robert Laneham's Letter* (1575), ed. F. J. Furnivall, for the New Shakespeare Society (London, 1890), pp. 5-6. George Gascoigne's description includes the porter's speech itself, *Works,* ed. J. W. Cunliffe (Cambridge, 1907-10), IV, 92-93. Steven Young made a general survey of inductions in his unpublished dissertation, "The Induction Plays of the Tudor and Stuart Drama" (1970, University of California, Berkeley). Young found no significant classical or continental models for the induction. He distinguishes three kinds: the "supernatural" induction, as in the *Spanish Tragedy,* which seems most like medieval plays; the "narrative" ones, as in Peele's *Old Wives' Tale* or *Taming of the Shrew,* similar to narrative frames in Chaucer; the "extradramatic" or apparently unrehearsed induction that we find in *Knight of the Burning Pestle* and *Every Man out of His Humor.* The third type seems to me to be indebted to courtly games such as Laneham describes. Similar things happened at the Inns of Court on Feast Days; see *Gesta Grayorum* (1594-95). I suspect that Jonson began experimenting with the induction in *EMOH* when he was searching for an English equivalent to the ancient chorus, and he repeated the device with variations in *CR, BF, Staple,* and *Magnetic Lady,* in different sorts of public and private theaters. The opening speeches by Envy in *Poetaster* and Sylla's ghost in *Catiline* seem more like the supernatural induction of *Spanish Tragedy.* The "accidental" opening of antimasques need not be derived from Jonson's dramatic practice, since it could as easily have come from Elizabethan courtly entertainments; see the antimasques to *Love Restored* (1612), *The Irish Masque* (1613), *Christmas His Masque* (1626), *For Honour of Wales* (1618), and *Neptune's Triumph* (1624).

[5]Middleton's *Mad World My Masters* (acted by the Children of Pauls, 1605-06) has a playlet called "The Slip" (referring to a coin), which may also glance at a farcical jig by Augustine Phillips of the King's Men. A brief discussion of the jig is in W. J. Lawrence's "The Elizabethan Jig," *Pre-Restoration Stage Studies* (Cambridge, Mass., 1927), 79-101. C. R. Baskervill prints thirty-six specimens in *The Elizabethan Jig* (Chicago, 1929), with an extensive introduction. He shows connections with balladry and with popular entertainment, and he traces the rise of the jig in the sixteenth and its decline in the seventeenth century. Baskervill corrects a number of Lawrence's points and says that independent jigs (i.e., not worked into texts of plays) were in both public and private theaters before 1600, and after that they continued mainly at the Fortune and the Red Bull. T. S. Graves in "The 'Act-Time' in Elizabethan Theatres," *SP,* 12 (1915), 115, suggested that after 1612, when Westminster magistrates suppressed jigs at the ends of plays, the jig was put into the ent'racte more often than before. But a variety of jigs were used in the texts of earlier comedies, and continued to be so in later comedies.

[6]See Michael Goldman, *Shakespeare and the Energies of Drama* (Princeton, 1972), pp. 147-50, for a sensitive comment on the epilogue to *The Tempest* in this respect.

[7]I mean "game" in the sense of "sport" or "play" as distinct from earnest, just as I accept V. A. Kolve's analysis of the traditional generic meaning of "playing" that pervaded medieval drama, in his study of *The Play Called Corpus Christi* (Stanford, 1966). Exactly how "playing" in this generic sense was transmitted to the sixteenth century and had declined by the early seventeenth century has not been fully explored, but Wickham deals with it at length in part two of his second volume. In the comic tradition, at least, the chain must have been unbroken since *Fulgens and Lucrece* (ca. 1497), and it was supported by the folk games,

mummers plays, and the like. (See chapters 4, 7, 8 below for Jonson's interest in comic games.) Muriel Bradbrook finds ample evidence that in the revels and in courtly "game" there survived the old kind of "conceited" drama. But she suggests that in tragic acting, Burbage as Richard III, for instance, achieved the final "objective" drama; *Rise of the Common Player* (London, 1962), pp. 119-38. I do not understand what she means about playing Richard III, since that role seems to be central to the most self-conscious and theatrical of Shakespeare's serious plays. In later tragedy, how objective could the boy actor have been who delivered Cleopatra's lines when she refuses to go to Rome a prisoner, only to see the players do their Alexandrian revels and some "squeaking Cleopatra boy my greatness/ I'th posture of a whore"? Shakespeare must have had a lot of confidence in the boy who played the part. The best discussion of theatricality in the court masque is Stephen Orgel's *The Jonsonian Masque* (Cambridge, Mass., 1965).

⁸G. K. Hunter's introductions to his editions of *Antonio and Mellida* and *Antonio's Revenge* (Lincoln, Neb., 1965) make the case for Marston's peculiar tone in self-referring drama.

⁹Alfred Harbage, *Shakespeare and the Rival Traditions* (New York, 1952).

¹⁰ Jonson, *Discoveries,* lines 2528-43. He is adapting Cicero's remarks in *De Oratore,* 1.16.70, and the pseudo-Ciceronian definition of comedy that comes down to us in the Donatan commentaries on Terence: *Comoediam esse Cicero ait, imitationem vitae, speculum consuetudinis, imaginem veritatis;* and comedy imitates the *mediocritatem fortunarum* of men. This was repeated in Erasmus' edition of Terence (1536) and elaborated in Philipp Melanchthon's school editions of the plays throughout the sixteenth century. Sir Philip Sidney's *Defense of Poesy* affirms that oratory and poetry are neighbors "in the wordish consideration" and that comedy imitates the common errors of life. In a popular comedy, *Common Conditions* (ca.1575), the trickster goes under that name. An alternative theory of comedy, which Sidney may have had a hand in forming, is discussed in chapter 2 below.

¹¹For instance the prologue, *2 Henry IV;* the epilogue, *Tempest;* prologue, *Henry V;* prologue, Beaumont and Fletcher's *Coxcomb;* epilogue, Ford's *Perkin Warbeck;* prologue, *Alchemist;* epilogue, *Volpone*; epilogue, *Magnetic Lady*.

¹²Earlier sixteenth-century comedies also had judicial endings, as in *Gammer Gurton's Needle* and *Promos and Cassandra.* Leo Salingar, *Shakespeare and the Traditions of Comedy* (Cambridge, 1974), pp. 298-305, comments on the conflicts of law and love in Shakespeare's comedies, which he found in Italian *novelle.* It should be noted that when the sources do not have a legal crisis, Shakespeare adds one, which Salingar convincingly attributes to Shakespeare's personal inclination. I suggest that some implications of comic form are involved too.

¹³Hamlet could have found a precedent in Cicero's story about the Greek poet Antimachus, who read a poem to the audience, but in the midst of his reading all his listeners left him but Plato. "I shall go on reading," he said, "just the same; for me Plato alone is as good as a hundred thousand." *Brutus,* 51, 191. All quotations from Shakespeare are from the New Cambridge edition, edited by J. Dover Wilson and others (1921-66).

¹⁴Jonson, we should remember, was a professional actor and hired playwright for the popular stage for at least two years before his better-known plays were written. On commission he revamped old plays and collaborated with various professionals (some mere hacks), as late as 1605 with Anthony Munday, Chettle, Henry Porter, Marston, and Chapman. Even *Sejanus* had another hand in certain scenes left out of the printed text. W. David Kay says more about Jonson *in* but not *of* the theater in "Jonson's Urbane Gallants: Humanistic Contexts for *Epicoene,*" *Huntington Library Quarterly,* 39 (1976), 251-66. Jonas Barish, in "Jonson and the Loathed Stage," *A Celebration of Ben Jonson,* ed. William Blissett, Julian Patrick, R.W. Van Fossen (Toronto, 1973), pp. 27-53, shows the depth of Jonson's antipathy to the theater and suggests that his antitheatricalism lends to his comic masterpieces "much of their unique high tension and precarious equilibrium."

[15]As noted by David Bevington, "Shakespeare vs. Jonson on Satire," *Shakespeare 1971*, ed. Clifford Leech and J. M. R. Margeson (Toronto, 1972), pp. 107-22.

[16]The folio text substitutes "child" for quarto's "Sal" since the reference would be meaningless in later performances after Salamon Pavy died (1602). Jonson paid tribute to his acting ability in his beautiful epigram, no. cxx.

[17]The dedication to *Volpone*, of course, addresses readers, not theater goers, which raises the question whether some of the preliminaries to Jonson's plays were literary revisions, like the folio revisions of *Poetaster* that aimed to justify the author some time after the first performances. I wonder if the induction to *EMOH* found in both quarto and folio texts was ever acted (and I wonder if anyone performed the induction to *Magnetic Lady*, although it is not as long). I agree with David Kay's interpretation of Jonson's conscious efforts to create a public image of himself in the 1616 folio; see the article "The Shaping of Ben Jonson's Career: A Reexamination of Facts and Problems," *Modern Philology*, 67 (1969-70), 224-37. In any case, texts that give us no reasons to expect literary revision have remarks to the audience with the same critical ideas as the obvious literary appeals.

[18]"Ben Jonson," *London Mercury*, 1 (1919), 184-91, a little-known and persistently narrow interpretation. Huxley accepted ideas from Gregory Smith's book for the English Men of Letters series, which he was reviewing. He assumed that Jonson was preeminently a theorist and reformer and that his plays were consistent with his literary theories in almost every respect. Nevertheless, Huxley recognized that Jonson had some hidden qualities, seen perhaps in his additions to the *Spanish Tragedy* and in his last work, the fragment of the *Sad Shepherd*. "But these qualities . . . he seems deliberately to have suppressed; locked them away, at the bidding of imperious theory, in the strange dark places from which, at the beginning and the very end of his career they emerged. He might have been a great romantic, one of the sublime inebriates; he chose rather to be classical and sober. Working solely with the logical intellect and rejecting as dangerous the aid of those uncontrolled, illogical elements of imagination, he produced work that is in its own way excellent" (p. 187). If Huxley had reread Jonson's plays and limited himself less to Smith's tidy view of the classicist, he might have seen more of the inebriate than he expected.

[19]Jonas Barish has elaborated on the contrast in his essay "Feasting and Judging in Jonsonian Comedy," *Renaissance Drama*, n.s. 5 (1972), 3-35.

[20]William Empson, "Volpone," *Hudson Review*, 21 (1968-69), 651-66, compares this ending with the freeing of Peter Pan by applause at the end of Barrie's play and with the end of the *Beggar's Opera*. I think the analogy is suggestive but not perfect, because Jonson, in effect, gives stern justice to Volpone; applause frees the actor, not the dramatic character.

[21]I incline to agree with E. K. Chambers' interpretation of the evidence and to doubt the Oxford editors' view that the revision came as late as 1612. J. W. Lever summarizes the facts in his excellent edition (Lincoln, Neb., 1971), pp. xi-xii. A. Richard Dutton, "The Significance of Jonson's Revision of 'Every-Man in His Humour,' " *Modern Language Review*, 69 (1974), 242-49, mounts on the revisions a general theory of Jonson's development as a playwright.

[22]Simpson's note on *EMOH*, Ind. 201-03, lists the places where Jonson quoted or paraphrased this statement. Horace wavers between a "mixture of" and "either/or" profit and delight, but Jonson consistently emphasizes the mixture. Paul Sellin, in *Daniel Heinsius and Stuart England* (Leiden, 1968), pp. 147-63, explains that Jonson did not indicate exactly how profit was related to delight in any consistent way. And I think that is a revealing observation, because most of Jonson's theories seem to have been invoked for specific purposes; he was not a systematic critic but mainly an apologist for his work. Furthermore, Sellin finds that Heinsius had little influence on Jonson's criticism. Horace apparently spoke more directly to him, and Heinsius' edition was the convenient one at hand.

[23]Jonson discusses the propriety of metaphors in *Discoveries*, ll. 1889-1918.

²⁴Decorum of character is mentioned in the "Conversations with Drummond," ll. 17-19, 64, 611-13; the tenor of a scene governs Mitis' remarks, *EMOH* I.iii.157, and Face's remarks, *Alchemist,* V.v.159; decorum of place influenced the setting of *Alchemist* in Blackfriars and *Epicoene* near Whitefriars, and in another way the locale of *Bartholomew Fair,* since both Smithfield and the Hope were filthy. On the use of decorum in sixteenth-century criticism, see Bernard Weinberg, *A History of Literary Criticism in the Italian Renaissance* (Chicago, 1961), and G. Gregory Smith, *Elizabethan Critical Essays* (Oxford, 1904), I.xli-xlvi.

²⁵He paraphrased Daniel Heinsius' commentary on Horace here, *Discoveries,* ll. 2602-78.

²⁶The dedication to *CR* is most explicit in depicting the court as the fountain of manners, which should teach men to hate their deformities and love their ideal forms. The mind shining through any suit needs no false light to help it, just like the court of Cynthia, assisted by Crites and Arete. In *The Courtier,* bk. IV, Castiglione describes the courtier as the truth teller and remover of self-conceit in the prince, keeping the prince's mind on worthy pleasures; Singleton translation (Garden City, New York, 1959), pp. 289-95. Jonson's quarrel with Inigo Jones was basically about the limits of accommodation, how much show is permissible for how much philosophic advice to a prince. See D. J. Gordon's essay, "Poet and Architect," *Journal of the Warburg and Courtauld Institutes,* 12 (1949), 152-78, reprinted in *The Renaissance Imagination,* ed. Stephen Orgel (Berkeley, 1975).

²⁷Muriel Bradbrook, *The Growth and Structure of Elizabethan Comedy* (London, 1955, reprinted 1963), p. 117, suggests various points of similarity between Jonson and Shaw—his comical satire like the discussion play, Jonson's inductions like Shaw's prefaces, both playwrights' relying on character and rhetoric, and both creating a public image, half heroic and half comic, which they manipulated with great skill; but she might have added their similar disdain for popular drama and their taunting or trapping an audience into untenable positions, even as the audience was entertained.

²⁸See chapter 8, p. 293.

²⁹G. E. Bentley, VI, 147. Moll Firth was cast as the heroine of Middleton and Dekker's *Roaring Girl* (1607-08) and the epilogue promises that she will walk on stage herself a few days hence. There were "high class" mannish women, too, as *Epicoene* reminds us. See Carroll Camden's delightful account, *The Elizabethan Woman* (Houston, 1952).

³⁰Jonson's satiric epigrams xxxvii, lxii, lxxiii, and cxv show his veiled hostility, as did his alter ego, Horace, in *Poetaster,* where patience is made much of. Self-ridicule of his body is in "My Picture Left in Scotland" (1619) and "The Poet to the Painter." His passion for drink is mentioned as early as the prologue to *EMOH,* line 334. The address to the reader of *Poetaster* says essentially what was later repeated in the two odes to himself (1629). The most suggestive essay on the contradictions in Jonson's public character is Arthur F. Marotti's "All about Jonson's Poetry," *ELH,* 39 (1972), 208-37. Donne's tenth paradox, "That a Wise Man is Known by Much Laughing," distinguishes three kinds of theater audiences — the wise who laugh at comedies, the fools who do not understand the jests but laugh so as to seem wise, and the completely ignorant who remain unmoved. The fourth kind is the comedian himself, a wise man who pretends to be a fool so that the wise (or seeming wise) will be flattered into laughing at him! (John Donne, *Selected Prose,* chosen by Evelyn Simpson, Oxford, 1967, pp. 16-17.) This idea of one who "affecteth the humor of jesting" and asks the wise to laugh at "both him and it" is close to Jonson's manner. In so far as the manner implies flattery it also suggests the danger that Jonson saw in the role of jester.

³¹William Gifford (1816) thought the first version *sake . . . ours* was an error for *sakes . . . his,* and De Winter (1905) agreed. The Oxford editors, however, retain the distinction between the two versions.

³²*London Music* (London, 1937), p. 29; the He-Ancient in *Back to Methusalah* (London, 1921, reprinted 1929), p. 282.

[33]He uses "meridian" in this sense again in the prologue to the court of *Staple* and in the induction to *BF,* meaning "suited to the locality or situation," considered as distinct from others.

[34]Epilogue to *CR.* Even Simpson, who often misses the joke, has seen this one, and he notes that Jonson's contemporaries teased him about his remark for many years (IX,532-33). I follow quarto text in my quotation "By God" rather than "By——" because that is surely what Jonson meant to have spoken, whereas the folio text abides by the 1606 statute against oaths.

CHAPTER 2. COMEDY OF ADMIRATION

[1]*English Literature in the Sixteenth Century* (Oxford, 1954), pp. 2-14.

[2]Walter Allen's translation in William Ringler and Allen's edition, "Princeton Studies in English," no. 20 (Princeton, 1940), p. 33. Also see Ringler's important essay, "The Immediate Source of Euphuism," *PMLA,* 53 (1938), 678-86. Another academic treatise in praise of poetry, *Ricardi Willieii poematum liber* (1573), deals with admiration as an effect of poetic frenzy; translated by A. D. S. Fowler. "Luttrell Reprints," no. 17 (Oxford, 1958), pp. 73-77.

[3]*The Dramatic Works of Thomas Dekker,* ed. Fredson Bowers (Cambridge, 1958), III, 122.

[4]*An Apology for Actors,* facsimile of the 1612 edition, ed. Richard H. Perkinson (New York, 1941), sig. B4.

[5]Erwin Panofsky, *Idea: A Concept in Art Theory* (German edition in 1924), trans. by Joseph J. S. Peake (Columbia, S. C., 1968).

[6]*Woe or Wonder: The Emotional Effect of Shakespearian Tragedy* (Denver, 1951). I am deeply indebted to this elegant and original little book.

[7]Cornelius à Lapide, the seventeenth-century commentator who gathered traditional glosses in his *Commentary of I and II Corinthians,* trans. W. F. Cobb (Edinburgh, 1908), VII, 34.

[8]The same point is made elaborately in *The Pretius Book of Heavenly Meditation* (1581), ch. 31, pp. 153-54, attributed to Augustine. Anglican sermons picked up the motif, for instance in the sermons publicly appointed for Rogation Week, on the theme "that all good things come from God." See *Certain Sermons or Homilies,* 1547 (facsimile of the 1623 edition, Gainesville, Fla.), p. 439; also see homily ix, bk. I, p. 60, "Against Fear of Death."

[9]The fourth book of *De Doctrina Christiana,* a guide to Christian rhetoric, makes this point especially clear. Quotations from Augustine come from the following editions: *Confessions,* trans. W. Watts (New York, 1912); *Christian Instruction,* trans. John J. Gavigan, "Fathers of the Church," (New York, 1947); *Exposition of the Psalms* (Oxford, 1847-57); and *On the Catechizing of the Uninstructed,* vol. IX of *The Works of Aurelius Augustine,* ed. Marcus Dods (Edinburgh, 1871-76).

[10]See the essay by J. A. Mazzeo, "St. Augustine's Rhetoric of Silence: Truth vs. Eloquence and Things vs. Signs," *Renaissance and Seventeenth-Century Studies* (New York, 1964), pp. 1-28.

[11]The glass of liberty in the English renaissance has been discussed by Gordon O'Brien in *Renaissance Poetics and the Problem of Power* (Chicago, 1956). A survey of ancient and medieval religious uses of mirror can be found in Sister Ritamary Bradley's "Backgrounds of the Title Speculum in Mediaeval Literature," *Speculum,* 29 (1954), 100-15. M. H. Abrams touches on the basicly Platonic implications of the mirror image in *The Mirror and the Lamp* (New York, 1958), pp. 42-46.

[12]*De Trinitate*, 15.9.6.

[13]*Expositio in Regulam Beati Augustini, Patrologia Latina*, clxxvi, 923D-924A, cited by Sister Ritamary Bradley, p. 111.

[14]Petrarch's place in the rhetoric of humanism before Ficino is clearly set forth by Jerrold E. Seigel, *Rhetoric and Philosophy in Renaissance Humanism* (Princeton, 1968).

[15]Sears Jayne's introduction to his translation of Marsilio Ficino's *Commentary on Plato's "Symposium"* (Columbia, Mo., 1944), pp. 20-33, is a useful statement of his importance. Raymond Marcel's *Marcile Ficin* (Paris, 1958) is the most thorough study of his thought. Jonson's debt to Ficino, Pico, and other Neoplatonists has been noticed often enough, particularly by D. J. Gordon, "The Imagery of Ben Jonson's *The Masque of Blacknesse* and *The Masque of Beautie*," *Journal of the Warburg and Courtauld Institutes*, 6 (1943), 122-41.

[16]Nicholas of Cusa had a similar conception of self-knowledge. Man re-reflecting upon himself sees that image of truth in the intellect of God. See Ernst Cassirer, *The Individual and the Cosmos in Renaissance Philosophy*, trans. Mario Domandi (New York, 1964), pp. 13-14.

[17]Commentary on *Timaeus*, 100.28, trans. D. P. Walker in his *Spiritual and Demonic Magic from Ficino to Campanella*, "Studies of the Warburg Institute," no. 22 (London, 1958), p. 9, and *De Triplici Vita* part III, *Coelitus comparanda*, as interpreted by D. P. Walker, pp. 15-24. The ability of music to cure troublesome humors is touched on again in *Symposium*, pp. 195-96; "poetic madness" that uses musical tones, harmony, and blending of different things tempers the various parts of the soul (p. 231).

[18]*The Heroic Frenzies*, trans. Paul Eugene Memmo, Jr. (Chapel Hill, 1964).

[19]Bernard Weinberg, *A History of Literary Criticism in the Italian Renaissance* (Chicago, 1961), pp. 87-88.

[20]Scaliger's classification of the three kinds of poetry, his view of the poet as maker, the fore-conceit, the reverence for Virgil as a wise man and model of art are all discernible in Sidney's *Apology*, and although some of these are commonplace notions, Sidney cites Scaliger as his authority for them. Neil Rudenstine, *Sidney's Poetic Development* (Cambridge, Mass., 1967), pp. 155-56, points out the likelihood of Sidney's debt to Scaliger in regard to *energia*. Jonson alluded to Scaliger's theories in his notes to *Hymenaei* (1606), in the dedication to *Volpone* (1606), and in the first chorus to *The Magnetic Lady* (1632). His marginalia in a copy of Chapman's Homer take specific exception to Chapman's "scurrilous" attacks on Scaliger (Herford and Simpson, XI, 593-94). The role of Scaliger's dramatic theories has been mentioned in J. A. Bryant's articles, "The Significance of Ben Jonson's First Requirement for Tragedy: 'Truth of Argument,' " *Studies in Philology*, 49 (1952), 195-213 and *"Catiline* and the Nature of Jonson's Dramatic Fable," *PMLA* 69 (1954), 265-77. Also see David McPherson, "Some Renaissance Sources for Jonson's Early Comic Theory," *English Language Notes*, 8 (1971), 180-82.

[21]*Poetices Libri Septem*(1561 ed.), III.ii, 83. See Sidney's *Apology* 98.28 and 141.37, and the praise of Virgil in Jonson's *Poetaster*, discussed in chapter four. Of course, Scaliger was not the first to hypostesize Virgil, for much of what he says survived from medieval opinion. His combination of the Virgilian model with a pervasive concern for a more earthbound Idea than the Neoplatonists constitutes his importance for Sidney and Jonson.

[22]III.xxv, p. 113, Bernard Weinberg's translation, in his article "Scaliger versus Aristotle on Poetics," *Modern Philology*, 39 (1941-42), 349.

[23]I.i, p. 4; Weinberg's "Scaliger," p. 354 and *Select Translations from Scaliger's Poetics*, trans. Frederick M. Padelford (New Haven, 1905), pp. 13-14.

[24]T. W. Baldwin, *Shakespeare's Five Act Structure* (Urbana, Ill., 1950), p. 296. Daniel C. Boughner, *The Devil's Disciple* (New York, 1968), pp. 20-29, elaborates analyzes the four parts of comic plots and their influence on Jonson.

[25]See Weinberg's account of tragic theory since Averroes, as admiration gradually

predominated over other effects, pp. 352-61; also Marvin T. Herrick, "Some Neglected Sources of *Admiratio*," *Modern Language Notes*, 62, (1947), 222-26.

²⁶Weinberg, pp. 389-97, and Marvin T. Herrick, *Comic Theory in the Sixteenth Century*, "University of Illinois Studies in Literature," (Urbana, Ill. 1950), appendix, p. 232.

²⁷Herrick, *Modern Language Notes*, 62 (1947), 224.

²⁸Owen Feltham, "Of the Worship of Admiration," *Resolves* (1628), pp. 42-43.

²⁹I am indebted to the commentary of Geoffrey Shepherd in his edition of *An Apology for Poetry* (London, 1965), and all quotations are from his text.

³⁰The mind that, with its *speculum vivens*, makes another world or better nature is dealt with by a number of humanists. Shepherd cites Charles de Bouelles' *Liber de Sapiente* (1511), but acknowledges that the same conception is in the Florentine Platonists as well as medieval Augustinian and Franciscan thought (p. 23).

³¹An analysis of the "speaking picture" in terms of sixteenth-century visual epistemology appears in chapters 2 and 3 of Forrest Robinson's *The Shape of Things Known* (Cambridge, Mass., 1972).

³²In 1580, about a year or two before the *Apology* was probably written, "A Comedie called Delight" was acted at Court by Leicester's Men (E. K. Chambers, IV, 195-98), and Delight was a character in *The Play of Plays and Pastimes* alluded to by Gosson in *Plays Confuted*, pp. 201-02 (Chambers, IV, 217-18).

³³The wise man or hero in the ignominious toils of female power had been a comic theme since the middle ages. Virgil caught in a basket below his paramour's window was an old favorite (J. Spargo, *Virgil Necromancer* [Cambridge, Mass., 1934], chap. 5); Aristotle down on all fours, bestrid by Phyllis, was engraved by Hans Baldung; the Wife of Bath tells how Xantippe cast piss upon Socrates' head; and numerous painters depicted Hercules under the power of Omphale. See the reproductions of the last by Lucas Cranach and by Bassano in Figures 1 and 2. *Sir Gawain and the Green Knight* also shows the embarrassment that a hero can suffer at the hands of a woman.

³⁴Neil Rudenstine in *Sidney's Poetic Development* has explored the implications of *energia*. His remarks on Sidney's energy in language are particularly fitting; the cool style of *Certain Sonnets* was transformed with energy in *Astrophel and Stella;* the *Apology*, presumably written between the two, put unusual emphasis on passion and forcefulness.

CHAPTER 3. LYLY AND SHAKESPEARE

¹*Promos and Cassandra*, reprinted in *Narrative and Dramatic Sources of Shakespeare*, ed. Geoffrey Bullough (New York, 1963), II, 442-44. This general view of Lyly is indebted to G. K. Hunter, *John Lyly: The Humanist as Courtier* (Cambridge, Mass., 1962).

²*The Works of John Lyly*, ed. R. W. Bond (Oxford, 1902), vol. II, *Sapho and Phao*, I.ii.17.

³A description of the technique is given by David Bevington, *Tudor Drama and Politics* (Cambridge, Mass., 1968).

⁴See the remarks by G. K. Hunter, *John Lyly*, pp. 190-91. Peter Saccio, *The Court Comedies of John Lyly: A Study in Allegorical Dramaturgy* (Princeton, 1969), finds the plays to be elaborately mythic and allegorical, especially *Campaspe* and *Gallathea*. He disposes of the others with brief strictures.

⁵The tradition of royal praise in these terms has been explained by Ernst Kantorowicz, *The King's Two Bodies* (Princeton, 1957).

⁶Don Cameron Allen, *The Star-Crossed Renaissance: The Quarrel about Astrology and Its Influence in England* (Durham, N.C., 1941).

[7]See L. L. Whyte, *The Unconscious before Freud* (New York, 1962).

[8]The best essay on the play is by Robert W. Dent, "Imagination in *A Midsummer Night's Dream*," *Shakespeare Quarterly*, 15 (1964), 115-29, although I disagree with his interpretation of the last act. David Young, *Something of Great Constancy: The Art of "A Midsummer Night's Dream"* (New Haven, 1966), has many good things to say. On the occasion of performance see Paul N. Siegel, *"A Midsummer Night's Dream* and the Wedding Guests," *Shakespeare Quarterly*, 4 (1953), 139-45, and Paul Olson, *"A Midsummer Night's Dream* and the Meaning of Court Marriage," *ELH*, 24 (1957), 95-119.

[9]C. L. Barber, *Shakespeare's Festive Comedy* (Princeton, 1959), pp. 119-62, gives an account of the fairies, but his emphasis is on folk tales and festivals. He does not recognize the fairies' identity as aerial spirits, and most disappointing, he accepts Theseus' view on the lunatic, lover, and poet as the nearly complete and satisfactory interpretation of the drama. According to Barber, we are not asked to think that the fairies exist, but imagination has played with the possibility. That's apparently all there is to it. For a more balanced view of the fairies see K. M. Briggs, *The Anatomy of Puck* (London, 1959).

[10]In *The Golden Ass*, Lucius is speechless, too, the moment after his transformation back to human form.

[11]Richmond Noble, *Shakespeare's Biblical Knowledge* (London, 1935), is usually helpful in these matters, but in this case he missed the word "bottom" in some translations of 1 Corinthians. Dent, p. 121, is much fuller and more accurate, but he is mistaken in saying that Coverdale's Bible reads "bottom"; it is in Tyndale, *The Great Bible*, and the 1557 Geneva New Testament, which I quote from. Geneva 1560 reads "yea, the deep things of God." One other possible influence has been pointed out by Thelma Greenfield, *"A Midsummer Night's Dream* and *The Praise of Folly*," *Comparative Literature*, 20 (1968), 236-44. In Erasmus, Folly tells listeners to put on asses' ears, and Folly quotes 1 Cor. 2.9 on fools glimpsing paradise who know not whether they are "waking or sleeping: remembering as little either what they heard, saw, said, or did then, seeing as it were through a cloud, or by a dream" (Cholner's trans., 1549, sig. P2).

[12]Frank Kermode, "The Mature Comedies," *Early Shakespeare* ("Stratford-upon-Avon Studies," no. 3, London, 1961), pp. 218-20. Kermode recognizes Bottom's dream as "blind love" and says that it is "ambiguous, enigmatic, of high import" as Macrobius distinguished one kind of dream.

[13]As Satan does in *Paradise Lost*, IV.803ff. Also see George Gifford, *A Discourse of the Subtle Practices of Devils* (1587), sig. F2v, cited by C. A. Patrides, *Milton and the Christian Tradition* (Oxford, 1966), pp. 106-07.

[14]But I do not understand what she means when she asks for "patience" (IV.i.57); patience with her doting, or with her delay of a few moments before she delivers the boy?

[15]Modern critics now seem to take an extraordinary interest in plays after the model of *Six Characters in Search of an Author*, where the subject of the play is about putting on a play, and some critics feel enormously satisfied if they can find this shopworn device in Shakespeare. There is a real difficulty in applying our attitudes in the modern theater to Elizabethan production, where theatrical "illusion" in our sense is hard to find. The basic distinction then was between playing and earnest, not between illusion and reality; the two pairs of concepts are very different, a difference that measures the gap between the old presentational theater and the modern representational one.

[16]J. Dover Wilson's emendation; the reading in Q1 and F1 is "strange snow."

[17]J. A. Bryant, *Hippolyta's View* (Lexington, Ky., 1961), pp. 1-18, thinks this implies a typological interpretation of the events, as "transfigured story." I find his view constricting, and I think Hippolyta means what she says: the "truth" of the lovers' accounts, suggested by their agreement, leads us to deduce that they talk of something more than fancy. She describes an attribute of admiration, a vague and exhilarating feeling of things beyond the apparent facts

of natural experience. Howard Nemerov is much closer to my interpretation in his witty essay, "The Marriage of Theseus and Hippolyta," *Kenyon Review*, 18 (1956), 633-41. Also see Nemerov on "Bottom's Dream," *Virginia Quarterly Review*, 42 (1966), 555-73, for a general discussion of the relationship of play and fact in poetry.

CHAPTER 4. THE WONDER OF COMIC SATIRE

[1] The comic Hercules is alluded to again in *The Haddington Masque*, performed in 1608, lines 165-67; Venus addresses Cupid about his triumphs; "Is there a second Hercules brought to spin?/ Or for some new disguise leaves Jove his thunder?" Cupid replies, "Nor that, nor those, and yet no less a wonder."

[2] "University of Texas, Studies in English," no. 1 (Austin, 1911). Alan Dessen in *Jonson's Moral Comedy* (Evanston, 1971), carries on where Baskervill left off, but with more discernment, pointing out analogies between Jonson and late moralities on social and economic themes. He singles out *Cynthia's Revels* as the only comical satire that resembles a morality, and I agree that it owes something to plays like Wilson's *The Cobbler's Prophecy* (1590). There is no doubt that Jonson was familiar with moralities, since he jokingly alludes to the conventions in *The Devil is an Ass* and *The Staple of News,* but the similarities with the "estates play" do not go far enough beyond a matter of themes.

[3] Oscar Campbell, *Comicall Satyre and Shakespeare's Troilus* (San Marino, Calif., 1938); Alvin Kernan, *The Cankered Muse* (New Haven, 1959).

[4] *The Growth and Structure of Elizabethan Comedy* (London, 1955, reprinted 1963), p. 109.

[5] See David Wykes, "Ben Jonson's 'Chast Book'—The Epigrammes," *Renaissance and Modern Studies,* 13 (1969), 76-87, and Edward Partridge, "Jonson's Epigrammes: The Named and the Nameless," *Studies in the Literary Imagination,* 6 (April, 1973), 153-98. Kernan and Campbell overemphasize the biting qualities of Elizabethan satire, prompted by the supposed etymology satire/satyr, but theories of satire in the sixteenth century were not that consistently narrow. In "Isaac Casaubon's *Prolegomena* to the *Satires* of Perseus," 1605 edition, trans. Peter Medine, *English Literary Renaissance,* 6 (1976), 271-98, Medine shows that satire was often singled out for its moral edification, its power to form great conceptions and to have a forceful *energia.*

[6] Dedication to the *Epigrams,* VIII, 26.

[7] I refer to the early version of the play, set in Florence, since the revised text in an English setting was made at least six years after *Every Man out of His Humor.* E. K. Chambers thought Jonson revised it for a known revival in 1605, although there are possible allusions to events of 1606 (III, 359-60). Simpson's arguments for a 1612 revision are not convincing — namely that the English locale suggests a date near *Epicoene* and *Alchemist* (1609 and 1610), and that the mention of a "tempestuous drum" and "monsters" on stage possibly refers to *The Tempest* (I,332-35; IX,346). We should remember that *Eastward Ho!* (1605) has an English setting, too, and storms and monsters were not invented in 1610.

[8] If Shakespeare played the part of Lorenzo Sr., as implied by the list of actors appended to the 1616 folio, his scornful remarks about poets must have been an extra joke for contemporary audiences. By that time Shakespeare's poetry was well-known enough to add sauce to the speech.

[9] III.i.157, quarto text. The folio reading is less precise about self-love in the definition: "It is a gentlemanlike monster, bred in the special gallantry of our time by affectation and fed by folly" (III.iv.20-22).

[10] W. David Kay, "The Shaping of Ben Jonson's Career: A Reexamination of Facts and Problems," *Modern Philology,* 67 (1969-70), 224-37.

322

[11]Jonson had written three plays for Henslowe in collaboration with small fry like Porter, Dekker, and Chettle, before the end of 1599. Henslowe's diary shows that he did at least two other jobs, the additions to *The Spanish Tragedy* and *Richard Crookback* in 1601-02.

[12]See Lawrence Babb's *The Elizabethan Malady* (East Lansing, 1951). Dudley North told of his melancholy, years later when he had recovered, in a series of essays written in imitation of Montaigne, *A Forest of Varieties*, 1645; see the article on him in the *D.N.B.*

[13]Confusion about Jonson's theory is mostly cleared up by Henry Snuggs, "The Comic Humours: A New Interpretation," *PMLA*, 62 (1947), 114-22, and James D. Redwine, "Beyond Psychology: The Moral Basis of Jonson's Theory of Humour Characterization," *ELH*, 28 (1961), 316-24. However, neither of those commentators observe that once Jonson has made the distinctions, he proceeds to blur them, and I think Redwine separates the moral from psychological implications of humors too sharply, since there was no available psychology not morally based. Just as one who pretends he is neurotic may very well be so for that reason, an obsession with pied feathers and shoestrings reveals a person's character — moral or psychological — as much as lust or envy.

[14]J. A. Bryant does not think these promises are fulfilled in the text as it stands; only the original ending does that, in his opinion (*Compassionate Satirist* [Athens, Ga.], 1972). But it is hard to imagine what these tricks do if they don't show spite.

[15]I quote from the fifth item in Jonson's note, appended to the quartos. The folio omits this explanation in its notes, and Herford and Simpson's text is so cut up and confusingly cross-referenced that it is hard to follow. The Malone Society's reprint of Q1, ed. F. P. Wilson and W. W. Greg, is the handiest place to see the whole of Jonson's postscript. W. J. Lawrence speculated that the original ending may have been prepared for a public performance at the Globe and that "some counterfeit presentment of Queen Elizabeth either came in or was disclosed" *(Shakespeare's Workshop* [Cambridge, Mass., 1928], pp. 99-103). A disturbance ensued and the "humorous man" was not allowed to finish his last speech. Lawrence guessed that Hamlet refers to the disturbance in his remark that the players would be welcome to Elsinore, especially he that plays the King, and "The humorous man shall end his part in peace" (Q2, II.ii.332). If the reference is to *EMOH*, as Chambers agrees, I should think that a court performance is as likely a place for the disturbance — moreover, Jonson's folio adds a heading to the final speech to the queen: "Which in the presentation before Queen E. was thus varied, by Macilente" (III, 599). Presumably the queen or other noble spectators broke up the performance, perhaps walking out as Claudius did during Hamlet's play. However, the Chamberlain's Men would have tried out the play before going to court. Simpson appears to accept Dover Wilson's suggestion that Hamlet's remark does not necessarily allude to *EMOH*, since the interruptions of the humorous man may be "by victims or their partisans of topical or personal allusions." However, we know that the ending of *EMOH* "seem'd not to relish" for an early audience; the trouble was about the queen's figure or presence and its influence on the humorous man. Hamlet is talking about his reception of the actors, and a similar situation develops involving a counterpart of the monarch on stage. Therefore, there is substantial evidence to support Lawrence's interpretation.

[16]I do not understand the last sentence of the dedication where Jonson gives ambiguous advice to the Jacobean court (the dedication was written for the folio). He says under Phoebus (James) it will be the court's province to make more noble minds, "Except thou desirest to have thy source mix with the spring of self-love, and so wilt draw upon thee as welcome a discovery of thy days as was made of her [Cynthia's] nights." It could be read as a warning against the errors of the Elizabethan court, but in that case the "welcome discovery" must be taken ironically. The easier reading is "If you condescend to mix the source of your spring (true minds) with the spring of self-love, you will purify it and draw the proper admiration to you that prevailed in the former court."

[17]Alvin Kernan, *The Cankered Muse*, pp. 162-63, thinks this was Jonson's artistic error, trying to turn the satirist into a reasonable, well-balanced person. If he had allowed Crites to

rail like the stereotyped satirist in Marston, it would have been a better play. But given a choice between *Cynthia's Revels* and *What you Will* or *Histriomastix*, I prefer Jonson's play.

[18] As I understand it, the antimasque is a false masque before the true one, and something like this can be observed in courtly pieces for Elizabeth's entertainment long before the *Masque of Queens*.

[19] E. M. Thron says some good things about this in "Jonson's *Cynthia's Revels*: Multiplicity and Unity," *Studies in English Literature*, 11 (1971), 235-47.

[20] It is difficult to say whether the changes for the folio text are revisions or restorations from a longer version that pre-dated the quarto, but R. W. Berringer, "Jonson's *Cynthia's Revels* and the War of the Theatres," *Philological Quarterly*, 22 (1943), 1-22, suggests that a passage, V.iii.601-02, was borrowed from John Davies of Hereford's *Witts Pilgrimage* ca.1605-10, hence part of the later revisions.

[21] J. Huizinga, *The Waning of the Middle Ages* (New York, 1954), p. 84.

[22] "I will hear the play;/ For never anything can be amiss/ When simpleness and duty tender it." *A Midsummer Night's Dream*, V.i.81-83. The parallel was first noticed by Peter Whalley in his Jonson edition (1756), but I have seen no critical use of it. Apparently the saying was not a proverb.

[23] Allan Gilbert first noticed the importance of this masque, "The Function of the Masques in *Cynthia's Revels*," *Philological Quarterly*, 22 (1943), 211-30.

[24] Vices disguised as neighboring virtues were used in court entertainment long before *CR*. An Elizabethan example was *The Cobbler's Prophecy* (1594) by Arthur Wilson, which Chambers thinks was for court production. A character named Contempt masquerades as Content, and one of the muses plans to write a pageant showing how Pain now wears the garment of Pleasure. See C.R. Baskervill, *English Elements in Jonson's Early Comedy*, p. 251, for a number of other instances of the device, going back to Skelton's *Magnificence*.

[25] Edward Partridge, "The Symbolism of Clothes in Jonson's Last Plays," *Journal of English and Germanic Philology*, 56 (1957), 396-409, discusses the negative implications of clothes.

[26] See Ernest Talbert's "Classical Mythology and the Structure of *Cynthia's Revels*," *Philological Quarterly*, 22 (1943), 193-210.

[27] Arthur B. Ferguson, *The Indian Summer of English Chivalry* (Durham, N.C., 1960); *The Autobiography of Edward, Lord Herbert of Cherbury*, ed. Sir Sidney Lee (London, 1906); Lawrence Stone, *The Crisis of the Aristocracy* (Oxford, 1965), p. 42.

[28] Jonson's letters, Herford and Simpson, I, 194-96. The same powers of shame and delight in reform are suggested in the satirical pamphlet, *Haec-Vir or the Womanish Man* (1620). The womanish man speaks after he hears his deformed character described: "You have both raised mine eye-lids, cleared my sight and made my heart entertain both shame and delight at an instant; shame in my follies past, delight in our noble and worthy conversion" (sig. C3v).

[29] The most valuable discussion of the intellectual form of the play is Ernest Talbert's long essay, "The Purpose and Technique of Jonson's *Poetaster*," *Studies in Philology*, 42 (1945), 225-52. I am also indebted to Ralph Nash, "The Parting Scene in Jonson's *Poetaster*," *Philological Quarterly*, 31 (1952), 54-62. The more conventional interpretations are O. J. Campbell's, pp. 109-34, Eugene Waith's, "The Poet's Morals in Jonson's *Poetaster*," *Modern Language Quarterly*, 12 (1951), 13-19, and Robert Knoll's in *Ben Jonson's Plays* (Lincoln, Neb., 1964), 57-65, all of whom have difficulty with the Ovid and Julia episodes. A long and careful study of style that has been neglected is by A. H. King, *The Language of Satirized Characters in* Poetaster: *A Sociostylistic Analysis 1597-1602*, "Lund Studies in English," no. 10 (1941).

[30] First published in the folio text but possibly written before publication of the quarto and spoken at least once upon the stage. See the address to the reader.

[31]Eugene Rice discusses this identity of knowledge and virtue in chapter 5 of *The Renaissance Idea of Wisdom* (Cambridge, Mass., 1958), pp. 156-63.

[32]Chambers, II, 204-07.

[33]Hatfield MSS, vii, 343, cited by Chambers, III, 353-55.

[34]Privy Council Register, XXII, 346, cited by Herford and Simpson, I, 217-18.

[35]*Lenten Stuff* (1599), ed. McKerrow, III, 213.

[36]*Palladis Tamia* (1598), ed. D. C. Allen (New York, 1938), pp. 285-86.

[37]Robert Pooley, a government spy 1588-1601, had been present after dinner at the death of Christopher Marlowe, and he was still alive when *Poetaster* was written. Parrot was another notorious spy. Mark Eccles, "Jonson and the Spies," *Review of English Studies,* 13 (1937), 385-97, suggests that these were the "two damned villains" who were put upon Jonson when he was imprisoned in the Marshalsea in connection with *The Isle of Dogs.* That Jonson did not lose his hatred of informers, we need only recall Sir Politic Would-be, an amateur version of Pooly, Parrot, and Lupus. Eccles also noted that a certain Henry Parrot wrote epigrams, once mentioning Volpone and alluding to a play about Ovidius Naso. Jonson's Epigram lxxi "On Court-Parrat" complains of one who praises him against his will.

[38]*Renaissance Philosophy of Man,* ed. E. Cassirer et al. (Chicago, 1948), pp. 387-93, gives the full text of Vives' theatrical vision of a Neoplatonic world. The burlesque banquet in *Poetaster* is probably based on a rumored private feast that Caesar took part in, in the role of Apollo, reported by Suetonius, *Augustus,* 70.

[39]Chapter 8 below deals with this parody of a litany at some length.

[40] "The Poet's Morals," pp. 13-19.

[41]Ernest Talbert, "Purpose and Technique of Jonson's *Poetaster,"* pp. 227-32, a valuable correction of Oscar Campbell's interpretation, although I do not consider Ovid the protagonist of the play as Talbert does.

[42]A parallel instance is found in V.xi.85-100 of *CR* where Cynthia shows how nicely she can "distinguish times" when indiscretions are proper and when improper. During revels Mercury is allowed to overstep bounds that must confine men on ordinary occasions.

[43]Eugene Waith, "The Poet's Morals," 13-19. A similar interpretation is in Frank Kermode's "The Banquet of Sense," *Bulletin of the John Rylands Library,* 44 (1961), 68-99.

[44]Ralph Nash comments on this passage well in "The Parting Scene," pp. 54-62; my account substantially agrees with his.

[45]*The Advancement of Learning,* I.vii.21. For the tradition of the adoration of Virgil see Domenico Comparetti, *Vergil in the Middle Ages* (New York, 1895), translated by E. F. M. Benecke. The tradition of consulting the *Aeneid* as an oracle is touched on in D. A. Slater's lecture *Sortes Vergilianae: or Vergil and To-Day* (Oxford, 1922). John W. Spargo, *Virgil the Necromancer,* "Harvard Studies in Comparative Literature," no. 10 (Cambridge, 1934) is the best survey of the legends of Virgil as a magician. However, there apparently is no history of sortilege with books.

[46]Nash, "The Parting Scene," pp. 54-62.

[47]*Discoveries,* VIII, lines 2466ff.

[48]Stephen Orgel, in *The Jonsonian Masque* (Cambridge, Mass., 1965), traces the most important uses of admiration in the masques to evoke an inner reality. This brilliant little book has influenced my views of Jonson and his audience.

CHAPTER 5. COMIC LANGUAGE IN *Volpone*

[1]Northrop Frye's example in "The Mythos of Spring: Comedy," *Anatomy of Criticism* (Princeton, 1957), p. 168.

[2] "The 'Uncanny,' " in *The Standard Edition of the Complete Psychological Works of Sigmund Freud*, James Strachey, general ed., (London, 1955), XVII, 219-52.

[3] *The Misanthrope* (New York, 1965), V.i, pp. 129-130.

[4] See Herford and Simpson, IX, 181-84, for an account of Dickens' revival of *Every Man in His Humor*.

[5] Lawrence Stone, *Crisis of the Aristocracy*, pp. 595-96, pointed out that John Cary offered his daughter in marriage to the aged and recently widowed Thomas Sutton, as a comfort in his grief. Sutton was a great moneylender, childless, and reputed to be one of the richest men in the kingdom at the time *Volpone* was written, and many devices were used to secure the inheritance of his estate. Sir John Harington tried to arrange it that the king would elevate Sutton to the peerage if Sutton deeded his property to Prince Charles. John Aubrey said that Sutton was Jonson's model for Volpone, but Gifford attacked this as slanderous gossip, arguing that Sutton was a pious, frugal man, a loving husband, and great benefactor. I think Gifford, and Herford, who agrees with him, put too much trust in the laudatory biographies of Sutton, that are mostly concerned with his generosity in founding Charterhouse, and they accept without question the fulsome praise of his funeral sermon. Stone's use of manuscript material and his evidence for the astonishing financial dealings of Sutton give some weight to Aubrey's story. We should also remember that Sutton did not die and found Charterhouse until 1611, thus gaining a reputation for benevolence. In 1605 his occupation was usury. No one knew what he would do with his money, and he was chiefly the object of solicitation by many noblemen in England.

[6] Preface to *An Evening's Love* (1671), reprinted in *Of Dramatic Poesy and Other Critical Essays*, ed. George Watson (London, 1962), I, 149.

[7] It is a pity that Richard Ohmann did not carry his analysis of Shaw's style beyond the great Prefaces and into Shaw's style in dramatic speech as well. See his *Shaw: the Style and the Man* (Middletown, Conn., 1962).

[8] W. Bosworth, *The Chaste and Lost Lovers* (1651), sig. A4, from remarks made by the editor, R. C., and cited by Herford and Simpson, XI, 145.

[9] Both Partridge, *The Broken Compass*, (London, 1958), and A.H. Sackton, *Rhetoric as a Dramatic Language in Ben Jonson* (New York, 1948), analyze Jonson's hyperboles, Partridge being the more acute critic.

[10] The earl of Somerset and the countess of Essex were most culpable, as later revelations showed.

[11] See further remarks on this device in chapter 1.

[12] *The Arte of English Poesie*, ed. Gladys Willcock and Alice Walker (Cambridge, Eng., 1936), pp. 191-93.

[13] Ralph Nash noticed the same habits of speech in his thoughtful and unjustly neglected essay, "The Comic Intent of *Volpone*," *Studies in Philology*, 44 (1947), 26-40.

[14] The distance between parasite and informer is not very great, suggesting traits shared by Sir Politic Would-be and Mosca, for Sir Politic collects gossip here and there, he would be a political spy, and he has a fertile imagination. Mosca is, however, so much better at his art than Sir Pol that he is in a wholly different class. See the discussion of spies in *Poetaster*, chapter 4.

[15] *Selected Essays* (New York, 1932), p. 134.

[16] *Drama and Society in the Age of Jonson* (London, 1937), pp. 200-06; *The Broken Compass*, pp. 70-113. Although I differ with Partridge's emphasis, I admire his sensitive and intelligent work, as all students of Jonson must.

[17] I am especially indebted here and elsewhere in this essay to William Empson's delightful and suggestive comments in "Volpone," *Hudson Review*, 21 (1968-69) 651-66, and to S. L. Goldberg's "Folly into Crime: The Catastrophe of *Volpone*," *Modern Language Quarterly*, 20 (1959), 233-42. They deal mainly with the trial scenes, and Goldberg thinks

that the strategy is part of the appeal of satire, but it seems to be essential to the art of dramatic speech, as I understand it.

[18]The critic I have in mind here is John L. Palmer, *Ben Jonson* (1934; reprinted 1967), p. 175.

[19]F. S. Boas, *An Introduction to Stuart Drama* (London, 1946), p. 108. Partridge cites this also.

[20]Partridge, *Broken Compass*, p. 92.

[21]Wallace A. Bacon, "The Magnetic Field: The Structure of Jonson's Comedies," *Huntington Library Quarterly*, 19 (1955-56), 137. C. G. Thayer, *Ben Jonson: Studies in the Plays* (Norman, Okla., 1963), in an otherwise suggestive book, implies this radical view. A. H. Sackton, pp. 139-40, takes another tack, saying that although hyperbole is involved in the dialogue of the scene, viewers are not supposed to feel any emotion; they should be completely detached because they know Volpone's rhetorical aims. The over-serious interpretation is much more persistent, as in Charles A. Hallett's articles, "The Satanic Nature of *Volpone*," *Philological Quarterly*, 49 (1970), 41-55; and "Jonson's Celia: A Reinterpretation of *Volpone*," *Studies in Philology*, 68 (1971), 50-69.

[22]Preface to "The Dark Lady of the Sonnets," in *The Works of Bernard Shaw* (London, 1930), XIII, 220-21.

[23]Edited by L. A. Beaurline for *The Dramatic Works in the Beaumont and Fletcher Canon*, gen. ed. Fredson Bowers (Cambridge, 1966), vol. I. A surprising number of these situations involve the woman as aggressor, beginning with Tamora's wooing of Aaron in *Titus Andronicus*. See Richard Levin, "The Eager Queen and the Melancholy Moor," *American Notes and Queries*, 4 (1965), 35-36.

[24]Hedwig von Beit's "Concerning the Problem of Transformation in the Fairy Tale," *Perspectives in Literary Symbolism* in "Yearbook of Comparative Criticism," ed. Joseph Strelka (University Park, Pa., 1968), I, 48-71, touches on the large problems of the myth. Also see Richard Bernheimer's *Wild Men in the Middle Ages* (Cambridge, Mass., 1952). The classical tradition of the catalog of delights has been traced by R. S. Forsythe, "*The Passionate Shepherd* and English Poetry," *PMLA*, 40 (1925), 692-742. J. B. Leishman's *The Art of Marvell's Poetry* (London, 1966) discusses its use in ancient and renaissance poetry with his usual subtlety. H. M. Richmond, "Polyphemus in England: A Study in Comparative Literature," *Comparative Literature*, 12 (1960), 229-42, adds many useful suggestions. But aside from Harry Levin's mention of it in *The Overreacher, A Study of Christopher Marlowe* (Cambridge, Mass., 1952), I have found little said about its use in the drama. Robert Jordan, "Myth and Psychology in *The Changeling*," *Renaissance Drama*, ns 3 (1970), 157-65, finds the myth of beauty and the beast in Beatrice and DeFlores, but for some reason he thinks this "substratum" should diminish our awareness of the psychological interest in characters.

[25]*The Complete Works of Christopher Marlowe*, ed. Fredson Bowers (Cambridge, Eng., 1973), vol. I.

[26]The handiest text is that edited by C. F. Tucker Brooke in *The Shakespeare Apocrypha; Being a Collection of Fourteen Plays Which Have Been Ascribed to Shakespeare* (Oxford. 1908).

[27]*Essays and Introductions* (New York, 1968), pp. 215-16. My colleague Robert Langbaum pointed this out to me.

[28]Numerous passages in the play create the impression of longing and gaping: "I long to have possession/ Of my new present" (I.ii.116-17); "How might I see her? . . . I must see her . . . I will go see her, though but at her window" (I.v.117-27); "but crown my longings" (II.iv.24); "all gaping here for legacies" (I.v.28); Volpone "takes his meat/ With other's fingers; only knows to gape" (III.vii.43-44); Volpone's mouth is "ever gaping" (I.iv.42); ravishing the money from the mouths of the clients, Volpone and Mosca delight to think of their victims "When they e'en gape, and find themselves deluded" (V.ii.74); see also

V.x.28. Nor should we forget the self-chosen emblem for Volpone—"a fox/ Stretched on the earth, with fine delusive sleights,/ Mocking a gaping crow" (I.ii.94-96). Philip Brockbank cites some of these pasages in his New Mermaids edition (London, 1968). Edward Partridge has gathered an especially complete list of speeches on feeding and eating in the play (*Broken Compass*, pp. 105-10), obviously the gratification of a gaping man. Jonson of course is not unique in using the analogy between hunger and the other appetites—for sex, money, or power. Shakespeare's *Antony and Cleopatra* and Middleton's plays are shot through with such comparisons (although in quite different ways). *Eastward Ho!*, written about the same time as *Volpone*, in collaboration with Chapman and Marston, uses the same analogies in an especially obvious way, signaled by the refrain "We do hunger and thirst for it."

CHAPTER 6. THE ILLUSION OF COMPLETENESS

[1]Madeleine Doran, on "Copy" of Words and Things, *Endeavors of Art* (Madison, 1954), pp. 46-52. Marion Trousdale, "A Possible Renaissance View of Form," *ELH*, 40 (1973), 179-204, speculates about the influence of copiousness on dramatic form.

[2]*On Copia of Words and Ideas*, trans. Donald B. King and H. D. Rix (Milwaukee, 1963), p. 47, cited by Trousdale.

[3]Ernst Curtius, *European Literature and the Latin Middle Ages*, trans. Willard Trask (New York, 1953; first German ed., 1948), p. 508. More recent studies of Spenser have shown the survival of numerological design in the *Epithalamion* and *The Faerie Queene*: A. Kent Hieatt, *Short Time's Endless Monument* (New York, 1960), and, ranging from Spenser to Dryden, Alastair Fowler's *Triumphal Forms* (Cambridge, 1970).

[4]*Endeavors of Art*, pp. 288-94.

[5] "Of the Colors of Good and Evil a Fragment," published at the end of Bacon's *Essays* (1597), sigs. F4-F4v. Indirectly, there is a link between the anatomy in rhetoric (born of the traditional topics or places of invention) and the Baconian tables of arrangement of instances, as aids to invention in science (*Novum Organum*, Book II). Paolo Rossi in his brilliant study of the intellectual context of Bacon's program, *Francis Bacon: From Magic to Science* (English edition, tr. Sacha Rabinovitch, Chicago, 1968), pp. 186-223, has shown how Bacon adapted the topics of rhetoric to his purposes, placing more emphasis on "exclusion" and restriction of a subject in the preliminaries of an investigation.

[6]Edited by Hoyt Hudson (Princeton, 1935), p. 22. Commenting on an earlier form of my essay, Ejner Jensen objected to this interpretation of the passages from Bacon and Hoskins; see "L. A. Beaurline and the Illusion of Completeness," *PMLA*, 69 (1971), 121-27.

[7]See Edward Partridge, *The Broken Compass* (London, 1958), and John Enck, *Jonson and the Comic Truth* (Madison, Wisc., 1957). The extravagant conceit as part of Jonson's debt to old comedy is explained by Ray Heffner Jr. in "Unifying Symbols in the Comedy of Ben Jonson," *English Stage Comedy*, ed. W. K. Wimsatt, Jr. "English Institute Essays," (New York, 1955), pp. 74-97; this article is the best account of the unity of these plays. Late morality form is discussed by Alan Dessen in *"The Alchemist:* Jonson's 'Estates' Play," *Renaissance Drama*, 7 (1964), 35-54, reprinted in *Jonson's Moral Comedy* (Evanston, 1971). Dessen is on the verge of making my point when he sees a "panoramic cross section of English society" in *The Alchemist* and *Bartholomew Fair*, pp. 49-50.

[8]Paul Goodman, *The Structure of Literature* (Chicago, 1954), p. 85, makes a similar observation. Also see the mention of *The Alchemist* in Richard Levin's thorough discussion of "The Structure of *Bartholomew Fair*," *PMLA*, 80 (1965), 176, reprinted in *The Multiple Plot in English Renaissance Drama* (Chicago, 1971).

[9]See Hugh Kenner's "Art in a Closed Field," *Virginia Quarterly Review,* 38 (1962), 597-613, to which I am generally indebted.

[10]An earlier form of this analysis appeared in the introduction to my edition of *Epicoene* (Lincoln, Nebr., 1966).

[11]In *The Broken Compass* and expanded in his introduction to his edition of *Epicoene* (New Haven, 1971).

[12]*Of Dramatic Poesy and Other Critical Essays,*ed.George Watson (London, 1962), I, 61, 66, 70-71, 129.

[13]Jonas Barish remarks on this, *Ben Jonson, and the Language of Prose Comedy* (Cambridge, Mass., 1960), pp. 176-77.

[14]I am indebted to Joyce Van Dyke, a graduate student at the University of Virginia, whose essay forthcoming in *Studies in English Literature* explains this aspect of *The Alchemist.*

[15]Ian Donaldson, " 'A Martyrs Resolution': Jonson's *Epicoene,*" *Review of English Studies,* n.s. 18 (1967), 1-15. Jonas Barish also sees much of the playfulness of the comedy, *Ben Jonson,* pp. 174-99, and observes that Truewit is an especially equivocal observer, for like Morose he sees the vanities of sophisticated life, but he does not recoil from them. For the moment he accepts them as a game. L. G. Salingar, in "Farce and Fashion in 'The Silent Woman,' " *Essays and Studies,* n.s. 20 (1967), 29-46, emphasizes the play with city taste. W. David Kay, "Jonson's Urbane Gallants: Humanistic Contexts for *Epicoene,*" *The Huntington Library Quarterly,* 39 (1976), 251-66, makes more of the detached and courtly playfulness, influenced by Erasmus and Castiglione. And it is worth remembering that the jests in *The Courtier* are often as callous as those in *Epicoene.*

[16]*The Life of the Drama* (New York, 1967), 219-56, 295-301.

CHAPTER 7. THE REAL PRESENCE OF VULGARITY IN *Bartholomew Fair*

[1]The moral inversions and their debt to earlier dramatic modes are abumbrated by Alan Dessen in *Jonson's Moral Comedy* (Evanston, 1971), pp. 138-210, and in Ian Donaldson's *The World Upside Down* (Oxford, 1970), pp. 46-77.

[2]Jonas Barish presents this view in *Ben Jonson and the Language of Prose Comedy* (Cambridge, Mass., 1960), pp. 187-289.

[3]The best account of the plot is by Richard Levin, "The Structure of *Bartholomew Fair,*" *PMLA,* 80 (1965), 172-79.

[4]W. David Kay, "*Bartholomew Fair:* Ben Jonson in Praise of Folly." *English Literary Renaissance,* 6 (1976), 299-316), points out the play's similarities to Erasmus' *Praise of Folly* and other works.

[5]See Dwight MacDonald's *Parodies* (New York, 1960), pp. 557-68, for a thoughtful attempt at distinctions that, unfortunately, cannot be observed in practice.

[6]Jackson Cope comments on vapors in "*Bartholomew Fair* as Blasphemy," *Renaissance Drama,* 8 (1965), 127, 141-46, and Barish makes equally important observations, essentially what I say here, pp. 217-19, 230-34. James E. Robinson, "*Bartholomew Fair:* A Comedy of Vapors," *Studies in English Literature,* I (Spring, 1961), 65-80, is also helpful, but he stresses the psychology of humors more than the play warrants.

[7]See Jonson's "Leges Conviviales" (VIII, 656), which forbids disputes, excessive drinking, and brawling. Barish cites "Inviting a Friend to Supper."

[8]*Unfortunate Traveller,* ed. McKerrow (Oxford, 1904-10, revised ed. 1958), II, 246-52.

Jonson and Elizabethan Comedy

[9]Anthony Nixon, *Oxford's Triumph* (1605), sigs. B3v-D2, commemorating the King's visit.

[10]Mark Curtis, *Oxford and Cambridge in Transition 1552-1642* (Oxford, 1959), pp. 88-90. William T. Costello, *The Scholastic Curriculum at Early Seventeenth-Century Cambridge* (Cambridge, Mass., 1958), pp. 14-31, the most detailed account of academic disputation.

[11]There was also an association of drinking games with academic spoofs, reflected in a little-known pamphlet *The Eighth Liberal Science or New Found Art of Drinking* (1650), surviving in a unique copy in the British Museum. That this travesty of college degrees, professors, and exercises has something to do with earlier tavern life is suggested by the formalities of drinking scenes in Sir John Suckling's plays, *The Goblins,* III.ii (about 1638) and *Brennoralt,* II.ii (about 1639-40), where the cavaliers "debauch—in discipline." More important is Thomas Randolph's *Drinking Academy* (1629). But these may have been influenced by *Bartholomew Fair* as much as by actual tavern games. Randolph was a Son of Ben, and Suckling had a love-hate relationship with Jonson, often impelling him to imitate and parody "good old Ben," the ancient wit.

[12]The same formalities recur in the dispute of Cutbeard and Otter, as two divines, about the twelve impediments to divorce, *Epicoene,* V.iii-iv.

[13]The earliest recorded use of "turd in the teeth," cited by John S. Farmer and W. E. Henley in *Slang and Its Analogues* (London, 1904), is from Thomas Harmon's *A Caveat for Common Cursetors Vulgarly Called Vagabones* (1567, reprinted and expanded 1573, reprinted 1592): "A torde in thy mouth," meaning "the devyll take thee," sig.G4v. Harmon's *A Caveat* is the best and most original of the cony-catching pamphlets, much borrowed from. However, the expression, "turd in thy mouth," must be somewhat older. A jest book Jonson possibly knew, *Howleglas* (1528?), tells of a trick played by Eulenspiegel on Jews who wished to prophesy the coming of the Messiah; in effect, the jest acts out the vulgar expression in order to silence prophets. Howleglas makes several magic "prophetuses" by putting excrement on figs, which he sells to the Jews. When they place the prophetuses in their mouths to inspire them to speak the truth, they cry " 'We are beguiled—for it is no other thing but a turd!' And they tasted and the turd hanged in their teeth, with the hair that he had cut from his arse, and then they knew well that they were deceived." The jest has been reprinted in *A Hundred Merry Tales and Other English Jestbooks of the Fifteenth and Sixteenth Centuries,* ed. Paul Zall (Lincoln, Nebr., 1963), pp. 189-92, where the offensive phrases are omitted. The association of *turd* and *dunghill* with religious disputation was firmly established in the public mind by the notoriously foul-mouthed Luther. "No marvel that he is so taxed for his obscenity . . . for his beastliness in his *Hans worst against the Jews:* for his filthy mentioning of hogs; for his stinking repetition of turds and dunghills in his *Schemhamphorise* . . . 'let the dog fill that [the Pope's mouth] with his excrements,' " Thomas Bayly, *Certamen Religiosum* (1649), pp. 194-95. In his reply to Henry VIII, Luther justified his rough language, among other reasons, because St. Paul inveighed against false prophets in the same way (Acts xiii), and Paul called his former Judaism "dung" (Philippians, iii.8). In Luther's terms, King Henry and his supporters are blockheads, silly asses, fatted swine, idiots, slimy sophists, Thomist swine (repeatedly), hogs, and damnable rotten worms. "Ye Thomist swine. Ye will have Luther as a she-bear in your way" (p. 11), *Luther's Reply to Henry VIII* (1522), trans. Rev. E. S. Buchanan (New York, 1928). I do not mean to denigrate Luther's ideas, for I respect them and admire his keen arguments in this tract. I merely point out that he set the tone for much religious dispute, associating it with turd, swine, and slurs on Judaism. Is there a connection between Busy's anti-Semitic eating of pig and the scatology of the play?

[14]I pass over the puppet show itself because it has been treated in detail by Barish in *"Bartholomew Fair* and Its Puppets," *Modern Language Quarterly,* 20 (1959), 3-17,

reprinted in *Ben Jonson and the Language of Prose Comedy,* pp. 225ff., but I have something to say of "Hero and Leander" in the discussion of Chapman's Homer, below. James E. Savage has some interesting conjectures in "Some Antecedents of the Puppet Play in *Bartholomew Fair,*" *Ben Jonson's Basic Comic Characters and Other Essays* (University of Mississippi, 1974), 145-64.

[15]*Table Talk* (1689), sig. G4v. That Selden forgot the third party in the dispute does not detract from the remark's evidential value.

[16]Herford and Simpson's account of this event in Jonson's life is incomplete (I, 65-67). The printed record of the controversy can be followed through five books. 1) Daniel Featley, *The Grand Sacrilege of the Church of Rome* (1630), STC 10733, whose appendix contains "The Summe and Substance of a Disputation . . . Sept. 4, 1612 . . . touching the Reall presence in the Sacrament," pp. 285-306. This is the version that "B.I." and John Pory certified as accurate, and it is the one I quote from. 2) S. E. (Edmund Lechmere), *The Conference Mentioned by Doctor Featley in the end of his Sacrilege* (Douay, 1632), STC 7436; the Catholic version, where the names of others in the party are identified, among them "M. Ben: Johnson." 3) Myrth Waferer (a nice pseudonym), *An Apologie for Daniel Featley . . . Against the Calumnie of one S. E. in respect of his Conference with Doctor Smith* (1634), STC 24930. This contains an especially humane and effective conclusion, pp. 101-03. 4) L. I. (Edmund Lechmere), *The Relection of a Conference Touching the Reall Presence* (Douay, 1635), STC 14053. 5) Daniel Featley, *Transubstantiation Exploded: or an Encounter with Richard . . . Bishop of Chalcedon* (1638), STC 10740. Pages 25-40 relate the circumstances surrounding the dispute in greater detail than earlier accounts, but make no mention of Jonson, just a general reference to the men who attested to the first account Featley issued. See also W. D. Briggs, "On Certain Incidents in Ben Jonson's Life," *Modern Philology,* 11 (1913-14). 279-88. Jonson had returned to the English Church sometime about 1610, so he was probably disposed to side with Featley's position against the Catholic view. And we can expect him to have disagreed with the extreme Puritans, but the differences between middle-of-the-road Anglicans and the Puritans (many of whom were still in the established church) on transubstantiation were not clearly discernible. John Jewel took a position indistinguishable from Bèze and other Calvinists, and Featley's loyalties seem to have been similar to Jewel's. Featley wrote a life of Jewel (1609), delivered the funeral oration on John Rainolds (the Oxford teacher of Lyly and Gosson), and wrote many controversial works after he became chaplain to Archbishop Abbot. He tutored young Raleigh at Oxford and gave him a bad report, according to Simpson. Jonson's unfavorable treatment of literal interpretations in *Bartholomew Fair* agrees with my assumption that he tended toward Featley's side, as his authenticating of the summary of proceedings also suggests. But Featley and Smith both behaved with such obvious ill nature and foolishness in the dispute that it would be a mistake to identify Jonson wholly with either side. I think he reserved his opinions and found wonderfully comic possibilities in the encounter.

[17]Theodore Bèze, *The Pope's Canons,* trans. T. W. (1584), is especially vivid about the beasts who eat unused communion wafers (sig. B6v). William Perkins, *A Reformed Catholic* (1598), p. 196, and W. Fulke (along with Jewel), *A Rejoinder . . . also the Cavils of Nicholas Sandar* (1581), p. 482 and passim, object to the Catholics' "carnal eating" and they emphasize the role of faith and preparation of a believer's heart. See Perkins' tenth point "Of Real Presence," pp. 185-203, and Fulke, pp. 476, 714, 742, and 786. Daniel Featley's "Summe and Substance of a Disputation," cited above, makes more of carnal eating. Busy's piggish gluttony was familiar enough in Puritan satire (like Parson Pigman in *The Widow of Watling Street,* 1607), but Jonson adds religious language to the analysis of the appetite, like these Protestant controversialists.

[18]The Bishop of Winchester told Isaac Walton that in Jonson's last retirement and sickness he was "much afflicted that he had profaned the scripture in his plays" (Herford and

Simpson, I, 181; also cited by Cope). Busy's veil over the face probably also alludes to Exodus 30:33-34, when Moses concealed his face with a covering, from all men, taking the veil off only in the presence of the Lord.

[19]W. Fulke, p. 476. Quoting Augustine, he goes on to say that Christians should eat "within, not without; he which eateth in his heart, not he which presseth with his teeth." The flesh should be "received with a pure and clean mind, not put in our mouth, nor swallowed down the throat" (p. 544). He objects to the "carnal manner of receiving into the mouth" (p. 546), in the "bellies of the beasts" (p. 599), what should be "eaten by faith not by the mouth" (p. 713). We should receive it with a "faithful heart and mouth" (p. 758).

[20]On travesty in *Volpone,* see Harry Levin, "Jonson's Metempsychosis," *Philological Quarterly,* 22 (1943), 231-39. The legal disputation on divorce in *Epicoene* may actually have been added to the text in revision about the same time Jonson wrote *Bartholomew Fair.* Hence it would have been after the disputation between Featley and Smith, and possibly influenced by it. Edward Partridge remarked that "Cutbeard sounds like a medieval Catholic and Otter a Puritan Protestant," and I agree; see *Epicoene,* ed. Partridge (New Haven, 1971), p. 197, note to V.iii.10. Gifford speculated that Jonson had in mind the divorce proceedings between the earl and countess of Essex in 1613, and Thomas Kranidas says that is "highly probable," given the specific allusions to claims of impotence — the earl's problem; "Possible Revisions or Additions in Jonson's *Epicoene,* " *Anglia,* 83 (1965), 451-53.

[21]Jonson alludes to Coryat twice in *Bartholomew Fair,* as the name of a foolish traveler (III.v.231) and as a low sort of entertainer at great city suppers (III.iv.126).

[22]A pamphlet, purported to have been written by John Dando and Harry Runt, wiredrawer and ostler, taken down from a conversation between Banks and his horse, contributed something to Jonson's conception. It is an imitation of Lucian's dialogue "The Dream," and is titled *Maroccus Extaticus, or Bankes Bay Horse in a Trance* (1595). The address to the reader gives it a mock puff, as "the finest philosophical discourse you can light upon . . . truely there was never horse in this world answered man with more reason, nor never man in this world reasoned more sensibly with a horse." This is surely a spoof on humanist dialogues, like Gelli's (cited below), but a specific association with "The Famous Voyage" is found in the same address, when the authors confess that they have on their consciences only the most venial kind of robbery, as if they had gone into "a cook's shop in Fleet Lane, and with the smell of roast meat filled our bellies, not emptying our purses." (Jonson makes the same joke in *Alchemist,* I.i.25-26, as Richard Bebee brought to my attention.) The conjunction of Banks, smells, and the cooks in Fleet Lane, in both *Maroccus* and "Famous Voyage" is probably not coincidental.

[23]Percy Simpson's notice (XI, 593-94) of Jonson's copy of *The Whole Works of Homer, Prince of Poets* (1616). Jonson also owned Chapman's 1598 selections from *The Iliad* (I, 263).

[24]The fragment is printed from manuscript by Phyllis B. Bartlett, *The Poems of George Chapman* (New York, 1941), pp. 374-78.

[25]*Works,* III, 151-52

[26]Chapman's *Odyssey,* ed. Allardyce Nicoll (London, 1957). In her edition Miss Bartlett inadvertently left out two lines of the dedication (p. 485) that involve the phrase "popular vapor."

[27]E. A. Horsman's introduction to his edition of *Bartholomew Fair, The Revels Plays* (London, 1960), pp. xx-xxi, gives full evidence.

[28]Barish is especially good on Overdo's oratorical style, pp. 204-15.

[29]Cope, pp. 127-52. This article has many keen observations about veiled allusions in the play, and they are highly suggestive. For instance, the black box containing Cokes' marriage license is like the Jews' Ark of the Covenant, because of echoes of Exodus 25:10, and I notice that Ursula's ale is offered as a "sup of Covenant" (II.iv.48). Cope's essay ought

to be consulted by anyone who wants an understanding of the play's images and allusions. He narrows the meaning somewhat when he allegorizes Trouble-All's blessing and Overdo's benediction at the end into a doctrinal tale of God, sin, and grace, in a Machiavellian commercial world.

[30]Ian Donaldson's point, *The World Upside Down* (Oxford, 1970), p. 58.

[31]Barish, p. 223; C. G. Thayer, *Ben Jonson: Studies in the Plays* (Norman, Okla., 1963), pp. 132-34; and John Jacob Enck, *Jonson and the Comic Truth* (Madison, 1957), p. 191.

[32]Topsell, pp. 675-77. Cicero's saying about the soul of a hog comes from *De Natura Deorum*, ii.160; but it was common in ancient writings. See Herford and Simpson's note on Jonson's use of it in the play, IV.ii.55.

[33]Nashe seems to be recalling Stephen Gosson here, who had applied these terms to poets, "the fathers of lies." "Pull off the vizard that poets mask in, you shall disclose their reproach, bewray their vanity, loath their wantonness, lament their folly, and perceive their sharp sayings to be placed as pearls in dunghills, fresh pictures on rotten walls, chaste matrons' apparel on courtesans. These are the cups of Circes, that turn reasonable creatures into brute beasts," *The School of Abuse* (1579), sig. A2v.

[34]Henry Howard, *A Defensitive Against the Poison of Supposed Prophecies* (1583). His comments on earth's vapors used by oracles are on sig. M2v.

[35]Gelli was a Florentine humanist with ideas similar to Pico and Ficino's. His *Circes* first appeared in 1549, the English translation by Henry Iden in 1557, another by Thomas Brown in 1702. The latter, revised by Robert M. Adams, with a handsome introduction and illustrations, was issued by the Cornell University Press (Ithaca, New York, 1963). Merritt Y. Hughes surveys more evidence in his "Spenser's Acrasia and the Circe of the Renaissance," *Journal of the History of Ideas*, 4 (1943), 381-99.

[36]Adams' introduction, pp. xxix-xxxiii.

[37]John Enck makes a similar point about the "positive aspects" of the Fair, pp. 198-208. Marvin Vawter, "The Seeds of Virtue: Political Imperatives in Jonson's *Sejanus*," *Studies in the Literary Imagination*, vol. 6, no. 1 (1973), 41-60, finds an implied disapproval of stoic passivity in the Germanican party. Jonson is sympathetic with stoic virtue, but he deplores the stoic's inability to assert himself in a crisis.

[38]Loeb translation, sec. 21.

[39]IV.ii.68-73. Images of St. Bartholomew often showed him with a knife in his hand or his skin over his arm, like a cloak he has taken off. I am indebted to John Steadman for this suggestion.

[40]Cope, pp. 151-52, and Thayer, pp. 149-50, give opposing interpretations of the many blessings in the play. Thayer says they are offerings of forgiveness which Jonson does not extend seriously, since he is "hardly a sentimentalist." Cope understands the blessings as granting mercy, which leads some characters to love, but others, like Quarlous, to hell on earth, that is, the commercial world like that of the Fair. Alan Dessen, *Jonson's Moral Comedy* (Evanston, 1971), pp. 148-220, taking a severe moralistic view, finds no blessing whatsoever, as if Overdo's old justice really ought to have prevailed. (See Barish's review of Dessen, *Modern Philology*, 71 (1973), 80-84.) Richard Levin, *Multiple Plot In English Renaissance Drama* (Chicago, 1971), pp. 213-14, implies the same interpretation as mine concerning St. Bartholomew and luck, but he does not acknowledge a degradation of sorts in Quarlous.

CHAPTER 8. ROMANCE IN A DIMINISHED MODE

[1]C. G. Thayer, *Ben Jonson: Studies in the Plays* (Norman, Okla., 1963); also Harriett

Hawkins, "The Idea of a Theater in Jonson's *The New Inn*," *Renaissance Drama*, 9 (1966), 205-26. Other essays on the play that deal with special topics are Frank Kermode, "The Banquet of Sense," *Bulletin of the John Rylands Library*, 44 (1961) 68-99; Barbara Everett, "Ben Jonson's 'Vision of Beauty,' " *Critical Quarterly*, 1 (1959), 238-44; Edward Partridge, "The Symbolism of Clothes in Jonson's Last Plays," *Journal of English and Germanic Philology*, 56 (1957), 396-409. Douglas Duncan, "A Guide to *The New Inn*," *Essays in Criticism*, 20 (1970), 311-26, recognizes a balance between irony and serious themes in the play; he is more discriminating about Platonic love, and he sees the importance of "public ideals" at the end of the play. Larry Champion, *Ben Jonson's 'Dotages'* (Lexington, Ky., 1967) sees a satire on court Platonism.

[2] See Epilogue, below, on Jonson's conception of the centered self.

[3] The best account of this is W. E. Houghton's "The English Virtuoso in the Seventeenth Century," *Journal of the History of Ideas* 3 (1942), 51-73, 190-219. Virtuoso activities were intimately connected with melancholy and the rise of "curious" scholarship. For a list of items in Tradescant's museum, begun in the 1620s and later to form part of the Ashmolean collection, see Allan Mea, *The Tradescants: Their Plants, Gardens and Museum 1570-1662* (London, 1964), appendix. Henry Peacham, *The Compleat Gentleman,* 1622, revised 1634, is a vivid contemporary advocate of the virtuoso ideal, and Burton's *Anatomy of Melancholy* 1621, the most permanent literary consequence of it.

[4] For the defense of love see Digby's *Loose Fantasies,* newly edited from the manuscript by Vittorio Gabrieli, "Temi e Testi," no. 14 (Rome, 1968), pp. 128-32. The vision of Venitia is related on pp. 84-87. Digby's memoir is an astonishing document, written in the form of a romance involving Theagenes and Stelliana. R. T. Petersson, *Sir Kenelm Digby, The Ornament of England* (London, 1956), is the fullest modern biography. So far as I know, the similarities between Lovel and Digby have not hitherto been noticed, and the analogy can be pursued, within reason, to the similarities in character between Lady Frances and Lady Venitia Stanley: both are rich, beautiful, aloof, vain, gay spirited, self-indulgent, and platonic (with suspicions of loose morals). Moreover, natural impulses overcame Kenelm and Venitia's scruples and vows of celibacy: first when Digby climbed into her bed naked and held her tightly as he told his whole story; second, when they allowed their will to pleasure to overcome their irresolvable philosophic conflicts (see *Loose Fantasies,* pp. 111-25). If Digby wrote his memoir in 1628 while in the Mediterranean as he claims, we must assume that Jonson heard the story of the romance by word of mouth, perhaps from Digby himself. Or else the specific associations could have been added to *The New Inn* in revision, after Digby's return to England in February, 1629. Certainly Digby, who was Jonson's literary executor, was close to the old dramatist in his later years. I suggest the analogy merely to establish the contemporary reality of the story in the play; these Platonic lovers were not simply literary or artificial lovers, because real passions seem to have been involved. Certainly Jonson's poems to Lady Venitia Digby seem ardent in their Neoplatonic praises, and they make Digby's association with *The New Inn* intriguing. Indeed, Sir Kenelm claimed that his generous passion for Venitia actually redeemed her from her former dubious character. More general descriptions of court Platonism and its impact on drama are in Alfred Harbage, *Cavalier Drama* (New York, 1936), and Kathleen Lynch, *The Social Mode of Restoration Comedy* (New York, 1926).

[5] The 1631 text, Gifford's, Schelling's, and the Oxford edition read "rag of love" but "rage of love" goes so much better with "burn," "tinder," and "spark" that it is probably the original meaning.

[6] A kiss as an inspirational beginning of mutual love and worthy of the "sun's light" (i.e., the benign rays of love coming from the king) works this way in Jonson's masque *Mercury Vindicated* (1616), lines 262-68:

There is no banquet, boys, like this,
If you hope better you will miss;
Stay here and take each one a kiss.
Which if you can refine
The taste knows no such cates, nor yet the palate wine.
                                    No cause of tarrying shun;
They are not worth his light, [who] go backward from the sun.

[7]Miss Bradbrook remarks that this shows Alleyn's sense of good fortune's instability (*Rise of the Common Player: A Study of Actor and Society in Shakespeare's England* [London, 1962], p. 206). I think it suggests a confidence that God is on his side — after all, Alleyn rose to fame and wealth at the Fortune Theatre.

[8]Douglas Duncan, however, thinks the disguises in *The New Inn* are consistent with Jonson's earlier use of them: "Disguise in Jonson, from *Volpone* onwards, are always treated critically as an evasion of identity, a calculated imposture practised on society or at best an irresponsible game" (p. 324). But neither Frank's nor the Host's disguises are irresponsible or evasive. I can see only good coming from their temporary dissemblings, as a character copes with his situation. Even the disguise of Pinnacia Stuff appears in a different light if we consider the consequences.

[9]The ceremony may have been familiar at rustic weddings, for there is the following rendition in "The Ballad of Arthur Bradley," about the tricks played on a groom:
                    To't, to't quoth lusty Ned,
                    We'll see them both in bed,
                    For I will jeopard [gib at] a joint,
                    But I will get his cod-piece point . . .
                    They got his points and garters
                    And cut them in pieces like quarters [martyrs].
An Antidote Against Melancholy (1661); another version is reprinted in Joseph Ritson's *Robin Hood,* (1795 edition), II, 214-15.

[10]Sir Kenelm Digby's dilemma with Lady Venitia reached a similar impasse—when both vowed for the best reasons never to marry or to see each other. Then both fell into silence, marred only by a few sighs. But after a few moments they followed their inclinations to satisfy their sexual pleasure, as dictated by will not reason, and in a trice the insuperable barriers disappeared (p. 125).

[11]E. K. Chambers, III, 373-74; W. W. Greg, "Some Notes on Ben Jonson's Works," *Review of English Studies,* 2 (1926), 129-45; G. E. Bentley, IV, 632-36. My own guess is that the original date of composition was 1613, based on two facts. (1) It is odd that Jonson has left no surviving work to commemorate the marriage of Princess Elizabeth to the Elector of Palatine, on St. Valentine's Day 1613, even if he was traveling intermittently on the continent in 1612 and 1613. And since *Tale of a Tub* contains an elaborate spoof on St. Valentine's Day, he may have drafted a masque or play for that occasion, but set it aside when Chapman and Inigo Jones were favored with the court appointment. (2) The country characters in Jonson's models — *John a Kent, Two Angry Women,* and *The Merry Devil* – are more or less gentry and not as low and common as those in *Tale of a Tub.* Puppy, Diogenes, Turfe, Awdrey, Clay, and Clench, suggest a much lower demotic mode, more like *Bartholomew Fair* (1614) than the fellows below stairs in *The New Inn* or the rustics of *The Sad Shepherd.* And since Medlay-Inigo and Lanthorn-Inigo both put on shows at the end of their respective plays, it is natural to expect that they were conceived at some fairly contiguous times. However, the layers of revision and the cuts demanded by the Master of the Revels in 1633 make it nearly impossible to go beyond Greg's conclusions about the date and quality of the final version of the script. (I am fairly certain, however, that the "Scene interloping," so headed in the 1640 folio, immediately following Act IV. Scene i, was one of the offending

335

scenes that the censor would not allow on stage. "Interloping" commonly meant "unlicensed, unauthorized." Our modern meaning of "introducing improperly" is first recorded by the *OED* in 1641 and was not common until later.)

[12]Medlay suggests this mock title to Tub, "Pancridge Earl" III.vi.6, and Jonson recommends it for Jones in "To Inigo Marquess Would Be," *Ungathered Verse*, vol. VIII, no. xxxv.

[13]A 1661 text of Suckling's "Ballad" identified the speaker as a west-country man, and the texts in *Fragmenta Aurea* 1646 and 1648 have dialectal spellings. See Suckling's *Non-Dramatic Works,* ed. Thomas Clayton (Oxford, 1971).

[14]Jonson himself was the city chronologer from 1628-31, and reappointed again at the behest of the king after being dropped for inactivity 1634-37, but according to Herford (I, 101) the stipend was no longer a fee for work but a pension.

[15]For tales of Puck that include his wild disruption of country weddings, see *Robin Good-Fellow, his Mad Pranks, Second Part* (1628).

[16]J. A. Bryant, Jr., *"A Tale of a Tub:* Jonson's Comedy of the Human Condition," *Renaissance Papers 1963* (1964), 95-105, and reprinted in *The Compassionate Satirist,* pp. 160-80, also comments on these transpositions of Saint Valentine. His essay is suggestive, although his general interpretation of the play as a myth or "submerged action" about the triumph of nature over human institutions allegorizes more than the text warrants. Mary C. Williams, *"A Tale of a Tub:* Ben Jonson's Folk Play," identifies the country festivals and suggests that the wooing of Awdrey resembles a dance routine, passing the girl from hand to hand; *North Carolina Folklore,* 21 (1973-75), 161-68.

[17]See F. P. Wilson, "Shakespeare and the Diction of Common Life," *Proceedings of the British Academy,* 27 (1941), 167-97.

[18]Herford and Simpson note only a few of these, but the *Oxford Dictionary of English Proverbs,* third edition, revised by F. P. Wilson (1970), is much fuller. Also see Mary C. Williams, cited above.

[19]From a manuscript in the Royal Library, Hague, Kon. Acad. MS Huygens 47, F 207, quoted by Rosalie Colie, *"My Echoing Song": Andrew Marvell's Poetry of Criticism* (Princeton, 1970), p. 211.

[20]An English version, published in 1658, has been reprinted by Basic Books (New York, 1957). My paraphrase comes from Book XVII, chapter vi, pp. 364-65 of that reprint.

[21]An analogy between Tub's masque and Quixote's dumb puppet show was pointed out by N. H. M. Zwager, *Glimpses of Ben Jonson's London* (Amsterdam, 1926), pp. 178-81.

[22]*The Muse's Looking Glass* (1638), epilogue.

[23]See D. J. Gordon's "Poet and Architect: The Intellectual Setting of the Quarrel between Ben Jonson and Inigo Jones," *Journal of the Warburg and Courtauld Institutes,* 12 (1949), 152-78. The irony is that Jonson and Jones agreed on basic principles of art but used them to defend their specific callings. So Jones probably assumed, too, that the real king and queen were closer approximations to the ideal he praises than his representations are.

[24]John Jacob Enck, *Jonson and the Comic Truth* (Madison, 1957), also notices a kinship of these two plays, pp. 227-30, 244, 251. Enck's witty phrase "catalogical imperative" (p. 155), is used to describe Subtle's long speeches. Enck does not, however, remark on the change in use of catalogs in later Jonson.

[25]Lady Venitia Digby died in 1633, Sir Kenelm grieved unconsolably, and Jonson wrote a series of poems in her honor, entitled *Eupheme.* Number 9, "The Elegy on my Muse" addresses her survivors with a vision of Christian paradise where they will be reunited with Venitia, but two earlier lyrics, numbers 3 and 4, praise Venitia as alive, her body and mind, in distinctly Neoplatonic language—as Aeglamor describes Earine. Otherwise, I have not recognized specific echoes of the play in the poems, but it is possible that the mourning Aeglamour could be Sir Kenelm, as I am certain Lovel represents his love for Lady Venitia, in

The New Inn. The whole tangled problem of the date and origin of *The Sad Shepherd* is examined by W. W. Greg, in his edition of the play (Louvain, 1905). I agree with him that *The Sad Shepherd* is a late composition, perhaps after 1633.

[26]*Poets and Playwrights* (Minneapolis, 1930), p. 149.

[27] "Have you seen a bright lily grow" first appeared in 1616, in *The Devil is an Ass,* but Simpson estimates that the ten lyric pieces were put together in about 1623.

[28]See Keith Thomas, *Religion and the Decline of Magic* (London, 1971), pp. 212-52, on the versatility and social uses of the cunning man.

[29]I quote from W. W. Greg's text, *Masque of Gipsies* (London, 1952). The most handy, readable edition is by Stephen Orgel, *Ben Jonson: The Complete Masques* (New Haven, 1969).

[30]Copies of a poem, blessing the King's senses, have been found in several early seventeenth-century archives. See A.H. Gilbert, "Jonson and Drummond or Gil on the King's Senses," *Modern Language Notes,* 62 (1947), 35-37, and C.F. Main, "Ben Jonson and the Unknown Poet on the King's Senses," *Modern Language Notes,* 74 (1957), 389-93. With the same refrain and with the senses in the same order, the poem contrasts nicely with Jonson's because the anonymous poem uses a sledge hammer rather than a feather. The author prays to save the king from his real vices: his bad conscience, his sexual deviation, his minions, his flatterers, and above all the duke of Buckingham's black deeds. The poem is a crude libel, a gross adaptation of Jonson's playful but slightly earnest jests. I incline to agree with Dale Randall in Jonson's *Gypsies Unmasked: Background and Theme of the Gypsies Metamorphos'd* (Durham, N.C., 1975), that there must have been a delicious irony for some members of the audience who recognized the similarities between Buckingham's crew and the gypsies they enacted in their masque. Randall comments only briefly on the mixture of telling and playful details in the blessing (p. 158), without mentioning the libelous satire. I presume that the innuendoes about Buckingham that worked so well at the first and second performances of the masque were, in the third performance, more daringly extended to the king himself. But I think Buckingham and the king enjoyed the jokes at their expense. That is the very nature of coterie humor and play.

[31]See George Philip Akrigg, *Jacobean Pageant; or The Court of King James I* (Cambridge, Mass., 1962).

EPILOGUE

[1]I, 148, lines 578-79.

[2]Allan H. Gilbert, *The Symbolic Persons in the Masques of Ben Jonson* (Durham, N. C., 1948), pp. 190-91.

[3]Edward Partridge, *The Broken Compass* (London, 1958), pp. 235-36.

[4] "Ben Jonson and the Centered Self," *Studies in English Literature,* 10 (1970), 325-48; and Jonas Barish, "Jonson and the Loathed Stage," *A Celebration of Ben Jonson,* ed. William Blissett, et al. (Toronto, 1973), pp. 27-53.

[5]Plantin published many emblem books with that device on the title page, including Geoffrey Whitney's *A Choice of Emblems,* 1528. Several of Plantin's devices are reproduced in Henry Greene's edition of Whitney (London, 1866).

[6]See the reproductions of these in D. J. Gordon, "Poet and Architect: The Intellectual Setting of the Quarrel between Jonson and Inigo Jones," *Journal of the Warburg and Courtauld Institutes,* 12 (1949), 152-78, reprinted in *The Renaissance Imagination* (Berkeley, 1975).

[7] "Donne's 'Valediction: Forbidding Mourning,' " *ELH, 30 (1963), 335-76.*

[8]He cites the following poems, as well as Jonson's epistle to Selden, to illustrate the twin movements of the human soul: Jean de Sponde's *Amores,* xviii, where the twin powers are "esprit" and "constance," and Pietro Bembo's canzone "Quantunque in altro clima io giri il piede . . ." which distinguishes "pensiero" and "core." Tasso's sonnet cix refers to "pensiero" and "costanza": "somiglia il mio pensiero / . . . / stella in cielo errante / per la costanza mia fatta incostante." Maurice Scève probably also uses the compass as a submerged image in his *Microcosme* to suggest a movement of the soul. See Freccero, pp. 352-53.

[9] "Il compasso, onde ella descrive il cerchio è perfetta figura fra le matematiche, & gli antichi ostervavano . . . che fatto il sacrificio, si bagnasse un circolo nell' altare col sangue delle vittime. . . . il cerchio del zodiaco è simbolo della ragione, & è debita, & il convenevole misura dell' attioni perfette." *Iconologia* (1630), p. 565.

[10]*Metamorphoses,* 8.236-55, trans. Frank Justus Miller (London, 1916).

[11]Ed. J. F. Nims (New York, 1965).

[12]A full discussion of this poem is in my essay on "The Selective Principle in Jonson's Shorter Poems," *Criticism,* 8 (1966), 64-74, but I did not mention the possible echo of Ovid in "Oh could I lose all father now," nor does Simpson cite it.

[13]Translated by Richard M. Gummere (London, 1925).

[14] "Plus fault celluy qui vient à presumer/ De mettre avant sa trop lourde Ignorance/ Et ne faict riens quo soit à estimer/ Des Muses n'a le port ne l'asseurance,/ Il est semblable au compas qu'on estand/ Pour faire ung rond, lequel on oeuvre tant/ Qu'on le corrompt, & le rondeau de faict/ Ja commencé est laissé imparfaict./ Parquoy l'ouvrier ne faict ce qu'il prétend./ Ainsi le sot faict semblant qu'il entend/ Sans jugement & sans discretion,/ Il se decoit, car au cas ou il tend/ N'y a propos, ordre & deduction/ Son faict demeure en imperfection/ Par ce qu'il a sur la force entrepris./ Et à la fin sera taxé, reprins/ Sy on congnoist son obstination" (Paris, 1540), p. 189, from a facsimile edited by Denys Janot (Paris, 1905).

Index

Abbot, George, Archbishop, 331
Abrams, M. H., 318
Accommodation, 24, 307, 317n26; Jonson's, 21-34
Accumulation, figure of, 174-77
Achilles, 63, 269
Acting: formal vs. natural, 2; styles of, 313
Actor, Jonson as, 315
Actors: Jonson instructs, 116; Shakespeare and, 10
Adams, Robert M., 333
Admiral's Men, 3, 275
Admiration: Augustinian, 92; comedy of, 68; comic, 71-72, 104; false, 118; Ficino on, 47; in Jonson's masques, 325; Neoplatonic, 56; silence as sign of, 41-42. *See also* Audience response
Aeneas, 232
Aerial spirits, 100-01, 321
Akrigg, George Philip, 337
Alberti, L. B., 41, 64
Alchemist, The, 160, 215, 256, 328, 332; compact tripartite, 7; decorum of place, 317; design of plot, 193-95, 200-09; ending, 213; English locale, 322; epilogue, 18; limited fullness, 199; parody in, 231; prologue, 15, 20, 315; Subtle vs. Virgil, 150; "To the Reader," 25
Alençon, duke of, 13, 70
Alexander the Great, 62-63, 68, 72
Allen, Don Cameron, 320
Allen, Walter, 318
Alleyn, Edward: and Dulwich College, 267; his sense of good fortune, 335
Ambition, Jonson's, 306-11
Ambrose, Saint, 44
Amplification, rhetorical, 195
Anacreon, 139
An Antidote Against Melancholy, 335
Anatomy. *See* Completeness
Antimasque, 297, 314, 324; Jonson's plays as, 299; like induction, 28
Apollo, 95, 140
Apuleius: *The Golden Ass*, 92-94; Lucius like Bottom, 321
Aretino, Pietro, 212

Ariosto, Orazio: *Cassaria, Suppositi*, 54
Aristophanes, 35, 51; *The Clouds*, 24
Aristotle, 40, 47; comic depiction of, 320; on laughter, 62
Arundel, earl of, 261
Ascham, Roger, 55
Astrology, 78
Aubrey, John, 326
Audience: better and worse, 115-16, 209, 317; diseased minds, 116; expectations, 197; Jonson's appeal to the better, 113; Jonson's indulging, 277; Jonson's new view of, 155; Jonson on, 257, 274, 316; Jonson's trapping of, 317n27; as judge and jury, 96, 99, 132-33, 155; their meridian, 318; potential for misunderstanding, 310; surrogate, 29; tempted, 185-87, 189; as understanders, 143
Audience response: admiration, 14, 36, 49, 51, 58, 61-65, 74, 80-81, 89, 101, 104-05, 115, 121, 128, 154-55, 291, 292, 319, 321; applause, 20, 316; charity, 8, 17, 98-100, 128; delight, 71-72, 74, 81, 210; dissembling, 25; to dramatic irony, 118; ethical judgment, 13, 56-65; Jonson on, 136; to language, 171, 177-92; laughter, 88, 104-05; laughter and love, 98; laughter mixed with wonder or delight, 61, 85-86, 90, 93, 109-10, 132, 152; light hearted, 258-60; mixed, 22, 105, 178-82, 209-12, 215-16; tears, 2; uncertainty, 83; understanding, 10, 86, 97, 91-92, 311; wider perspective, 194. *See also* Admiration
Augustine of Hippo, Saint, 92, 226, 332; *Christian Instruction*, 45, 318, on interpretation, 44; *Confessions*, 318, on interpretation, 44; *Exposition of the Psalms*, 45, 58, 318; Law of Love, 44-45, 65; *Of Catechizing of the Uninstructed*, 45, 318; on silence, 41-42
Augustinian piety, 42-46
Augustus, Caesar, 140-42
Averroes, 319
Awareness, comic knowledge, 249-55

339

351

DATE			